SPEARHEAD

BY ADAM MAKOS
Spearhead
Devotion
A Higher Call

SPEARHEAD

Atlantic Books
London

Adam Makos

SPEARHEAD

★ ★

An American Tank Gunner, His Enemy,
and a Collision of Lives in World War II

Published by arrangement with Ballantine Books, an imprint of Random House, a division of Penguin Random House LLC, New York.

First published in Great Britain in 2019 by Atlantic Books, an imprint of Atlantic Books Ltd.

1 2 3 4 5 6 7 8 9

A CIP catalogue record for this book is available from the British Library.

Hardback ISBN: 978-1-78239-578-2
E-book ISBN: 978-1-78239-580-5
Paperback ISBN: 978-1-78239-581-2

All interior maps by Bryan Makos of Valor Studios, Inc.
Photo credits can be found on p. 383

The image on the front cover is taken from the film of cameraman Jim Bates and shows the Pershing crew in Cologne on March 6, 1945. Left to right: Smokey Davis, Bob Earley, Woody McVey, Clarence Smoyer, John DeRiggi.

Book design by Simon M. Sullivan

Printed and bound in Great Britain by TJ International Ltd, Padstow, Cornwall

Atlantic Books
An Imprint of Atlantic Books Ltd
Ormond House
26–27 Boswell Street
London
WC1N 3JZ

www.atlantic-books.co.uk

To those brave American tankers—the "power and might"
of the New World—who went to the rescue of the Old

CONTENTS

Introduction   xi

1   **The Gentle Giant**   3

2   **Baptism**   14

3   **"Bubi"**   25

4   **The Fields**   31

5   **The Foray**   43

6   **Beyond the Wall**   49

7   **Respite**   58

8   **The Fourth Tank**   68

9   **Hope**   77

10   **Something Bigger**   88

11   **America's Tiger**   103

12   **Two Miles**   115

13   **Hunting**   137

14   **The Fire Department of the West**   143

15   **Going First**   155

16   **Victory or Siberia**   178

17   *The Monster*   201

18   *The Conquerors*   218

19   *The Breakout*   232

20   *The American Blitz*   244

21   *The Fatherless*   256

22   *Family*   268

23   *Come Out and Fight*   280

24   *The Giant*   292

25   *Getting Home*   307

26   *The Last Battle*   313

     Afterword   337

     Acknowledgments   345

     Sources   349

     Notes   351

     Photo Credits   383

     Index   387

Some stories begin with a roll of the dice.

It was a Sunday morning in 2012 when I approached a brick row house in Allentown, Pennsylvania. The working-class neighborhood was quiet and no one paid me any notice.

I had come chasing a story.

My former college classmate Pete Semanoff had given me a lead on a World War II veteran living here in relative obscurity. Pete said this veteran had a tale to tell, maybe a book in the making. Supposedly, he had been a tank gunner in one of the war's most legendary tank duels, and an army cameraman had filmed the whole thing.

But did he want to share his story? And would anyone want to read a book about tanks? This was before Brad Pitt strapped on his three-buckle boots for the filming of *Fury*, and before *World of Tanks* became all the rage.

And there was another question looming in my mind. The veteran had served in the 3rd Armored Division—the "Spearhead" Division. Most history buffs know of the Screaming Eagles. The Big Red One. Patton's Third Army.

But the 3rd Armored Division?

The only 3rd Armored soldier I knew of had joined them during the Cold War. His name was Elvis.

. . .

I checked the house numbers against the address I had noted on my phone. This was the place.

I knocked, and Clarence Smoyer answered. He was eighty-eight and surprisingly tall, dressed in a simple blue polo shirt that stretched over a robust stomach. His thick glasses made his eyes seem small. Clarence welcomed me inside with a chuckle and pulled up a chair for me at his kitchen table. There, I'd make a discovery.

It was true. All of it.

This gentle giant held the keys to one of the last great untold stories of World War II, and he was ready to talk.

I've always visited the battlefields before I write about them. *A Higher Call* took me to a dusty airfield in Sicily. *Devotion* led my team and me into the misty mountains of North Korea.

To bring you the deepest level of historical detail for this book, we went to new lengths in our research. This time, we traversed the battlefields of the Third Reich—*with* the men who made history.

In 2013, Clarence Smoyer and three other veterans traveled to Germany and allowed us to tag along, to interview them on the ground where they had once fought. We recorded their stories. We recorded what they remembered saying and hearing others say. Then we verified their accounts with deep research.

We drew from four archives in America and one in England. We even traveled to the German Bundesarchiv in the Black Forest in search of answers. And what we found was staggering. Original orders. Rare interviews between our heroes and war reporters, conducted while the battle was raging. Radio logs of our tank commanders' chatter, allowing us to time their actions to the minute. Daily weather reports. And much more.

Prepare to mount up.

In a few short pages you'll find yourself behind enemy lines with the 3rd Armored Division, a "workhorse unit," one of the "most aggressive" American divisions, and arguably the best in the armor business.

Even General Omar Bradley saw something special in Clarence and his comrades. When asked to gauge the personality of his units,

Bradley wrote that Patton's tankers adopted his "flair." Simpson's in the Ninth Army were known for their "breeziness." And the 3rd Armored? They led the fighting march across Europe "with a serious and grim intensity."

Serious. And grim. That's who you'll be riding with.

But this is not a story about machines, how one tank stacked up against another. This is a story about people.

We'll drop you inside the tanks with Clarence and his fellow crew members, strangers from across America who became family.

We'll lift you outside, into the elements and enemy fire, with an armored infantryman fighting to clear a path for the armor.

And we'll explore the other side, stepping into the boots of a German tanker and into the shoes of two young fräuleins caught in the crossfire.

Ultimately, we'll see what happens when these lives collide, leaving aftershocks that still shape the survivors more than half a century later.

Is the world ready for a book about tanks?

There's one way to find out.

Shut the hatches.

Tighten your chin strap.

It's time to roll out.

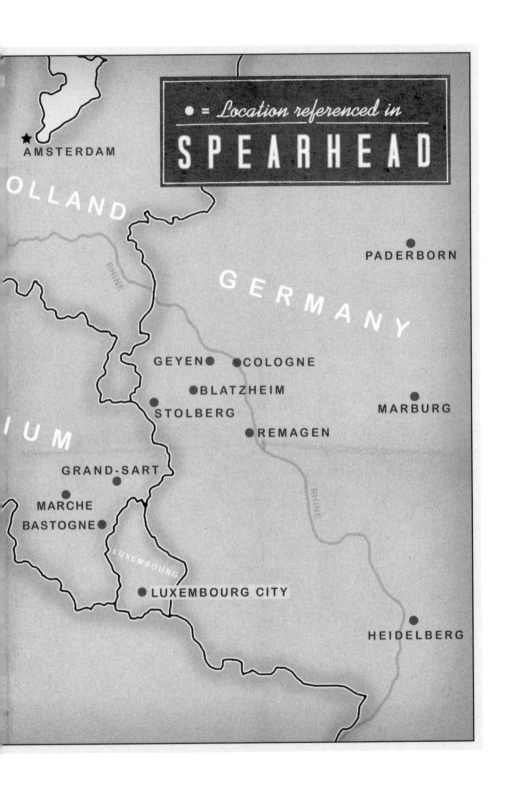

★ AMSTERDAM

HOLLAND

● = *Location referenced in*
SPEARHEAD

GERMANY

RHINE

PADERBORN

GEYEN ● ● COLOGNE

● BLATZHEIM

● STOLBERG

MARBURG

● REMAGEN

BELGIUM

GRAND-SART ●

● MARCHE
BASTOGNE ●

RHINE

LUXEMBOURG

● LUXEMBOURG CITY

● HEIDELBERG

SPEARHEAD

CHAPTER 1 **THE GENTLE GIANT**

September 2, 1944
Occupied Belgium, during World War II

Twilight fell on a country crossroads.

The only sounds came from insects buzzing in the surrounding blue fields, and something else. Metallic. The sound of hot engines ticking and pinging, decompressing after a long drive.

With silent efficiency, tank crewmen worked to rearm and refuel their tired Sherman tanks before the last hues of color fled the sky.

Crouched behind the turret of the leftmost tank, Corporal Clarence Smoyer carefully shuttled 75mm shells into the waiting hands of the loader inside. It was a delicate job—even the slightest clang could reveal their position to the enemy.

Clarence was twenty-one, tall and lean with a Roman nose and a sea of curly blond hair under a knit cap. His blue eyes were gentle, but guarded. Despite his height, he was not a fighter—he had never been in a fistfight. Back home in Pennsylvania he had hunted only once— for rabbit—and even that he did halfheartedly. Three weeks earlier he'd been promoted to gunner, second in command on the tank. It wasn't a promotion he had wanted.

The platoon was in place. To Clarence's right, four more olive-drab tanks were fanned out, "coiled," in a half-moon formation with twenty yards between each vehicle. Farther to the north, beyond sight, was Mons, a city made lavish by the Industrial Revolution. A dirt road

Clarence Smoyer

lay parallel to the tanks on the left, and it ran up through the darkening fields to a forested ridge, where the sun was setting behind the trees.

The Germans were out there, but how many there were and when they'd arrive, no one knew. It had been nearly three months since D-Day, and now Clarence and the men of the 3rd Armored Division were behind enemy lines.

All guns faced west.

Boasting 390 tanks at full strength, the division had dispersed every operational tank between the enemy and Mons, blocking every road junction they could reach.

Survival that night would hinge on teamwork. Clarence's company headquarters had given his platoon, 2nd Platoon, a simple but important mission: guard the road, let nothing pass.

Clarence lowered himself through the commander's hatch and into the turret, a tight fit for a six-foot man. He slipped to the right of the gun breech and into the gunner's seat, leaning into his periscopic gun sight. As he had no hatch of his own, this five-inch-wide relay of glass prisms and a 3x telescopic gun sight mounted to the left of it would be his windows to the world.

His field of fire was set.

There would be no stepping out that night; it was too risky even to urinate. That's what they saved empty shell casings for.

Beneath Clarence's feet, the tank opened up in the hull, with its white enamel walls like the turret's and a trio of dome lights. In the bow, the driver and bow gunner/assistant driver slid their seats backward to sleep where they had ridden all day. On the opposite side of the gun breech from Clarence, the loader stretched a sleeping bag on the turret floor. The tank smelled of oil, gunpowder, and a locker room, but the scent was familiar, even comforting. Ever since they'd come ashore, three weeks after D-Day, this M4A1 Sherman had been their home in Easy Company, 32nd Armor Regiment, of the 3rd Armored Division, one of the army's two heavy tank divisions.

Tonight, sleep would come quickly. The men were exhausted. The 3rd Armored had been charging for eighteen days at the head of the First Army, leading two other divisions in the breakout across northern France. Paris had been liberated, the Germans were running back the way they'd come in 1940, and the 3rd Armored was earning its nom de guerre: the Spearhead Division.

Then came new orders.

The reconnaissance boys had spotted the German Fifteenth and Seventeenth Armies moving to the north, hightailing it out of France for Belgium and on course to pass through Mons's many crossroads. So the 3rd Armored turned on a dime and raced north—107 miles in two days—arriving just in time to lay an ambush.

The tank commander dropped into the turret and lowered the split hatch covers, leaving just a crack for air. He slumped into his seat behind Clarence, his boyish face still creased by the impression of his goggles. Staff Sergeant Paul Faircloth of Jacksonville, Florida, was

COMMANDER

LOADER

DRIVER

GUNNER

BOW GUNNER/
ASSISTANT DRIVER

M4A1 (75mm) Sherman

Paul Faircloth

also twenty-one, quiet and easygoing, with a sturdy build, black hair, and olive skin. Some assumed he was French or Italian, but he was half Cherokee. As the platoon sergeant, Paul had been checking on the other crews and positioning them for the night. Normally the platoon leader would do this, but their lieutenant was a new replacement and still learning the ropes.

For two days Paul had been on his feet in the commander's position, standing halfway out of his hatch with the turret up to his ribs. From there he could anticipate the column's movements to help the driver brake and steer. In the event of a sudden halt—when another crew threw a track or got mired in mud, for instance—Paul was always the first out of the tank to help.

"I'm taking your watch tonight," Clarence said. "I'll do a double."

The offer was generous, but Paul resisted—he could handle it.

Clarence persisted until Paul threw up his hands and finally swapped places with him to nab some shut-eye in the gunner's seat.

Clarence took the commander's position, a seat higher in the turret. The hatch covers were closed enough to block a German grenade, but open enough to provide a good view to the front and back. He could see his neighboring Sherman through the rising moonlight. The tank's squat, bulbous turret looked incongruous against the tall, sharp lines of the body, as if the parts had been pieced together from salvage.

Clarence snatched a Thompson submachine gun from the wall and chambered a round. For the next four hours, enemy foot soldiers were his concern. Everyone knew that German tankers didn't like to fight at night.

Partway through Clarence's watch, the darkness came alive with a mechanical rumbling.

The moon was smothered by clouds and he couldn't see a thing, but he could hear a convoy of vehicles moving beyond the tree-lined ridge.

Start and stop. Start and stop.

The radio speaker on the turret wall kept humming with static. No flares illuminated the sky. The 3rd Armored would later estimate there were 30,000 enemy troops out there, mostly men of the German Army, the Wehrmacht, with some air force and navy personnel among them—yet no order came to give pursuit or attack.

That's because the battered remnants of the enemy armies were bleeding precious fuel as they searched for a way around the road-blocks, and Spearhead was content to let them wander. The enemy was desperately trying to reach the safety of the West Wall, also known as the Siegfried Line, a stretch of more than 18,000 defensive fortifications that bristled along the German border.

If these 30,000 troops could dig in there, they could bar the way to Germany and prolong the war. They had to be stopped, here, at Mons, and Spearhead had a plan for that—but it could wait until daylight.

Around two A.M. the distinctive slap of tank tracks arose from the distant rumble.

Clarence tracked the sounds—vehicles were coming down the road in front of him. He knew his orders—let nothing pass—but doubt was setting in. Maybe this was a reconnaissance patrol returning? Had someone gotten lost? They couldn't be British, not in this area. Whoever they were, he wasn't about to pull the trigger on friendly forces.

One after the other, three tanks clanked past the blacked-out Shermans and kept going, and Clarence began to breathe again.

Then one of the tanks let off the gas. It began turning and squeaking, as if its tracks were in need of oil. The sound was unmistakable. Only full-metal tracks sounded like that, and a Sherman's were padded with rubber.

The tanks were German.

Clarence didn't move. The tank was behind him, then beside him. It slowed and sputtered then squeaked to a stop in the middle of the coiled Shermans. Clarence braced for a flash and the flames that would swallow him. The German tank was idling alongside him. He'd never even hear the gun bark. He would just cease to exist.

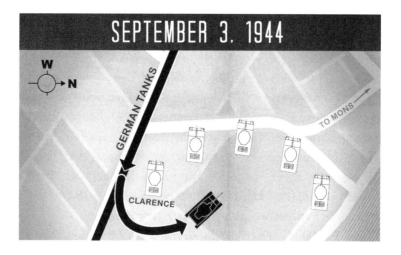

A whisper shook Clarence from his paralysis. It was Paul. Without a word, Clarence slipped back into the gunner's seat and Paul took over.

Clarence strapped on his tanker's helmet. Made of fiber resin, it looked like a cross between a football helmet and a crash helmet, and had goggles on the front and headphones sewn into leather earflaps. He clipped a throat microphone around his neck and plugged into the intercom.*

---

* A WWII tanker's helmet was in fact patterned after a 1930s-era football helmet and carried the manufacturer's stamp of sporting goods companies such as Rawlings, A. G. Spalding & Bros., and Wilson Athletic Goods.

On the other side of the turret, the loader sat up, wiping the sleep from his eyes.

Clarence mouthed the words *German tank*. The loader snapped wide-awake.

From his hatch, Paul tapped Clarence on the right shoulder, the signal to turn the turret to the right.

Clarence hesitated. The turret wasn't silent, what if the Germans heard it?

Paul tapped again.

Clarence relented and turned a handle, the turret whined, gears cranked, and the gun swept the dark.

When the gun was aligned broadside, Paul stopped Clarence. Clarence pressed his eyes to his periscope. Everything below the skyline was inky black.

Clarence told Paul he couldn't see a thing and suggested they call in armored infantrymen to kill the tank with a bazooka.

Paul couldn't chance some jittery soldier blasting the wrong tank. He grabbed his hand microphone—nicknamed "the pork chop" due to its shape—and dialed the radio to the platoon frequency, alerting the other crews to what they likely already knew: that an enemy tank was in the coil. In a Sherman platoon at that time, only the tanks of the platoon leader and platoon sergeant could transmit. Everyone else could only listen.

"No noise, and no smoking cigarettes," Paul said. "We'll take care of him."

We'll take care of him? Clarence was horrified. He had hardly used the gun in daylight and now Paul wanted him to fire in pitch-darkness, at what? A sound? An enemy he couldn't see?

He wished he could return to being a loader. A loader never saw much. Never did much. On a tank crew, the loader was pretty much just along for the ride. That was the good life. A gentle giant, Clarence simply wanted to slip through the war without killing anyone or getting killed himself.

No time for that. The German tank crew had likely realized their mistake by now.

"Gunner, ready?"

Panicked, Clarence turned and tugged on Paul's pant leg.

Paul sank into the turret, exasperated. Clarence rattled off his doubts. What if he missed? What if he got a deflection and hit their own guys?

Paul's voice calmed Clarence: "Somebody has to take the shot."

As if the Germans had been listening, they suddenly cut their power. The hot engine hissed, then went silent.

Clarence felt a wave of relief. It was a reprieve. Paul must have been biting his lip in anger, because he said nothing at first. Finally, he informed the crew that now they would have to wait to fire at first light.

Clarence's relief faded. His indecision had cost them whatever advantage they'd had. And against a German tank, they'd need every advantage they could get, especially if they were facing a Panther, the tank of nightmares. Some GIs called it "the Pride of the Wehrmacht," and rumor had it that a Panther could shoot through one Sherman and into a second, and its frontal armor was supposedly impervious.

That July, the U.S. Army had placed several captured Panthers in a field in Normandy and blasted away at them with the same 75mm gun as in Clarence's Sherman. The enemy tanks proved vulnerable from the flanks and rear, but not the front. Not a single shot managed to penetrate the Panther's frontal armor, from any distance.

Clarence checked his luminescent watch, knowing the Germans were probably doing the same. The countdown had begun. Someone was going to die.

The loader fell asleep over the gun breech.

Three A.M. became four A.M.

Clarence and Paul passed a canteen of cold coffee back and forth. They had always joked that they were a family locked in a sardine can. And like a family, they didn't always see eye to eye. Unlike Paul, who was always running off to help someone outside the tank, all Clarence cared about was his family on the inside—him and his crew.

This had been his way since childhood.

Growing up in industrial Lehighton, Pennsylvania, Clarence lived in a row house by the river, with walls so flimsy he could hear the neighbors. His parents were usually out working to keep the family afloat. His father did manual labor for the Civilian Conservation Corps and his mother was a housekeeper.

With the family's survival at stake, Clarence was determined to contribute. When other kids played sports or did homework, twelve-year-old Clarence stacked a ballpark vendor's box with candy bars and went selling door-to-door throughout Lehighton. Just a boy, he had vowed: *I've got to take care of my family because no one is going to take care of us.*

Clarence checked his periscope. To the east, a faint tinge of purple colored the horizon.

He kept his eyes glued to the glass until a blocky shape appeared about fifty yards away.

"I see it," he whispered.

Paul rose to his hatch and saw it too. It looked like a rise of rock, highest at the midpoint. Clarence turned handwheels to fine-tune his aim.

Paul urged him to hurry. If they could see the enemy, the enemy could see them.

Clarence settled the reticle, as the gun sight's crosshairs were known, on the "rock" at center mass and reported that he was ready. His boot hovered over the trigger, a button on the footrest.

"Fire," Paul said.

Clarence's foot stamped down.

Outside, a massive flash leapt from the Sherman's barrel, momentarily illuminating the tanks—an olive-drab American and a sandy-yellow German—both facing the same direction.

Sparks burst from the darkness and a sound like an anvil strike pierced the countryside. Inside the turret, without the fan operating, smoke hung thick in the air. Clarence's ears throbbed and his eyes stung, but he kept them pressed to his sight.

The loader chambered a new shell. Clarence again hovered his foot over the trigger.

"Nothing's moving," Paul said from above. A broadside at this range? It was undoubtedly a kill shot.

The intercom came alive with voices of relief, and Clarence moved his foot away from the trigger.

Paul radioed the platoon; the job was done.

Through his periscope, Clarence watched the sky warm beneath the dark clouds, revealing the boxy armor and the 11-foot, 8-inch long gun of a Panzer IV tank.

Known by the Americans as the Mark IV, the design was old, in service since 1938, and it had been the enemy's most prevalent tank until that August, when the Panther began taking over. But even though it was no longer the mainstay, the Mark IV was still lethal. Its 75mm gun packed 25 percent more punch than Clarence's.

More light revealed the tank's dark green-and-brown swirls of camouflage and the German cross on the flank. Clarence had nearly placed his shot right on it.

"Think they're in there?" One of the crewmen posed the question, seeing that the Mark IV's hatch covers hadn't budged.

Clarence envisioned a tank full of moaning, bleeding men and hoped the crew had slipped out in the night. He had no love for the Germans, but he hated the idea of killing any human being. He wasn't about to look inside his first tank kill. A shell can ricochet like a supersonic pinball within the tight quarters, and he'd seen maintenance guys go inside to clean and come out crying after discovering brains on the ceiling.

"I'll go." Paul unplugged his helmet.

Panzer IV

Clarence tried to dissuade him. It wasn't worth looking inside and getting his head blown off by a German.

Paul brushed away the concerns and radioed the platoon to hold their fire.

Through his periscope, Clarence watched Paul climb the Mark IV's hull and creep toward the turret with his Thompson at the ready. With one hand steadying his gun, Paul opened the commander's hatch and aimed the Thompson inside.

Nothing happened.

He leaned forward and took a long look, then shouldered his gun.

Paul sealed the hatch shut.

CHAPTER 2 **BAPTISM**

That same morning, September 3, 1944
Mons, Belgium

After the tense standoff of the previous night, the tanks were on the move.

Traveling solo or in pairs with the rising sun at their backs, multiple companies of Shermans flooded across the Mons countryside to extend the division's reach, pressing the enemy into an ever-tightening cordon.

Every country lane, every farmer's path, had to be roadblocked, which meant that Easy Company, too, would operate piecemeal today, and its crews would do their fighting alone.

With his goggles lowered, Paul rode head and shoulders above his open hatch, his jacket flapping in the wind. Thirty-three tons of tank churned beneath him, going about 20 miles per hour, following the road uphill between foggy fields.

The machine seemed alive. Everything vibrated: helmets and musette bags hung from the turret, a .30-caliber machine gun on a mount, spare tracks and wheels tied down wherever they would fit. The tank cleared its throat with each gear change. At the heart of its power was a 9-cylinder radial engine that had to be cranked awake by hand if it sat overnight.

This Sherman was a "75," owing to its 75mm gun, but to Clarence's crew it had a name—Eagle—and someone had painted an eagle head on each side of the hull. For recognition purposes, every tank's name in Easy Company began with the letter *E*.

Paul raised his field glasses to his eyes and studied the terrain ahead. The tank was bound for the tree-lined ridge, the source of the night-time commotion.

One by one, the neighboring Shermans vanished from sight. They plunged into patches of woods or slipped around edges of fields and set their guns toward the enemy.

While Clarence and the crew inside assumed that a mighty force still surrounded them, Paul could see that his tank was alone. Every swaying tree, every shifting shadow now assumed a sense of hostile intent.

Paul held his course. His orders were to set a roadblock atop the tree-lined ridge where the German tanks had originated the night before.

His crew hadn't been the only one to experience a fraught encounter. At one American bivouac, a fatigued MP had directed a Panther tank off the road and into a parking space meant for Shermans. The German crew realized their mistake and came out with their hands up.

As the tank barreled toward the ridge, Clarence pestered Paul on the intercom.

"Are you sure?" Clarence asked, again, from his perch in the gunner's seat.

Paul wasn't deviating from his story. "Don't worry, they all got out."

Paul had assured Clarence that the German crew escaped the Mark IV alive, but Clarence had a suspicion that his friend was just trying to protect him. Paul had done it before.

It happened after the last furlough before the unit shipped overseas in September 1943. Clarence had been on a date in a park in Reading, Pennsylvania, and was so enjoying the young woman's company that he missed the bus back to base. By the time he hitchhiked back, he'd been declared AWOL.

When Easy Company arrived in the English village of Codford, Clarence's punishment was handed down. Every night after the evening meal, Clarence was ordered to cut the grass around the company's three Quonset huts with just the butter knife of his mess kit. He'd take a fistful of grass, saw away, and then move to the next clump, from about seven to eleven each night.

Paul wasn't one to frequent the local pub or foray on a pass to London, so he'd sit against a Quonset hut and keep Clarence company while he worked. Over the course of three months, they talked. Clarence learned that Paul's father had been an engineer for Georgia Southern Railroad and that his mother was a full-blooded Cherokee and convert to Evangelical Christianity.

When Paul was in sixth grade, his father had died, so he quit school and became a clerk at a general store to support his mother and sisters. Surprised by Paul's keen mind for numbers, the store owner soon had him doing the bookkeeping.

A few tankers from the company found Clarence's punishment amusing and took to urinating behind the huts on grass that Clarence was due to cut. Paul called them together. "It's the latrine that separates us from animals," he said.

That put an end to it.

At the crest of the ridge, Clarence's periscope filled with sky as the mighty tank's nose lifted from the road.

He'd never get to see what lay on the other side.

As the tank settled forward, a crack rapped the gun barrel with a spit of sparks. Clarence reeled from the periscope. *We're hit!* A gong-like sound resonated through the steel walls.

Paul dropped into the turret and screamed for the driver to reverse. Gears ground and the tank tilted and backtracked downhill. At the base of the hill, Paul guided the driver backward into a sunken road lined by trees, until only the top of the tank was visible.

Paul and Clarence climbed out to inspect the damage. Atop the turret they froze at the sound of thunder in a perfectly blue sky.

A battle was raging beyond the nearby hills. Smoke rose into the sky, and P-47 fighter-bombers powered overhead, bound for a distant

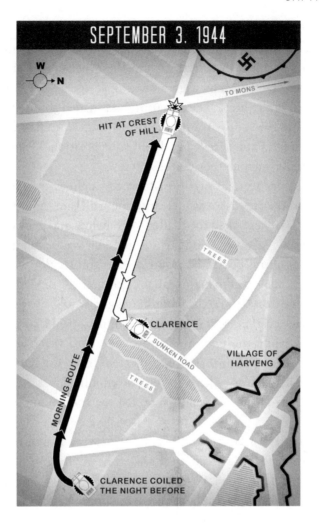

SEPTEMBER 3. 1944

HIT AT CREST
OF HILL

TO MONS

W N

CLARENCE

SUNKEN ROAD

TREES

TREES

VILLAGE OF
HARVENG

MORNING ROUTE

CLARENCE COILED
THE NIGHT BEFORE

tangle of roads where German vehicles were reportedly snagged in a "delicious traffic jam."

Clarence eyed the gun barrel with concern. A shell had struck the side and removed a scoop of metal before deflecting over the turret. A few more inches to the right and the shell would have come straight through his gun sight, killing him instantly. They had probably driven into the sights of an antitank gun—an enemy tank would surely have maneuvered to take a second shot.

Clarence gave Paul the bad news. The gun barrel was likely collapsed internally, and if he fired, the shell could get jammed and its backblast could come into the turret, wiping out the crew.

That settled it. It was simply too risky to fire.

Back in the safety of the turret, Paul radioed Easy Company's head-quarters for permission to retreat. On the other end, a shaky voice reported that the Germans were attacking across a wide front, probing for holes in the lines. The situation had turned so dire that clerks and men from the supply train were being sent out to fight.

The orders to Paul were firm: "Hold your position." Paul asked for reinforcements, anyone they could spare.

Transmissions were always broadcast throughout the tank, for the awareness of the crew, so it was clear to them all that the situation was desperate. Clarence asked the loader to go below and get extra ammo for the coaxial—a .30-caliber machine gun that was set on the loader's side with its barrel protruding outside the gun shield, where it was fixed to fire wherever the main gun was pointed. A second trigger on Clarence's footrest, left of the cannon trigger, would fire the coaxial.

Paul reviewed their roles. He and Clarence would cover the tree-lined ridge, while the bow gunner would guard the front with his .30-caliber machine gun, which projected from the tank's frontal armor. The driver was to keep the engine running.

Paul rose from his hatch and swiveled the roof-mounted machine gun.

Everything revolved around him as the turret swung to the right then stopped sidelong from the tank. The main gun and coaxial elevated toward the ridge.

From between his partially open hatch covers, Paul took aim.

About two hundred yards away, on top of the ridge, the silhouettes of men appeared.

A dozen soldiers waded cautiously down the gentle slope as more soldiers appeared behind them. They spread out, clambering down the field in staggered groups. There were about one hundred of them, wearing German gray, some with green smocks. Sunlight beat down on their faces.

The turret slid beneath Paul; Clarence was tracking them too.

The enemy had come far enough.

Paul clenched his trigger, sending fire leaping from the muzzle. He worked his gun side to side as the bolt blurred and spat empty casings. Clarence's coaxial added its earsplitting roar, its smoke rising in front of Paul.

The Germans fell in droves—many killed or badly wounded. Others pawed for cover in shallow gullies. A few fired back, their bullets snapping the air around Paul.

Inside the tank, Clarence held an eye to his 3x telescopic gun sight. It was kill or be killed—them or his family. Clarence's foot came down, the coaxial thumped, then he turned a handle, an electric motor whined, and the turret swung his reticle to the next target.

A German working the bolt of a rifle. An officer screaming into a radio. A soldier running away. Clarence's foot came down again. The action was so fast, there was no discerning.

Almost as quickly as they had appeared, the enemy stopped coming over the hill.

"Cease fire!" Paul shouted.

Clarence lifted his foot and caught his breath. From above the turret, Paul gazed upon a massacre. More than a dozen German bodies dotted the slope and survivors limped away, dragging their wounded. The enemy attack appeared uncoordinated, desperate, and blundering. But it was over. Or so Clarence hoped.

Within thirty minutes, engines revved behind the Sherman.

An American M3 half-track armored personnel carrier pulled up, followed by an M8 Greyhound, a scout car with a 37mm gun. A squad of armored infantrymen leaped from the half-track and took up firing positions. Known to the tankers as "doughs," in homage to the "doughboys" of World War I, they were the division's infantry arm and often rode tanks or half-tracks into battle. The reinforcements that Paul asked for had arrived.

A sergeant stood in the Greyhound's open turret, gripping a machine gun.

Paul was about to brief the reinforcements when popping sounds came from the ridge, as if the Germans were opening champagne bottles.

Shouts of "Mortars!" resounded through the sunken road. The

doughs took cover. Paul slammed the hatch cover to secure the turret. From his seat, Clarence heard shells whooshing down. Explosions and shrapnel thumped the tank's steel hide. With the Sherman blocking their route homeward, this was the Germans' reply.

Above the chaos of the barrage came bone-chilling screams. The horrifying sounds leaked through the cracks into the turret. Clarence twisted in his seat, wanting to plug his ears and bury his head. Something terrible was happening outside. The shells kept bursting as the screams cycled up into inhuman wails.

A hand shook Clarence by his shoulder. "Clarence, you're in charge!"

Clarence turned and found Paul swapping his tanker's helmet for a steel pot. He was going out there.

Paul grabbed his Thompson and opened his hatch. The cacophony of battle flooded the tank.

Clarence sprang from his seat and grabbed Paul's leg, desperately trying to hold him back from something foolhardy. No stranger's life was worth throwing away his own.

"We gotta help those guys!" Paul shouted, and kicked free from Clarence's grasp.

Clarence rose from the turret and spotted Paul running through dark smoke, toward the source of the cries.

The Greyhound had taken a direct hit into the turret and the men inside were suffering.

The sky whistled as a fresh round of mortar shells rained down.

Clarence hollered—"Get back here, Paul!" But Paul didn't look back as he rushed through the inky haze, determined to save what lives he could.

A dark streak punched the road with a burst of orange and a shock-wave of smoke. Another orange burst leapt from the road, then another. Clarence ducked from the force of the blasts, which were so strong that they blew the leaves off the surrounding trees. He rose back to eye level. Paul had almost reached the Greyhound when a mortar shell landed to his right. The explosion lifted him from his feet and flung him askew through the smoke. Clarence's legs became weak at the sight and he collapsed into the turret.

The barrage soon lifted. Clarence stood and frantically searched for his friend.

Paul had landed almost upside down on a bank. The blast had shattered his arm, and his right leg had been blown completely off below the knee.

Clarence stared, horror-struck.

This can't be happening.

He fumbled for the pork chop and called company headquarters, stuttering, and begging for any medics they could spare.

Before Clarence could move to Paul's aid, a rifle barked. Then more rifles joined in, crackling like a string of firecrackers. The doughs fired feverishly in the direction of fresh silhouettes pouring over the ridgeline. The timing couldn't have been worse. The Germans were back in force.

On the intercom, Clarence heard his crew panicking, some wanting to drive away. He was the ranking crewman; they wanted to know what to do.

Clarence felt an emotion welling, one he barely recognized. He glanced at Paul. His friend still hadn't stirred.

Dropping back into the gunner's seat, Clarence told the crew, "We aren't going anywhere."

He swung the turret into action.

The Germans were moving tactically, hitting the dirt every few yards then advancing and repeating. Clarence's foot smashed down on the trigger. The coaxial hammered, spitting a tracer downrange every four bullets, venting his rage.

The manual instructed gunners to fire in bursts, but Clarence still thought with the instincts of a loader. He swept the hose of fire across the enemy. There were so many silhouettes, he nearly stood on the machine gun button.

The gun consumed one belt of ammunition after another as the loader kept them coming. When Clarence finally lifted his foot, the gun didn't stop, it kept firing every few seconds. He'd overheated it and now heat was flowing back from the red-hot barrel and "cooking off" the bullets.

"Turn the belt!" Clarence shouted to the loader. The loader twisted the bullets and jammed the gun by hand.

Clarence yelled for a "barrel change." Using asbestos gloves, the loader could unscrew the barrel—but it would take time. Time they didn't have facing the enemy's onslaught.

Clarence emerged from the commander's hatch and swung the roof-mounted machine gun into play.

Now halfway down the field, the Germans were coming into focus. Clarence could see their camouflaged smocks, wire helmet netting, and faces shouting orders or contorted with fear.

Taking the grip hand over hand, Clarence resumed firing, this time in bursts.

Germans fell. His bullets danced across the dirt and through them. It was impossible to tell who had been hit and who was taking cover.

The gun rhythmically shook its mount. The belt of bullets sank lower and lower until the box was empty and the gun was silently smoking. Clarence grabbed the pork chop. He needed the coaxial but the loader was saying he needed more time.

The Germans seized upon the lull to strike back. Bullets began pinging off the tank and buzzing from the turret, forcing Clarence lower in the hatch.

Frantic voices drew Clarence's attention. Two young doughs lay behind the tank as bullets sliced the air above the sunken road. They begged for permission to hide beneath the tank.

"Fine," Clarence said, but with a disclaimer: "If you hear the engine revving, get the hell out of there!"

The doughs disappeared beneath the tank.

The Germans were back up on their feet and charging. As they raced toward the tanks, the loader came on the intercom. The coaxial was ready. Clarence returned to the gunner's seat and pressed his eyes to the periscope. The enemy was closer than ever, seventy-five yards, then sixty, fifty . . .

Clarence heard voices beneath him. Somehow, over the engine's idling and the crackle of gunfire the voices rose through the tank's hollow confines. It was the young doughs beneath the hull, making promises to God if he'd only save them now.

Clarence violently stepped on the trigger and drowned out their prayers with gunfire.

· · ·

The field in front of the tank was a graveyard.

Morning had become afternoon and the cacophony of battle had faded.

The remains of German soldiers littered the slope to the ridgetop. From the midst of the motionless gray and green lumps, those left alive were struggling to step over fallen comrades on their way down to surrender.

"You Americans don't want to fight," said one prisoner, "you just want to slaughter us."

Countless scenes like this played out across Mons.

"As though drawn to the city by a fatal fascination, German troops kept pouring in to 3rd Armored Division road blocks," the unit recorded. "Tanks and tank-destroyers enjoyed a brief field day, the crews firing their big guns until the tubes smoked."

The American victory was resounding.

The 1st Infantry Division, the "Big Red One," would come in to finish what the 3rd Armored had begun, and out of the 30,000 Germans who came to Mons, 27,000 would leave as prisoners, including three generals and a lowly sailor who had hitchhiked from his port in western France.

"Probably never before in the history of warfare has there been so swift a destruction of such a large force," concluded the 3rd Armored Division history.

The turret floor was slippery with bullet casings as Clarence rose half-way from the commander's hatch and eyed the sunken road.

Reinforcements had arrived in the form of more doughs, but it was too late. Paul's lifeless body lay at the medics' feet. Clarence silently pleaded for his friend to cough or flinch or show any sign of life.

That time had passed.

The medics packed up their bags to move on. "Can we take him back with us?" Clarence asked with a trembling voice from his perch in the turret.

The medics were sympathetic. "Graves Registration will be along soon."

At the words, Clarence buried his face in his sleeve. Paul's body. The field of dead Germans. He sank down into the turret and shut the covers.

The Sherman belched a grunt of smoke before rolling from the sunken road, bound for the bivouac.

Inside, Clarence folded over in the commander's seat and wept. The night before, he and Paul had shared a thermos of cold coffee. And now Paul was dead. It had not even been twenty-four hours. But for a Spearhead tanker, this was just another day in the hard-fighting division that would suffer more men killed in action than the 82nd or 101st Airborne Divisions, and would lose the most American tanks in World War II.

And Germany was yet to come.

Five days later, September 8, 1944
Eighty-five miles southeast—Luxembourg

The thunder of heavy artillery rippled over the village of Merl, on the western outskirts of Luxembourg City.

Beneath leafy trees on a country lane, a young German tank crewman performed a balancing act as he carried five mess kits brimming with food.

Shells burst in the fields to his left, tossing embers and vaporized dirt into the morning sun.

Private Gustav Schaefer watched the explosions in awe. Far beyond the forests that ringed the fields, the Americans were firing blindly, hitting nothing, putting on a fireworks show seemingly just for him.

Barely five feet tall, Gustav resembled a child in camouflaged tanker coveralls. He was seventeen, blond, and square-jawed, with a disposition so quiet that his lips seldom moved to speak. His dark eyes did his talking for him—there was nothing they couldn't convey with a glance. On this, his first day in combat, his eyes

Gustav Schaefer

spoke volumes. Despite the explosions detonating nearby, Gustav was having fun.

The thunderclaps grew louder as they landed closer and closer.

Gustav increased his pace to a brisk walk, but refrained from running. As the crew's radioman, who doubled as the bow gunner, he was known as the "girl for everything," because his role also entailed fetching food and fueling the tank. Gustav accepted the tasks—and the title—without complaint. Hot stew rocked in the mess kits, the crew's meager rations for the day. He couldn't afford to spill a drop.

About one hundred yards up the road, his crewmates were running back to their tank, which was parked in the shade alongside a hedge. A web of hand-cut branches served as camouflage and further masked the sharp lines of a Panther. Before disappearing inside, the men shouted for Gustav to hurry.

Another thunderclap rippled. This one was so close that the shockwave slapped Gustav's cheek. Brown clouds of vaporized dirt floated closer than before. He broke into a jog, holding the mess kits high as the stew sloshed inside. Another thunderclap shoved him. He felt its heat and smelled burnt powder.

The tank was bouncing in his vision, he was nearly there. He had only about forty yards farther to go and he'd be safe, a returning hero with the crew's rations. But before he could make it, the field to his left exploded.

A blinding flash. A deafening crack. An invisible hand seemed to pick him up and sweep him across the road into a ditch.

Gustav opened his eyes to a rain of dirt. His eardrums throbbed with pain and he felt a burning sensation on his chest.

I'm hit!

He pawed at his coveralls and his hand came away wet, which sent him into an even greater panic. Then he saw the spilled mess kits oozing with stew and knew what he was feeling. Another shockwave rippled overhead. He had to move before he ended up a casualty along with the rations.

Scooping up his black overseas cap, Gustav bolted for the tank. Thirty yards away, twenty, ten . . .

With an athletic leap he grabbed the gun barrel and swung himself

COMMANDER

LOADER

GUNNER

RADIOMAN/
BOW GUNNER

DRIVER

Panther G

onto the frontal armor. Scampering higher, he parted the camouflage branches and entered his hatch.

Safe in the tight, oil-scented confines, he collapsed against his machine gun. The others couldn't see him. A wall of spare shells, stacked horizontally, separated him from the driver to his left, and more shells obscured the three men in the turret basket behind him. It was too soon to show them his fear.

They were all veterans who knew him as *Bubi,* or little boy. After their units had been devastated on the Eastern Front, they, together with rookies like Gustav, had been placed into the 2nd Company of the newly formed Panzer Brigade 106, and sent to Luxembourg City, just twelve miles west of the German border.

With a strength of forty-seven vehicles—thirty-six Panthers and eleven Jagdpanzer IV self-propelled guns—the brigade's orders were hopelessly overreaching: delay the American advance at any cost.

Like a U-boat crew in the ocean depths, the men listened to the explosions thumping outside. Gustav eyed the hull's ceiling, expecting it to burst at any moment. He would have given anything to be back on his farm in Arrenkamp, in the windswept fields far in the German north.

Home was a humble ranch lit by candles, with a stable attached to the entrance and swallows fluttering inside. Abiding by folklore tradition, his father always cut a hole in the roof so the birds could build their nests within the walls and bring the family luck.

Gustav's parents had one bedroom while Gustav and his younger brother shared the other with their grandparents. His best friend was his grandmother Luise. A short, sturdy woman who wore her blond hair in a bun, she would read fairy tales to the boys, including Gustav's favorite, "Snow-White and Rose-Red." It was a simple life, but far better than in any tank.

No one spoke after the shelling tapered to nothing. Was that it?

The tank wasn't big enough for Gustav to hide forever. Sooner or later his crewmates would notice that he was wearing their supper.

His gut instinct told Gustav to blame the kitchen crew. They had parked a half mile from the tanks to protect their own necks.

But his emotion couldn't overcome his upbringing. "Always be modest," his grandmother had taught him, "and always be honest."

Facing an entirely different kind of fear, Gustav broke the silence. "I lost it . . . I lost all our precious food!"

The men were furious, as Gustav knew they'd be. "What about our smokes?" one asked.

Gustav retrieved five small cigarette packets from his pockets. Each held four cigarettes and was badly crumpled. Gustav passed the packs through the shells to the other men, which sparked a fresh round of cursing.

Gustav pulled a wooden box from a cloth bag he kept beside his seat. Inside were numerous packets of cigarettes and a bed of cigars. He slipped the crumpled cigarettes inside and returned the box to the bag.

As the crew continued to grumble, the commander reassured them: "He'll be punished."

Once the shadows had shifted with the afternoon sun, the camouflage branches were cleared.

The Panther idled on the dirt road, its steady growl reverberating between the fieldstone homes of Merl.

A Panther G model, the tank was sandy yellow with green and brown swirls of camouflage. A forward-leaning turret sat atop a sleek hull and housed a gun that stretched more than half the tank's length. Everything flowed from a slanted two-ton slab of frontal armor, known as the upper glacis. Equivalent to 5.7 inches thick, it dwarfed the 3.5-inch front plate on an M4A1 75mm-armed Sherman.*

The Panther gave a snort.

Drive sprockets cranked, steel tracks clanked, and sixteen interlacing wheels turned on each side. When the machine rolled forward and away, it revealed Gustav lying on the road, a hammer and tools at his side.

The little radioman sat up, coughing from the dust that the tank had kicked back in his face. Normally after a road journey it was the driver's job to tighten or replace the pins that held the tracks together. Today it had been Gustav's punishment. His hands were greasy and his knuckles were bloody as he wiped the tools down with a cloth.

In front of the Panther, the commander guided the driver toward a barn where they'd park for the night. Second Company was in reserve, with its twelve Panthers dispersed throughout Merl, hidden wherever the machines could be concealed. After parking the tank, the commander approached Gustav.

Staff Sergeant Rolf Millitzer was tall and lanky. Beneath a black forage cap, his face was long and lined with the stress of command. The war had aged him far beyond his twenty-six years.

Rolf squatted to Gustav's level, his dark eyes friendly in spite of Gustav's earlier accident. There were larger concerns. In the early hours that morning, their three sister companies had crossed the border into France before running into American lines. They hadn't radioed back since. The silence could only mean one thing: the Americans were on the doorstep of Luxembourg and coming here next.

---

* Armor took on additional thickness when laid at an angle. For example, a Panther's upper glacis was 3.149 inches thick when stood vertically, but when laid at a 55-degree angle, it took on the *equivalent* thickness of 5.7 inches. In this book, the author will refer to armor by its equivalent thickness.

"I told them they can open the emergency rations, so they'll lay off you," Rolf said, referring to Gustav's fellow crewmen.

Each tanker carried a ration of spreadable pork, biscuits, and a tin of Scho-Ka-Kola—dark chocolate infused with caffeine, which was only to be opened in an emergency.

Gustav was relieved and he apologized for his actions.

"You need to be more careful," Rolf said. "There's no need to push too hard any longer. The main thing now is to stay alive."

Rolf departed, leaving Gustav puzzled.

They were German soldiers on the eve of battle, on the verge of losing the war, and Rolf was urging thoughts of survival already?

Gustav held no illusions, himself—victory was impossible. He had known it that autumn day in 1943 when his mother took him to the train station to report to the military.

The 6th Army had been wiped out at Stalingrad, the Afrika Korps had surrendered in Tunisia, and Germany was at war with the entire world. There was no way to win.

But what about their "duty"?

As Gustav carried his tools back to the tank, Rolf's admonishment wouldn't leave him.

The main thing now is to stay alive.

Coming from a battle-hardened veteran, what kind of words were those?

The next morning, September 9, 1944
Merl

The farm courtyard was cool and quiet around seven A.M., as Gustav prepared to shave.

The sky was warming overhead. Seated on a stool, he leaned into a mirror propped on a well, gazing contentedly at himself as he lathered his face with soap and dipped his razor into a bucket of cold water. The farmer who had provided the water must have chuckled at the little German who barely showed any stubble to shave.

Today was Gustav's eighteenth birthday and this was his gift to himself.

He wasn't about to tell the crew about the occasion; no one was in the mood anyway, after what had happened to their sister companies. The previous night, the survivors limped back with stories of a massacre.

Under the confusion of darkness they had mistakenly wandered into American lines in a forest and were surrounded, losing twenty-one tanks and self-propelled guns, nearly half the unit, in the first day.

Still, Gustav didn't feel right about fighting Americans. As a boy, he had enjoyed reading books about cowboys and Indians and even Mickey Mouse. And back home, nearly every farmer had relatives who had emigrated to the New World or sent their children there when there were too many mouths to feed. Even his grandmother's family had gone, and Gustav had pondered the idea too.

Gustav had barely swiped the razor when a courier bolted into the courtyard looking for Rolf. His spirits sank. The courier could only mean one thing.

It was time to fight.

Sizzling with power, the line of twelve Panthers rolled into the fields of Merl and headed west.

Churning slowly through the soft earth, the machines seemed to chomp at the bit, eager to run. The throaty growl of their engines coursed through the air as puffs of smoke rose from their exhaust stacks.

The tanks were fresh off the assembly line. Crisp black numbers lined the turrets and their hides were covered in smooth concrete ridges called *Zimmerit,* for shaking off magnetic mines.[*]

But even brand-new, the Panther came with worrisome defects. All that armor made the tank front-heavy, which wore out the drivetrain, and the tank's interlacing wheels were easily clogged, so that when one wheel jammed, all were affected. A year earlier, 200 Panthers had debuted at the Battle of Kursk. After five days of action, wear, and tear, only 10 remained operational.

Gustav and the driver rode with their hatches open.

Behind them smoke rose in Luxembourg City. The German administrators were destroying the city's phone grid, water lines, and other infrastructure as they fled. In the process, they were also leaving Gustav's brigade to operate without these necessities.

Gustav wore a throat microphone around his neck and a headset over his cap. A purr filled his ears, coming from the FU5 radio mounted over the transmission to his left. As radioman, he listened simultaneously to the intercom and the company frequency.

Rolf stood in the commander's position, ribs-deep in the turret, with his hat turned backward so the brim wouldn't hit his periscopes. The radio antenna waved behind him.

---

[*] Gustav's was one of more than 6,000 Panthers built during the war, a number eclipsed by the 49,234 Shermans that would roll off the Allies' assembly lines. His tank's turret identification numbers, unfortunately, are long forgotten.

The Panthers were driving toward a gap in the distant forest, where they expected the Americans to arrive. The 5th Armored Division was on the way. A "regular" division with 32 percent fewer tanks than the 3rd Armored, it was now contending for a historic feat.

With Allied units in Italy running up against the Germans' defensive Gothic Line north of Florence, and the Soviets stalled in Poland along the river Vistula, the 5th Armored found itself in position to reach Germany first, after Spearhead's unexpected detour to Mons. All that remained was to charge into Luxembourg City and then springboard to the border.

With just twelve Panthers, 2nd Company would try to spoil that feat.

The Panthers had barely traveled a mile when a voice erupted in Gustav's ears—"Fighter-bombers!" High above Gustav to his two o'clock, a dozen silver planes with red noses were curving around from the right. They were American P-47s, Thunderbolts of the 50th Fighter Group.

Gustav stared in awe as the planes leveled their wings and dove toward him.

Rolf disappeared from above the turret; the driver sank from sight and sealed his hatch. But Gustav wasn't moving. He held his gaze on the lead plane, captivated. The propeller spun hypnotically. The closer the plane came to him, the wider and wider apart the wings seemed to stretch. Sunlight sparkled from the canopy glass.

"Bubi!" Rolf shouted on the intercom. "Button up!"

Snapped free of his trance, Gustav dropped into his compartment and slammed the hatch cover just before a torrent of bullets sprinted across the tank, leaving a high-pitched ringing noise that reverberated through the hull.

Gustav wanted to slap himself for being so foolish.

The radio squawked with the company commander's order to disperse. It was every crew for itself. The hull in front of Gustav vibrated as the Maybach engine surged in the rear of the tank. Seven hundred horsepower coursed through the floor.

Outside, the tanks accelerated in the field and fanned out in an effort to put more space between them and become more difficult targets for the planes.

Rolf's Panther took up the left flank of the formation. Smoke now blasted from its stacks. Its tracks chewed the farm dirt like a coffee grinder before spitting it out the back. The interlacing wheels rose and fell with the terrain, absorbing the bumps, while the cannon stayed level, ready for anything.*

At 18 miles per hour the tank hit its stride. But the American planes were hot on their trail. Over the deafening throb of the engine, Gustav heard a clinking and clanging above him, then the thunderous roar of a P-47 ripping overhead. Gustav made himself small and held on for dear life. The tank was barreling along like a runaway train.

The P-47s made pass after pass, mercilessly targeting the vulnerable air intakes over the Panther's engine. But without bombs or rockets underwing, those grates were too small for the Americans to land a deadly blow. The planes abandoned the hunt and departed, off into the horizon.

Gustav could breathe again, but he couldn't relax for too long. A new order came on the radio: take cover. Rolf ordered the driver to move the Panther toward a thick grove of woods on their left. Gustav opened his hatch and stood to help the driver steer. Even in the midst of combat, his job was to stick his head out and watch for threats from the side.

Bathed in the sharp shadows of spruce trees at the end of the forest, the Panther halted with a sigh. Rolf had chosen this position for its proximity to a potential escape route, a shady cut in the neighboring woods. The frontal armor faced westward toward the gap.

With the Panther in position, its hatch covers were flung open. After being enclosed in the tight space during the race for their lives, everyone rose hungry for air.

Gustav was surprised to find they had traversed the farthest distance of anyone in their company. Across a field to the right lay a road that led to the gap. Everyone else was on the other side. Just the turret of a Panther tucked beside the road was visible. Two other tanks had

---

* Although the average American tanker believed that he had the more nimble tank, the Panther was deemed faster and more maneuverable, both on- and off-road, in a U.S. Army wartime test.

slipped among the trees of a hilltop estate. None of the tanks moved as they waited in ambush.

After taking fire from the planes, Gustav's once pristine tank was scarred. Bullets had raked the turret numbers, stripped the *Zimmerit,* and blasted away the tow cable.

Rolf lowered himself to the hull, directly between Gustav and the driver. "I need your mirror, Bubi," he said. "Mine caught bullets."

Gustav removed the mirror from his periscope and gave it to Rolf. It was more important that the commander could see outside than that he could.

Rolf was an enigma. He received letters from Dresden but never spoke of his family. He wore the silver Panzer badge for surviving twenty-five tank engagements, but never told stories. All Gustav could deduce with any certainty was that he had held a white-collar job before the war, because he spoke fluent English and sometimes sang to himself in English.

The Panther's engine labored as the massive tank idled. An hour, maybe two, passed. Gustav had lost track of time and didn't own a watch.

Farmers waded into the fields among the tanks, men and women pushing wheelbarrows and digging for potatoes. Life went on. Gustav envied the men and women with their boots caked in soil. He had always loved farm work. The vision before him brought back fond memories of harvesting rye with a scythe in fields similar to these, which his family sometimes did by the light of the moon.

Gustav was a reluctant fighter. Hitler Youth membership had been mandatory since 1939; he'd had no choice but to join. Although he enjoyed the camping, marching, and sports, he'd never wanted to be a soldier like the other boys. Gustav's dream was to be a locomotive conductor.

Every Sunday, after church, he'd pedal his bicycle far from home to watch the trains chug past on the Hamburg–Bremen line. After the war began, he'd even applied to work in a factory that built locomotives. He hoped it would be a first step toward becoming a conductor.

But when his father was drafted into the army, the family found itself shorthanded and Gustav's grandmother asked him to remain on the farm. What could have been a difficult choice for some was easy for him. To Gustav, his duty came first, before any personal wishes or desires. He had a duty to his family. To the farm. It was that simple.

When Gustav's own army orders arrived in autumn 1943, he wrote to the War Office and secured a four-week reprieve to help with the harvest. Only after fulfilling his duty to his family did he board a train to serve his country.

When Gustav finally stood before an army doctor for his physical, the doctor took one look at his compact frame, a perfect fit for tight spaces, and sent him straight to the armored forces.

Gustav's headset crackled with voices. The transmission was scratchy but alarming.

The voices were American. Gustav alerted Rolf—if he was picking up the enemy's transmissions, they had to be close. Possibly close enough to shoot.

Except for Rolf, who stood lookout with field glasses, the crew withdrew inside and buttoned their hatches.

Since his periscope mirror had been requisitioned by Rolf, Gustav pressed an eye to the rubber ring sight of his MG 34 Panzerlauf machine gun, a special stockless variant. The barrel and sight protruded from the slant armor and gave a view no wider than the diameter of a coin.

The Germans retreating into their tanks spooked the local farmers, who scattered from the fields, leaving their tools behind. As if on cue, the Shermans appeared two miles away in the forest gap.

From the turret, Rolf called out their range and heading, which Gustav copied in a pad before alerting the company commander.

Following the road, the column of the U.S. 34th Tank Battalion flowed into the fields without hesitation, obviously intent on liberating Luxembourg City that day.

A motorized whine sounded behind Gustav. The gunner was tracking the column with the nearly 17-foot-long gun known as the *über lang,* or extra-long. The turret crept agonizingly slowly. Finally, the extra-long stopped directly over Gustav. It was a 75mm gun like the older Mark IV's, but chambered with a larger, nearly 3-foot-long shell that fired with earsplitting "super velocity."

"Wait for my call," Rolf told the gunner. The enemy was in range, but Rolf wanted to hold his fire until they couldn't retreat.

Sweat trickled down Gustav's face. The whites of his knuckles showed as he gripped his machine gun. It was useless against tanks, but comforting to hold. Peeking above the stacked shells that separated them, he saw the Panther's driver gazing through his periscope, its light spilling around his eyes. The man was utterly relaxed.

The Shermans motored farther from the safety of the forest toward where Rolf and the Panther lay in wait. They were now only a mile away. But Rolf wanted them closer. He'd learned on the Eastern Front to wait until the target was within a half mile's distance, then to shoot the last tank in the column, then the first, which created a deadly logjam. After that, the hunting was easy.*

Suddenly, a shaft of green tracer zipped from the right and slammed into the lead Sherman.

Gustav couldn't believe it. *Someone fired too soon!* He watched as the Sherman's hatch covers flung open and the crew came tumbling out.

---

* The extra-long was at its most accurate at the range of a half mile, as evidenced by a postwar test when a Panther put every shot within a 12-inch circle at that distance.

Rolf cursed. He must have traced the fire back to its origin and seen it. There, on the hilltop to the north, sat a Panther in the trees, smoke floating from its muzzle. The golden opportunity was squandered.

The column of Shermans halted. In unison their turrets turned toward the hilltop Panther and began firing, driving it and a second Panther into retreat.

Rolf had to act. He directed the gunner's attention to the second Sherman in line. Its crew had turned nearly broadside to join in the firing.

The extra-long was typically a "point-and-shoot" weapon—the gunner had no need to compensate for distance.

Gustav sat back from his gun sight and braced for the shot. Rolf gave the order as if perturbed to have to do so. "Fire."

With an earsplitting bark, flames leapt from the extra-long's muzzle and a 16-pound warhead blasted downrange. The green tracer covered the mile in barely two seconds. The Sherman shuddered and swayed on its suspension as it absorbed the punch. The gun's recoil rocked the Panther back on its heels.

"Hit," Rolf said.

Gustav returned to his gun sight. A hole flickered with flame where the Sherman's engine sat. Gustav watched the crew come pouring out of the Sherman as it burned in the field. Gustav was pleased to see them escape. Even if they were the enemy, they were fellow tankers who endured the same miseries that he did.[*]

Shielded by the two smoking wrecks, the remaining Shermans turned back the way they'd come.

Gustav glanced over at the driver—*That's it?*

He'd barely finished the thought when a shell smacked the Panther's front armor with a low-pitched resonance. The battle was just beginning.

The intercom came alive with cursing as Gustav reeled from the attack. Returning to his gun sight, he saw a brilliant white cloud

---

[*] Amazingly, of the two Shermans that the 34th Tank Battalion lost that day, no men were killed in either vehicle. Their commanding general would comment in his report: "It soon was apparent from the skillful tactics of the enemy, that the engagement was considerably more than a hastily planned rear-guard action."

enveloping them, billowing larger and larger. Fiery sparks popped and danced.

The smoke wafted inside the tank through an air intake in the ceiling, stinging Gustav's eyes and nostrils, and he tasted acid on his tongue. "What is this?" Gustav asked, wiping his watering eyes. The others couldn't stop coughing. No one answered because none had seen white phosphorus before.

It was an incendiary weapon used primarily by the Western Allies. A chemical substance so volatile that it was stored underwater for safety reasons, when packed into exploding shells it ignited on contact with the air, burning at 5,000 degrees for almost a minute. A single waxy flake could burn a man to the bone. And this was just the smoke from it.

Gustav was still pawing his eyes when another, heavier, shell slammed the Panther's slant with the noise of a cathedral bell.

As the tank lurched backward, the gun sight punched Gustav in the forehead, sending him sprawling against his seatback.

Rolf called for the driver to reverse—"Get us out of here!"

The tank shifted gears, lurched backward, and began clanking slowly toward the shady cut in the woods, which was behind and to the left of them. Nursing his forehead and with ringing ears, Gustav crept back to the gun sight to resume his post. A dark shape, probably some sort of armored vehicle, had moved into the gap during his absence.

It was an American M7 self-propelled artillery vehicle, housing a massive 105mm gun.

Nicknamed the "Priest" by the British, an M7 normally fired skyward as mobile field artillery, but now its gun was leveled at the Panther.

A muzzle flash blinked from the Priest's direction. Gustav jumped back before the shell slammed the armor directly in front of his face. The lights flickered. The ringing in his ears returned. He stared in terror at the walls of the tank. The cream-colored paint was flaking.

A second shell slammed the slant armor. Then a third. Gustav gripped his ears. It was like a battering ram striking just inches from his face. In the corner of the hull, he could see fissures forming up and down the welds.

Despite the pounding fire, the driver swung the tank into the cut in the forest, striving to get behind the wall of trees. For a brief moment, the turn to safety presented the Priest with a clear view of the Panther's side. The enemy took advantage. Yet another shell slammed the Panther, this time finding the left track. The brutal impact flung the driver sideways against the shells and Gustav against the steel wall.

Gustav clutched his shoulder. The driver regained the controls from the midst of the chaos. He reported to Rolf that he could feel the damage—a shell had probably severed the left track.

"Keep going!" Rolf urged.

The tank kept rolling deeper into the cut, behind the wall of spruce trees, just before its wheels rolled off the last track link and sank into the earth.

The Priest reluctantly shifted its aim to fire on someone else.

A hatch slid open from the turret and Rolf stood in the shade.

In the sun-swept fields, Panthers were retreating left and right. They had no choice but to leave behind two of their own—one abandoned by the road, one burning on the hilltop.

A soft, puttering noise from above drew Rolf's attention from the carnage.

Two thousand feet above the battlefield, an American L-4 spotter plane was circling with one wing pointed toward the earth. Known as a "Grasshopper," the L-4 was used to direct artillery fire.

Gustav and the others gripped their hatches, awaiting Rolf's command. They were eager to flee, but didn't dare. To abandon a tank without orders was tantamount to desertion. It was a crime that the German Army wouldn't hesitate to punish—with extreme prejudice. By the end of 1944, they would execute 10,000 of their own soldiers.

Rolf gave the command, "Everybody out!"

The turret was empty in seconds. But in the hull, Gustav had a problem. His hatch cover wouldn't open more than a few inches. He put his back into it, but without luck. One of the shell hits had jammed the hinges. He was trapped. The confines suddenly felt tight, uncomfortably tight.

On the other side of the stacked shells, the driver lingered. "Don't wait for me!" Gustav said. The driver was gone in a flash.

Faint whistling sounds seeped through the open tank, followed by the thunder of exploding shells. Artillery was falling outside. Gustav frantically unbuckled the thirty-pound shells and began sliding them, one at a time, back into the turret until he created a path to the driver's side. He crawled for freedom.

Outside, Gustav rolled over the side of the Panther, scrambled to the tree line, and dove into a pile of fallen leaves. He looked up and tried to get his bearings.

Behind the tank, the driver was already two hundred yards away, running through the fields as artillery shells burst in his wake. Every fiber in Gustav wanted to stay glued to the forest floor. Even Rolf himself had admonished him: "The main thing now is to stay alive." The Americans would be coming soon. Gustav didn't fear capture, because the Americans seemed cautious with the lives of their men and he assumed, by extension, that they would be humane toward him.

Out in the fields, a shell burst changed everything.

The driver hobbled then fell and rolled on his back, clutching his left knee. The shelling didn't let up. A gear clicked in Gustav. He had a duty to help a comrade, even a comrade who had not hesitated to leave him behind.

Gustav leaped to his feet and sprinted for the driver, across smoking craters, shielding his face from flaming tree bursts. Another crew-member must have seen the driver fall, because he was approaching from the opposite direction, pushing a wheelbarrow. They arrived at the driver's position at the same time. Behind the wheelbarrow was the gunner, Senior Lance Corporal Werner Wehner, a stocky veteran with a round, ruddy face and precious little patience.

The driver was screaming, his knee split open. Werner gripped the man in a bear hug and dumped him in the wheelbarrow, eliciting an animal howl of pain. Werner took one handle, Gustav took the other, and they began pushing the wounded man toward Merl. They steered around undetonated shells that sizzled in the dirt, flinching as shells burst and dirt rained down upon them.

Finally, they dropped into a flat stretch of hard-packed soil and backtracked over the same ground they'd covered that morning. It was easier to push the wheelbarrow here, in their tank's tracks, as they outran the bursts of artillery over their shoulders.

The irony was not lost on Gustav.

They'd traded their Panther for *this*.

That same night
West of Merl

Clutching a wooden box, Gustav followed Werner through the dead of night.

The moon lay low on the horizon, casting the patchwork fields in shades of blue. It was around ten P.M. The men crouched low and moved silently. Every so often, Werner paused to touch the earth and check their course.

The box grew heavy in Gustav's arms. Although the night was cool, he found himself sweating beneath his coveralls. He knew what they had come to do.

And it was crazy.

Like knights stalking a sleeping dragon, Gustav and Werner were creeping back toward their abandoned Panther. It lay untouched against the forest, the hatches open to the breeze, the gun still facing where the enemy had been. But where were they now?

Standing absolutely still, Werner listened. In the forest to their left, leaves were rustling. Could this be an American trap? Gustav's eyes darted in pursuit of the noises. He wore a pistol, but that brought little comfort. What could a pistol do if they were confronted by men with rifles?

Gustav's company commander had ordered him and Werner here, and with good reason. It was their tank. Their duty. Their mess to clean up. And besides, they were all that remained of the crew.

The medics had taken the driver off their hands for treatment and Rolf and the loader were still missing. Werner had last seen them dart into the forest during the shelling. And now Werner was stuck with Gustav, whom he viewed as a liability in this precarious situation. The thirty-two-year-old veteran had been offered many chances to lead a crew of his own, but he had turned down every promotion to avoid the headache of looking after anyone other than himself. If Werner had it his way, he'd have done this mission alone too.

Gustav followed Werner in a dash to the Panther. Taking cover on the field side of the tank, they braced for the forest to erupt with gunfire. But to their surprise, nothing happened.

Gustav crept forward toward his compartment on a quick, personal foray.

Werner's grip stopped him.

"I left my bag next to my seat," Gustav said in a whisper. Inside were his diary, letters from his grandmother, and his cigar box.

"Forget it."

Gustav's spirits sank.

Werner climbed up to the engine deck and cast a glare at his partner. "Get up here!" he said.

"But my things!" Gustav protested.

Werner had bigger concerns. A half mile to the north, a Panther smoldered at the hilltop estate. In attempting to retreat, its commander had presented the tank's vulnerable flank and rear to the enemy, who made good on the targets.

Across the field and beyond the road sat another Panther with just its turret showing. It had been immobilized by the P-47s but hadn't burned. It was still partially operational.

And therein lay the problem. A captured Panther could be repurposed, an eventuality that would happen across multiple theaters during the war. On the Eastern Front, the Russians had seized enough Panthers that they printed instruction manuals in Cyrillic. And in Italy, the Seaforth Highlanders of Canada would soon capture a Panther and gift it to the British 145th Regiment of the Royal Armoured Corps, who'd use it under the ironic code name "Deserter." Later, in Holland, the British Coldstream Guards would find their Panther, "Cuckoo," in a barn, and fight with it into Germany.

Gustav and Werner couldn't let this happen in Luxembourg.

Gustav carefully handed the wooden box up to Werner and then climbed aboard himself. The two men disappeared into their Panther's turret. For a moment, they were home again. Werner sat in the gunner's seat, situated to the left of the gun breech—opposite where his American counterpart would sit—and he turned the turret by handwheel. With a shell in his hands, Gustav served as his loader.

Outside the tank, the Panther's turret crept to the right so slowly that its movement was barely perceptible. The turret stopped with its barrel aimed at the Panther across the road.

The muzzle barked a spout of flames as long as a telephone pole and the shell punched the abandoned tank in the turret numbers. The sound rippled across the fields like a church bell.

But still, the tank wouldn't burn. The Panther seemed impervious to friendly fire. After the ten seconds needed to reload, Werner and Gustav sent another green projectile zipping across the field. This strike accomplished Werner's goal. A glow appeared behind the two holes in the turret, pulsing brighter and brighter until a blowtorch of flame blasted upward from the turret hatches.

The fire from the abandoned Panther lit up the fields and forest.

Gustav leaped down from his tank and took off running. Werner followed, hot on his heels. They still didn't know the enemy's position, but the two shots in the night were sure to reveal their presence.

Werner had taken the explosives from the box that Gustav had brought along with them and slid the charges into the Panther's gun breech before lighting the fuse. Anticipating the blast that they thought was sure to follow, the men dived to the ground and covered their heads.

Thirty seconds turned into a minute, which turned into two. But the explosion they were expecting didn't resound.

The men lifted their heads. Silence.

Gustav couldn't believe it. This day refused to end.

The tank was a powder keg, but would it blow?

Maybe twenty tense minutes had passed and still it hadn't exploded. The silence was broken by new sounds coming from the opposite side of the forest. Sherman tanks had pulled up and parked. Now hatches were opening and Americans were talking as if they'd never heard the Panther firing just shortly before.

"Did you bring your knife?" Werner asked.

"Yes?"

Whatever Werner was thinking, Gustav didn't like it.

Gustav's feet felt like lead as he and Werner returned to their Panther. He waited while Werner disappeared around the front of the tank and eyed the turret with trepidation, hoping the explosives weren't smoldering inside. He no longer cared about his sack of personal effects.

Sounds of hammering and wood splitting were now traveling through the forest from the Americans' position. They were probably adjusting their tracks or removing ammunition from wooden cases. Whatever they were doing, they were too close for comfort.

Werner returned from inside the tank holding the driver's leather seat cushion. Using his knife, Gustav split open the cushion and Werner gutted the wool filler and twisted it into a six-foot rope. Werner climbed onto the engine deck and fed the rope into one of the Panther's gas tanks, drenching it. Leaving one end in the gas, he fed the other to Gustav, who strung it from the tank like a tail.

Werner came down and with a flick of a lighter, a flame raced up the rope.

Gustav and Werner fled as fast as they could into the field behind the tank. They reached safety just as a roaring volcano of flames burst from the Panther's engine deck and licked the night sky. The heat from the flames triggered the plastic explosives and the gun barrel ruptured with a thunderous crack. Side by side, Gustav and Werner watched as their tank became charred. The ammunition began cooking off, popping and hissing.

Gustav cringed. It was like losing a friend. The tank had taken a beating, shielding him from six hits so violent that people four miles away in Luxembourg City reported seeing the shells ricocheting into the air.

Earlier in the war, a German crew might have towed their Panther back for repair instead of risking their lives to destroy it. Gustav blamed Hitler, who had personally ordered the brigade rushed into Luxembourg without aerial reconnaissance or artillery support or even a recovery vehicle to retrieve disabled tanks.

A sweet, smoky scent caught Gustav's nose. It may have been his imagination, but he swore he smelled his box of tobacco burning. He had intended it to be a gift.

His father was a supply soldier on the Eastern Front, tasked with bringing up essentials by horse-drawn cart. In a letter, he'd lamented to Gustav the lack of good tobacco available there. For months, Gustav had stashed away his cigarette rations and bought any cigars he could find. Now his parcel for his father was gone, along with his diary and mail. Would they even find another tank for him, or would they send him to the infantry?

Gustav wanted to cry.

Werner must have recognized that the young radioman needed some encouragement. He gently elbowed Gustav and extended an open hand. In the flickering light, the two men shook to the success of their mission.

The moon was high at midnight when Gustav and Werner rode back to Merl on a Panther.

Their company commander walked ahead of the tank, on the lookout for tree stumps. The tank was his, but he had relinquished command.

For the return journey, Gustav was the tank commander. Werner sat on the tank's front hull, holding on by the gun barrel, and Gustav rode in the commander's position with earphones pulled on over his cap. No one could remember why the company commander had deputized Gustav. Perhaps it was a reward, or perhaps he had seen the duty roster and this was a birthday present. But one thing was clear— Gustav was loving every second of it.

For the first time in the war, and maybe his entire life, he felt important, riding in the turret's high perch with the engine surging through the steel ring around his ribs. He held the reins of a 49-ton machine, but it came with a responsibility: to make sure the driver didn't feed the Panther too much gas, which would send blue flames leaping from the exhaust, revealing their position. But it probably didn't matter anyway; the Americans already had an eyeful.

Behind them, Panthers were burning like oil wells.

Beneath an overpass hidden from the moon's reach, Gustav spread a blanket on the tank's engine deck.

His eyes drooped with exhaustion. He could barely stand. It was nearly two A.M. in Merl and the others had gone to scrounge for food or to plan their next moves. At first light, their brigade would retreat for the West Wall and then on to the city of Trier to be reequipped.

The Americans would soon be hot on their trail. Later that morning, American Shermans would roll into Luxembourg City, where ecstatic locals would swarm the tanks with chalk, scribbling patriotic messages on their hulls. And a day after that, on September 11, the war would enter a new season.

That's when a 5th Armored foot patrol would lay first boots on German soil and gaze upon the pillboxes of the West Wall.

That's when Allied troops who had landed in Normandy would link up with Allied troops who had landed in southern France to form a wall of their own, of men and machines stretching from the Belgian coast to Switzerland.

And that's when the Supreme Allied Commander, General Dwight Eisenhower, would be unleashed to act on his mandate to "undertake operations aimed at the heart of Germany and the destruction of her armed forces."

Gustav curled on the deck of the Panther and pulled the blanket over him, blissfully unaware that seven Allied armies were now converging on him. Residual heat from the engine still warmed the deck beneath him.

His birthday had come and gone, leaving him with just the uniform on his back. But that was good enough. He had done his duty and survived, convinced that the days ahead would be easier. How could they be worse than this?

Gustav fell fast asleep.

CHAPTER 6 **BEYOND THE WALL**

Eight days later, September 14, 1944
Seventy-five miles north—Germany

A dozen or more Sherman tanks of Easy Company rumbled to a stop by the side of a country road about four miles west of Stolberg.

No crewmen climbed down. Alongside the column stood a darkened farmhouse, a white bedsheet flapping from a dark second-story window.

The air tingled with tension—a storm was boiling over the lifeless surrounding forests.

Sergeant Bob Earley, of Fountain, Minnesota, stood like a statue in the lead tank's turret, a pipe clenched between his teeth. At twenty-nine, Earley was a hardened old man among a unit of boyish tankers. His black hair was receding and his face was flat and stoic, with eyes often locked in a squint. He was the replacement for Paul Faircloth.

Earley's piercing gaze settled on the farmhouse. Not a candle flickered.

Behind him, other tank commanders kept low, ready at their machine guns. This was Germany, the enemy's home turf. Before the men could stretch their legs and take a breather, someone would have to investigate.

Smoke rose about two miles behind the column. The day before, the 3rd Armored had opened the door to Germany, becoming the first Allied unit to punch through the West Wall and to also capture a

Bob Earley

German town. But the day after the triumphs, Easy Company showed the scars. Normally sixteen tanks strong—three platoons of five, plus a tank for the company commander—the unit was missing five tanks and crews.

It could have been worse. Had they not stopped 27,000 German troops at Mons, the division concluded that piercing the West Wall would have been "next to impossible."

The farmhouse door cracked open. A half dozen machine guns swung toward the sign of motion. Then, a hand emerged, waving a white cloth. A short German farmer stepped outside. He looked to be in his seventies, with bushy gray hair and a tired face bristling with gray stubble.

The farmer spoke to the tankers as they glared down menacingly from behind their guns. They couldn't hear him over the tank engines, and even if they could hear him, they couldn't understand him.

"Smoyer!"

The radio call came from the company commander, whose tank traveled last in line.

Earley leaned into the turret and spoke, then stepped down to the engine deck with a Thompson submachine gun in hand. He cradled the gun, keeping an eye on the farmer.

Earley had come with his own tank too. The tank beneath him was one of the new M4A1 Shermans known as a "76." With a barrel that was three feet longer and a millimeter wider than before, it was chambered to fire a larger 76mm shell, which was capable of penetrating an extra inch into enemy armor.* In the 3rd Armored Division, each company received about five 76s and they often went to the best fighters.

Inside the tank, also christened "Eagle" by the crew, Clarence grumbled. Someone had leaked that he spoke German. Regulations said to wear a steel helmet whenever outside the tank, but he didn't bother, and climbed down with a knit cap on his head. Since no one else could do this job, they were in no position to object.

Clarence drew his 1911 pistol, racked a round into the chamber, then holstered it. Despite the white flags, Clarence kept a hand near his pistol as he approached the farmer.

M4A1 (76mm) Sherman

* The British had up-gunned their Shermans as early as 1943, swapping the 75 mm gun for a 17-pounder and re-naming it the "Firefly." They offered to convert American tanks—their gun was even more potent than the 76 mm—but U.S. forces couldn't take their Shermans off the line, due to lack of reserves. Besides, there was the promise of new M36 tank destroyers coming and the brass's underestimation of the enemy, evident that September when Eisenhower's Armored Chief wrote: "Probably the problem of the Panther will no longer be with U.S. for the remainder of the war. The German, we believe, has lost most of his armor."

Easy Company had been placed in reserve and was trailing the task force, a multicompany fighting unit of tanks and doughs. It was a pause for the men of Easy Company to catch their breath and lick their wounds, but that didn't mean they were safe here or anywhere. Often, the enemy would let one column pass in order to strike another that had lowered its guard.

Was an ambush waiting around the next bend? If anyone knew, it would be the farmer.

Clarence towered over the small man, who looked at Clarence and saw a grimy, imposing giant in his battledress—a tanker's short khaki jacket with a knit collar, olive-drab trousers, and spats stained by life in a machine.

What Clarence saw was a tired old man. Clarence greeted him in German. The farmer's face came to life.

"You're German?" he inquired hopefully.

"No," Clarence said. He explained that his parents were Pennsylvania Dutch. "When I was a kid, they spoke German when they didn't want me to know what they were saying."

The farmer laughed and Clarence cracked a smile. The mood lifted and the tankers came down to smoke or relieve themselves in the nearby grass.

"Where are the German soldiers?" Clarence asked.

The farmer pointed back the way the Americans had come.

Clarence wasn't sold. He had seen the enemy's fanaticism just the day before. At one particularly stubborn blockhouse, they had given the German defenders an ultimatum to surrender, only to hear their leader shout in reply: "Go to hell, we will fight it out." So, a few tanks went *around* the blockhouse and pumped fire into the undefended doorway. The result? "Soon afterward the 12 man bunker crew filed out, half blinded and dazed from the concussion of heavy shells hitting their retreat," recorded the division history.

Clarence pressed his interrogation. With each question, the farmer became more and more emphatic. "No National Socialists here," he said. "Just farmers."

The prospect was so absurd that Clarence had to hold back a laugh. They'd come all this way and now the Nazis had eluded them?

Possibly the farmer's neighbors weren't National Socialists *any-*

more. In the nearby village of Langerwehe, with liberation in sight, the civilians had already turned against their own soldiers. When men of the German 89th Grenadier Regiment had marched through, the civilians taunted them: "You will not stop the Americans."

Finally satisfied that the German farmer knew little more than they did, Clarence thanked the man and turned to leave. A bony hand reached out and grabbed Clarence's arm, stopping him in his tracks. Clarence wheeled around and broke the man's grip, clenching his fists to defend himself. His expression softened at the sight of tears welling in the old man's eyes.

The farmer told Clarence that he hated the National Socialists. He had two sons on the Eastern Front and had not heard from them for a year. "Good, healthy boys," he said as the tears slipped down his cheeks. "Good, healthy boys."

He lowered his chin to his chest and began sobbing. Some of the tankers looked away.

Clarence had always thought of the Germans they killed in battle as faceless soldiers without an identity. Not as sons, with fathers or mothers who worried about their safety.

It wasn't until now that he saw an awful truth in the old man's eyes.

War touches everyone.

Clarence placed a hand on the man's shoulder and leaned in close. "I'm sorry about your boys," he said. "We lost some good people too."

With one foot on a bogie wheel, Clarence pulled himself back up and onto the tank. From the turret, he glanced back at the farmer, who was still drying tears from his face. Clarence shouted to him: "*Jetzt wird alles gut werden.*"

The farmer nodded and raised a hand in farewell.

Earley's eyes asked the question without him speaking—*What was that about?*

"I told him that he's going to be okay now," Clarence said.

Earley approved. Now that the Americans were here, that much was true.

Clarence disappeared into the turret.

A week or two later, Stolberg, Germany

This was the end of the road—for now.

Scattered throughout a neighborhood nestled on a hillside, the tanks of Easy Company sat parked between houses with their guns pointed up the slope in the evening light.

Behind the Shermans lay a valley straight out of a fairy tale. A castle was tucked into the valley's center, in the middle of the Rhineland town of Stolberg, which was divided by a winding stream.

The leaves were beginning to turn as a late September chill laced the air. After a summer spent slugging across western Europe, Spearhead had driven six miles inside the West Wall before grinding to a halt, here.

On this hillside, the silent tanks were the front line.

Stolberg was locked in stalemate. The German 12th Infantry Division held the eastern side of the hill, opposite them. They sometimes sent patrols in the direction of Easy Company, but their probing missions were halfhearted.

It was finally dim enough to cloud a sniper's scope.

A tank crewman dashed from a battle-damaged house to cover at the rear of Eagle. Dropping to his knees, he crawled beneath the tank, moving forward. An escape hatch in the belly of the hull allowed for crew to come and go unnoticed.

Moments later, Clarence crawled out from beneath the tank. Rising to his feet he darted successfully into the house. No bullets gave chase.

Clarence joined Earley and the rest of the crew inside the house. The others were slumped in stuffed chairs and on a couch. The dwelling was in ruins from artillery damage. Wooden slabs covered the windows, and the roof leaked also.

Each crew took refuge in the home nearest their tank. It didn't offer much in the way of shelter, but it was better than nothing.

No one was in the mood to talk. The men were homesick, and edgy with inaction. The war wasn't going to end by them just sitting there. Anything could set them off, even something as simple as opening a magazine from home and seeing a pinup girl, or hearing a familiar song on Allied radio.

"Honey I don't see where candle and lamp light is so romantic," wrote one tanker. "I am about to go nuts on them. To see a room lighted again would be a pleasure."

In the kitchen, Clarence lit the crew's small Coleman stove and heated a can of food from his K-ration. He took one of the remaining porcelain dishes from the cupboard and poured his supper onto the plate, then took a seat at a table in the main room and ate in silence.

The Clarence Smoyer from before the war would hardly have recognized himself now. Back in Lehighton, he had one love above all others—roller-skating. He would go to Graver's skating rink, pay the 50 cents admission, clip rollers to his shoes, and skate to organ music, past massive wall murals, for hours and hours on end.

Now, he could barely muster the energy to shovel his food, let alone skate a lap, if Germany even had skating rinks.

The pervasive sense of fatigue—and borderline depression—was felt across Spearhead.

A division designed to pierce enemy lines, "to race amok, cutting the German supply and communications channels, the organization of reserve forces, and the very will to fight," now had barely 1 of 4 tanks combat ready, according to the unit history.

"Tanks were tied together with baling wire," wrote *The Saturday Evening Post*. "The men had been pushed to the limit of human endurance."

Supply lines were stretched so thin that they were holding together only through superhuman effort. On a given day, nearly 6,000 trucks of the "Red Ball Express," crewed primarily by African American drivers, ferried supplies more than three hundred miles from Normandy. By night, their headlights cast a river of light from France to Germany.

If the Spearhead Division was to return to its feet, it would take time, and something special.

The unmistakable sound of a jeep pulling up outside penetrated the crew's malaise.

The engine cut out, someone banged on their tank. Voices were heard.

After a pause, the door to the house flew open, and a lieutenant ducked inside.

He stood before the crew, every inch of six-five, with a slender frame, a long face, and gray eyes. Behind his back, the men called him "High Pockets." He'd attended college for a year, where he studied theatre. In these times, even such meager credentials were enough to make him their superior.

The crew forced themselves to their feet. High Pockets's eyes roved back and forth as he counted them. He had come to inspect them, to ensure that someone was manning the gun in the tank and no one had slipped down to Stolberg for some unauthorized R&R. Clarence pitied the guys in 1st Platoon who were stuck with High Pockets as their lieutenant.

Seemingly out of nowhere, the shrill whistle of artillery arced over the hilltop. The shells were coming from twelve miles away on the German side, in the direction of the Rhine River.

High Pockets's eyes went wide as he tracked the noises shrieking overhead.

The first shells landed downhill. Subsequent barrages thundered steadily uphill—closer and closer to their position. The house shuddered. The crew cursed—they were certain that High Pockets had brought this attack on them; a German artillery spotter must have seen his jeep pull up.

Since the house didn't have a basement, Earley and the others darted into the kitchen and took cover behind the brick stove. High Pockets hit the floor and wrapped his arms over his head. Clarence folded his arms where he sat at the table. After all that he had seen and done, he no longer cared what happened.

The house jumped anew with each blast. Water and plaster rained down from above. Clarence's supper bounced up off the plate in front of him. The window slats blew open. It sounded like a freight train was roaring past outside.

High Pockets tried to crawl under the couch but got stuck. Trapped, he started clawing at the floorboards. When Clarence saw High Pockets's long legs flailing behind him, he couldn't help himself any longer. In spite of the chaos outside, he broke into uncontrollable laughter.

Just as abruptly as it began, the shelling ended.

Earley and the others came back dusting themselves off. High Pockets stood away from the couch, panting for air and disheveled. When the officer turned, he found Clarence casually eating his meal as if nothing had happened.

"You'd be just as dead there as I would here," Clarence said.

High Pockets glared and departed in a huff.

Earley and others erupted in laughter.

When Clarence had finished eating, he took the dirty plate and opened the rear window. Outside lay a pile of broken china. Their first few days in the house, the crew would shout, "No KP duty tonight!" then let fly with the plates, but not anymore—that joke had gotten old. Clarence tossed the plate from the window, watching it shatter on the pile.

A month later, October 29, 1944
Stolberg, Germany

Jubilant whoops pierced the quiet of residential Stolberg.

The Easy Company beer party had just ended.

In the faded light of evening, Clarence and Earley followed the excited voices through the neighborhood south of the castle. They each had been allocated two beers poured from German kegs, but Earley abstained and passed his allotment to Clarence. Somehow, Clarence was still on his feet.

It was their week off the line. Easy Company had begun a rotation with G-Company whereby each unit spent one week in the tanks on the hillside followed by a week recuperating in the valley. The fall weather had turned temperamental. A dreary drizzle was an almost daily ritual, and the precipitation had turned the Rhineland roads into "sticky ribbons of mud." No one was going anywhere anytime soon, which was fine by Clarence.

Stolberg was beginning to feel like "home."

The street where Easy Company was billeted was lined by tall trees and tall homes with porches. Two crews shared each house. The homes were more modern than any they'd seen in France or Belgium, with hot running water for baths and dry floors for their sleeping bags.

On the sidewalk ahead of Clarence and Earley, a private was pulling aside passing tankers, whispering in their ears, and motioning to his house. Whatever he said had them almost tripping over one another in a dash to get inside.

Clarence and Earley reached the private, a tanker from their platoon. He looked around them, keeping a hesitant watch for officers. When he was sure he was in the clear, he told them in a hushed, conspiratorial voice that a beautiful blond German fräulein was inside.

"She's taking all comers."

Clarence was confused.

"She wants to have sex with GIs!" the private said.

Earley scoffed; he was true to a girl back home. Clarence was incredulous. The private reminded them that the German men of Stolberg had been away fighting the war for years. As a result some women were craving affection. He described the fräulein as a bombshell.

Clarence had to see this. The private assured Clarence that he would not regret it. Earley cautioned Clarence against it. A man could get fined just for talking with a German, let alone being caught under the same roof.

A month prior, the army had banned "fraternization" with the foreign civilians. It was a policy that left many Stolberg residents, who were eager to put the war behind them, "a little astonished and dismayed."

It all came about after photos of American GIs and smiling German civilians landed in American newspapers. The White House was quickly flooded with complaints from citizens who considered the images objectionable.

Clarence promised Earley it would be a quick investigation. The private smiled and showed Clarence the way.

Inside the home, the host crews had a system. A sergeant welcomed Clarence and directed him toward a staircase leading up to the second floor. The action was happening in a first-floor bedroom situated near the back of the house.

Clarence stopped at the foot of the staircase, astonished. At least six men lined the steps waiting for their chance to enter the den of debauchery. The sergeant gave Clarence a nudge to move to the back of the line. Clarence complied. He wasn't about to turn back now.

Moments later, a tanker exited the room and approached the

staircase. He wiped his brow and straightened his shirt. "That's good stuff!" he testified to the men in line.

Clarence raised an eyebrow. Something was amiss. The disheveled man. The private outdoors. The sergeant working the staircase. They were all part of the same crew. Why were they being so accommodating?

The sergeant gave the next man in line—a big burly tanker—the go-ahead to enter the bedroom. From his spot in line, Clarence caught a glimpse of the bedroom. It was dark, lit by only a single bulb dangling from the ceiling. The burly man shut the door behind him and took in the view of a figure kneeling on the bed, facing away from him. Long blond hair. Lacy night garments. Smooth skin. As he came closer, the figure turned to face him. Puckered red lips. Smoky eyes and black lashes.

All at once, the room exploded with beams of light. The closet door flung open and five tankers jumped out, shining flashlights on the burly man's face while muffling their laughter. The man was shocked and dismayed. The "girl" added another flashlight to the swirling beams and the burly man looked closer. This was no fräulein. Looking back at him was a young male tanker in a blond wig, full makeup and all, making kissy faces.

The burly man was boiling mad.

Normally, the hosts would have shoved him out the back window to keep the prank alive, but the burly man burst from the door and stormed toward the stairs to warn those still waiting in line. Men from the host crew tried to hold him back and cover his mouth to keep their secret under wraps. But the burly man wasn't having it. After he'd been humiliated, the attempt to silence him was the last straw. He threw the first punch and all playfulness went out the door.

The host crew swung back. The burly man's crew flew to his defense from the steps. In the midst of the chaos, more combatants poured in from outside, likely seething victims of the prank. A crew fight raged throughout the house.

Clarence had never been in a fistfight and saw no need for this pointless scuffle to be his first. *His* crew was his family, not these guys. He sidled toward the exit as the brawl swirled around him. Before he could make it out under his own power, a solid grip on his collar yanked him backward, dragging him toward the front door. It was Earley.

"I'm not getting a new gunner over this," the commander muttered.

Safely outside the melee, Earley steered Clarence toward their quarters, and not a moment too soon. Whistles shrilled behind them in the semidarkness as MPs converged on the fracas.

Several days later, Clarence, Earley, and the other men of Easy Company stood in ranks at the company motor pool in a field behind the houses.

A six-foot-tall officer paced between the men and their tanks. The tanks were parked side by side with their covered barrels leveled. It looked like a fearsome mechanical firing squad.

For several nights, the host crews had relived the prank. It only took a flicker of a flashlight to bring the men to stiches. But not anymore. The company commander, Captain Mason Salisbury, was furious. He was just twenty-four years old, and his square, boyish face reflected his youth. He wore an overseas cap atop blond curly hair.

Salisbury hailed from Long Island high society. He'd been attending Yale in 1942 when he gave up his studies, and football, crew, and glee

Mason Salisbury

club, to join the army. He was still new to this post and to his men, having taken command at the West Wall when his predecessor was seriously wounded. Before joining Easy Company, he had served as secretary on the board that conducted the firing test on the Panthers that July.

Salisbury stopped in front of 2nd Platoon. They had acquired the most black eyes from the melee by far. Clarence and Earley stood ramrod straight as his glare drifted across them. They had escaped the MPs, but would the platoon be punished?

Salisbury recounted the repulsiveness of their behavior—lining up to have sex with the same woman and then fighting over her. The perpetrators eyed one another with a glimmer of hope. If Salisbury knew that they had dressed up one of their men as a woman, they'd be dead already.

"I should court-martial each of you," he said.

Salisbury asked them to ponder the morality of such a woman. "Did you consider that she might have venereal disease?"*

He really thinks it was a girl! Clarence thought.

Some of the culprits eyed the young tanker who had played the woman. The young tanker grinned.

Salisbury informed them that a court-martial for fraternizing would be unnecessary, however, because they already had their punishment: shame. "If this woman is seen again, you are to report her to your platoon leader," he concluded.

The culprits' faces tightened with smiles. After the first sergeant dismissed them, their barely contained laughter exploded across the company. Even Clarence had to chuckle.

By the standards of the U.S. Army, they had just gotten away with murder.

Six weeks later, early December 1944

Under the cover of darkness, Clarence slipped from his house and darted across the street where Easy Company remained billeted. No

---

* *Yank* magazine would later crusade to prevent venereal disease in a cartoon that reminded GIs to avoid the temptation of Veronika Dankeschön ("V.D.")—a caricature remembered by one GI as "chubby with braided pigtails and a fondness for sauerkraut."

one spotted him as he followed a cobblestone road up toward a hilltop neighborhood. He wore a mackintosh against the persistent chilly drizzle, and carried a package under his arm. The gas lamps no longer functioned but he knew the way.

The castle was shadowy, and Stolberg was quiet behind him. Tankers followed their flashlights to the nightly movie or other functions.

Life had gotten better.

In November, the 104th Infantry Division, the "Timberwolves," had pushed out the front lines, ending the artillery barrages, and the port of Antwerp had been opened in northern Belgium, unleashing a much-needed flood of supplies. The company mess now served such luxuries as pancakes with butter, Nescafé, and chocolate pie.

Clarence's package contained leftover food that the cooks had slipped him under the table. Tonight, he had a different, but no less dangerous, mission: a date.

He had seen her sitting on the steps of her home. Starved for companionship, he approached her, in spite of the rules. Almost everyone was guilty of fraternization by then, many as a distraction from the looming dread of a return to battle.

Tankers kept an eye on where the prettiest women lived, so they would know exactly where to seek cover during an air raid. When a sergeant named Donovan tried this trick, a woman opened the door only to reveal none other than Captain Salisbury. Salisbury gave Donovan a bottle of whiskey to buy his everlasting silence. The bribe was apparently not enough, because the entire company soon knew of the story.

At the top of the hill, across the street from a park, stood a row of brick townhouses. On her front step, Resi Pfieffer waited beneath an umbrella, keeping an eye out for MPs. She was a full-faced eighteen-year-old with gentle green eyes who usually wore her brown hair pulled back into buns.

The coast was clear.

Resi and Clarence slipped inside her front door. The date would be confined to the home—where they would play board games and share the food that Clarence had brought—all while under her parents' supervision. And whenever the MPs came knocking, they'd cover for him: "No Americans here."

Resi Pfieffer

To Clarence, still new to dating, this was a fine first step toward something more.

The days of smashing plates felt far behind him.

A week or two later, December 18, 1944

It was a good afternoon to be indoors. Wintery gray clouds hung over Solberg, threatening to burst with snow.

The townspeople braced themselves for a storm. It was common to see young mothers and children hauling little wagons to collect kindling from the forest, or an elderly couple emerging from their shell-damaged house, checking the roof with dismay.

Inside their billet, the tankers had a stove roaring. Clarence checked his watch, counting down the hours until he could see Resi again. She wasn't just his secret anymore. His whole crew knew about her.

A Christmas tree stood in the corner. They had cut it from a forest full of West Wall bunkers and draped it in chaff, the thin strands of aluminum dropped by bombers to confuse German radar.

It was a time for hope. Everyone in the platoon had chipped in two dollars to buy a cow for Christmas dinner.

It was a time for faith. Some of the men had taken to going to church with Germans, even sharing the same pews.

And then Earley blew through the front door. "Get ready to mount up!" he said. "We're leaving!"

Clarence and the others leaped to their feet. "The Germans broke through somewhere," Earley said. It was all he knew.

In actuality, that "somewhere" was the Ardennes Forest in Belgium. Reputed to be a "quiet paradise for weary troops" and a place to park untested units, that was where the Germans had struck with a surprise offensive.

Intelligence coming from the Ardennes was murky, even for the Spearhead brass. Their maps showed the enemy in "vague, general zones of contact," although a pattern was forming: the Germans were making a bulge in the American lines as they pushed westward toward an objective yet unknown.

Clarence was stunned. The Germans were supposed to be falling apart. They were taking a pounding—even while Spearhead sat here— from the air and from the Soviets in the east. The enemy was supposed to be reeling ever backward on multiple fronts.

Someone asked Earley if they could kill the cow and bring it along. Clarence asked if he could say goodbye to his sweetheart.

There was no time for either.

Earley told the crew to gather any warm clothing they could find. They had been issued only rain gear and wherever they were headed, they would be fighting in winter. Clarence had an idea. It would not hurt to have extra food, so he volunteered to approach his friends in the kitchen crew. Everyone scattered to his task.

Stolberg had descended into pandemonium. The streets were a crisscross of men. Tankers emptied from chow halls and MPs waved through urgent, honking traffic. Taking advantage of the bedlam, an Easy Company bow gunner set out to the nearest farmyard with a gunnysack and stole three or four chickens.

The division's armored infantrymen were packing up too. As one dough loaded his half-track, a rear echelon soldier said, "My God, it's just like a movie, you guys running off to war!"

No one knew exactly how desperate the situation was.

The fighting in the Ardennes had been raging for two days by then and the Germans were steamrolling the American forces. The enemy had a tremendous tactical advantage, a three-to-one edge in infantry, and a two-to-one disparity in tanks. They cut field telephone lines, jammed American radio wavelengths, and filled the airwaves with broadcasts of bells ringing from German towns.

To slow the onslaught, GIs were fighting fiercely and trying everything, felling trees across the roads, dragging chains from trucks to imitate the sound of tanks, and lobbing bazooka shells to mimic artillery. But the German forces were simply too many.

The motor pool was a flurry of tankers tending their mounts. Clarence finished his preparations for Eagle's departure, cinching tight the wooden boxes of rations that he had secured.

The Shermans had become battlewagons. Freshly cut logs now hung from the flanks, ready to be unfastened and laid down to drive across muddy patches, and black tarps lay across the tails like bedrolls. Shovels, sledgehammers, and spare fuel cans were lashed wherever there was space. Even the tracks below were wider, due to the addition of "duck bills"—attachments that broadened the outside of each link by four inches for buoyancy on slushy terrain.

Clerks brought out bags of Christmas mail and shouted names. One man came back with a package of roasted peanuts that had already turned rancid. Another received a letter notifying him that his kids were sick. No one was receiving good news.

When he heard his own name—"Clarence Smoyer!"—Clarence seized up with trepidation. He returned from the mail scrum eyeing a box wrapped in wax paper and hoping it contained what he thought it did.

German citizens were congregating on the street, whispering and pointing as they watched the motor pool. Clarence was distraught that he had not said goodbye to Resi and her parents. They had all but adopted him and treated him as if he were their own son.

The tank commanders huddled for a final briefing before the race to the front lines. Spearhead's parent unit, the First Army, was sending veteran divisions to stanch the hemorrhaging and a relief force of 60,000 men was already in transit.

"If one of your men is wounded," some commanders were told, "give him a shot of morphine, a blanket, tag him, and leave him along the road. If your vehicle is disabled, the vehicle behind will push it off the road. We will be at the battle site at first light."

Darkness had already descended at five thirty P.M. when Easy Company fell in line with the convoy that wound through Stolberg. The tanks' headlights glowed through blackout shades as they set out to "destination unknown." Seated at his periscope, Clarence didn't need a map to tell him that they were leaving Germany. The route was leading them southwest out of Stolberg, toward Belgium.

The column turned the corner and the tankers beheld a sight they would never forget. The sidewalks brimmed with German citizens of all ages, many holding lanterns and candles. Clarence was not the only tanker who had been "adopted" by the enemy.

Earley relinquished his place in the turret and Clarence stood to look for Resi as the tank held course between the crowds. As Clarence looked left and right, countless faces swept past his vision. Women dabbed their eyes, overcome with emotion. Men waved handkerchiefs, wishing the troops good luck. And even Stolberg's children got in on the act as they ran alongside the convoy shouting farewells. If the German Army returned, anyone on that street could be branded a sympathizer or collaborator, yet still they waved goodbye.

Clarence tore off his helmet in the hopes that Resi would recognize him, but the crowds slipped by too quickly. As the tanks plunged into the dark outskirts of the city, he kept his eyes on the panorama behind him. Residents continued waving to other passing crews, their lights gently swinging. Those three months in Stolberg had brought Clarence back to himself, giving him and his crew a taste of freedom from fear. Now they were leaving it all behind for some far-flung winter battlefield.

In a nearby Sherman, a bow gunner was plucking the stolen chickens in a hurry.

CHAPTER 8

THE FOURTH TANK

Five days later, December 23, 1944
Southern Belgium

One after another, the tanks of Easy Company followed their leader on the road flanked by snowy fields.

A fuzzy shell of snow blanketed each Sherman. Their engines throbbed and puffed exhaust into the cold. The afternoon sun was beaming brightly after a "Russian High" of frigid winds had wiped away the clouds. Beyond the fields, the jagged pines of the Ardennes Forest slipped past. The chaos here now had a name: "The Battle of the Bulge."

Four tanks back in the column, Earley rode low in Eagle's turret, goggles in place and a mackintosh topping multiple layers of clothing in an attempt to stave off the bitter cold. Exhaust fumes suffused the winter air as the column crept south on the N4 highway.

After the ease of their sojourn in Stolberg, 2nd Platoon was now "spearheading," or leading in the crews' parlance. There was a rotation. Each platoon took a turn, and then within the platoons, individual tank crews alternated the duty. The tanks were arrayed in combat formation, with a spacing of thirty yards between vehicles. The lead tank set the pace, gun aimed forward. The second tank shadowed the first, in case the leader missed something. The third guarded the right flank, and the fourth watched the left.

Every minute took them farther from the safety of the American foxholes that ringed the city of Marche and deeper into what would be the largest battle ever fought by the U.S. Army. But the tank crews remained confident. One commander was annoyed by the need to evict the Germans from Belgium "for a second time in less than a year." Victory was all but assumed, a sentiment captured by the unit's history, in which someone noted: "It was a good try, but the Krauts have lost."

Inside the fourth tank, Clarence felt like he was sitting in an igloo. One piece of technology the Sherman sorely lacked was a heater. With a gloved finger, he'd etched his name in the frost that wrapped the wall. If he brushed the ceiling he could make it snow inside. Beneath his helmet, Clarence wore a tanker's winter hood—similar to a medieval skullcap—and had pulled a standard-issue GI blanket over his shoulders, but it didn't stop his teeth from chattering.

Through his periscope, Clarence marveled at Belgium's beauty. A stream lined by brambles. A mismatched fence stepping into a field. Gaps in a dark forest and snowy, hidden paths. It was a winter wonderland.

Easy Company had been sent to fight in the deepest portion of the bulge in the Allied lines. After an eighty-six-mile journey, their task force had arrived the prior evening and joined the 84th Infantry Division, the "Railsplitters," in the defense of Marche, an ancient town of cobblestone streets and narrow homes built around a fourteenth-century Catholic church.

The Battle of the Bulge might hinge upon what happened here.

Hitler's forces were racing to reach the Meuse River before the Allies' superior manpower arrived. Across the Meuse lay an open road to the Germans' ultimate objective: the port of Antwerp. Hitler was gambling that if German troops could drive a wedge behind the American and British forces and capture the port, the shocking setback might bring his enemies crawling for peace.

The German battle plan relied on speed.

The twisty Ardennes roads passed through four major crossroad towns that the Germans desperately needed to control to pull off their grand designs. They had already sacked La Roche and St. Vith, and laid siege to Bastogne, where the 101st Airborne was holding out. All that remained was Marche, closest to the Meuse. A stand at Marche was shaping up to be the Allies' best chance to repel the German offensive.

But the fight would be won—or lost—outside the city.[*]

About three miles south of Marche, the terrain gently rose ahead of Easy Company.

The gray roofs of Hèdrée, a settlement that straddled the road, came into view about one hundred yards ahead. The lead tank radioed for a halt, then stopped with a lurch.

Clarence removed his gloves and unwrapped the wax paper from the package he'd received as they departed Stolberg, revealing a white inner box full of chocolate fudge. It was a treat he'd been looking forward to ever since he smelled it.

Back home in Lehighton, Melba Whitehead, a friend from the skating rink, had made it for him as a Christmas present. Clarence had promised himself that he wouldn't touch it until he reached the combat zone. He figured this was close enough, and dug into the fudge. He wasn't sure if it was the tension of his environment, or the memories of the home he hadn't seen for more than a year, but it was the best fudge he'd ever tasted.

He could live on chocolate. He'd done it before. On the first day of the Atlantic crossing, a seasick GI vomited on Clarence's mess tray. No one saw Clarence after that. He skipped meals and his bunk was empty, his bed untouched. Eventually, Paul Faircloth found Clarence above deck, sleeping beneath a tall exhaust pipe. Wrappers from Hershey's chocolate bars were scattered everywhere. Paul urged him to come back belowdecks, but Clarence declined. He was adamant that his days in the chow line were through. He had worked out a rou-

---

[*] When the Germans delivered a demand for the surrender of Bastogne on December 22, they falsely claimed that they'd already taken Marche, writing: "The fortune of war is changing. This time the U.S.A. Forces in and near Bastogne have been encircled by strong German armored units. More German armored units have crossed the river Our near Ortheuville, have taken Marche and reached St. Hubert by passing through Homores-Sibret-Tillet."

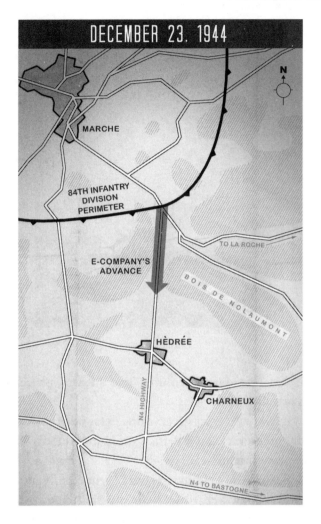

DECEMBER 23. 1944

N

MARCHE

84TH INFANTRY
DIVISION
PERIMETER

TO LA ROCHE

E-COMPANY'S
ADVANCE

BOIS DE NOLAUMONT

HÈDRÉE

N4 HIGHWAY

CHARNEUX

N4 TO BASTOGNE

tine. When the ship's store opened every other day, he'd buy a box of
Hershey bars. And for ten days that was all he ate.

The tank felt warmer now that they had stopped and the cold air
was no longer whistling inside. Or maybe it was the fudge. Clarence
slowly savored every bite.

Sitting fourth in line made all the difference in the world. In most of
the battles he had seen, the first tank did the fighting while the others
waited.

From the towering vantage point in the turret of the lead tank, a
slender young commander scanned the horizon through his binocu-

Charlie Rose

lars. It was his first day of combat and he was proceeding with caution—by the book.

In tank warfare, vision was everything. The side that saw the other first typically fired first, and a British study found that 70 percent of the time, whoever fired first survived.

The man behind the field glasses was Lieutenant Charlie Rose. A dark-haired twenty-two-year-old, he had a cleft chin that—when he smiled—perfectly framed an All-American grin. He was a rookie lieutenant who'd joined another platoon at Stolberg. But today he was leading 2nd Platoon to build experience.

His personnel file read like a war-bond advertisement.

Rose was popular—high school class president and the star fullback on the football team. After graduation, he'd stayed close to home in Chicago and enrolled at DePauw University. As the war raged, he'd left school behind to enlist in the army together with his father, a stockbroker. Back home, Rose had a wife, a child on the way, and plans to sell tractors alongside his father-in-law—who owned a series of Caterpillar dealerships across Chicago—after the war.

But all that would have to wait. Today, he was hunting enemy tanks.

His orders were to clear the road to the next crossroads, and expect resistance.

Easy Company was headed down the same road that the German 2nd Panzer Division had come up the day before to attack Marche, only to be beaten back.

But where were they now? Someone had to go looking.

That morning, the commanding general of the 3rd Armored, Major General Maurice Rose—of no relation to Lieutenant Rose—had ordered his chain of command: "Impress on every individual that we must stay right here or there will be a war to be fought all over again and we won't be here to fight it."

On Lieutenant Rose's word, the tanks resumed clanking toward Hèdrée. With its homes made of stones stacked like wafers, the settlement resembled colonial New England.

Clarence reluctantly closed his box of fudge. The frigid flowing air was back. Rose's tank was pulling even with the doorstep of the first dwelling when the crack of a German gun stopped the tank cold in its tracks. With a vicious clang of steel on steel, Rose's Sherman shook on its suspension from the blow. A cloud of snow billowed from the tank like dust shaken off a sheet.

They had found the 2nd Panzer Division. But not before the 2nd Panzer Division had found them.

"Lead's hit," Earley said.

Clarence turned the gun forward.

The second tank, commanded by the platoon sergeant, idled at the entrance to the settlement as its turret swung side to side, searching desperately. Neither the platoon sergeant nor his gunner had seen the shot.

After recovering from the shock of the hit, Rose and his crew bailed out of their tank and came bolting back through a ditch. Rose urged the men to keep going, but he wasn't coming with them. He backtracked to the second tank and climbed aboard.

Standing behind the turret, Rose drew the platoon sergeant's attention forward and to the left—where he'd last seen the enemy tank. The platoon sergeant sank into the turret to direct his crew while Rose kept watch for movement.

From ahead, a fiery green German tracer cut through the frozen air and slammed into the front of the turret. A glowing chunk of shrapnel punched straight through Rose's gut, nearly tearing him in half. His body tumbled over the side of the tank, lifeless.

Clarence reeled back in his seat, spilling what remained of his precious fudge. Earley dropped inside the turret, muttering that a fragment of the shell had nearly taken off his head. Clarence returned to the periscope. Did that just happen? Was the lieutenant really gone? Sure enough, Rose's body was seeping blood into the snow, and the platoon sergeant and his crew were pouring from their damaged tank.

"Situation report!" Captain Salisbury radioed from the rear of the column. "Situation report!"

No reply came from the front. All the tanks that had two-way radios had been abandoned.

Clarence's eyes darted back and forth over the chaotic scene as his mind swirled with panic. Nearly three months spent in Stolberg had dulled his reactions. The first two tanks were useless shells. Only one tank remained operable ahead. The relative safety that had sheltered Eagle was rapidly diminishing.

Earley got back on his feet and stood tall in the turret. "Keep your gun up there," he told Clarence. "If it's a Panther, you know what to do."

Clarence felt his stomach turn cold. The army had finally found a chink in the Panther's frontal armor, but it was a small one. At close range—less than 250 yards—the 76mm gun had enough punch to penetrate the Panther's mantlet, the armored shield where the gun barrel entered the turret. With his periscope fixed forward, Clarence waited for the enemy tank to slide into view. His heart pounded in his ears as he waited.

The commander of the tank directly in front of Clarence's, Sergeant Frank "Cajun Boy" Audifred, couldn't take it anymore. His tank veered to the right and drove off the road into a shallow gully.

Clarence couldn't believe his eyes. Was Cajun Boy abandoning them?

Cajun Boy was a twenty-three-year-old wild card from the Louisiana bayou, and his toughness was almost legendary in Easy Company. Somehow, he had survived having four tanks shot out from under him in battle. This time, only he and his crew knew where they were going.

Clarence kept his reticle trained on the rise. A sudden realization terrified him: They had been the fourth tank a moment ago. Now they were the first.

Farther to the right, Cajun Boy's tank reappeared, climbing uphill this time. Clarence marveled at his audacity. Cajun Boy wasn't running. He was circling around the village to try for a side shot.

Cajun Boy's 75 Sherman churned slowly in the snow. In a twist of daring, Audifred, a former gunner, had a high-explosive (HE) shell locked and loaded in the breech. This type of shell was typically used on soft-skinned vehicles, buildings, and troops—not tanks—but the tactic had worked for him in Normandy when he used an HE shot to stun a German Mark IV before switching to an armor-piercing (AP) shell and maneuvering in for the kill shot.

The radio squawked to life. A tank commander's voice sounded the alert from farther back in the column. "They're outflanking us!"

One of the crews had spotted movement in the forest to the left. It was a sure sign that German infantry were coming to finish the job that their tank had started.

Salisbury ordered a company retreat back to the Marche perimeter. Tanks began turning around haphazardly. In front of Clarence, Cajun Boy's tank carved a slow reversal in the snow. They had no choice but to turn their backs to the enemy.

It was complete and utter chaos. In the midst of it, Bob Earley realized that no one had a gun on the rise. If the German tank—which was undoubtedly still up there—simply moved to the edge, it could pick off the retreating Shermans one by one as they fled.

Earley told Clarence to lay down suppressive fire using HE while they retreated. "We gotta scare this guy from coming at us."

Clarence was confused. Since the German tank hadn't shown itself, he had no idea where to aim. "What do I fire at?"

"Anything."

Earley told the driver to get them out of there. Eagle pulled a sloppy K-turn, then the engine roared as the tank barreled after the others. Clarence swiveled the gun behind the tank and took aim at the settlement's entrance. Even if he didn't have an enemy in his sights, orders were orders. His foot came down on the trigger.

The explosion rocked the hilltop settlement. Riding and firing backward, Clarence shifted his fire from side to side. Gravel and snow leapt from the road, stone walls turned into dust, and trees shattered as he sprayed the area in front of the abandoned Shermans. After every shot, the gun breech jumped back like a piston before excreting a smoking shell casing. The loader quickly fed the gun a fresh shell and Clarence took aim again.

In the midst of Clarence's firing, Cajun Boy's tank reemerged, plowing through the cover of the thick brush alongside the road.

Clarence kept thumping shells toward the rise. The reticle was bouncing, but accuracy didn't matter. The world was bursting between them and the German tank, almost like an artillery barrage falling from above, a storm that no enemy tank would want to move through.

And that was Earley's plan.

Cajun Boy's tank rumbled back onto the road to join the retreat, and Clarence held his fire. Cajun Boy could take it from here.

Steam rose from the gun breech next to Clarence. Earley eyed the rise through binoculars as the abandoned Shermans shrank in his rearview.

It had worked. The enemy tank had never moved forward to follow up its first two kills.

Clarence set his foot aside the trigger and caught his breath. Shell casings and fudge littered the floor.

That same night, December 23, 1944
Several miles southeast of Marche, Belgium

The three Shermans sat silent beneath snow-filled evergreen boughs. So far, it was quiet.

The frozen landscape glistened in the moonlight. Behind the tanks, the Bois de Nolaumont woods rose into the darkness. Nearby, a platoon or two of doughs had ditched their vehicles and dug in beneath the trees. The temperature hovered around zero.

The camouflage was complete. The tank crews had draped their mounts in evergreen branches and the shell of snow on the hulls had hardened in the frigid air. Even when the moon shone directly down on them, the tanks were almost impossible to see.

About seventy yards across a field and to the right lay a tiny Belgian village. Now and then, the glow of candlelight would appear in the windows of the village's houses, taunting the crews with thoughts of warmth.

Three tanks. They were all that remained of 2nd Platoon. Captain Salisbury had ordered them to this sleepy side road with orders to shoot anything that moved, while the bulk of Easy Company was a mile and a half away, covering the N4. Every road mattered in the defense of Marche. A tank could drive overland anywhere it wanted to go, but these days, the Germans were sticking to the roads for speed.

There was nothing to do now but wait.

The bitter cold seemed to seep through the tank's walls. In Eagle's gunner's seat, Clarence wrapped himself in a blanket, stepped inside his sleeping bag, shoes and all, and brought the ends of the bag around his neck. If the tank was hit, he probably wouldn't be able to get out, but he didn't care.

The day's events weighed on him. Everything felt futile. No matter what he did, it wouldn't matter. His Sherman's armor was simply no match for the ferocity of the German guns.

Private John Danforth, an Easy Company gunner, would vent the unit's frustration in a written statement that reached all the way to the desk of General Eisenhower: "I have had two tanks shot out from under me. . . . The people who build tanks I don't think know the power of the Jerry gun. I have seen a Jerry gun fire through two buildings, penetrate an M4 tank and go through another building."

Periodically, Clarence scraped his periscope with a gloved finger when it frosted over from his breath. The radio was turned low. Cold wind whistled through Earley's hatch, where he sat with the cover cracked, listening for the enemy. Flurries plastered themselves on his steel helmet. Now and then he sprinkled instant-coffee granules into his mouth.

Back at a convent in Marche, Carmelite nuns served soup to warm the men of the Railsplitters Division, who were defending the city proper. The Reverend Mother had asked a GI if there were many Germans in the area.

He assured her that there certainly were.

"We will pray for you," she promised.

"Thanks," said the GI. "Yes, pray a lot."

The next Sherman over from Clarence's was named Eleanor. An old 75, it bore battle scars from its time in Normandy, including a deep gouge on one side of the turret.

In the gunner's seat—lost in thought—sat Corporal Chuck Miller. A wry midwesterner from Kansas City, Chuck was nineteen, with heavy cheeks and narrow eyes that made him always look to be in pain—even when he was smiling. Beneath his tanker helmet he wore a hooded sweatshirt that his mother had sent to him.

Chuck Miller

It didn't sit right with Chuck, the way they had left Lieutenant Rose out there in the snow.

After the company had pulled back to friendly territory, a message had arrived. Through some miracle of family connections, the War Department had sent word to Lieutenant Rose that he had become a father. His son, Charles Crane Rose, had been born about a week and a half earlier. The news cut everyone deeply, and perhaps Chuck the deepest. A father would never know his son. A son would never know his father. Chuck recognized his own story in the tragedy. He had few memories of a father of his own.

Chuck had been just a child when his father abandoned his mother, leaving her to raise Chuck, his older brother, and five older sisters on a seamstress's salary. She was Chuck's hero. Somehow, she held the family together and even now still scraped money together to send him adventure novels to read between battles.

Midnight had come and gone. It was now Christmas Eve.

Chuck had a plan, and now was the time to act.

Illuminated only by the sparse light of a half-moon, a jeep set out through the silvery fields.

At the wheel, Chuck took it easy on the gas and leaned from side to side to keep an eye out for fence posts. A dough volunteer sat in the passenger seat clutching his rifle, probably entertaining a slew of second thoughts. They went off-road, to avoid the Shermans on the N4. Captain Salisbury could never know of this unauthorized mission. The short mile or two that they traveled felt like an eternity. As the terrain began to rise, Chuck parked the jeep and they got out.

Celebratory German voices leaked from a nearby farmhouse. It sounded like the soldiers were singing and likely drinking beer in the Christmas spirit. They were a blocking unit of the 2nd Panzer Division. The main force had already abandoned their attack on Marche in favor of detouring west, seeking a route around the city.

With rifles at the ready, Chuck and the dough crept forward and followed a roadside ditch up to the two abandoned Shermans. There they found Rose's body covered in snow, though the snowfall couldn't hide the gaping hole in his midsection.

His combat time in a Sherman had lasted less than a day.

When the men tried to move the body, they discovered that it was frozen to the ground, so they drew their knives and finally pried it free. With their arms looped beneath Rose's, Chuck and the dough slipped away.

Chuck climbed aboard Eleanor and knocked on the turret.

The hatch cover opened and Chuck's commander greeted him. Sergeant Bill Hey bore a resemblance to the cleft-chinned film star Errol

Bill Hey

Flynn due to the way he trimmed his mustache thin. He spirited Chuck inside, as if he were harboring a fugitive.

Chuck fell into his seat, pale and convulsing. He had been in the cold so long that he was nearly hypothermic. Bill covered Chuck in a blanket and called for the blowtorch. The crew typically used the blowtorch for repairs, and the men relayed it up to Bill, who lit the flame and handed the torch to Chuck. Chuck huddled over the flame's warmth and slowly came back to life under Bill's watchful eye.

At twenty-eight, Bill was a little older than most of his counterparts and new to command. He had just been assigned a tank of his own a month earlier. A devout Methodist, he often had his nose in a prayer book and was particularly fond of a soldier's poem entitled "And God Was There."

Back in the doldrums of Stolberg, when Cajun Boy had lamented that he could not think of anything to write to his girlfriend, Lil, Bill volunteered to give the young woman an update on the company's comings and goings. There was one unintended consequence, as Cajun Boy would note: "He's a nice fellow honey. Now he has everybody in the platoon asking me if they can write (you). You know how a bunch of soldiers are."

Of his commander's many attributes, there was one that Chuck appreciated the most that night: Bill Hey could keep a secret.

The night wore on. Clarence dozed on and off in his sleeping bag. He was bent at the waist when an icy drip stung the back of his neck. Another splattered on his helmet.

The frost was melting.

Beneath the turret basket, a faint glow and hissing sound came from the bow gunner's compartment at the tank's front right corner. A di-minutive, ornery scrapper named Private Homer "Smokey" Davis was down there. Twenty-year-old Smokey came from a hard life in Morehead, Kentucky, as evidenced by the thick bags beneath his eyes. He was seldom without a cigarette and wore his tanker's hood everywhere.

Clarence leaned in his sleeping bag and saw shadows dancing in the bow. He knew it. Smokey was using the crew's

Homer "Smokey" Davis

Coleman stove to keep warm, and the heat was rising to the turret. Clarence returned to his seat. He felt bad for his friend, down in the coldest reaches of the ice cave.

The icy drips kept coming. Clarence's collar and shoulders were getting soaked. *It'll run out of fuel, eventually,* he thought.

Earley grumbled. He was getting it too. He grabbed the pork chop and spoke. "Smokey."

Smokey's voice came back weakly. "It's so cold, I can't stand it anymore." His feet were freezing because he had nowhere to move them, so he had removed his boots and was holding his feet over the stove's flame.

Earley reminded Smokey of the need for noise-and-light discipline— just the night before a German panzer division had come this way. "You can afford to lose a few toes."

The stove stopped hissing and once again the tank went dark.

A mechanical rumble shook the night, jolting all three tank crews awake.

Clarence sat up in his sleeping bag. He crinkled as he moved. His jacket—once damp—had frozen. Something was out there. He cleared the frost from his sights and flicked the switch that illuminated his telescopic gun sight.

Earley opened his hatch farther and a mechanical rumble poured inside: engines puttering, gears shifting, tracks clanking. It was coming from a forest to the front left, and was growing louder.

Dim headlights beamed from the forest as they swept the field in front of the tanks.

Clarence freed himself from his sleeping bag and settled an eye to the telescopic sight, which shook as he trembled. An armored scout car led the column as it emerged from the forest, traveling from left to right across Clarence's field of vision. Only the scout car had its headlights turned on, and they were dimmed by blackout shades. The others followed with their lights blacked out, the vehicles silhouetted only by the moon.

They were Germans, traveling by night to avoid Allied fighter-bombers.

"Track 'em, Clarence," Earley said.

The moonlit shapes kept coming.

Almost every German war machine seemed to be represented in the nighttime convoy, including Kübelwagens, Opel Blitz trucks, and blunt-nosed half-tracks.

The distinctive sounds of each vehicle rose and fell as they passed. Then came a noise that drowned out all others. Squeaking metal tracks clawed the road as a German tank rumbled into the open, followed by a second, and then a third. Their Maybach V-12 engines snarled and blue flames leapt from exhaust stacks as each roared past. It seemed like the earth was shaking.

Clarence followed the silhouettes with the reticle, left to right, then back again. The nearby village appeared to swallow them whole until they came out the other side. The turret traversed with an electric whine. It was fast, capable of spinning a full circle in fifteen seconds.

"They're gonna hear us!" Smokey whispered over the intercom. The plea went unanswered.

The tanks kept coming. Clarence swore he could smell their amassing exhaust.

Earley had eyes on them and told Clarence to be ready to fire on his call.

Clarence's heart pounded. Much of him wanted to take a shot now. They were arrogant machines, most likely the rear guard of the 2nd Panzer Division, racing to catch up with the main force. He gauged the silhouettes, attempting to ascertain what they were up against. Some were sharp, possibly Panthers. Some were blocky, maybe Mark IVs or even the legendary Tiger, a 60-ton behemoth so heavy that it couldn't cross most bridges and so wide that it had to be fitted with narrower tracks to ride a rail car.

But now Clarence could kill any of them. Every German tank was vulnerable broadside.

He could avenge Lieutenant Rose.

"How's it looking?" Earley asked Clarence. The commander sounded hesitant.

Clarence felt a lump in his throat. His answer to Earley's question might steer the situation in one direction or another.

The moonlit German tanks were slipping away. Three Shermans

could each knock out a tank or two and maybe the doughs could get some with their bazookas. But what would happen if just one of those German tanks turned to face them? The Shermans had a forest at their backs. There was nowhere to run. They certainly couldn't take a hit. A muzzle flash would be the last thing he'd see. *It'd be suicide.*

"Not good, Bob. There's too many."

If it was a smaller column, they could handle it. But attacking now would be like poking a bear.

Earley agreed, but reminded Clarence that if one of the other guys fired they would have no choice but to join in. Without a radio transmitter to communicate with Cajun Boy or Bill Hey, he couldn't tell them to hold their fire.

The turret's whine ceased when Clarence stopped tracking the targets.

He hated letting the Germans get away like this, but had little choice. The moral calculations were different in the dark. Those suddenly weren't machines out there with men in them; they were steel monsters hunting for something to kill.

"Let 'em pass," Earley muttered beneath his breath.

Outside, the American line of tanks and doughs remained silent. *Choose your battles,* they told themselves. *Their day will come.*

Every man inside Eagle remained still, as if some German soldier would hear them over the putter of his Kübelwagen. They second-guessed their camouflage. *Did we skimp on the branches?*

Clarence had never pondered being captured like he did now.

In the sponson bin next to him, Clarence kept a German officer's Luger that he'd acquired in France. Rumor had it that if the Germans found one on a man they'd captured, they'd put the barrel in his mouth and pull the trigger. Where could he hide it now?

"Let 'em pass."

Clarence felt the cold seep back into his bones and his shivers returned. His wristwatch began clinking against the gun breech like a dinner bell. He gripped his left wrist with his other hand to arrest the noise.

As a youngster, Clarence had never known quite how to pray. It wasn't until a neighbor bought him a suit that he regularly attended church, and by then, he simply mimicked what he saw the other parishioners doing. In lieu of a primer on how to pray or what to pray, Clarence began to do what came naturally: he simply spoke to God.

Clarence sat back from his sight and drew his arms tight against his chest for warmth. The tank encircled him, it bound him, he couldn't run or hide from the roar of the German column.

Silent, Clarence had never spoken so hard in his life.

When the sun cracked the horizon, it revealed an empty road torn to shreds by German tracks.

Tankers emerged from the three Shermans. After the harrowing night, Clarence eyed the dawn from his periscope with a new sense of appreciation.

No one would tell headquarters that a German column had been allowed to pass or how Lieutenant Rose's body mysteriously appeared outside the command tent, lashed to the hood of a jeep.

If they weren't there, they'd never understand.

The next day, Christmas morning

The tankers huddled behind their vehicles in a field like hobos and warmed their hands with the engines' exhaust. It was around eleven A.M. The boom of artillery rippled through the clear sky. Sun glinted from the snow.

In addition to Easy Company, two more companies each of tanks and doughs were spread over the neighboring fields. Their task force had been ordered back to friendly territory and held in reserve, six miles north of Marche. If the Germans broke through the lines, they'd get the call.

American engineers were laying mines at the lower entrances to Marche, rigging everything—even the sidewalks—to explode. And outside the city, artillerymen were firing so furiously that they worked bare-chested despite the cold. Their shells arced southward from the perimeter to disrupt the enemy. New German units had arrived to take the place of the 2nd Panzer Division, which had resumed its drive toward the Meuse.

Once his hands were warm again, Clarence had to step away from the tank. The exhaust fumes were a great heat source, but they could put a man under. Smokey stomped around cursing. When he sought medical attention for his frostbite, all the medics did was warm his toes and send him back. There were more serious cases to treat.

It was "Shades of Valley Forge" here, as the unit history put it. "A bitter wind whipped over the white Belgian hills and tankers found that their steel battle wagons were so many mechanized ice boxes."

There were no glad tidings or toasts of cheer this Christmas. Clarence had never felt more homeless and forgotten. Back home in Lehighton, he knew, Christmas bulbs would be strung from lampposts, the store windows on First Street brimming with displays. Families would stream from churches bundled in long coats as the bells rang out news of Christ's coming.

As a boy, Clarence had gone downtown and stood in line with the other needy children at the Eagles Club. After a moment inside with Santa, he would leave with a gift. He'd take it to the park, where he'd enjoy his favorite part of Christmas: a box of candy and an orange.

Clarence's upbringing gave him a healthy sense of perspective. No matter how bad things seemed, someone else always had it worse. He thought of Paul's mother, and Lieutenant Rose's young widow, Helen. What kind of Christmas were they having?

Around noon, a truck parked behind the tanks. Clarence pried himself from the huddle to see if the truck had brought them more ammo.

The lift gate dropped and Clarence couldn't believe his eyes—the delivery was far better than ammo. The company cooks were crouching behind steaming containers of hot food. It wasn't too late for a Christmas miracle after all.

Clarence and his crew retrieved their mess kits and joined a fast-forming feeding line. At each man's turn, the cooks wished him a Merry Christmas. At the front of the tank, Clarence and the crew set their food and cups of coffee on the fenders as they ate. It was a Christmas dinner with all the fixings: drumsticks, stuffing, mashed potatoes, gravy, and even a slice of freshly baked bread.

With every bite, Clarence's mood lifted. Someone still cared about them after all.

Soon after, the sky started buzzing.

Across the field, Clarence and his comrades craned their necks to see what was making the noise. American bombers were flying westward and shimmering like tinsel as they raked the sky with white vapor trails.

The Eighth Air Force was heading home.

Nearly 400 B-24s had just bombed western Germany, precision-targeting railroad marshaling yards and road junctions. The offensive was designed to amplify the previous night's raids, when more than 300 Royal Air Force planes had struck airfields used by German transport aircraft. The raids aimed to strangle the enemy in the Ardennes by denying them resupply. And the German soldiers definitely noticed. One tank crewman observed, "Over our head, floods of bombers are flying towards the Reich. With a heavy heart and helpless in my rage I can only stare after them, full of despair."

The waves of bombers slipped overhead for thirty minutes, reverberating through the frozen sky as Clarence and his fellow tankers relished their Christmas dinner.

Clarence smiled for the first time in days. A great military force stood behind them and was finally back to swinging.

There would be no losing this battle.

CHAPTER 10 **SOMETHING BIGGER**

Nearly two weeks later, January 7, 1945
Grand-Sart, Belgium

The tracks clacked harder with increased effort as the Easy Company Shermans climbed uphill through a tunnel of dead trees.

It was around eight thirty A.M. and the road was coated in an icy veneer of snow. A blue sky beckoned through a craggy canopy of branches overhead.

Several tanks from the front, Eagle was a mess. Icicles hung from its fenders and frozen branches stuck like stubble to the hull. With his hatch cover open, the driver tried to keep the 33-ton machine from rolling off the slick track into the nearby ravines. He gripped both steering-brake levers and pulled back on one or the other to turn.

Smokey leaned from his hatch to gauge how close they were to leaving the road. The men had battled thirty-six miles east from Marche and had the grime to show for it. "Enough dirt on us that you could plant spuds," wrote Cajun Boy. "Sometimes I wonder how I'll ever scrub it off."

But the end of the battle was in sight.

The 2nd Panzer Division had been stopped within three miles of the Meuse. Marche was safe and Bastogne had held. The British were about to take La Roche, and St. Vith was next in line for liberation. The tide was turning. It was time to reverse the bulge.

Light beamed from the crest of the hill above. They were almost there.

At the crest, the tanks passed through the lines of A-Company, 36th Armored Infantry Regiment. Doughs huddled in foxholes dug between splintered black tree trunks, the snow around them sooty. They looked like bandits with their faces wrapped in scarves and GI sweaters against the cold.

The doughs stopped the lead tank, Eleanor, and shouted a warning to the commander, Bill Hey. The night before they had been shelled by a Mark IV and worried that the tank might still pose a danger to anyone approaching the village.

In Eleanor's turret, Bill stood with goggles over his eyes as ice gathered on his thin mustache. From the crest, he gazed upon an idyllic scene straight from a Currier and Ives Christmas card.

A bed of white snow stretched down to the village of Grand-Sart then up to the bluish-gray tree line of another hilltop. Hay bales dotted the fields. If it had been anywhere else in the world, it would have been beautiful.

Easy Company had orders to take and hold this solitary piece in a jigsaw puzzle of forests, ravines, fields, and hills, all of which needed to be wrested from the Germans' grip. Already the enemy's tenacity was defying explanation. A German soldier said it best in his diary when he wrote, "The town is in ruins, but we will defend the ruins."*

It was Bill Hey's turn to lead the company.

A dozen or more Shermans filed down into the fields. Some had been hastily whitewashed with paint; others were still olive drab, like Eagle, but caked with snow. Easy Company had lost two tanks since Marche—one to an artillery strike and another to a rollover.

Bill steered Eleanor to a point farthest into the field before turning toward Grand-Sart and idling in the snow. Three more Shermans took their places to his side. Today, 2nd Platoon would be spearheading. Anchoring the left flank was Eagle, nearest the woods. Clarence sat back

---

* Technically speaking, the Germans reached the Meuse during the Battle of the Bulge. In late December, British soldiers came across an American jeep that a mine had destroyed on a riverside road. The occupants wore American field jackets on the outside, but German uniforms underneath. They were believed to be reconnaissance troops from the 2nd Panzer Division.

William "Woody" McVey

from his sights, concerned about the prospect of firing in snowdrifts that were as much as two feet deep. The top layers were powder and the 76's sizeable muzzle blast was bound to kick up quite a cloud. In a normal field, the dirt cloud would blind the gunner for up to thirty seconds.

Eagle's driver—a nineteen-year-old Irish American from Michigan named Tech Corporal William "Woody" McVey—didn't share Clarence's burden. Dark-haired, with darting eyes, the youngster launched into his pre-battle routine. Feigning seriousness, he asked the crew if they would pray with him. By now, they knew better than to bow their heads.

"Lord, please keep the big bullet away from us." After a solemn pause he concluded—"Amen."

The tank's interior echoed with laughter. It never failed to break the tension.

Trapped inside the tight confines of Eleanor, Chuck Miller sat brooding with his hood drawn over his ears.

He didn't like it one bit. Two thousand yards—more than a mile. That's how far they were being asked to go—without cover and likely under fire. At that range, the 75mm gun's muzzle velocity would be its Achilles' heel.

The 75mm had been a fine gun when the Sherman first entered production in early 1942. The British, who received more than 17,000 Shermans over the course of the Lend-Lease program, even reported "great satisfaction" when they first employed the tank against the Mark IV G at El Alamein. But that was two years ago. Since then, the Germans had bolstered the armor of their vehicles and the muzzle velocity of their guns, while the 75mm gun's muzzle velocity remained the same—comparatively low.[*]

"This is a bad idea," Chuck said.

Bill agreed, but was powerless to change the orders. Some of the crew scoffed. Chuck was reinforcing the nickname bestowed on him by the driver.

The crew's driver, a heavyset corporal by the name of Fahrni, had it out for Chuck. Possibly it was because Chuck had said he was the baby of seven kids. Or maybe it came from Chuck's payday ritual. With each check he received, Chuck saved some money for candy before sending the rest to his mother. But for whatever reason, Fahrni had given Chuck a nickname that spread like wildfire throughout the company: "Baby."

And whenever Fahrni went looting, he usually brought back a doll for Chuck.

The company was in place. Captain Salisbury radioed the order for the attack to commence.

From his hatch in the lead tank, Bill relayed the signal: a raised hand, lowered forward. Second Platoon began rolling. The four tanks

---

[*] The Sherman had been designed for everything in 1941—supporting infantry breakthroughs, sowing chaos behind enemy lines, firing skyward as artillery, *and* battling other tanks. Tank-on-tank engagements had rarely occurred in the First World War, when the Kaiser's forces built only twenty tanks. However, by the German blitzkrieg of 1940, it was the Allies' turn to catch up.

plowed deep lines in the snow, their tracks shuttling lumps of snow forward as if they were conveyor belts.

The second row of tanks, belonging to another platoon, waited until there were seventy-five yards between them and the lead platoon before setting into motion. The third rank then followed the same procedure as the second. The doughs would follow later on foot.

With the flick of a switch, Chuck turned on his gun's gyrostabilizer. An American advantage, the device employed hydraulics to limit the gun's bounce, aiding a gunner's target acquisition when on the move and if the tank stopped suddenly to fire. As much as Chuck feared that they were rolling into a snowy shooting gallery, he also accepted his role as just a small part of something bigger.

The Allied counteroffensive had just begun that week and already it was redrawing the map. The 3rd Armored and the First Army were pushing from the north, while the British XXX Corps pushed from the west, with Patton's Third Army pushing from the south. In the battle for this real-world jigsaw puzzle, every piece mattered.

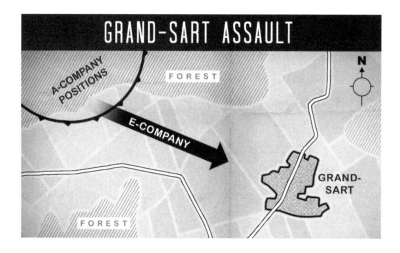

Chuck swept the field with his telescopic sight. A couple yards ahead and to the left there was a dark mass—a dead German soldier. Chuck could see the black bread spilled from his bread tin. But what was he doing out there?

· · ·

It was 10:13 A.M., and the tanks were almost halfway across the two thousand yards when machine-gun fire crackled from the village.

Bill Hey ducked lower in his hatch as bullets whizzed by.

The remnants of two Wehrmacht regiments—the 20th Panzer Grenadiers and the 48th Grenadiers—had remained to defend Grand-Sart to cover their comrades' retreat. Behind them, the roads to Germany were a traffic jam of vehicles with individual soldiers slipping past "on foot, on bicycles, on horses."

German forces in the Ardennes were losing faith in their high command, yet many found personal motivation to continue fighting. As a German general later reflected, "It was only the realization of the immediate danger of the homeland and its frontiers, which spurred the troops to increase their effort against an unmerciful enemy."

The armored assault crawled forward, steadily gaining ground.

To Eleanor's left, an explosion erupted from the snow beneath a Sherman two vehicles away. The blast left a black cloud blossoming around the tank.

"Mines!" Bill shouted into the pork chop.

Up front, Fahrni hauled back on the steering-brake levers. But by that point it was too late.

A massive explosion erupted beneath the left track, lifting the tank's nose a few inches off the ground before slamming it back down. The tank swayed on its suspension. Dark smoke—intermingled with Fahrni's cursing—filtered into the turret. Bill called for an injury report.

Chuck gripped a bloody nose, which he'd smashed against the periscope. But he wasn't about to give Fahrni the satisfaction by admitting to an injury. He reported that he was fine.

He was no "Baby."

In the aftermath of the blast, the company idled in place as they took stock of the situation.

They'd driven directly into a minefield hidden beneath snowdrifts. Everyone was thinking the same question: *Will we turn back?*

Clarence turned his turret. He had friends in every tank.

A smudgy hole ringed the next tank over. It was commanded by Donovan—the sergeant who'd caught Captain Salisbury with the

German woman. Donovan and his crew came stumbling out in a daze. Luckily, only one crew member was wounded.

Three tanks away, a halo of smoke and snow settled around Eleanor. Clarence thought of his friend Chuck, and hoped he was unharmed.

The crews never expected to see what transpired next.

Bill Hey jumped down into the minefield.

He worked his way to the front of Eleanor before dropping to his hands and knees to inspect the damage. The blast had stripped the rubber pads from several links and two of the tank's bogie wheels were sheared in half. But somehow, the tracks themselves were intact.

The hull floor escape hatch wasn't damaged either. Mines had been known to blast the hatch up and into the tank, which sometimes killed the bow gunner.

Bill climbed back up to the turret. He was facing a difficult choice. No one would blame him if he turned back. But he wasn't about to give up now. From his hatch, he raised his hand and signaled "Forward."

Eleanor's tracks started turning again and everything held together. The trailing tanks funneled directly behind the three lead tanks, to narrow their exposure to mines. Minutes felt like hours; another blast could come at any moment.

Bill stood tall in his turret, determined to spot the next threat. Grand-Sart was just a small piece of the puzzle in the Bulge, but it was *their* piece. And they weren't going to let their fellow fighting men down.

Bill raised a clenched fist, which stopped all three platoons of tanks. Through his binoculars, he saw something. "Chuck, we've got an enemy tank," he said calmly.

Chuck felt a tap on his left shoulder and turned the turret in that direction.

"Steady, steady," Bill said.

When the gun was aimed where Bill wanted, he stopped Chuck—"On!" He gave a range estimate of about a thousand yards.

Chuck spotted the enemy. At the end of a short barn, a long white-washed gun barrel jutted from behind a woodpile. The German's barrel's length was visible, which meant it wasn't aiming at them. But it was aiming at someone. Probably one of Chuck's friends. No one else was firing, and without a two-way radio, Bill couldn't warn them.

Chuck couldn't tell if the tank was broadside or narrow, so he followed the gun barrel back and set the reticle on the wooden barn where he estimated the turret should be. A few inches of wood wouldn't stop an AP shell. He stomped his foot on the trigger.

The gun thundered and the shell struck the barn with a shatter of splinters. The breech kicked out the empty casing. Stinging white fumes rose in the turret. Chuck coughed and waved a hand to clear the smoke. His head spun. The turret exhaust fan had never been repaired after a hit in Normandy.

Chuck returned to his sight, hoping to see fire rising from behind the barn like a Roman candle. But he saw nothing. Did the shot deflect? Did it even hit? The German tank seemed to be unscathed.

"He's coming out!" Bill said.

The German tank pulled forward and stopped with a lurch as it swung its gun toward Eleanor.

Chuck moved to adjust his aim, but it was too late. The enemy's long barrel had disappeared. It was now aiming straight at him.

The muzzle flashed.

Chuck watched the green tracer flying toward him, seemingly in slow motion. Suddenly it gained speed and zipped above his telescopic sight. The shell slammed the turret, the tank hiccupped, and a red flash filled Chuck's field of vision, sending him reeling backward.

Bill did not duck in time. The ricocheting shell cut a V through his tanker helmet. He fell dead onto Chuck's shoulder, showering the young gunner in blood and brain matter. Chuck screamed and flailed, and his commander fell to the turret floor. Bill Hey's tenure as a Sherman commander had lasted just eight days in combat.

The tank heaved to a stop. The intercom came alive with panicked voices from the bow. The loader stared in horror at Bill's body.

There was no time.

"Get out!" Chuck shouted over the intercom. "Abandon tank!" The enemy was known to pump shells into a tank until it burned.

To avoid Bill's remains, the loader wove down through the tank and followed the bow gunner out his forward hatch.

Get out!

Chuck stepped around his fallen commander and pushed himself out from the turret.

Get out!

Chuck rolled back across the turret, expecting to land on the engine deck, but he had forgotten that he had left the turret askew—turned leftward—and now its rear was dangling over the snow. With nothing to catch him, Chuck fell almost nine feet, face-first into the snow.

He sat up, stunned. Snow matted his bloody nose and tanker jacket. He was by no means out of the woods. Bullets pinged against the tank. The Germans in Grand-Sart were targeting him. He crawled behind Eleanor for cover, but his reprieve lasted only a moment.

Eleanor mysteriously sprang to life.

The dual exhaust pipes growled and spewed hot exhaust in Chuck's face. He heard the unmistakable noise of a gear shift before the tracks began clanking backward.

Chuck rolled to the right, narrowly missing being crushed.

As the tank reversed, the gun centered itself. It seemed as if it were being operated by a ghost. Eleanor stopped, a hatch opened, and Fahrni slid over the side, fuming mad.

When he saw Fahrni, Chuck immediately realized his mistake. Since he left the turret pointing leftward, the gun had blocked the driver's hatch, trapping Fahrni alone inside the vehicle. However, the Sherman had a function that automatically centered the gun when the tank was in motion, a trick Fahrni used to escape.

The crew took cover in a frozen creek bed. When Fahrni caught up there was no curse too vulgar for him to throw Chuck's way. Chuck ignored him and peered over the bank just in time to catch a glimpse of the German tank retreating from the barn. Its tracks were kicking up snow as it galloped across the field. Its whitewashed paint made the shape hard to discern, but here in the Bulge there stood a nearly one-in-three chance that it was a Panther.

And this maneuver resembled a strategy that Panthers often employed—after firing they would pull back half a mile and seek cover before resuming their assault.

Using the village as a shield, the tank slipped away into the nearest forest.

· · ·

Easy Company approached Grand-Sart, shooting as they went.

Dark clouds were brewing in the distance, signs of another snow-storm approaching.

There was nothing to be gained by watching, so Chuck and his crew set out for the woods they had come from earlier—retracing their steps without the safety of their tank.

Long coats swishing, the A-Company doughs poured from the tree line to join the assault. Usually they would have ridden in half-tracks, but their drivers weren't about to take their chances on the snow-covered minefield.

The doughs ran past the four haggard tankers toward the promise of warm houses. Only at 5:07 P.M. would Grand-Sart be fully secured, just in time for the doughs to take shelter from the storm.

One of the medics, seeing Chuck covered in blood, veered over to the young tanker.

"Where you hit?"

"It's not mine," Chuck said. He assured the man—he was fine.

The medic moved on, but incredulously glanced over his shoulder.

Chuck's breath puffed from his hood as he plodded toward the trees—and safety. His mind was slowly catching up to the chain of events that had befallen his crew.

Did I shoot too high? Too short? Chuck could ask himself these questions for the rest of time, but would never know the truth.

"Cajun Boy" Audifred would later write to his girlfriend—who had continued writing to Hey—to break the news.

"It's miserable darling and I am suffering cold day in and out for weeks. . . . I need sleep now. Yesterday I could hardly lift my legs. . . . Darling by the way don't write Bill Hey anymore. I don't have to tell you why, it's not nice."

Sometime after the attack

The snowstorm howled through the darkness.

Light leaked from the windows of a battle-damaged Belgian farm-house and illuminated snow flurries flying sideways.

Private Malcolm "Buck" Marsh stepped out the back door of the home and into the swirling snow. He tugged his helmet lower and his scarf higher, framing his dark eyes and prominent cheeks that flowed to a pointed chin. Buck had already vowed never to make snowballs for fun again. An affable, twenty-one-year-old Southerner, he felt for the boys out roadblocking in the tanks. At least he and the other doughs had a place to warm themselves between sentry duties.

A slightly taller, burlier dough slogged behind Buck. Private First Class Bob Janicki had his head down and collar turned up, obscuring a face of close-set eyes and tightly balled cheeks all set on a heavy jaw. He couldn't be bothered by the elements. Janicki was Buck's foxhole buddy. Combat had aged him and he seemed a decade or two older than his twenty-three years.

It was almost midnight and time for them to relieve the ten P.M. shift manning the squad's .30-caliber machine gun.

Malcolm "Buck" Marsh   *Bob Janicki*

With his M1 rifle at the ready, Buck led the way toward the dark forest.

He was relatively short, and the bottom of his overcoat touched the knee-deep snow. Too new to be sufficiently fearful, Buck was one of nineteen replacements rushed into the Ardennes to join A-Company.

Although the village had been secured, the neighboring woods remained dangerous ground. Buck and his fellow doughs had captured thirty-seven enemy prisoners in the area of Grand-Sart but had also sent an alarming number of German troops fleeing into the woods. There the enemy wandered, searching for Belgian civilians they could implore for shelter.

Beneath the lip of his helmet, Buck saw the outlines of two men shuffling toward him. Apparently the ten P.M. shift couldn't wait to get indoors. Huddled in their long coats, the men passed without a glance. It was too cold to stop and chat.

Buck and Janicki arrived at the tree line and found two doughs clustered close together at the machine gun.

Buck was puzzled. Did he get the shift schedule wrong?

The doughs stood and gathered their gear. They were just as eager to head inside as the two men Buck had passed earlier. Buck eyed the outline of the farmhouse. It was only then that he realized what he'd seen a few moments before.

"Oh, shit." Buck alerted the others. They'd just walked past two Germans.

Janicki unslung his rifle. "Come on," he said, his voice deep and perturbed.

Buck followed Janicki toward the house. The veteran trudged with little visible urgency. They hadn't heard any gunshots. Their squad was inside the home and the Germans were outnumbered anyway.

"Not so fast!" The other doughs reminded them whose shift it was before darting around Buck and Janicki to block their route. These doughs were more eager to face the enemy than to face another minute in the cold.

Buck and Janicki took their places at the gun and hunkered down for their shift in front of the spooky black woods. Hunched over the gun, Buck couldn't stop replaying their encounter with the Germans earlier in the evening. What if they were German commandos? He had heard that some English-speaking Germans—dressed in American uniforms—had infiltrated the lines at the start of the battle. The only way to identify these scouts and saboteurs, aside from questioning them about baseball or Ginger Rogers, supposedly was to check their trousers for German underwear.

Janicki didn't seem worried. His eyes appeared perpetually glazed over—the only time they sparked to life was in a firefight. Back in Illinois, he had been a motorcycle mechanic. Now all he wanted was to get home to his wife, Ruth.

Buck had grown up well-to-do in a large Southern home on the edge of Florence, Alabama. Gregarious and approachable, he had been voted the "Boy with the Best Personality" by his high school classmates.

As foxhole buddies went, the duo were an odd pair.

Two hours' worth of snow had collected on Buck's helmet by the time the next shift arrived. They told Buck and Janicki that two German deserters had knocked on the door—looking for a place to surrender—and surprised a sleepy dough who "nearly pissed himself" before he took them prisoner.

Buck felt an immense wave of relief and laughed.

When they got back inside, coffee was simmering on the wood stove in the candlelit kitchen. Buck did a double take. There sat the two Germans, in chairs against the far wall. They wore their long coats and soft-brimmed caps without their helmets. When they tossed away the helmets, it meant they were done fighting.

A dough kept an eye on the Germans from his seat at the kitchen table. The rest of the squad was sleeping near a crackling fireplace in the main room.

The Germans were pale, gaunt, and itchy, probably stricken with lice. One was older and larger, with a black beard, while the other was slight, fair-haired, and in obvious pain. He was in bad shape. When they removed one of his boots, part of his frostbitten foot had come off with it.

Only the Germans knew how long they'd been watching them from the woods.

Janicki removed his helmet, which revealed a long red scar on the side of his face. That fall, he'd been hit by a sizzling chunk of shrapnel. Unimpressed by the spectacle of the German prisoners, he went to sleep by the fire.

Buck sat with the guard at the kitchen table and laid his rifle against the wall. Between sips of coffee, he wrote his nightly diary entry. He was fastidious at this, a carryover from his previous life as an engineering student at Tennessee Tech. Since the guard was getting dopey and Buck was too wound-up to sleep, he volunteered to watch the prisoners. The guard hurried off to bed before Buck could change his mind. The gesture wasn't unusual for Buck. Quietly, he aspired to be a veteran like Janicki and often sought to exceed others' expectations of him by going above and beyond.

The only people awake were Buck and the larger of the two Germans.

Buck eyed the soldiers as they sat five feet away. The one with the bandaged foot dozed with his face against the stone wall. Now and then, he whimpered in pain. The larger one with the black beard was closest to Buck. His tired eyes were leery of the young American, and perhaps the uncertainty of his future.

The Nazis' orders had made it perfectly clear that any unwounded soldier who allowed himself to be captured "loses his honor and his dependents get no support." Heinrich Himmler, Reich Leader of the SS, had been unsparing in his thoughts on deserters when he messaged the 5th Fallschirmjäger Division: "If there is any suspicion that a soldier has absented himself from his unit with a view to deserting and thus impairing the fighting strength of this unit one member of the soldier's family (wife) will be shot."

As the night wore on, Buck fished a K-ration from his musette bag and dumped the boxed contents onto the table. At the appearance of food, the bearded German perked in his seat. Buck set a can of processed cheese aside—he abhorred the stuff—and searched for something else: canned pork, or biscuits, or caramels, anything would be better than the cheese. After he finished eating, the canned cheese still sat on the table.

With eyebrows raised, the bearded German motioned to the can.

Buck pondered the suggestion. Was he allowed to feed the prisoners? In the main room the fire was dying and everyone was asleep. Did he even want to? They were the enemy, after all.

The wind was howling outside. The candles around him were melting to nothing. Buck was all alone with a bigger, harder enemy soldier. But the prisoner seemed docile.

"Sure." Buck tossed him the canned cheese.

The German caught it, smiled, and muttered his thanks.

Buck set about tidying up from his meal, when a noise stopped him in mid-motion.

It was the unmistakable sound of a knife sliding from a metal sheath. Buck's heart raced as his eyes slowly shifted.

The German held an eight-inch knife that he had slid from his boot.

Buck eyed his M1 rifle where it stood against the wall. It was only an arm's length away, but the safety would need to be turned off and in his present circumstances an arm's length felt like a mile. He slowly inched his hand toward the rifle. The German's boots shifted as he leaned forward in his seat. It would be close.

Before Buck could lunge for his rifle, the German plunged the knife blade into the can and began sawing around the lid.

Buck resumed breathing.

The German cut the cheese in half before waking his younger companion to pass him the food and knife. The two soldiers made quick work of the cheese and didn't leave anything behind. They were clearly starving.

With their supply lines cut for weeks, the only source of sustenance these German soldiers likely had to rely on was plundering Belgian homes. In one farmhouse, a woman resisted, begging the soldiers to not take everything, only to have a German officer throw her aside with a warning: "Our men haven't eaten in eight days. They come first."

The bearded German wiped the blade on his trousers and handed it, hilt-first, to Buck.

"Thank you," Buck said.

The German nodded and sat back.

Buck marveled at the instrument, a Hitler Youth knife. It featured a wide blade, a black fish-scaled hilt, and a red-and-white inlay with a swastika in the center. Weighing it in his palm, Buck felt a shiver.

Another German at a different time might have buried the blade directly in his gut. If he was to survive as a dough in the Spearhead Division, Buck knew he had a long way to go.

The "Boy with the Best Personality" award counted for nothing here.

A month later, February 8, 1945
Stolberg, Germany

It felt like springtime in the valley, even though winter still held the region solidly in its grasp.

Tankers and doughs crisscrossed Stolberg on their first morning back from the Ardennes. The men were in a hurry to reunite with their German girlfriends and adopted families.

Stolberg was "home" once again. For now, at least.

They had departed on a moment's notice before, and it would happen again after this pause for rest and recuperation—it was just a matter of when.

Clarence huffed up the hill toward Resi's house. He had to see her, to talk with her about their future together.

The experience of the Ardennes lingered. He had seen the Allies emerge victorious in the Battle of the Bulge through sheer sacrifice and stubborn will. The tactics of the day had sent tank crews on suicide missions down icy roads or through snowy fields, yet still the men saddled up and went forward, often to their deaths.

The 3rd Armored had lost more tanks than it destroyed—163 losses against 108 German tanks and self-propelled guns, including 31 Panthers that American crews had claimed. And the U.S. Army as a whole had to borrow 350 Shermans from the British just to replenish their losses. As a result, many tankers became frustrated with the tools at their disposal, an attitude that stretched beyond Clarence and the men of Spearhead.*

A *Stars and Stripes* reporter caught up with tankers of the army's other heavy tank division, the 2nd Armored Division—widely known as "Hell on Wheels"—while the men recuperated from the Ardennes. In his story, "Shells 'Bounce Off' Tigers, Veteran U.S. Tankmen Say," the reporter recorded their words. A tank commander: "We're just out-tanked and outgunned, that's all. We don't mind the lack of armor on our tanks as much as the lack of firepower. But it's mighty aggravating to let fly with everything you've got and just have the shells bounce off the front of the Jerry tanks."

His bow gunner concurred: "Don't misunderstand us, all we want is a better gun, and we'll be ready to tackle any of them."

Their company commander: "Our morale would be a lot better if there weren't so many cock-and-bull stories in the papers about how our tanks are world-beaters. We lose four or five tanks, and then the boys on the busted-up tanks have the guts to go out and do it again."

A platoon sergeant had the last word—grudging praise for the Panther: "If they'd give me a Mark V, I'd take on any of the bastards."

When Resi opened the door, she couldn't believe she was looking at Clarence in the flesh.

"You're back!" She started kissing and hugging him in full view of the street.

Once indoors, Resi became emotional as she told Clarence the news she had heard on the radio. "Hitler said he destroyed the 3rd Armored Division."

The absurdity of the propaganda gave Clarence a good chuckle.

As the reunited couple sat together, Resi was so talkative that Clar-

---

* In a letter to Eisenhower, Spearhead's General Rose reported his division's "excessive" casualties in the Ardennes and declared the Sherman to be "inferior" to the Panther. So how was his division still successful? "The answer," he wrote, "is that we compensate for our inferior equipment by the efficient use of artillery, air support, and maneuver and in final analysis a great step toward equalizing our equipment is taken by the individual tanker and gunner, who maneuvers his tank and holds his fire until he is in a position most favorable for him."

ence couldn't get a word in edgewise. He had a speech prepared, but he couldn't find the opening to launch into what he wanted to say.

Resi's mother—a dark-haired, neatly dressed woman—was clearly delighted that Clarence had returned. Unlike Resi's easygoing father, a merchant in town, she intimidated Clarence.

She had to talk with him—privately. Once they reached the kitchen, Resi's mother lowered her voice to a conspiratorial whisper. "Deutschland is kaput," she said. "There is nothing good for Resi here."

Clarence sympathized. The sentiment was widespread. A woman in nearby Aachen had spoken for many when she lectured a German soldier, "We have been lied to and cheated for five years, and promised a golden future, and what have we got?"

But Clarence sensed something more was coming.

"You marry Resi now," her mother said. "Take her to America later."

"We aren't even supposed to be talking," Clarence said. "I can't marry her—they'll throw me in jail."

The mother's face soured. She wasn't about to watch him leave Stolberg again without trying to ensure her daughter's future. She grabbed Clarence by one hand and retrieved Resi with the other, and led them to Resi's bedroom. She pushed them inside and shut the door behind them.

The front door slammed. The mother's shoes could be heard on the cobblestones outside as she departed. Her intent was unmistakable. She hoped that if they were left alone, hormones would persuade Clarence where she had failed.

The young couple sat on the bed. Conversation wasn't as easy as it had been moments before. Resi giggled at the awkwardness—she must have seen this coming.

Clarence looked at her. She was youthful, whereas he felt old and tired. She was cheerful while he felt hopeless. And above all she was loyal—she had waited for him even after he left without saying goodbye.

Other men weren't so lucky.

When the platoon's mail had caught up with them, several men received discouraging news. "A lot of guys are getting two timed by their wives and girlfriends," wrote a tanker. "It hit them like a spell I guess.

I hope I won't have to worry about that. Fellows going home after the war won't know what kind of a girl he'll find."

Resi moved in to kiss Clarence. But to her surprise, he pulled back.

Clarence finally came around to what he had been waiting to say. There was a reason why they shouldn't be together: the next battle. He didn't know where the war would take him or whether he had any chance of survival.

"I might not be coming back," Clarence said.

Tears streamed down Resi's face. As he gripped her hands, Clarence also became emotional.

He had come back from the Ardennes resigned to his fate. But as he held Resi, he admitted his greatest fear aloud. "I may die."

Resi threw her arms around him and sobbed. Clarence held her tenderly. He was convinced that he was doing the right thing for both of them. The war had robbed Resi of more than enough already. And Clarence was certain that sooner or later, his Sherman would be his hearse. When Resi's tears had dried, Clarence took her hand in his and led her out of the bedroom.

For her sake, they had no choice but to say goodbye.

Two weeks later, February 22, 1945

It was a good day for shooting.

On a hilltop northeast of Stolberg a crowd of tankers buzzed around a lone tank. From across the regiment, a large crowd had gathered for a firing demonstration. "All you hear is 'what a beautiful day to be home,'" wrote one tanker.

A vast valley spread out below them in the midday sun. The men wore helmets only for formality's sake; the front lines were eight miles away.

The Rhineland was soaked. Its pale green fields were marshy and flooded and stands of dead trees stood like islands above the tide. Melted snow was partially the problem, but most of the blame rested on the German military, who had unexpectedly opened dams in the north to flood the area to delay any Allied advance. Until the Rhineland dried out, Spearhead wasn't going anywhere—the tanks simply couldn't navigate the sodden terrain. For American armored units, the reprieve was a blessing.

Across the theater, ordnance officers and maintenance men were scrambling. Something had to change for their Shermans to survive the next push. Their solution? Homemade armor.

The Seventh Army was building steel baskets filled with sandbags around their Shermans. Another popular do-it-yourself solution involved pouring concrete over the tanks' frontal armor to reinforce their strength.

The Ninth Army welded steel tracks over their tanks' frontal plates before adding sandbags secured by nets.

Patton had ordered his Third Army to double the Shermans' frontal armor using steel plates salvaged from the wrecks of both American and German vehicles.

And in the First Army, Spearhead was experimenting with additional steel plates and concrete armor in select vehicles. But it wasn't the only solution on the table. They had something even better.

Clarence and the crew wove toward a tank sitting on the firing line. A staff sergeant's rank now lined Earley's sleeves, indicating his recent promotion to platoon sergeant. A murmur arose as the crew broke free of the crowd and approached the tank. It was no Sherman.

A wedge of frontal armor flowed into a sleek body with widely spaced tracks. The turret was set so far forward it seemed as if the tank were looking for trouble, and the gun was almost as long as the tank itself. This was "America's answer to the Tiger," the T26E3 Pershing tank.

A secret weapon, the Pershing had yet to be unveiled to American taxpayers. The first forty tanks had just rolled off the assembly line at the Fisher Tank Arsenal. Half of the inventory had been sent to Fort Knox for testing, while the other twenty tanks went to Europe to the ultimate proving grounds—the trial of live combat.

Two days before this, Captain Salisbury had called Clarence and the crew together to deliver good news: one of the Pershings was all theirs. It was serial number 26 off the factory floor.

The crew had no trouble handing over their Sherman.

The Pershing wasn't just a small step forward. It advanced tank technology by leaps and bounds. It was equipped with a monstrous

90mm cannon, not to mention an automatic transmission that could move the tank in reverse at high speed. With twice the effective armor of a 76 and twenty thousand pounds more heft, the Pershing weighed in at 46 tons, just three tons short of a Panther.

The allocation of the Pershing befuddled Clarence. *Why us?* Personally, he thought the crew of a crack gunner named Danforth should have received it, because they led the company more often.

Clarence asked the regimental ordnance officer how the decision was made. Like a number of consequential decisions, it happened around a conference table far from any battlefield. "Everyone figured that Earley's crew was the best one to get the tank," the officer said.

But what made them the best? Earley had his own theory: "We just never got knocked out."

Clarence and the crew climbed aboard while cameramen jockeyed to document the event. The Pershing had the designation E7 painted on its front fender. The crew accordingly christened their new tank "Eagle 7."

T26E3 Pershing Eagle 7 *during the demonstration*

Standing atop the engine deck, Clarence felt a wave of anxiety. All eyes were on him. His first time firing the 90mm would serve as a demonstration for the entire 32nd Regiment. Hardened tankers had come to see if this alternative to the Sherman offered any hope. Was the Pershing a machine that could go muzzle to muzzle with anything the Germans put on the battlefield?

The paint inside of the Pershing was fresh white. Clarence took his seat alongside the 90mm gun, which was touted by the army as "the most potent weapon we've ever mounted in a tank." A powerful 6x telescopic sight had been set within the periscope mount, an advance that all but negated the need to lean from sight to sight.

Clarence flipped through his notepad one last time. The targets in the valley for this demonstration were prearranged, and every home in the impact area had been verified as abandoned. The notepad shook in his hand. Once again, Clarence was flying by the seat of his pants.

Civilian specialists had walked him through the basics of how to operate the gun, but that was in a classroom and hardly a complete education, especially considering that he had never been formally trained as a gunner in the first place.

If anything, Clarence had tripped into the role by accident.

In fall 1943, the battalion was on the southwest seacoast of England for long-range gunnery training, which involved blasting table-sized targets located high up on the coastal dunes. After the gunners fired, each loader was given a turn so that he could operate the weapon if the gunner was ever incapacitated. The officers devised a competition among the crews of two companies and offered a large bottle of whiskey as a prize to the winner.

Clarence should have missed. The target was set a thousand yards away and yet he hit it all eight times without breaking a sweat, leaving everyone to question his secret. That night, as the crew celebrated with whiskey, Paul Faircloth had confided in Clarence: the first chance he got, he would make Clarence their gunner.

Behind the Pershing, the crowds parted for a group of officers.

They were all attired in knee-length mackintoshes except for the man in the center, who wore a tanker's jacket and riding pants tucked into tall brown boots.

Maurice Rose

As the commander of the 3rd Armored Division, two small silver stars lined Major General Maurice Rose's helmet. He was a strikingly tall forty-five-year-old with black eyebrows that arched over stern, determined eyes. The son of a Polish rabbi who had immigrated to Denver, Rose had enlisted in the army as a private at the tender age of seventeen and climbed the ranks from there.

He'd already commanded tank units in Africa with the 1st Armored Division, "Old Ironsides," and Sicily with the 2nd Armored Division, "Hell on Wheels." Now came Germany, where he was the leader of the division he named Spearhead—a group of men and machines that he called "the greatest tank force in the world."

"He goes himself wherever he sends his men," wrote the *Chicago Tribune*. Rose's men loved him for it and would follow him almost anywhere.

General Rose and his entourage took their places to the left of the Pershing so that they were even with the tank's barrel. No one had seen the Pershing fire. Not even Eisenhower, who had rushed the tanks to the front lines, or General Omar Bradley, who had assigned half of the tanks to Spearhead.

Rose watched intently, eager to assess the capabilities of the gun and gunner. The Pershing was essential to the success of his plans. Thirty miles away lay Cologne, the "Queen City" of Germany. With a massive twin-spired Gothic cathedral that stood against the Rhine, the city was a symbolic guardian of German territory.

That's where Rose would take Spearhead. If the division could conquer Cologne and leap the Rhine, they could charge deep into the heart of Germany and bring the enemy to their knees.

Rumors were circulating that Cologne would be the climactic battle of the war, and Rose's presence seemed to confirm the gossip. But first, the general had to make sure that the Pershing was everything it was advertised to be.

"You won't believe who's here," Earley said as he assumed his position in the turret.

He told Clarence that General Rose was standing fifty feet away.

Clarence wanted to groan. The revelation added another layer of pressure. He had only dry-fired the 90mm. He had no "feel" for the weapon and now the general was watching? They had given his crew the Pershing, but could they take it away?

Earley gave the command. It was time for the show to begin.

The loader hefted a 3-foot-long armor-piercing shell and slid it into the breech. The 102-pound breech block slammed shut with a clang. Two civilian technicians took their places on the tank's rear deck and plugged their ears.

With a pair of binoculars pressed to his eyes, Earley directed Clarence's aim. "Traverse right."

Clarence set an eye to his 6x zoom sight and twisted the pistol grip to the right. A 15.5-foot barrel swept the air as the turret began turning. At the tip was a football-shaped muzzle brake with holes to funnel the blast out the sides, which would stir less dust in the gunner's line of sight.

The roofs of a small community floated across Clarence's sight. He stopped turning when a damaged farmhouse filled the reticle.

Earley gave a range estimation: "One, two hundred"—tanker-speak for 1,200 yards, about two-thirds of a mile. "The chimney."

Clarence wanted to throw up his hands in defeat. They wanted him to shoot the home's brick chimney? This was a tank gun, not a sniper rifle.

"Fire when ready," Earley said.

Clarence fine-tuned the reticle onto the target.

Gone was the foot trigger button from the Sherman. Clarence's index finger tensed on a red trigger on the pistol grip instead. *Don't miss,* he told himself. The secret to his marksmanship was simple: fear of letting down his crew.

He took a deep breath. There was no going back now. Clarence squeezed the trigger.

A blinding flash filled his sight and the 46-ton tank jumped as the cannon blasted the warhead downrange with an earsplitting crack.

A haze of hot propellant gases obscured Clarence's vision.

Outside the tank, the muzzle brake vented a sidelong blast that blew General Rose and his entourage clear off their feet. Onlookers watched a bright orange tail of tracer zip forth with such tremendous muzzle velocity that the 24-pound shell flew without arc, straight into the chimney. A shower of red bricks somersaulted through the air.

Inside the tank, Clarence gripped his ears. The gun's report was like an ice pick to the eardrums. When his hearing returned, Clarence heard grumbling behind him. When he turned, he found Earley nursing his face.

No one had warned the crew—if they even knew—that when the gun breech kicked out a spent shell, it also belched a flaming orb of propellant gases that would travel up through the commander's hatch as it exited the tank. The fireball had whisked Earley's face and singed his eyebrows.

Up front, McVey opened and shut his hatch in a fit of laughter.

He reported that General Rose and his officers had been "blown over like bowling pins!" After hearing this, Smokey had to see it for himself. And when he did, he joined in the chorus of laughter. As Rose and his entourage picked themselves up from the soggy ground, the hardened crews fought to keep straight-faced.

"Target two." Earley was back to business.

Clarence swung the gun farther to the right. The target this time was another farmhouse, which was set back at 1,500 yards, about a mile from the tank. This house had two chimneys. One was located on the near side, and a second on the far side. "I'll try for the near one," Clarence said. A white stone chimney, it was the easier of the two to hit.

Earley flattened himself against the wall of the turret and said he

With infantry aboard, this Spearhead M4 probes for resistance during the fighting in France, August 1944.

A Panther G, fresh from the floor of the MAN factory in Nuremberg, September 1944.

The real Fury, *seen here in Normandy. This M4 belonged to the 2nd Armored, the army's other heavy armored division.*

A Panzer IV H races to the front lines in Normandy, June 1944.

A Spearhead Sherman crosses a floating bridge, likely during the liberation of Belgium, as evidenced by the patriotic scribblings on the hull.

A Spearhead Sherman rolls through Stolberg on September 24, 1944, at a time when only half of the town had been wrested from the Germans.

Tanks were literally parked between houses in the early days at Stolberg. Seen here is "Cajun Boy" Audifred (far left) and some of his crew aboard their Sherman.

At the onset of the Bulge, Easy Company tankers take a meal alongside Clarence's Sherman Eagle. *Left to right: Smokey, unidentified, Earley, McVey, and Clarence.*

A view through the periscope. Jim Bates snapped this photo from the bow gunner's seat of a Stuart during the Battle of the Bulge.

"Cajun Boy" Audifred and his M4A1 during a lull in the Bulge. "Duckbills" can be seen extending from the tracks.

Spearhead crews assess their next move in the Ardennes. To the right of the M4A1 is one of the division's sought-after M4A3E2 tanks, an up-armored assault Sherman.

Clarence (left) and McVey display a 76mm high-explosive shell. Their tank Eagle, *seen later in the Bulge, is now missing its logs.*

This Spearhead M4 struggles for grip on the icy streets of Baneux, Belgium, during the American counteroffensive in January 1945.

An M4A3 Sherman passes a vanquished Panther in the northern salient of the Bulge.

The Pershing drew a crowd wherever it went. Here, troops crowd the turret for a peek inside Eagle 7.

The muzzle brake protrudes from the 90mm gun of Clarence's Pershing.

Captain Salisbury inspects the barrel of an M4 during a Saturday morning inspection in Germany. The Pershing is next in line, on the far left.

Easy Company driver-turned-tank-commander Joe Caserta, with his Sherman, named Everlasting.

An Easy Company Sherman juxtaposed against Clarence's Pershing.

The Sherman Eleanor, *seen in France with some of her original crew. Left to right: Peter White, Bill Hey, Robert Rowe, and Chuck Miller.*

At Blatzheim, Clarence would see gunner Hubert Foster (far left)
"walk on air" as he exited the tank.

An Easy Company Sherman abandoned at Blatzheim after taking a hit. The commander likely reversed the turret so his men in the bow could escape.

One of Spearhead's new M4A3E8 Shermans crosses the Erft Canal during the drive on Cologne. The "Easy Eight" featured twenty-three-inch wide tracks for better ground flotation.

The Pershing idles while a dozer tank moves to clear the underpass leading into Cologne.

Beyond the overpass, the Pershing leads Task Force X past a white flag and into Cologne. DeRiggi can be seen riding above the turret, and Earley is behind him.

A Spearhead dough advances toward Cologne's ancient Römerturm, *or Roman tower, while firing his machine gun from the hip.*

Kathi Esser cares for her nephew, Fritz.

Kathi and her three sisters, each of whom lost a husband to the war. Left to right: Anna, Kathi, Barbara, and Maria.

Behind the door of the Opel P4, Spearhead medics tend to their patient while the Pershing keeps a vigil for any threats ahead.

was ready. Clarence's finger hovered in front of the trigger. Between the savage crash of the gun and the disconcerting change in air pressure that followed in the blast's wake, firing the 90mm actually scared him.

Don't miss, Clarence reminded himself.

He fired again.

With another ear-piercing crack, a shell launched forward and the breech leapt back. When the haze of propellant had cleared, the target was down a chimney. A cloud of white dust hung where the bricks had been.

Cheers streamed into the turret from outside.

I like this gun! Clarence thought.

The outpouring of enthusiasm encouraged Earley. "See that little one?" he asked Clarence.

A small brick chimney—which probably came from a pantry—stood on the back of the house and just the top was showing.

Clarence didn't like it. At about a mile's distance, it would be like trying to shoot a helmet off a soldier's head. Clarence admitted that he'd rather quit while they were ahead. It would be better than disappointing everyone.

"Oh, come on," Earley said. "Try it."

Clarence reluctantly laid an eye to his sight. The chimney looked as narrow as a pencil point. This would require something special. He set the aim point on the chimney. Another, less talented, gunner would have stopped there. But Clarence estimated that the periscope and its sights were set about two feet to the right of the gun barrel, so he worked the hand crank and shifted his aim to the right of the target to compensate.

Don't miss.

Clarence squeezed the trigger. Another ear-piercing crack sent the shell downrange at 2,800 feet per second. The chimney burst into red dust. Clarence eyed the target in disbelief. He had not only hit it, he'd evaporated it.

Inside the tank, the crew erupted in a din of astonished praise. Earley leaned forward and gave Clarence a pat on the back.

• • •

Clarence followed Earley outside to thunderous applause. A grin lined his face as he gave a bashful wave.

General Rose and his entourage were muddy, but proud and clapping with the rest of the troops. Rose would soon write to Eisenhower: "There is no question in my mind . . . our gunnery is far superior to that of the Germans."

On the ground, the crews mobbed Clarence, Earley, and the others. Captain Salisbury approached his men and doubled over in laughter at the sight of Earley's singed eyebrows.

Roughshod tank crews became schoolboys. There was more back-slapping and bravado than there'd been in a long time, complete with proclamations of "Look out, Hitler, here we come!" These men had resigned themselves to eventual death or dismemberment, but now they had hope.

Clarence told his admirers, "The army needs to rush a whole bunch of these over here."

Instead of hurrying back to Stolberg to drink beer or frolic with women, the crews lingered. Clarence saw men posing for photos with the tank as the cameramen snapped away. Earley, McVey, and Smokey gave tours of the tank in the background.

The enthusiasm was infectious. In the distant haze, Clarence could envision the spires of Cologne and, more important, somewhere beyond the spires, the end of the war.

Stolberg was the closest he'd been to home during his time in Europe. Now, for the first time since he'd arrived, he was restless to leave.

He and the boys were ready to go back to work.

Four days later, February 26, 1945
Golzheim, Germany

A light drizzle fell as the tanks of Easy Company idled on a highway that ran beside the German village of Golzheim.

It was a cold morning, around eight thirty A.M. Fog drifted across the surrounding spongy fields. Rain spiraled from the tanks' barrels.

Vibrations from the Pershing thrummed around Clarence's waist as he stood in the commander's hatch, watching for Earley to return from a briefing. The crew had a running wager and only Earley could reveal the result.

Today, their lives might depend on it.

On the highway ahead, a dozer tank rammed aside a log roadblock. Beyond the logs, the highway was open and inviting, with neatly interspersed trees on either side. Clarence looked past the scene with little more than a yawn. Spearhead had set out from Stolberg in the early morning hours, going east and spreading its task forces across the Cologne Plain in a coordinated drive of the First Army.

For Clarence's "Task Force X," it had been smooth sailing—sixteen miles without a shot so far—thanks to the Timberwolves. To the left of the column, the infantrymen, in wet helmets and muddy spats, were moving between the puddles of Golzheim, preparing to move on, having secured the village the night before.

Golzheim, like every town on the Cologne Plain, had been fortified since the prior fall, and they all bore a resemblance to one another, as the division recorded, "each with its main streets barricaded, vehicles overturned and buildings smoldering in ruin. German dead lay by the roadside among the pagan effects of their falling empire: the swastika flags, the official papers of Nazi government, and the litter of cross-marked personal belongings."

The tank commanders were returning with their map cases under their arms. Clarence leaned forward for a better view of Earley among the men. Clarence and the crew believed they could predict how dangerous a mission would be solely by the weathervane of Earley's pipe. But sometimes it was better not to know.

Erratic puffs of smoke sifted upward as the pipe rose and fell in Earley's teeth. Clarence sank into the turret. He was almost afraid to speak the words. "It's jumping."

The crew's groans could be heard outside. If Earley was nervous, they were in for a tough one.

The highway was a no-go, Earley told them. Engineers had concluded that it was likely mined. As a result, the tanks would have to go cross-country, line abreast, through bleak, barren fields. Easy Company funneled from the road and the tanks fell in line with their backs to Golzheim.

Clarence brought himself close to his periscope. The lens was streaked with water. Two miles to the east, behind a misty wall of dead trees, lay the town of Blatzheim, another fortified enclave on the road to Cologne. Cologne itself was now just twelve miles away. Aerial reconnaissance had confirmed enemy trenches ringing the town, but Clarence was optimistic. This time, Easy Company wasn't leading the charge.

Three M5 Stuart light tanks queued at the starting line.

Today's would be a full task force attack with Easy Company and its two sister tank outfits combining forces. A few Stuarts of B-Company would go first, scouting for a spot to cross the trenches. Then the Shermans of F-Company would cover the left flank while Easy Company went straight up the middle to the doorsteps of Blatzheim.

Idling in Easy Company's lineup was a 76 Sherman with the name "Everlasting" written on its flanks. Inside, Chuck Miller sat in the gunner's seat. Gazing through the periscope, he was on the verge of traumatic flashbacks. The empty field, the spongy terrain, it was Grand-Sart all over again.

Chuck had transferred to this crew after hearing that the commander needed a gunner. Any tank was better than Eleanor. After Grand-Sart had fallen, Chuck, Fahrni, and the crew drove the battered old tank into a Belgian garage. Cleaning the tank was typically a job for the maintenance guys, but somehow, in this instance, it fell to Chuck's crew. They unloaded the blood-splattered radio and shells and scrubbed the white walls. It only then that Chuck forced himself to stomach the task that the others refused. He removed Bill Hey's brain matter from the commander's seat.

The division buried Bill in his uniform and a mattress cover. After the makeshift funeral, the army sent his belongings, a pad of addresses, and a prayer book, to his mother, Lauretta.

Normally after a man died in a tank, the unit would transfer the machine to another company—the army didn't want the remaining men seeing the ghost of their fallen comrade at inopportune times. But for some reason, Eleanor remained in Easy Company's possession and Fahrni was promoted to commander. Chuck couldn't escape fast enough.

After detouring from the road, they were off. The three Stuarts raced toward Blatzheim in a wedge formation with exhaust puffing from their Cadillac engines.

To Chuck's eyes, the boxy little tanks looked like little more than bait.

Aside from its speed—the tank was capable of traveling 40 miles per hour—the Stuart was "obsolete in every respect as a fighting tank," according to the general who commanded the Hell on Wheels Division.

A far cry from the engineering marvel of the new Pershing, the Stuart had only a 37mm gun and weak frontal armor with just an inch and a half of effective thickness. As if that wasn't bad enough, its belly was so thin that if the tank hit a mine, the blast could punch the floor into the legs of the crew.

About a third of the way across the field, the Stuarts came to a screeching stop. The gun of the lead tank turned toward some distant haystacks.

M5 Stuart

Don't do it! Chuck implored the distant tanks. If the enemy were watching, any pause could prove deadly.

The commander of the lead tank "forgot" his objective and blasted a hole through one haystack. As he prepared to shoot another, a German shell brought him back to his senses. A green shaft of tracer streaked from the left, punching through the Stuart and flying out the other side. Smoke in the shape of ominous black rings rose from the tank as wounded men rolled over the sides. The remaining Stuarts spun on a dime and came racing back.

Chuck tracked the shot back to a farm complex about a mile north.

It felt like a warning.

After the inauspicious beginning for the Stuart tanks, it was Easy Company's turn. The tanks rolled into the soggy field arrayed in their usual three-row phalanx.

At the periscope, Clarence breathed easy. McVey had blessed their maiden voyage—"Lord, please keep the big bullet away from us"—and his prayer had already been answered.

The Pershing was surrounded. Everywhere Clarence looked were the whirling tracks and rising exhaust from other tanks. Five Shermans drove ahead, five followed behind, and his platoon bracketed the Pershing's flanks. The lead tanks held back their speed—they were traveling at just 20 miles per hour—so the slightly slower Pershing could hold formation. As added insurance, the A-Company doughs were also with them, advancing on foot, alongside the highway. Additional doughs of B- and C-Companies were held in reserve, should anything go wrong.

Salisbury had put the Pershing in the middle rank for safekeeping. No one wanted to see the brand-new tank suffer needlessly in its first battle.

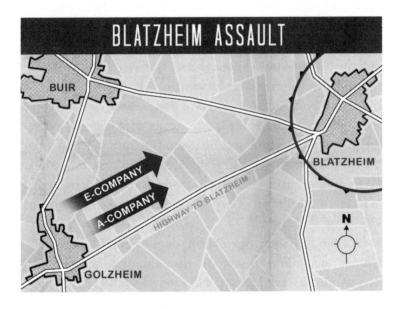

Clarence wasn't complaining. The Pershing was worth protecting. Thanks to the longer turret it was roomier than a Sherman, and even with a bigger gun there was more space to slip behind the gun to the loader's side or to escape down to the bow gunner's position. A well-placed step for entry and exit into the turret didn't hurt either.

The formation split to avoid the burning Stuart, its steel skin sizzling in the rain. Earley shielded his face against the heat as they passed.

This time, the crews were ready.

The lead Shermans swung their guns toward the farm complex that the earlier shot had come from, all but begging the Germans to try again.

It was an invitation the Germans were happy to accept. From the left, another green lance streaked toward the tanks. It narrowly missed before it burrowed through the muddy soil.

The doughs hit the dirt. The tank drivers hauled back on the steering levers. The dull rumble of engines returned as the formation stopped. Clarence felt a twinge of trepidation. This was no warning shot. Another green lance—likely from a 75mm antitank gun—sliced through the air, followed by another.

The lead row of tanks returned fire. Gun barrels recoiled into turrets with each shot. Their shells dismantled the farm complex and whoever had attacked them from it. All eyes were on the enemy to their side when another shot came from the front. A green bolt zipped through the formation with the crack of a massive bullwhip.

Clarence wheeled the turret forward.

More green bolts came flying from Blatzheim in what appeared to be slow motion, at first. At the last moment, they seemed to accelerate as they rocketed through the formation. Clarence flinched in his seat while Earley ducked from the whipcracks. The first volley narrowly missed everyone, but revealed a troubling truth by its sounds: These weren't just any shells. The Germans were firing their tank-killer gun, the 88.

A fearsome gun with an 88mm mouth, the 88 was an "anti-everything," according to one American soldier. When used as an antiaircraft gun it could throw a 20-pound shell for six and a half miles into the sky. But when used to target tanks, it was even deadlier. Leveling the gun extended its lethal range by three more miles.

The radio—which had been silent with discipline—now crackled with curses.

The German guns on the left had resumed firing and Easy Company found itself caught in a net of fire from at least six guns as tracers crisscrossed the field.

Clarence made himself small in his seat. With friendly tanks surrounding the Pershing he was powerless. All he could do was watch. A green bolt struck a 76 Sherman to his front-right with a flash of sparks.

Hatches were flung open and the crew nearly tripped over one another in their hurry to escape. It was every man for himself.

When topped off, a Sherman held around eighty shells and 170 gallons of gasoline—a recipe for disaster if the tank were struck by enemy fire. "Once you get hit in a tank there's fire to worry about," wrote a gunner, "and your only goal in life then is to get the hell out of there."

Clarence was relieved to see his friend Corporal Hubert Foster worm his way out of the turret, apparently unhurt. A lanky man with big feet and pimply skin, Foster frantically jumped to the engine deck. As he ran off the back of the tank he kept running in midair and his feet continued bicycling like crazy until he hit the ground.

Clarence burst into nervous laughter.

"What's so funny?" Earley asked on the intercom.

"I just saw a man walk on air," Clarence said.

From Earley's viewpoint outside the sanctuary of the turret, there was no time for humor. The lead rank was in disarray. Some tanks were firing forward while others shot sideways. Everyone stuck behind them was idling with impatience. Some commanders even made angry gestures reminiscent of drivers caught in a traffic jam.

To top it all, the airwaves were just as clogged as their route forward. Captain Salisbury was trying to get a handle on things from Golzheim, where he was using his Sherman as a mobile command post. One crew reported a jammed cannon and another came running from what appeared to be a sound tank after a mechanical failure.

It was chaos.

With the clang of metal on metal, another of the lead Shermans took a heavy hit and exploded. Covers blasted upward from the rear deck and the commander was thrown headlong into the air. Another crewman stumbled from around the front, his shirt flapping wildly where his arm had once been.

Now reduced to two fully operational Shermans in the lead rank, Salisbury called for a retreat. Earley ordered the platoon to lay down a smokescreen to cover their fellow tankers. Each Sherman had an M3 smoke mortar launcher, a British invention, like a flare gun, that the loader fired from a hole in the turret. A cascade of smoke shells arced over the two lead tanks and sizzled, spewing a massive white wall of smoke.

Sporadic green bolts cut corkscrews through the haze as the twelve American tanks carved U-turns in the slush.

It was the Ardennes all over again.

If they were supposed to retreat, no one told the doughs.

Buck Marsh paced through the shroud of smoke with his rifle at his hip. The Germans had stopped firing and now the only thing that permeated the smoke was the hiss of a flaming Sherman.

Buck was cold and wet; his teeth chattered uncontrollably. His pace slowed as he imagined German soldiers charging at him through the mist. He was the first scout, chosen to strike out alone ahead of the company. He'd thought the assignment was an honor, until Janicki corrected the naïve misconception. The first scout was usually the first one to step on a mine, or become separated in a firefight, or get outright shot.

Buck wiped his eyes from the stinging smoke. Were they close to the German trenches? He was disoriented. Each step was slower than the last as he waded through the man-made cloud.

"Buck! Keep going!"

Over his shoulder, Buck saw the reassuring outline of a six-foot-two officer standing taller than his fellow doughs. Second Lieutenant William Boom was waving him forward. Buck's platoon leader was eager to gain ground.

Always eager to please, Buck picked up the pace. The smoke thinned and bits of green vegetation appeared beneath his boots as he stepped from the haze. The highway was to their right and Blatzheim still lay a mile ahead. They were only halfway there. With every step, the mist slipped behind Buck and, one by one, other doughs appeared. At full strength, A-Company fielded 181 officers and men.

"Keep going, Buck!" It was Boom again, urging him on as a teammate would. A former college basketball star, Boom was more of a coach than a platoon leader.

As first scout, Buck was supposed to stay one hundred feet ahead of the main body so that he could watch for irregular terrain or motion from the enemy. He felt naked now that he was no longer shrouded in smoke. The grenades jingled on his harness, as did the shovel on his back. His palms were sweating beneath his gloves. He eyed the ditches along the highway. They were full of inviting dark leaves.

What are they waiting for? he wondered.

Surely, the Germans were watching from behind their Flak 41 guns, an antiaircraft model of the 88. This region had been a flak belt, bristling with at least two hundred 88s and crews.

It was a good time to pray. Buck had grown up Presbyterian, in a Southern family that had occupied the same church pew for fifty years. He had prayed regularly when he was first deployed, but sharing a foxhole with Janicki had changed that. In the Ardennes, with mortar shells bursting all around, Buck had prayed aloud to beg God for deliverance. After the bombardment, Janicki turned to him and said, "Why do you think God will help you? So you can climb out of this hole and go kill Germans?"

There was no good answer to that question then, and since he still didn't have an adequate answer now, he kept his prayers to himself.

Buck glanced back toward Golzheim. The tanks were just sitting there. If A-Company reached the trenches without armored support, they'd be annihilated, World War I–style.

It made Buck want to shout, *What are you waiting for?*

Easy Company idled back at the starting line.

The tank with the jammed gun had fallen out and the eleven machines remaining were itching to roll.

Inside a 75 Sherman, Sergeant Frank "Cajun Boy" Audifred had traded his commander's position for the gunner's seat for now. The tough but good-natured tanker had the looks of bayou country, with thick black hair, a sharp nose, and deep-set dark eyes. Hunting water moccasins had been his favorite after-school activity before the army found better use for his talents. Audifred set an eye to his telescopic sight. What he saw outside wasn't pretty.

The doughs were blindly forging ahead. Meanwhile, stranded tank crews were sheltering in shell holes. One tanker was even hopping back on one foot—where the other foot had been was now a stump. A

Frank "Cajun Boy" Audifred

mile to the left, F-Company's Shermans were assaulting the farm complex, but until that flank was clear, Easy Company was stuck here.

Audifred sat back and fidgeted. He wasn't one for watching from the sidelines. He wasn't one for riding in the gunner's seat either, but it was only temporary.

That morning, Captain Salisbury had asked him for a favor. The captain had a new lieutenant who had just transferred over from B-Company after being wounded in the Ardennes. Salisbury asked if Audifred would serve as gunner for the day, to give the lieutenant experience.

Lieutenant Robert Bower now sat in the commander's seat behind Audifred, still shaking from the earlier attack. Tall, with blue eyes, brown hair, and a pale complexion, he looked like a college kid to Audifred, even if the twenty-six-year-old lieutenant was five years older than he was. Bower carried a chess set in his musette bag and possessed a boyish eagerness to learn anything he could about Shermans. He was also quick to acknowledge that it was Audifred's tank—he was just borrowing it for the day. Audifred liked him instantly.

The radio crackled. Audifred listened in as Salisbury briefed Bower.

The farm complex was clear. Their attack could resume. Since 2nd Platoon was at full strength, they would lead, which meant that Lieutenant Bower would be in command.

Salisbury's order ended on an ominous note: "There will be no turning back."

Bower's eyes met Audifred's. "He's serious?"

Audifred nodded. It was their job to saddle up and go forward, even if it meant their deaths. Audifred was numb to any qualms about his own mortality by now. Once during a rainstorm in France, his crew had elected to sleep beneath the tank even though that meant likely getting wet. But Audifred found a better option. A P-47 had crashed upside down in the field and stood propped up by its tail. The locals had respectfully laid the dead American pilot beneath the rear fuselage. The space was dry there—much drier than beneath the tank—so Audifred spent the night there, right beside the dead pilot.

It was time to move out. As the tank began rolling, Audifred's pistol rattled against the sidewall, so he switched it over to his left hip.

Lieutenant Bower's voice was shaking as he radioed the platoon.

"Just keep your head down when the shooting starts, Lieutenant," Audifred said, speaking with his slow-rolling Southern-French drawl. "You'll be just fine."

Bower appreciated the tip.

He has no idea what he's in for, Audifred thought.

The stranded crews cheered as the 2nd Platoon tanks roared past. Six more Shermans followed close on their heels.

Nothing stood between the lead tanks and the doughs.

Audifred's 75 Sherman anchored the left flank, while the Pershing was assigned the right, nearest the highway, in the safest estimable position. In the middle was Everlasting, the 76 Sherman whose gunner's seat was occupied by Chuck Miller. Try as he might, Chuck hadn't completely escaped Eleanor. The battered old tank was holding formation in a slot to the left.

Behind Chuck in the commander's position stood his best friend, Sergeant Raymond "Juke" Juilfs. Juke hailed from a small speck of a town in Iowa. Twenty-two, with blond hair and flat dark eyebrows, he

Raymond "Juke" Juilfs

looked like he belonged on a base-ball diamond, not captaining a tank.

But here they were.

In Blatzheim, 88s began blinking. Chuck watched through his periscope as the doughs flattened themselves before the green bolts could shave their helmets. The terrible sound of metal on metal cut the air. Someone had been hit.

"It's Eleanor!" Juke reported from above.

"How bad?" Chuck asked.

Juke swiveled in his hatch. A bow strike had stopped Eleanor in her tracks. Fahrni was rolling from the turret while other survivors were pulling the driver out by his arms. He was Peter White, who had stolen the chickens in Stolberg. Both his legs were mangled and destined for amputation.

The platoon kept going, now down to four tanks strong.

Chuck struggled to hold an eye to his periscope, and when he managed, he found the reticle was bobbing wildly despite the gyro-stabilizer. He was hungry for retribution. But each bounce on the rough field tossed him from his seat. With the gun breech bouncing just as violently, there was no way that the loader could reload even if Chuck managed to fire off a shot.

A glimpse of a green bolt zipped toward Everlasting. Chuck leaned sideways in his seat, as if he meant to dodge it. The shell thudded to the ground before skipping off to hit someone else.

Juke reported that another Sherman had fallen out of the formation. It looked to him that it suffered from a thrown track.

The platoon kept going. They were now down to just three tanks. With fewer targets, the enemy narrowed their aim to the middle tank. The whip began cracking over Juke's head as the green bolts plowed the soil around Everlasting. An enemy shell descended right in front of the tank and left a smoking hole in the ground. The driver tried to haul back on the steering levers but there was no time.

"Brace!" Juke shouted.

Chuck gripped the bulkhead as the Sherman dove nose-first into the crater with a crunch.

Track links went flying as the engine ground on and whined with immense effort before mercifully quitting.

Chuck's head was swimming beneath his helmet after slamming into the periscope. He tried to move his limbs but realized that he was pinned in his metal corner by an avalanche of fallen equipment. This was not the time to be unable to think straight. He braced himself for the telltale hiss and whoosh of flames, a nightmare that could arise at any moment.

"Abandon tank!" Juke called.

In the crew's frenzy to worm their way out of the Sherman, they left Chuck behind. Tankers the world over recognized the Sherman's reputation as a tinderbox. It was known to British crews as the "Tommy Cooker," to free Poles as the "Burning Grave," and to Americans as the "Mobile Oven," and even the "Crematorium on Wheels."[*]

To prevent a spark, Chuck shut off the gun's electrical switches. He unplugged his helmet and began digging free from the ammunition belts, shell casings, maps, and other debris. Then he climbed for daylight. Chuck vaulted from his seatback to Juke's hatch and pulled himself outside, emerging into a world of noise. The trailing row of tanks was peeling around Everlasting to go forward.

Chuck slid down the hull into the crater and scrambled to join the crew, who had taken shelter behind a pile of straw-covered potatoes. He hit the dirt next to Juke. Juke and the others were banged up, with black eyes and bloody noses. With each explosion, the men pressed their helmeted heads into the soil. They couldn't stay here, but could they survive a run to Golzheim?

Chuck looked back at the disabled tanks and the men taking shelter. A shell landed amid a group of tankers. From the roiling cloud of

---

[*] The Sherman owed its fire-prone reputation to the early 75 models, where ammunition was racked along the tank's vulnerable sidewalls. In those tanks, a penetrating hit triggered a fire 80 percent of the time. In later models, the shells were moved to bins set in antifreeze in the hull floor. This "wet stowage" lowered the chance of a fire to around 15 percent. However, for crews, the tinderbox reputation proved hard to forget.

dirt, a tanker bolted in a frenzy. Chuck watched, horrorstruck, as the man's gait slowed. He managed several last steps before dropping dead. He had no face.

As Chuck turned forward, a flash burst in front of the potatoes. A crack like thunder come to earth. The shockwave sucked all the air from his lungs. Ringing filled his ears as he came up panting and disoriented. Dust hung in the air. The driver, Corporal Joe Caserta, was writhing in pain as he clutched his shoulder.

Chuck turned to Juke. "We need to get out of here!"

But Juke didn't stir. Chuck shook his friend and Juke's head rolled toward him, limp. Smoke rose from a black shrapnel hole in the top of his tanker helmet.

Juke was dead, never to return to his wife, Darlene, or Jimmy Ray, the baby son he had yet to meet. Chuck couldn't believe it. His best friend was gone. The crew around him were wounded and stunned and the shells continued popping. At a time like this, another man might fall to pieces and cry like a baby.

But not Chuck Miller. "Let's go," he hollered as he lifted Caserta, wounded but still ambulatory, to his feet. Offering a steady shoulder, Chuck steered his injured friend toward Golzheim, leading the way for the others.

The platoon kept going, despite the fact that their numbers had been whittled to just two tanks.

Audifred's Sherman charged side by side with the Pershing. They had just eight hundred yards left to go. Inside, Audifred talked to himself nonstop. Whether Bower could understand him or not didn't matter; the drawl of the bayou filled the tank.

He muscled the gun from target to target, but every time he landed his sights where he had seen a gun flash, the reticle would jump or dive and he would lose the target. Audifred glanced over his shoulder to check on Lieutenant Bower, who—on Audifred's advice—was staying low in the turret and waiting for the moment when they would hit the trenches and he could spring into action.

That moment would never come.

A shell struck the turret with the clang of a bell, and a blast of molten steel punched through the loader's side. The blast swallowed the loader and Lieutenant Bower before throwing Audifred into the sidewall, knocking him unconscious.

Seconds later, maybe minutes, Audifred came to and opened his deep-set eyes. Dark, acrid smoke filled the turret as sparks danced in the darkness like fireflies. Crashing waves filled Audifred's ears; both eardrums were ruptured. He was still seated, but was so numb he couldn't tell if the tank was still moving.

We got hit.

The left side of his body was naked. The sleeve of his tanker jacket and a pant leg had been completely incinerated. Blood seeped from shrapnel holes up and down his body. It looked like he had been hit with a meat tenderizer. His jaw tingled and his head itched. When Audifred's fingers traced his scalp, his black hair fell out in clumps. The steel gun breech had shielded his eyes, but that was the only part of him that emerged unscathed.

The lieutenant.

Audifred turned. Where once a promising "college kid" had stood, a blistered body now lay on the turret floor, its skull crushed beyond recognition.

Once outside the tank, Audifred sank to his knees in the soil. At the ripe old age of twenty-four, he had just lost his fifth tank. Audifred looked around. He was alone and had no recollection of exiting the tank. Enemy shells were still popping. Instinctively, Audifred went for his 1911 pistol, which he'd switched to his left hip. But the leather holster was gashed and he had to tug the pistol to break it free.

Looking down, he saw why. A jagged shard of shrapnel was wedged in the pistol's slide. The gun was holding together by a thread. The pistol had shielded an artery and possibly saved his life.

It was then that Audifred collapsed into the dirt. The pain had caught up to him.

The Pershing was now in the lead—all by itself.

The trailing Shermans had fallen behind, ensnared in the traffic jam of dead tanks and stranded crews.

John "Johnny Boy" DeRiggi

Inside, Clarence was glued to his periscope as explosions shook the mighty tank.

He had yet to fire a shot.

Across the turret, Corporal John DeRiggi gripped a shell, eager for a reason to reload. The twenty-year-old loader had the looks of a young Robert Mitchum and wore a French-made tanker's helmet, black with generous leather earflaps, something that he had traded to get.

Growing up in an Italian-American household in Scranton, Pennsylvania, he was known as "Johnny Boy," because his mischief gave his parents reason to shout, "Johnny, boy, if I get hold of you . . ." But the typically fun-loving DeRiggi was now deadly serious as his eyes and ears tracked the shells outside. He couldn't take any more. A battle was raging around them and Clarence wasn't fighting back.

"Do something!" he shouted across the turret. "We're being wiped out!"

Clarence's temper flared as he snapped back, "I've got no shot!" The enemy guns were dug in below ground level, making them all but invisible.

Five doughs bolted for the highway seeking cover. But they didn't make it. An explosion sent their bodies flying and an American helmet rolled twenty feet into the field.

From what Clarence could discern, most of the flashes came from where the highway met the town—right beneath the trees.

The trees.

The enemy had tried to hide their trench line by digging it beneath an umbrella of trees.

Clarence asked Earley to stop the tank to give him a stable firing platform. DeRiggi and others protested—it would be suicide. Stopping would make them sitting ducks.

Clarence ignored them and turned to Earley. "Stop the tank, I need to shoot!"

Earley had never seen Clarence so inflamed. He called for the driver to stop the tank. McVey released the accelerator and hauled back on the levers.

Clarence turned to DeRiggi. "WP!"

DeRiggi looked confused—they normally used white phosphorus shells to mark targets.

"Now, goddammit!" Clarence leaned back to his periscope.

DeRiggi swapped out the shell in the breech for one with a gray-painted warhead.

With the Pershing stationary, the Germans' green bolts converged on it. Geysers of soil leapt from the field as dirt showered them from all sides.

Clarence looked past the chaos to where the highway met the town. He blocked out the noise and settled the reticle on the trunk of a single tree.

Don't miss. It was the usual pep talk he'd give himself, but this time, the stakes were life or death. Clarence squeezed the trigger. The 90mm barked as it blasted the special gray-painted shell at its target.

Downrange, the tree trunk shattered into matchsticks, but not before the shell gave birth to something more. Where the tree had stood, a white cloud billowed, sparkling with particles of white phosphorus, each burning at 1,000 degrees. The glittering tentacles floated down into the trench.

Clarence saw the outcome from his periscope—in that stretch, an 88 stopped flashing.

It worked!

Clarence could have cried with joy. There was hope, but no time to celebrate. Enemy shells were landing closer and closer. Before Clarence could fire again, Earley told the driver—"Reverse!"

Almost instantly, the Pershing rolled backward and a shell exploded where the tank had been. Stationary again, Clarence depressed the trigger, shattering another tree and silencing another gun with white phosphorus. Clarence called for more shells while Earley ordered more tank movements—forward, backward—to keep the enemy gunners off balance.

Casing after casing ejected from the 90mm's breech and Earley dodged the flaming spheres as Clarence directed his fire at tree after tree.

A pale mist, like a ground fog, hovered over the trenches. The German guns had all but stopped flashing. Earley radioed the trailing tanks and instructed anyone who had white phosphorus to help finish them off.

A safe distance from the trenches, A-Company hugged the dirt as American shells streaked overhead.

Buck tugged his helmet over his ears to hide from the "all-consuming noise."

When the firing finally tapered off, he lifted his head. The fog of white phosphorus was dissipating. A runner dashed from platoon to platoon. It was time to rush the enemy trenches.

On Lieutenant Boom's shout, Buck sprang to his feet as the entirety of A-Company charged forward. With a generous head start, Buck outdistanced the others. Blatzheim's thatched roofs and stone church bobbed in his vision. Before he knew it, he'd reached the trenches. He threw a grenade into the trench and watched it explode with a rise of dirt. The scout's job was to find the enemy, and Buck took his duty literally. He jumped into the trench and found them.

Twenty yards to the right lay a gun pit, where a German gun crew—still stunned by the use of white phosphorus—was huddled around an 88. After one German noticed Buck, four or five others turned toward him with their weapons lowered. Buck took aim with his rifle in reply. He froze. They froze. Buck's finger tightened on the trigger. Everyone's eyes were bulging in fear.

Before anyone could pull the trigger, A-Company hit the trench. Dough after dough jumped to the muddy floor and pointed gun muzzles in the Germans' faces. Others forcefully disarmed them, kicking aside rifles and tugging machine pistols from trembling hands.

Up and down the trench, pockets of Germans removed their helmets and surrendered. Five of the gun pits held abandoned 88s. But many more German guns were missing, having been towed away through getaway corridors behind each pit.

Buck sank to the trench's muddy floor. His mouth felt as if it were stuffed with cotton, so he took a swig from his canteen. The water didn't help.

German prisoners stepped over Buck's feet as doughs herded them past. A-Company claimed 173 prisoners, most of whom were older men from the 12th Volksgrenadier Division, a group of draftees made to honor pacts of "unconditional defense."

Janicki located Buck and helped him up as their squad gathered around. Together, the ten men were the 3rd Platoon's second squad, known as 3/2, or three-two.

The others were amazed that Buck had survived. To them, he was "Shorty," and they even had a saying about him: "Shorty thinks he's invisible!" Every time that Buck heard it, he had to wonder if they knew the difference between "invisible" and "invincible." He wasn't about to correct them now. They were hard-nosed veterans and he was not. And after today, he felt further from joining their ranks than ever.

When Janicki and the others unslung their weapons, Buck did the same. He wished he could stay there, but gunfire was popping in Blatzheim and there was a log roadblock to clear on the main street.

The veterans led the way.

The Pershing's wheels rose and fell over the uneven terrain as its tracks snaked across the trench.

On the edge of Blatzheim, the Pershing shut down with a battle-weary sigh, and the remaining six Shermans parked haphazardly around it. The logs that hung from the Shermans' flanks were splintered and flayed. Hatch covers flipped open and crews hopped down. A religious shrine stood nearby, pockmarked with bullet holes.

Clarence steadied himself against the Pershing. The sights of the battle's aftermath nearly made him sick. Four of the company's Shermans and a Stuart lay derelict in the field with their guns frozen, pointing at phantom targets. A few broken tanks limped back to Golzheim. And that was just the mechanical carnage. The human bloodshed was even worse. Medical jeeps raced forth to tend to sixteen wounded tankers, not to mention the injured doughs.

And the dead? They were still riding in cold, steel sarcophaguses.

Out in the middle of the field, a tank commander named Truffin stood up from a crater to wave down a Sherman sputtering back to Golzheim.

Truffin had lost a tank of his own, but he wasn't seeking help for himself.

When the Sherman stopped, Truffin carried an unconscious "Cajun Boy" Audifred from the shell crater. With the crew's help, Truffin placed Audifred on a fender and sat beside him to help hold him in place as the Sherman rumbled away.

In a field hospital, doctors would find the shape of a pistol bruised into Audifred's thigh. But when Cajun Boy awoke several days later in a French hospital, his good fortune wasn't his first thought. Or even his second. Instead, he was possessed by a singular thought: *That poor lieutenant!*

Lieutenant Robert Bower's combat time in a Sherman had lasted two hours.

Having safely delivered Caserta to the medics, Chuck Miller hobbled to the curb in Golzheim and took a seat. A fresh pain in his ankle had seemingly arisen from nowhere.

Chuck removed his right boot, lowered the sock, and found blood seeping from a hole on the outside of his ankle. A medic came along and fished around, but the shrapnel was embedded too deeply for him to retrieve. He bandaged the wound and called for a stretcher.

Having lost two tanks and two commanders, Chuck would be sent to Stolberg for care and reassignment to a new job with the supply sergeant. As far as the 3rd Armored Division was concerned, Chuck Miller had seen and done enough.

• • •

Shadows stretched across the field in the day's waning moments as Clarence and crew replenished the Pershing. With its sooty muzzle brake, mud-caked tracks, and countless claw marks left by shrapnel, the tank had taken on a stalwart, rugged appearance.

Passing doughs gaped at the "Super Tank" and asked if it was a captured German tank. Easy Company tankers came by to rib the crew, claiming that the Pershing had been "too slow" on the battle-field.

"I never saw any of you try to pass us," Clarence said. That shut them right up.

At one point, Earley took Clarence aside to praise his quick think-ing with the white phosphorus. Earley had also noticed a change in Clarence. For the first time since he'd been under Earley's command, Clarence was displaying confidence and forcefulness, the traits of his profession.

Earley looked his friend in the eye.

"From now on you fire when *you* want to," Earley told Clarence. "No more waiting on me."

Clarence was flattered by the gesture and promised Earley that he wouldn't let him down.

Personally, Clarence credited the Pershing with their survival. The automatic transmission, the accuracy of the 90mm gun—the tank wasn't just a tank anymore, it was a partner in the only mission that mattered to Clarence: keeping his family safe.

That night, however, someone would come to see the Pershing differently.

Captain Salisbury drifted sullenly around his company, disgusted by their losses. Five men dead. His company had lost five men taking one small German town, and this wasn't even Cologne, the city they were gunning for.

Salisbury was known to dwell on his unit's casualties, especially over the men killed in action. To him, each death was a personal fail-ure to someone's mother. Now he had to sign five letters of consola-tion and send death inventories home with the belongings of the boys who didn't make it. They included a lighter, a ring, religious articles, twenty-seven souvenir coins, and a chess set.

For all this, Salisbury blamed one person: himself. He had chosen to spare the Pershing. He had wrapped his company around the Super Tank only to see his Shermans be decimated before the Pershing could even throw a punch.

Never again.

It was February 1945. Although it was a painful choice, Captain Salisbury had made his decision. If his company was to live to see the end of the war, he'd have to risk one crew to protect the rest.

From now on, the Pershing would lead.

Four days later, March 2, 1945
Near Oberaussem, Germany

Buck stepped lightly along the path through the cold, dead woods about seven miles northeast of Blatzheim.

Snow flurries floated through the canopy of trees. Stands of white birch swayed in the wind. It was afternoon, and winter was refusing to make way for spring.

All of A-Company followed behind Buck in single file. They had not assigned him to be first scout this time. He had volunteered.

While the tanks stuck to the roads, the doughs were clearing the woods toward Oberaussem—another fortified town on their march to Cologne. The city was now just eight miles away.

Buck was actually enjoying the role of first scout. There was nothing quite like the rush of stalking the enemy and trying to shoot them before they could shoot you. It was just like the cowboy movies that he had loved to watch.

In some respects, Buck had exponentially more training for his job than the company's city slickers, many of whom had never seen a cow heap. He was no stranger to the woods. His father—a rugged outdoorsman—had overseen the construction of dams in Tennessee and highways in northern Alabama and first put a rifle in Buck's hands when he was just twelve. In no time, Buck and his younger brothers had built a cabin in the woods, where they spent their free time playing and hunting.

• • •

The woods were thinning out. Buck slowed his pace and tuned an ear to the sounds filtering through the trees. There was no telling what lay around the bend. It was a lesson that one Spearhead patrol would never forget.

The doughs had stumbled upon a ghastly scene inside a barn—an entire German family, a father, mother, and a teenage daughter, were all hanging from the rafters. Even their dog, a loyal dachshund, lay strangled at their feet. There were no signs of a struggle. Possessed of a fanatical devotion, the family had taken their own lives just before the Americans arrived.

The men of the patrol took the spectacle in stride. They had seen worse, and besides, the world was now three Nazis fewer.

A journalist from Spearhead headquarters recorded one man's reaction: "An American soldier surveyed the group perplexedly, then snapped his fingers. 'I got it,' he said. 'The dog was disgusted—he hanged the family and then committed suicide!' "

The woods in front of Buck opened up to a narrow footbridge that crossed a babbling creek. On the other side, in the backyard of a stone hunting lodge, stood a large oak tree. Shovelfuls of earth ringed the base of the tree—it looked like a fighting position. Something was moving in the tree's shadow, something gray.

A German helmet.

Buck pumped his rifle overhead to signal "enemy in sight." Behind him, the company hit the dirt. Buck took cover behind the nearest tree to study the enemy emplacement.

A German soldier rose into view. He was in profile to Buck as he took a peek at some woods to the left, then sank from sight.

Moments later, a burst of flame shot from the emplacement. Bullets from a machine gun tore the air and chewed into an empty patch of woods farther up the tree line from where Buck had taken shelter.

The Germans had to be spooked—they were firing in the wrong direction.

Another burst ripped from the gun. When it ceased, the German gunner rose to see if he'd hit anything. Buck balanced his M1 rifle on the nearest tree knob and centered his sights on the man's helmet, taking aim just above the curved earflap.

His gun barked. The helmet dropped from sight as the shot reverberated through the woods. Surging with adrenaline, Buck fired the rest of the clip toward the emplacement.

An eerie silence filled the forest air.

Lieutenant Boom crawled behind Buck and stopped within the tree line. Boom, the former college basketball star, still looked the part. The twenty-three-year-old was gangly, with a narrow face featuring close-set eyes and jug ears. He and Buck had bonded over a shared love of sports. Buck had been captain of the college tennis team and Boom had played basketball at Arizona State until his senior year, when he left to enlist.

Buck pointed out the emplacement to his friend, across the short bridge spanning the creek. "I'm pretty sure I hit one," Buck said.

William Boom

Boom looked through his field glasses. Even if Buck had killed one gunner, another could easily take over on the machine gun. They had no idea how many of the enemy were hiding in the emplacement.

Instead of taking a chance and sending the platoon across the bridge, Boom requested mortar support. Several minutes later, dark blurry streaks whooshed down from the sky and slammed the lodge and the oak tree, punctuated by orange bursts. Bits of the lodge's roof and branches from the oak showered down.

Satisfied that the gun emplacement was sufficiently silent, Boom summoned his squad leaders. The men took a knee as Boom doled out assignments. He ran his platoon like a sports team. Everything was a competition that came down to "us versus the enemy," and in this match there could only be one winner. However, his pep talks often ended with a sober reminder, delivered almost as an after-thought: "And be careful, so no one gets shot."

"Okay, let's go," Boom said, breaking the huddle. He then took off running across the narrow bridge, leaving Buck and the rest of the platoon to give chase.

As Boom and other doughs carefully encircled the emplacement, Buck recklessly bounded straight onto the lip to see the results of his marksmanship. But to his surprise, the pit was completely empty. No Germans, no machine gun. The only evidence that the emplacement had recently been occupied was an escape trench that led to the wall of the lodge.

Buck turned to Boom in disbelief. "I swear I got one!"

"If you live through this war you're going to deserve a medal," Boom said, amused.

Buck picked up a trail of blood in the trench. He followed red drops along the lodge's exterior, around a corner, and over to a basement staircase. Others stacked up behind him, including Boom. A well-meaning sergeant reminded the lieutenant that this wasn't an officer's job. Boom was known for his reckless disregard for his personal safety. Sometimes it seemed like he was trying to get himself killed.

Buck crept down the basement steps, leading the way. He was living up to his reputation: *Shorty thinks he's invisible.* A dough urged him to lead in with a grenade, but Buck refused—civilians sometimes took shelter in basements and he didn't want their blood on his hands.

At the foot of the stairs, Buck gave the "hold" signal and opened the door. When no shots rang out, he stepped inside the dimly lit basement.

The Germans were just standing there. Eight enemy soldiers hud-dled around something with their backs to him. When Buck shouted, the soldiers turned with their hands raised in surrender. Their faces were creased with dismay. Buck motioned them away so he could see what they were hiding. The soldiers stepped back, revealing a young German soldier lying on the floor.

Buck stepped closer.

The soldier was blond, blue-eyed, and around Buck's age, twenty-two. He was breathing, but bloody gray brain matter was oozing from holes on both sides of his head. Buck almost gagged. His hearing faded, and time seemed to stand still. He felt so lightheaded that he was afraid he was going to faint. This was his victim; no other dough had fired a shot. It was the first time Buck had seen the results of his bullets up close.

Buck turned to the other Germans and saw grief-stricken faces. Several wiped away tears, while others were on the verge of crying. They probably weren't just fellow soldiers; they were more likely friends who had known one another for years, belonging to a unit recruited from the same town.

Buck hollered for a medic.

A staircase's worth of doughs burst into the room, sweeping their rifles from side to side on the lookout for threats. Moments later, Boom arrived with a medic in tow.

The medic knelt over the young German. Buck couldn't look away, as if he could somehow will the young man back to health with his stare. The wounded man's eyelids fluttered, his breaths were shallow. The medic shook his head. The young German was going to die.

Buck struggled for breath as his chest tightened uncontrollably.

Boom must have recognized Buck's anguish because he ordered him to go upstairs to search the lodge. As Buck's feet carried him away, he looked over his shoulder, yearning to see the damage undone.

Dazed and ashen, Buck drifted aimlessly through the commotion of the hunting lodge.

Beneath the ceiling's wooden rafters, doughs crowded around gun cases, examining rifles and claiming the enemy's best specimens for themselves.

Janicki noticed Buck's indifference to the free-for-all and took him aside. Buck shared what he had just seen.

"He wouldn't have hesitated to turn his gun on us," Janicki said, referring to the soldier Buck had shot. "You just happened to fire first."

Buck wasn't about to accept that he had *possibly* saved lives by *certainly* taking one. In an effort to distract Buck, Janicki led him to the gun cases and reminded him that there was space in the squad's half-track to stash a rifle.

Buck picked up a triple-barreled shotgun and rifle combination with two 16-gauge shotgun barrels on top and a .44 rifle barrel underneath. Janicki suggested that Buck send the weapon home to his younger brother, which Buck thought was a good idea.

Buck departed the lodge with his M1 on one shoulder and the triple-barreled weapon on the other. Despite Janicki's best efforts, Buck's eyes were distant and his mind was elsewhere. He couldn't stop replaying the moment when he'd pulled the trigger. His life had changed forever.

Should I have shot over his head or into that oak tree?

Would he have dropped the gun and run?

He couldn't shake what was happening in the lodge behind him or forget the faces of those German soldiers as they watched their friend die. He'd heard in church that God knows every hair on a person's head, and how "when you take your last breath, God is with you."

Looking over his shoulder, the thought gave Buck a chill. God was probably in that basement, about now.

In his rush to become a veteran, he'd overlooked the downside: war is an ugly business to be good at.

CHAPTER 14 **THE FIRE DEPARTMENT OF THE WEST**

A day or two later, early March 1945
About 130 miles south—Germany

Darkness blanketed the countryside in all directions as the German
military train raced north, parallel to the Odenwald Mountains.

The Kriegslok steam locomotive was working hard. Drive rods
pumped, wheels spun; it was chugging a rhythmic four beats to the
bar and making 30 miles per hour.

Running with its lights turned off, the train was difficult to hide. A
steady stream of sparks flowed from the smokestack into the darkness. Glowing embers sailed backward, illuminating flatcars carrying
German tanks. With his goggles lowered, Gustav rode in the radio
operator's seat of a Mark IV tank three cars from the front.

His blond hair blew in the wind; his head bounced to the train's
rhythm above the open hatch. The coal smell was comforting and it
reminded him of home in winter.

With the countryside north of Heidelberg blurring past him,
Gustav couldn't stop smiling.

He was right where he wanted to be.

He'd stolen away to ride in his tank while the other crewmen rode
in freight cars, in strict obedience to regulations. But Gustav wasn't
about to miss the chance to see the rails as a conductor would—at
least for a few hours. If only his grandmother had let him follow his
dreams to become a railwayman, he could have been doing this every
day.

Dawn was approaching and light was creeping from behind the rounded mountains as the clouds above turned pink. But the fields were still black, with the nearby villages nestled in sleep.

The train was chasing the darkness, beating a steady lullaby as the wheels crossed the rail joints, luring Gustav toward much-needed sleep.

Ever since the battle on his birthday the fighting had been brutal.

Panzer Brigade 106 had been sent to the hotly contested Alsace Province, in the southwest corner of Germany. Alsace had belonged to the French before the war. After the Germans seized the territory, first the Americans, and then the French First Army, fought to take it back.

Deemed too essential to fight in the Battle of the Bulge, Panzer Brigade 106 had been rushed wherever there were holes in the line, which earned them the nom de guerre, "the Fire Department of the West."

The label came at a great cost.

After being decimated in the line of duty, the brigade had recently been dismantled and redeployed northward in pieces. One battered company went ahead to defend a bridgehead at Bonn, two went to the Rhineland, and now the final piece of Panzer Brigade 106 was riding the rails toward its fate.

On the flatbeds behind Gustav, chains bound approximately seven more tanks belonging to 2nd Company. Theirs was now a mixed fleet of tanks that consisted of about three Panthers, three Mark IVs, and a leftover Jagdpanzer IV or two.[*]

Gustav's days in a Panther were behind him. After the unit's losses in Alsace, where he often filled in as the tanks gunner, he had been assigned to a Mark IV H for future fighting. The dark-green-and-brown camouflaged tank had been requisitioned from a disbanded unit. Its battle scars showed: the skirt armor had been stripped from both flanks, leaving only a halo of skirt armor around the turret for added protection.

The increasing warmth of the sky signaled trouble.

The engineer would have to park the train soon. With 5,000 Allied

---

[*] The Panther, ever mechanically sensitive, typically had to travel by rail after the German military issued a warning: any road march longer than sixty-two miles was known to inflict heavy wear on its suspension.

fighter-bombers patrolling the skies over western Germany, it was too dangerous to travel the rails during daylight.

Gustav leaned in his seat to see around the locomotive. Tunnels were a train's only sanctuary these days. Surely one was coming soon?

At the start of the journey, Gustav had traveled in one of the two cargo wagons at the rear of the train. Thirty men rode in each car, playing cards on a bed of hay as the train chugged along. But the car's wooden ceiling and walls offered little protection from the increasing likelihood of an aerial attack. So Gustav had sneaked forward to live in his tank. He would reappear at each stop just in time for muster—no one any the wiser about where he'd been.

During a layover, the train's brakeman confided in Gustav that when they passed his hometown, he planned to jump from the brake van—consequences be damned. He knew where they were headed and wanted no part in it.

The train was bound for Germany's "Fortress City"—Cologne.

The Wehrmacht was preparing the city for an American onslaught by sending 88s to augment the city's flak ring. The Volkssturm militia—a force comprised of the few, mostly older, men who hadn't yet been conscripted—was jamming underpasses with streetcars and digging fortifications in parks as the showdown approached. Orders were cut for Gustav's company.

They would provide the tanks.

From the brake van, the brakeman signaled the engineer by applying a tap of the brakes. He hadn't abandoned them yet. The engineer leaned from the locomotive for a glimpse behind the train. Something he saw in the dark sky sent him into a frenzy. He shouted to the stoker before returning inside the cab.

The Kriegslok's whistle bellowed a bloodcurdling wail.

Every time the stoker opened the firebox to toss in a shovelful of coal, strobes of orange light burst from the locomotive, illuminating both the landscape and the engine's red underbelly.

When the engineer opened the throttle, the driving wheels momentarily lost their traction as they spun from the burst of power. The train accelerated to 35 miles per hour, maybe 40. Sparks gushed from the smokestack with a deafening roar. They were running from something, but Gustav wasn't sure what. He looked over his shoulder in a panic, but the turret blocked his view.

Gustav sank lower in his seat. The tank lurched at its chains as the flatbed leaned and swayed beneath him. More than 600 tons of train were speeding down Germany's badly patched tracks. He held on tight.

The locomotive throbbed with light. It looked ablaze to Gustav, as if everyone up front were dead and the train was a runaway.

A howl rose in pitch behind him. It was the unmistakable sound of air whipping through radial engines. Now Gustav knew what they were running from—Allied fighter-bombers were hot on their tail. Gustav descended into the tank and closed the hatch cover behind him, entrenching himself in the dark confines.

Machine guns clattered. Tracers slanted through the dark. Bullets walked the length of the train from back to front, chewing on wooden cars and clinking metal as they went. The sounds danced over Gustav's steel ceiling and kept going. The locomotive gave a scream— its external pipes were fractured. A second plane roared overhead and smothered the machine's cries with a racket of blazing guns.

The planes kept running low and straight, ahead of the train. The Kriegslok kept chugging but it was living on borrowed time. If the nearly half-inch-thick plate of the boiler ruptured, it would explode with the force of a bomb.

Gustav cracked the hatch to peek outside. Were they gone?

Steam jetted from the locomotive's veins, billowing into a wide, hot mist that Gustav felt against his face. The elusive enemy was now even harder to spot. But through the vapor Gustav located them. Higher in the sky and far away, a shadowy pair of P-47s peeled around from the front, setting up for another pass.

The wolves were not finished with them yet.

Gustav closed the hatch cover and made himself small.

The first plane came in gunning for the train's nerve center—the locomotive. Tracers raked along the top of the locomotive and chopped through the coal tender, leaving clouds of black dust that swirled in the plane's wake.

The Kriegslok was breathing hard and bleeding, but it wasn't going down without a fight.

The P-47s were done with half measures. The second plane came at them higher and slower, then it let loose with a bomb that crashed down, tossing up a cloud of cinders directly ahead of the train.

The engineer must have seen it, through the cab's forward windows. The tracks in front of them had been severed. If they didn't stop, they were heading straight for a derailment.

Brakes screeched under the strain of trying to arrest the train's forward momentum. Sparks flowed from the brake blocks and slipped around the locomotive like the bow wake of a ship. The drive wheels locked, throwing up sparks of their own as the train skidded on the rails.

The train slowed to 30 miles per hour. Then 20.

Behind Gustav, tankers jumped off the moving cars, willing to take their chances at this point. If the train derailed at 10 miles per hour, its 400 tons of cargo would slam forward with the violence of an avalanche. Even at just 5 miles per hour a man would be thrown from his feet.

The train was almost at a standstill. But it wasn't enough. The whistle shrieked—it was the signal for the remaining tankers and crew to assume crash positions. Gustav braced himself for impact with outstretched arms.

The locomotive barreled blindly over the edge of the bomb crater before nosing into the hole with a sickening crunch. Car after car violently slammed together. Beneath the weight of the tanks the train compressed like an accordion. Gustav lurched forward. His face came to a rest against his gun sight.

It took a moment to shake the cobwebs.

Gustav raised the hatch and surveyed the damage. Every train car except the locomotive was still sitting on the tracks. A roar of steam rose from the bomb crater. The locomotive's safety valves were venting boiler pressure.

The P-47s purred past to admire their handiwork for a moment before continuing on. Gustav watched them shrinking into the distance as they flew away in pursuit of other quarry.

Nobody emerged from the wrecked locomotive. In crashes like this, the coal often shot forward and crushed the men against the scalding boiler.

Gustav wished he could hug his grandmother. That could have been him.

The following afternoon, a cluster of about ten German tankers strolled through Old Town Heidelberg.

Gustav marveled at the old baroque buildings, ornate and full of color. Painted signs hung over sidewalks, and Byzantine church domes stood like mile markers. The Neckar River lay a few streets away and in the other direction, mountains and a crumbling castle abutted the town.

The most remarkable thing about the city was that it was still fully intact. So far, Heidelberg, home to Germany's oldest university, had been almost entirely spared by the bombings. Wandering these streets, Gustav could almost convince himself that the war was nothing but a bad dream.

He and the other tankers were in high spirits. It felt good to be back in a German city, especially after their close call on the rail lines. After a locomotive had towed them back to Heidelberg, they were given a furlough until workers repaired the damage.

Gustav was surprised that the other men let him tag along. He was the youngest among them and even after his promotion to private first class, he was the lowest-ranking soldier in the group, which was composed of corporals and sergeants.

Luckily, Rolf had vouched for him.

Gustav's commander was back, walking beside him, in the flesh. In the scramble to escape the disabled Panther in Luxembourg, Rolf and the loader had chosen the forest over the fields and hidden there, returning just before the brigade evacuated without them.

Gustav and Rolf were the only remaining members of their original crew. Werner, the stern veteran gunner, had been transferred from the company, as had the loader, due to wounds or needs of the war.

Passersby drifted to the other side of the street to give the tankers a wide berth. Some averted their gaze, while others made no effort to look away and glared at them.

The citizens of Heidelberg saw something they didn't like.

Gustav wondered if his comrades sensed the hostility. Maybe it was their uniforms?

Having left their oil-stained coveralls behind on the train, the men wore their standard-issue Panzer Wrap uniforms, all black like a Luftwaffe mechanic's and featuring wide, overlapping lapels. The color was a practical choice, designed to hide the grease stains that were an inevitable part of the job.

The trouble was, the feared SS also were known to wear black uniforms, and to the untrained eye Wehrmacht tankers like Gustav could be confused with the men of the Nazi Party's private fighting force.

The tankers' collar tabs didn't help. On the collars of Gustav's uniform were silver skull patches. German cavalrymen of the Brunswick Corps had worn the same skulls on their caps when they fought alongside the British at Waterloo—the skull symbolized one placing his loyalty over his own life—and now Wehrmacht tankers claimed the emblem as their heritage, despite the fact that it looked a lot like the skull insignia adopted by Hitler's SS during its rise in the 1920s.

But it wasn't just the uniforms. There was something more at work.

During his time away at the front, Gustav had not been privy to the latest propaganda. He hadn't heard the "terror stories." To instill fear and a fighting spirit, Propaganda Minister Joseph Goebbels was employing state media to paint a horrific picture for Germans of what the country's future would hold should they be defeated.

Goebbels claimed the Americans had cut a deal with the Russians to send prisoners to camps in Siberia. Any men left in Germany would be shifted from city to city to shovel rubble and break rocks. Goebbels told his people that American officers would flog German women with riding crops and civilians would be imprisoned in their homes for all but two or three hours a day.

The propaganda quickly took root among the German people. But the campaign had an unintended consequence—a vicious blame game that was crippling morale and turning German civilians against their own troops.

One German sergeant turned POW described Heidelberg to his captors: "The mood there is shit, yet the hatred is not directed at the enemy, but against the German regime." The word on the street was, "If only the Allies would hurry up and come to end the war."

In countless towns and cities, German civilians in the west now called their soldiers by a new name: "Prolongers of the War."

During his short time in Heidelberg, Gustav hadn't heard those words specifically, nor would he need to. The unspoken display of scorn was enough to set his mind in motion.

If his people were now against him, then who was he risking his life for?

Everything was better inside the brewery. Beer kept the harsh realities of war at bay—for the time being.

The tankers sat together at a table beneath an arched wood ceiling. Radio music streamed from speakers, matching the tankers' renewed festivity. The beer hall exuded comforting smells of the hearth and food.

There were other customers besides the tankers, but few businesses were crowded anymore. Seated near Rolf, Gustav felt comfortable again. Frothy mugs of beer arrived. No one took the toasts seriously any longer. Most were delivered in jest and received with guffaws.

"Many enemies, much honor!" was a tongue-in-cheek favorite.

On any future battlefield they would be outnumbered, there was no running from that reality. So, German tankers joked about it. "One of our tanks is better than ten of yours," they wanted to tell the Americans—"But you always have eleven!"

Every unit had its fanatics, to whom such jokes were blasphemy, men who still believed in Hitler's *Endsieg*, or final victory—an impossible triumph over the numbers arrayed against them. But none of them sat with Gustav that day.

Gustav took a sip. The beer was watery. As he looked around the table he saw the others puckering at the flat taste as well. Beer was another casualty of wartime ingredient shortages, along with butter, marmalade, honey, and coffee, which were all artificial now.

A veteran tanker slipped a hand into his tunic and removed a bottle of Kümmel schnapps, a grain alcohol flavored with caraway. Gustav looked to Rolf with concern. Since they were technically on duty, hard alcohol was forbidden. But Rolf didn't bat an eyelash. Under the table, the veteran poured half the bottle into his mug while the others kept a lookout. There was no need to hide from their fellow officers—they would have asked for a taste.

Their greatest fear was German civilians. They were hiding from the very people they were fighting for. The Goebbels propaganda machine had transformed anyone and everyone into a potential mole. Apart from a swastika pin on a lapel, it was impossible to tell whether someone was a loyal Nazi Party member who would tip off the Gestapo.

The 1938 "Subversion of the War Effort" law made it criminal to undermine the war effort in any way, shape, or form, and the punishment for breaking the law was death. Did drinking in uniform while making unpatriotic toasts qualify? At this point, after all they'd been through, they didn't care.[*]

After a test sip or two, the veteran tanker passed the mug to the next man. Gustav took a tentative sip. It tasted fragrant, like a combination of spice, anise, peppermint, honey—and beer. He liked it. When the mug was emptied, another sergeant spiked a second beer beneath the table. Almost every man had a hidden flask. As the mugs continued to make the rounds from one tanker to another the songs got louder and the jokes cruder. Gustav grinned and laughed more than he spoke.

A side effect of the alcohol was a desire to reminisce. One of their favorite often-told stories was of 2nd Company's one—and only— Texan. A German American, he had been visiting his ancestral homeland when the war broke out and he was drafted by the Germans soon after. As a radio operator, his accent came in handy in Alsace. When the Americans were firing artillery, he'd call them on the radio. Hearing his thick Texan drawl, American troops were convinced he was one of their own. It was an assumption the Texan would use against them to redirect their fire into the wrong field.

---

[*] The "Subversion of the War Effort" law, Section 5 reads: "Whoever openly challenges or incites others to refuse to fulfill their duty to serve in the German armed forces or their allies, or otherwise openly tries to self-assertively put up a fight to cripple or subvert the will of the German people or their allies . . . will be sentenced to death for undermining the military."

One soldier, an older tanker seated close to Gustav, was especially emboldened by the liquor-laced beer. He requisitioned a metal trash vessel from the center of the table, then emptied it and held it to his mouth to re-create the resonance of a radio broadcast. "From the Reich Ministry in Berlin," he said.

Gustav looked over his shoulders. This was fun, but dangerous.

Speaking with a crooked mouth, the older tanker launched into a mocking impression of a Goebbels speech: "If our enemies think we Germans have no art, then we can prove the opposite! Every day there is a full train wagon of *art*-ificial honey being sent to the Eastern Front! And what about our *art*-ificial coffee? And . . ."

The table broke into a fit of drunken laughter.

Gustav laughed with the rest of them, but held back from contributing any jokes of his own. He had learned long ago to fear the wrath of the National Socialists.

Gustav was twelve on November 9, 1938, the "Night of Broken Glass," when church bells awakened his entire family from their slumber. Flames were rising from the neighboring village of Wehdem. Gustav's father was in the local fire brigade, so he shouldered his tools and pedaled away on his bicycle to fight the blaze. Other firemen followed steering a horse-drawn water pump.

In the village, they discovered that the fire was coming from a burning synagogue and the town's Jewish homes. The fire brigade was able to rescue one family's belongings from the flames and were moving to another home when the Nazi Brownshirts returned. A gang of local troublemakers unified by the same uniform, the Brownshirts had set the fires on Goebbels's suggestion as part of a wave of violence in retaliation after a Jewish teenager murdered a German diplomat in Paris. The Brownshirts outnumbered the fire brigade and forced the men to stand aside. As if that wasn't bad enough, the Brownshirts threw everything the fire brigade had managed to save right back into the fire.

When Gustav's father returned home that night, he wept.

Germany's anti-Semitic fervor made no sense to Gustav. He knew only one Jewish person—a neighboring farmer who had loaned the family a cow during tough times, without ever asking for, or expecting, anything in return. To Gustav's way of thinking, the Jews were ordinary, hardworking Germans just like his parents. Even though he was only twelve at the time, he was aware enough to know that whatever was happening, it was wrong.

It had gotten late and the party was winding down.

Each man drank to the voice in his own mind as the mug slowly circled the table.

Bursts of war news interrupted the music. As frontline updates drifted across the beer hall, any last traces of revelry were dampened. The Red Army had entered East Prussia. Soon, millions of civilians from those territories would be refugees, forsaking more than seven hundred years of German history.

The news made Rolf especially melancholy. He was worried for his family back home in Dresden, Germany's seventh largest city. Like other men from eastern Germany, he didn't even know if his home was still standing. Several weeks earlier, nearly eight hundred British bombers had flown over the city in the dead of night, raining enough incendiary bombs to light a firestorm in the city center.

Word of the horrors of Dresden spread quickly. Survivors spoke of a tornado of flames that drew air so violently into its vortex that it tore people from their handholds as it sucked them into the red glow. Marching walls of flames transformed air-raid shelters into ovens. Molten rivers of tar flowed as the asphalt streets boiled over from the heat.

Rolf desperately awaited word from his family. He had no idea whether they had survived or not, and Gustav was worried for his commander's sake. Rolf was more than a commander; he was a friend. But at the moment, Dresden felt like it was a world away. Their real concern was in front of them—the Fortress City.

No matter how much he drank, Gustav couldn't forget where the "Fire Department" was headed. They were the last fragments of the Wehrmacht in the west, the "Prolongers of the War." With just a few tanks they would fight the most technologically advanced killing force the world had ever known. Eisenhower had 73 divisions, 17,000 aircraft, and 4 million soldiers at his disposal for accomplishing one purpose—to kill Germans like Gustav.

That knowledge engendered a crippling sense of doom.

As the mug made its way around the table, an old hunter's saying came to mind: "Many dogs bring death to the rabbit."

The tracks would soon be repaired. Another train would come, and there would be no turning back. The train to Cologne was a one-way trip, and Gustav knew it.

When the mug reached him, he drank in gulps.

CHAPTER 15 **GOING FIRST**

A day or two later, March 5, 1945
Cologne, Germany

The gate to the city was barred.

Easy Company halted behind the Pershing as it shuddered to a stop on the street. Commanders sank lower in their turrets. Two companies of doughs sought cover in the yards of nearby houses. It was around noon and the residential outskirts of Cologne were freezing cold. Rusty leaves fluttered beneath gnarled trees. Ominous clouds were forming on the horizon—a storm was brewing.

Inside the lead tank of Task Force X, Clarence pressed his eyes to his periscope to survey the scene. The road ahead led directly to an underpass jammed with white trolley cars lashed together with steel cables.

"Could be an ambush," Clarence said to Earley.

On the other side of the overpass stood blocks of factory-like apartments. It was a perfect location for observers to spring a trap.

Earley broadcast a warning to the whole company.

The tanks' turrets swept the horizon. All it took was one German soldier wielding an infamous Panzerfaust for a tank to meet a fiery end. American crews had been briefed to expect the weapon, a deadly combination of a bazooka and a grenade launcher, in urban combat.

Clarence scanned the high banks on either side of the tank, bracing for the enemy to appear. Thunder rippled from the sky to the north. A parallel task force was running into Flak 88s at the Cologne airfield.

"Hold your fire," Earley radioed the platoon, sounding relieved. The infantry would handle this. A rush of doughs moved forward and secured the overpass without firing a shot.

A bulldozer tank was coming to clear the blockade that stood in their way, but it would take a while for the specialists to arrive.

Earley left the tank to confer with the other commanders. Captain Salisbury was away in Paris—having earned a well-deserved furlough—but before he left, he had installed a veteran platoon leader, Lieutenant Bill Stillman, as the acting company commander.

Clarence was fidgety. Sitting in the lead tank—the most exposed target—was harrowing. But he wasn't alone. Smokey came down from the tank and paced back and forth, puffing on a cigarette like a chimney. The ornery bow gunner wore his pistol low on his hip, like the gunslinger he fashioned himself as. Back in Stolberg, he became notorious for the quick-draw contests he organized with a fellow tanker to pass the time.

The two would square off and dry fire at each other. The rules called for them to clear their pistols, but one time Smokey forgot and actually shot his "opponent" in the groin. The repercussions? No furloughs for the rest of the war. Keeping Smokey in a tank was a better punishment than jail time.

Clarence lowered himself from the turret and walked forward to the bow wearing his favorite knit cap instead of a helmet. Even here, he was willing to take his chances. If there were snipers around, a helmet wouldn't stop a bullet anyway, he figured.

Clarence gestured to Smokey's cigarette. "Can I have one?"

Smokey was incredulous. Clarence—the man who traded the cigarettes in his rations for chocolate—wanted to smoke?

"Please, I really need something," Clarence said.

Smokey grinned. He was all too pleased to corrupt his friend, and even gave Clarence a light.

Clarence took a long drag from the cigarette. The rush of nicotine was soothing, so soothing that he nearly fell off the tank. Steadying himself against the barrel, he returned to the turret, where he smoked and settled his nerves.

A sign nearby marked the city limits of Köln, the German name for Cologne. In the distance, the famous cathedral stood blackened and

The cathedral, as seen from Cologne's western outskirts

burned above a cityscape still smoking from an RAF raid mounted three days earlier. The cathedral's twin spires stared back at Clarence like sinister, all-seeing eyes.

He wished his parents could see him now: one of five crewmen on the tank that would lead the 3rd Armored Division into the Queen City of Germany. He had come a long way from peddling candy back in Lehighton, Pennsylvania.

A jeep lurched to a stop behind the Pershing. The task-force commander, Colonel Leander Doan, a lanky, six-foot-three Texan, stepped out. The unit's PR men sang his praises: "an old Cavalryman . . . he still roars into action like a Texas Cowboy. He grinned like a cat when things were hot, and is said to have no nerves at all."

Doan's eyes scanned the progress at the underpass before settling on Clarence. "Soldier!"

Clarence looked down, startled out of his reverie.

"Get your helmet on!" Doan snapped.

Clarence flicked the cigarette away and saluted instinctively.

Doan had ruined his smoke, not to mention his brief moment of reflection. Clarence ducked into the turret as Doan returned to his jeep, satisfied that order had been restored. But Clarence wasn't about to obey the command. He simply went inside, where the colonel couldn't see him helmetless.

Situated to the north of Clarence's position on a parallel road, Buck sat atop an idling Sherman with Janicki, Lieutenant Boom, and three or four other doughs.

During this attack, they would ride the tanks of F-Company.

The doughs wore green fatigues with gloves and scarves that were cinched at the neck or draped over their ears, but the layers were becoming too much. Buck was sweltering. He unraveled his scarf and opened his collar. Heat was rising from the blistering grates in the engine deck. And it wasn't just the heat—the smell of oil was nauseating.

There was only one way to get off the scorching, static-bound tank. Buck asked Lieutenant Boom if he could investigate the holdup ahead. Always one to value a display of initiative, Boom approved Buck's request.

Buck set out alone. He had no intention of relinquishing his solidified position as first scout, especially not to some new replacement who might get them killed. Even if the job was dangerous, at least he held his fate in his own hands.

Turning the corner, Buck found a lone Sherman idling in front of another blocked underpass. The Germans were doing everything in their power to keep the Allied troops outside their city.

GI engineers were already on the scene. The Sherman commander was standing in his hatch talking to the engineers as Buck joined them. They were waiting on a dozer tank to clear the barricade so they could keep advancing.

Movement stirred in their peripheral vision. Someone was walking on the bridge that ran above the underpass. Buck snapped his rifle to his shoulder as the engineers fumbled for their carbines. One by one, the men lowered their guns.

It was just a German couple out for a leisurely stroll.

But even after he lowered his rifle, Buck kept an eye on them. Something wasn't quite right about the pair. The man and woman both wore white medical aprons bearing the Red Cross. They were dawdling, taking their time studying the Americans below. When they had seen all they needed, they acted. The man reached under his apron and lifted a Panzerfaust beneath his arm, taking aim at the Sherman. The Americans scattered. Buck spied an automotive garage to his left and bolted for cover.

The Panzerfaust fired with a burst of black powder, propelling a football-shaped warhead that flew down like a meteor. The warhead hit in front of the tank, but didn't explode. Ricocheting off the street, the missile kept traveling and skidded beneath the tank's undercarriage and out the backside before exploding against a curb.

The shockwave lifted Buck and threw him against the garage.

With his chest heaving from exertion and the force of the impact, Buck leaned out from his covered position and took aim in conjunction with the Sherman, which had elevated its gun in the direction of the bridge. But it was too little, too late—the couple had disappeared.

Buck and the others had just met a new breed of German soldier.

A seat of Nazi power, Cologne held 125 local offices of the Party and many neighborhoods had "block leaders," who kept tabs on which households hung swastika flags and also monitored who participated in Stew Sunday, when Germans were asked to consume only stew and donate the money they saved to the poor. Were the German couple a pair of rogue block leaders with no one left to harass? Had they been recruited by the military to wage guerrilla warfare in the streets? It was anyone's guess.

Buck was fuming. Being nosy had nearly gotten him killed. It had been a close call for the tank crew too. A Panzerfaust's warhead worked by spurting a jet of flaming plasma through a tank's armor, spraying anyone inside with molten metal.

Buck was in the midst of berating himself when he again noticed motion on the bridge. The pair was back. Their faces rose from the bridge to take a glimpse at their handiwork. They had heard the explosion and assumed they'd destroyed the tank. One stood brazenly, then the other.

Buck took aim with his rifle, but before he could squeeze off a shot, the Sherman fired first. The shell punched the bridge, sending a hail of shattered concrete and shrapnel directly into the fanatics with more force than a close-range shotgun blast.

When the dust settled it revealed a crumbling hole in the side of the bridge. Where the couple once stood, only a pair of long red streaks remained.

Lieutenant Boom and the platoon arrived and started securing the area. Buck came out to greet them as if everything were normal. They couldn't know the truth of how close he'd come to becoming a red splatter himself. If they did, he'd never hear the end of it.

One dough glanced from side to side, as if he had lost something. Private first class Byron Mitchell spotted Buck and broke from the pack. Byron looked to Buck like he was of Scandinavian descent. But it was Byron's bright blue eyes that no one could place. They radiated skittishness, like those of an animal that had been abused. A former baker from Atlanta, Byron had grown up poor, so poor that some wagered he might have raised himself.

Byron wielded the squad's Browning Automatic Rifle, or BAR, their most potent handheld weapon. He also had the aggressiveness to match it. "Where'd they go?" Byron asked furtively. He was after the German couple.

Buck told him that the couple had been blown to pieces. Byron looked disappointed and lingered for a moment to gauge if Buck was telling the truth.

Byron's objective was no secret. As the top looter in the company, he wanted the first souvenirs from Cologne.

Whenever he came across a dead German, Byron would search him for souvenirs. Pistol. Watch. Jewelry. Pockets. Byron had it down to a science. He could even determine a German's time of death, like an amateur medical examiner. Because of their wartime diet, a German soldier's skin often took on a yellowish tinge within a few minutes after his demise.

So when Byron once came across a young SS soldier whose skin hadn't turned yellow yet, he sat back on a nearby bank cradling his BAR and waited for twenty minutes. When the SS soldier started crawling away, Byron stuck the muzzle of the BAR between his eyes.

But his looting wasn't solely for personal gain. Sometimes Byron came away with valuable intelligence for Lieutenant Boom, which allowed the others to look the other way, regardless of how they felt about his habit.

Buck ran to catch up to his platoon. He knew how careless he'd been and how narrowly he'd escaped. It almost felt like fleeing the scene of a crime.

The Pershing idled on the far side of the underpass. The tank was quivering with the engine's power, eager to get moving again.

Clarence kept looking, expecting the sight to change. The boulevard into Cologne was vacant, dotted with nothing but empty stone flower boxes. The Reich lay before him, but where were its soldiers?

Behind him, Easy Company wound back through the newly cleared underpass, followed by a stretch of about thirty-six half-tracks brimming with doughs of B- and C-Companies.

It was now four P.M. and Easy Company's march into Cologne had been delayed for four hours—a tactical victory for the Germans. The radio crackled with static and the acting company commander finally addressed his tankers.

"Gentlemen, I give you Cologne," he said. "Let's knock the hell out of it!"

The words brought a smile to Clarence's face.

It was about time.

The Pershing churned down the empty boulevard with half of Task Force X trailing close behind. The other half of the task force paralleled Easy Company on a road to the left. There were three routes into the city, but only Easy Company's led to the cathedral—directly into the heart of Cologne. Black tarps draped like bedrolls across the Shermans and colored panels were stretched like flags on each tank's engine deck. These adornments identified them to friendly aircraft. The assault on Cologne was the linchpin of Operation Lumberjack, a synchronized push by three American armies to secure a foothold up and down the west bank of the Rhine.

Clarence felt like a vandal who had breached the walls and sneaked into an enemy's camp. The comparison was especially fitting, since Cologne had once been an outpost on the fringe of the Roman Empire. Teeming with nervous energy, Clarence searched for a target. Any target at all. But he couldn't seem to find one.

The armored column roared past the parched soil where a park had once stood. But when Clarence gazed through the periscope, it re-sembled no park that he'd ever seen. Most of the trees had been felled for firewood. Vents poked from the soil, revealing underground air-raid bunkers. The terrain was littered with bomb craters, which were pooling with water.

Clarence was astonished.

This was 1945.

This was the time of the *Endkampf,* the "final battle," when Germans were urged to fight blindly for Hitler, even if the possibility of victory was almost nonexistent. This was the day when the city's Nazi gauleiter, as the regional leader was known, had called for the "unrelenting defense of Cologne until the end."

Yet, Germany's fourth largest city appeared empty. It seemed as if everyone had already been wiped from the earth and there was no one left to put up a fight.

In the 76 Sherman behind Clarence, Chuck Miller was thinking the exact same thing.

The resilient youngster was back in the gunner's seat. Chuck had enjoyed several days in the supply depot, before the company sent word that his skills were needed back on the front. A gunner at Blatzheim had gotten drunk and fallen off a horse, which resulted in a bad knee injury and a crew in desperate need of an experienced gun-ner. Despite an ankle wound of his own, Chuck had stepped forward. Even after losing two commanders, it didn't feel right, the idea of his buddies fighting without him.

It was just a glint, but Clarence caught it out of the corner of his eye.

A clock tower stood about a mile ahead to his left. High in the tower, something had sparkled. It was just one flash—possibly a burst of light bouncing off broken glass or the clock's white enamel face—but Clarence wasn't taking any chances.

Enemy observers were known to place themselves high above the fray. What if one was up there now, with binoculars and a field phone that connected to an artillery battery? If so, the doughs in their open-topped half-tracks were in serious danger.

"Bob, I'd better get that clock," Clarence said. That was all he had to say.

Earley called for a halt. The Pershing, and the entire column behind it, rolled to an abrupt stop. Everyone watched and waited in silence.

Without a fuss, DeRiggi switched to an HE shell and Clarence sent the projectile flying toward the clock. The 23-pound shell landed smack in the middle of the clock's face. The tower ruptured with a sidelong blast as bits of clock and brick came tumbling down, generating a massive cloud of dust.

The crew roared in approval as Clarence smirked at the sight of the truncated tower. He had been half hoping to hear a giant chime. In the opening shot of the battle for Cologne, time stood still.

Easy Company drove onward, but the smooth sailing couldn't last forever.

The column slowed and tank commanders consulted their maps as they approached the ring of Cologne's urban neighborhoods.

When the main boulevard ended, it branched into smaller streets, each leading toward the cathedral. At the first two streets that Easy Company came to, a platoon of its tanks peeled off, followed by a company of doughs in half-tracks. The company's remaining platoon of tanks would operate in reserve. Between these two streets, Easy Company and the doughs would fight side by side to clear one block at a time, all the way to the train station. Once there, they would stand before the ultimate prize: the cathedral.

At the spearhead of 2nd Platoon, the Pershing idled over the median. From the gunner's seat, Clarence kept his eyes peeled for any movement.

The street ahead was a gauntlet. Stately townhouses lined both sides. Their once-beautiful turn-of-the-century flourishes were now heavily damaged or destroyed and rubble spilled from the shattered buildings over the sidewalks, choking the Pershing's path forward.

The RAF had bombed the city so often—262 times over nearly five years—and so severely that the Nazis had ordered the evacuation of all but the essential war-industry workers. And just like that, a cultured major city with a prewar population of 445,000 dwindled to merely 40,000 residents.

Lines of doughs moved up the sidewalks past the Pershing and began going door-to-door. The tanks had cleared the way, but this was their show now.

"Rubble and broken glass crunched beneath the feet of the infantry," wrote a GI observer. "An unnatural silence had settled over the great metropolis."

Clarence felt for the doughs. Each block held more than thirty homes and each of those homes was comprised of multiple floors that all needed to be searched. And the doughs' search had to be thorough. No German soldier could be left behind.

From his perch in the Pershing, Clarence scanned the buildings up and down. His thumb rested alongside the machine-gun trigger, a red button on top of the pistol grip. The urban environment of Cologne presented an entirely new set of challenges. He had been briefed to expect all-out resistance, including Molotov cocktails thrown from the upper-story windows and fire from mobile 88s placed in ground-level shops. And those were the least of their worries. In this environment, the deadly thump of a Panzerfaust could come from anywhere.

The crackle of gunfire echoed through the streets as doughs broke down doors with boots, hammers, and axes. It was late afternoon, and the army's biggest house-to-house battle of the European war had officially begun.

Start and stop. Start and stop. The column of tanks inched through the streets of Cologne.

Inside an idling Sherman, Chuck Miller held his breath. The Pershing in front of him spewed a steady stream of exhaust from its 80 octane gas, which was trapped by the residential streets. The fumes left his head swimming. He felt hot and claustrophobic; the width of his periscope was the extent of his vision and the rattle of idling engines drowned out all other sounds.

While the doughs worked on a hostile block, the tanks waited behind them on a secure block, holding close enough to respond with fire support. This was the art of block clearing. It was a time-consuming, nerve-racking means of traversing a city.

The enemy was near. Chuck had seen doughs escorting back German prisoners, though he hadn't seen a hostile enemy soldier yet. What he didn't know was that the enemy was spread thin in Cologne. The city was guarded by the 9th Panzer Division farther north and the 363rd Volksgrenadier Division here and to the south. Both were divisions in name only at this point. After getting battered in the Rhineland fighting, they were essentially whittled down to the size of regiments.

Through his cloudy mind, Chuck could see that the doughs had cleared another block and were on the move. The Pershing rolled forward and Chuck's tank followed. Chuck swung his gun from side to side, guarding the Pershing's flanks. As the reticle passed from doorway to doorway, Chuck was reminded of his paper route. They crossed an intersection, and he could see other Easy Company tanks on their left, working in the same direction.

As he swung his gun back from the left, Chuck caught a flash of gray in the lower-right corner of his periscope. The gun crept farther and he saw more. Someone on the sidewalk was running along the right side of the Pershing. It was the unmistakable gray sleeve of a German uniform. Chuck couldn't believe it. The doughs had missed someone.

The German soldier ducked into a doorway ahead of the Pershing, where he was fumbling with something. Chuck caught a glimpse of the yellowish warhead of a Panzerfaust.

Hot damn!

It was a perfect storm. The Pershing was on course to drive right past the enemy soldier. The doorway was in Clarence's blind spot and Earley was looking the wrong way as he talked into the pork chop.

Chuck wanted to shout a warning to the tank ahead of him, but there was no time. The Pershing was about to become a smoking hulk. He slammed his turret control all the way to the right, spinning the turret directly toward the threat, and hovered his foot over the tank's triggers—the main gun on the left and the machine gun on the right.

As soon as the barrel reached the German, he'd fire the machine gun—the tank was too close for anything else. *Faster!* Chuck urged the turret onward. The German stepped out from the doorway, raised the warhead from his hip, and aimed it toward the Pershing.

Like a shotgun chasing a clay, Chuck's gun caught up to his target.

Chuck stomped for the trigger.

But in the heat of the moment, his foot found the wrong firing button. Instead of a machine gun's measured response, the muzzle flash from the 76mm lit up the surrounding shadows as the gun kicked.

The HE shell blasted the German soldier straight through the house he was standing in.

A backblast of stone and wood pelted Chuck's tank. Debris crumbled from the building onto the turret. A cloud of plaster dust rose from the rubble and seeped inside. Chuck and the crew coughed. The smell of paint infiltrated the tank.

When the dust cleared, Chuck returned to his periscope to see his handiwork. Where just a minute before the German had stood, a pink mist had settled around the edges of the doorframe.

Chuck's whoops of elation could be heard over the tank's engine.

The crew erupted in cheers and praise. Bob Earley radioed, his voice shaking from the emotion of the close call: "Thanks, Chuck." Chuck beamed with pride.

Later, Chuck would feel a pang of guilt over the use of excessive force. But not now and not here, where survival was the goal by any means necessary.

No one in Easy Company would ever call him "Baby" again.

Two streets over from Clarence, Buck moved quickly along the sidewalk as he ventured into a new residential block.

The crack of sniper fire and boom of grenades echoed from the side streets around him.

Whenever the wind shifted, the acrid smell of death wafted into Buck's nostrils. Bodies littered the streets from the latest air raid. More than 300 casualties remained unburied.

To accomplish their house-clearing mission, Squad 3/2 had split into two fire teams of five men each. Buck's fire team surrounded him as they made their way down the street. Besides Janicki, there was

Members of Squad 3/2. Standing, left to right: Slim
Logan, Bill Carrier, Jose De La Torre, Buck Marsh,
Z. T. Burton. Kneeling: Fred Schoener, Frank Alaniz.

Private First Class Jose De La Torre from El Paso, a former doorman at the Hollywood Palladium Ballroom. Sharp and streetwise, he wore a tanker's coveralls in place of trousers and was particular about his appearance—even as he tramped through a war zone.

There was also Tech Corporal Frank Alaniz, a quiet soldier with a gift for operating and fixing radios. Before the war started he had driven cars from Detroit to Mexico. And then there was the always-grinning Private First Class Bill Carrier, who hailed from the back-woods of Kentucky. The short, moonfaced soldier was dangerously persistent in befriending German girls. No one remembered what he had done before the war.

Together, they had cleared houses all morning.

They had found what they expected. As one soldier recorded, "Closets are crammed with Nazi leaflets and Nazi books and Nazi uniforms and Nazi ceremonial daggers." And they had found the un-expected as well. Tunnels. Lots of them.

Cologne's remaining populace had moved into their basements and knocked "mouse holes" in the walls as air-raid escapes, in case bombs collapsed the structures above them. The tunnels ran the length of entire blocks, and in the running street fight, German soldiers were now using the passageways to move between basements and elude capture.

Four Germans burst from a doorway ahead like quail being flushed during a hunt, sprinting frantically to escape.

Buck shouted for them to stop as Janicki fired warning shots over their heads. Buck was surprised; the veteran apparently had qualms about shooting a man in the back. The Germans hung a right and took cover inside the nearest house.

Squad 3/2 followed in hot pursuit.

The squad leader led his fire team one house beyond where the Germans had entered—they'd wait as a blocking force in the next basement.

Buck and his team followed the Germans through the front door. In tense moments like this, De La Torre and Alaniz sometimes spoke to each other in rapid-fire Spanish. The upstairs was clear. Buck and the others cautiously eyed the steps descending to the basement. There was nowhere else to hide.

The team was supposed to alternate who led the way through each house. But more often than not, the job fell to Buck or De La Torre. This time was Buck's turn.

Since a grenade was not an option due to the potential for civilian casualties, Buck shouted the only German he knew: *"Raus kommen! Wir nicht schiessen."* It meant "Come out! We don't shoot."

In one of the first houses they cleared, German civilians had come up laughing and shaking their heads after Buck had employed his German. They corrected Buck, telling him that he had been shouting *"Wir nicht scheissen."* It was a transposition error of just two letters but it made a difference. He had been saying, "Come out! We don't shit." It provided a much-needed moment of levity.

This time, Buck got the pronunciation right. But no one came out.

Buck set aside his rifle. It was unwieldy in close quarters. He drew a German P-38 pistol from his shoulder harness and chambered a round. He had picked it up a few days earlier and had a feeling that it was going to come in handy. In the half-track he'd oiled it religiously.

Buck hunched down to make himself small, and gingerly laid his boot on step after step as he descended the stairs. The ancient floor-boards creaked in protest. He held a flashlight in his left hand—away from his body—in case it drew their fire. The others crept behind him.

When he reached the bottom of the stairs, Buck kicked the door to ensure no one stood behind it. The door swung all the way open, nearly popping off its hinges from the impact. Buck and the others burst inside. To his left, a window set at street level cast a narrow slant of light into the otherwise dark basement.

Sometimes one could smell German soldiers by their diet of smoked fish and black bread. Here all Buck smelled was musty, stale air. All four walls were intact. There were no tunnels to provide an escape route. So where were they?

Against the wall stood a wooden bin that opened in the front for loading potatoes. It was as tall as a man, and deep. The soldiers had to be hiding in there. Buck could toss a grenade into the bin like a basketball into a hoop and never look back. But if it worked there would be one problem: living with himself.

Buck raised a clenched fist, signaling the others to hold back. He cocked the pistol's hammer. Taking a knee, he aimed the pistol across the open front of the bin and fired. A long blue flame shot from the gun's muzzle like the lick of fire from a flamethrower. In the close quarters of the low-ceilinged basement, the crack resounded like a cannon.

Buck was startled. So were the Germans. Frantic voices shouted, "Comrade, comrade!" as four Germans nearly trampled one another in their race to come out with their hands up.

Janicki gave Buck a nod of approval as he helped secure the prisoners.

The enemy soldiers were tired and haggard, and possibly not professional soldiers in the first place. To prop up its ranks, the 363rd Volksgrenadiers had taken in Volkssturm militiamen and deployed its forces in small, ad-hoc combat groups. They consisted of a sergeant, five trained soldiers, and two Volkssturm recruits, some of whom had only been in uniform for three days. It was hardly a fine-tuned fighting force.

The fire team marched the prisoners out of the basement toward daylight, which left Buck to examine his pistol. The muzzle was black.

He'd over-oiled the pistol so much that the shot had ignited a pool of oil in the barrel, causing the blue flame.

Buck searched the food bin and found the Germans' pistols buried beneath some shriveled potatoes. By rights, the guns were his. And they were worth taking to trade with his fellow soldiers. Tankers didn't get as many chances to loot as the infantry did and would pay as much as five cartons of cigarettes for a pistol—especially if it was a Luger.

Buck stuffed the pistols into his musette bag, glad that he hadn't used the grenade. He didn't hate the Germans. They were soldiers too, in the same ugly line of work. But that didn't mean Buck was going to start shooting over heads or asking forgiveness for the young German he had killed. In Buck's mind, asking for forgiveness meant he wouldn't commit the same sin again. There in the midst of Cologne, it was a promise he just couldn't make.

On the cusp of evening, shadows squeezed the streets as Earley and the crews of 2nd Platoon milled around their tanks.

The tankers stretched their legs and tried to unwind from the day's action. It was always jarring to transition from the adrenaline-fueled rush of battle to the uneasy calm of downtime.

Now was about time for a breather. The front line stopped moving and the doughs ahead were forting up in houses for the night. Clarence remained inside the Pershing, stationed at the gun. He was suspicious of the city, even if Cologne hadn't been the bloodbath that everyone expected.

In taking the outer city, Easy Company hadn't lost a man and Spearhead had ticketed 1,027 prisoners. "No [German] unit above company size was organized in a defense," the 3rd Armored unit history would record. "Even kitchen battalion personnel were taken prisoner."

Spearhead had paved the way into Cologne and Colonel Doan wanted everyone to know it. He had given the order to put up signs stretching all the way back to the underpass that read: YOU ARE ENTERING COLOGNE THROUGH THE COURTESY OF TASK FORCE X.

Sylvester "Red" Villa

But despite their success, the day's tension lingered. The crews had been going since four A.M. and had spent nearly twelve hours inside their tanks among loaded guns, on constant guard for enemy soldiers who wanted to kill them.

Each man burned off his nervous energy in his own way. To Chuck Miller's amusement, Earley repacked his pipe countless times. Some men paced circles on the sidewalk. Chuck's new commander, Sergeant Sylvester "Red" Villa, burned through cigarette after cigarette.

Beneath his helmet, Red was, in fact, bald. He was a boisterous ex-detective from the Midwest, and the crew always heard him coming well before they could see him. When shells were flying in Normandy, Red had lost his composure and laid his forehead on the ring of his hatch. Inside, his crew could hear him reading the Bible aloud. As punishment, he was busted to private and demoted to bow gunner. But over time, he became accustomed to the terror of combat and assiduously worked his way back to being a commander—and redemption.

A tall, unusually shaped soldier approached the tankers, wearing a helmet and jacket with an armband bearing a white C, the designation

Ann Stringer

for a war correspondent. The "soldier" was Ann Stringer of the United Press, one of the three female reporters there on the front lines who'd soon be dubbed the "Rhine Maidens." She wore her curly brown hair pulled back to reveal a shapely face with bright eyes.

"Would any of you grant me an interview?" she asked.

Almost all of the tankers were willing to talk. Chuck hoped his mother would read the story.

The men jostled closer, enamored with the journalist. Stringer's smile entranced them. They hadn't seen lips that red in ages. Earley told Stringer that—for reasons of secrecy—they couldn't talk about the Pershing, but anything else was fair game.

Stringer whipped out her notepad. She asked the men about their mounts. How were their tanks holding up? The crews let out a harrumph of disgust and aired their grievances, as her story would record.

"We pushed into this town with our old M-4 tanks, which the Nazis have been knocking around all through France," said Red Villa. "It made us feel pretty blue."

Chuck Miller chimed in and told her: "It makes us feel pretty bad to have everyone at home talking about having the best equipment when we know our tanks lack a lot of things being the best."

Stringer voiced her surprise that Easy Company's tanks weren't adorned with hand-painted names. Earlier in the war, one might come across Spearhead tanks with scrolling, creative monikers such as "Eliminator," "In the Mood," and "Plenty Tough II."

A driver had an answer. "What good would it do?" he said. "We wouldn't even have time to get used to the name, so we just drive it blank. It's less trouble that way."

The men explained that Easy Company had lost almost half of their tanks—and plenty of friends—just a week earlier at Blatzheim.

Stringer was sympathetic; she had recently suffered a loss of her own. She and her husband, William, also a journalist, had reported together until that August, when he was killed in his jeep by sniper fire while approaching Paris. Eisenhower's headquarters reprimanded Stringer for journeying closer to the front than any women—even nurses—were allowed to travel. But that admonishment only spurred her to press harder.

Earley didn't have to say a word. He was captain of the "Super Tank," and had no complaints about it. And he had already made an impression upon Stringer, who would astutely observe: "Earley was tired, and he was shaking."

But this wasn't just about him. Earley felt the need to speak for the tankers whose voices were forever silenced by German guns. Of the twelve Shermans that Easy Company had driven into the Fortress City, seven of them were 75s, equipped with an underpowered gun that had gone three years of war without modifications. It simply was no longer up to the task of keeping its crews safe, and someone had to say it.

So, Earley gave Stringer a punctuation mark for her story: "Our tanks are not worth a drop of water on a hot stove. We want tanks to fight with, not just to drive over the countryside."

Stringer smiled. She knew she had something explosive. Stringer rushed off so fast that Chuck second-guessed giving an interview. How would the brass react to them sounding off in the papers? They'd just spoken for every Sherman tanker in the 3rd Armored Division.

Earley shrugged away any concern. They'd only spoken the truth.

Three streets away, Buck glanced across the avenue from the safety of a doorway.

Behind him, the platoon entered through the townhouse's back door and stomped up the stairs. They would spend the night here, less than two miles away from Cologne's cathedral. Their destination was almost within reach.

Dusk had settled over the wealthy neighborhood. Buck's eyes landed on a cream-colored corner house across the street. It was stone and stately, with a gray roof and carved window flourishes. Cracks of light shone from behind the second-story windows.

Lieutenant Boom said that someone had to investigate the source of the light. If there were civilians, they should be warned that A-Company's side of the street was now the MLR, or main line of resistance, and whoever was over there was now on the wrong side of the front lines.

It was a job for the first scout.

Buck was wary. The beckoning lights looked like a trap to him. All the civilians he'd seen that day had been living in basements. It was simply too brazen. Scoping out his approach, Buck visualized how he could react if he drew fire. His squad set up a machine gun in a window above him to provide cover.

"Ready?" Buck shouted. There was no avoiding this and waiting wouldn't make it any easier.

Buck dashed across the avenue, bracing himself for the snap of a sniper's bullet. In one leap he bounded the streetcar tracks before throwing himself against the front door of the stately home.

Perturbed, Buck rapped at the door. *All for a bunch of Germans!* No answer.

He raised his rifle to smash the butt against the door. This would get their attention.

The door flew open and Buck held back his blow. He lowered the rifle to his side and stared. He was speechless. Looking back at him was a stunning young woman. Her blond hair was swept back from her beautiful face. Her blue eyes sparkled beneath dark eyebrows. She was nineteen and wore a classy dress befitting her opulent surroundings.

When she saw Buck at the door, the young woman's face lit up. She was deliriously happy, laughing and crying at the same time. She threw her arms around Buck and kissed him on the cheek and then on the lips. Buck was taken aback. What was happening? Whatever it was, he would go with it. Buck set his rifle against the doorframe and savored the attention.

Shadows moved inside the home behind her. Maybe it was a trap after all.

Buck started to reach for his rifle, but stopped short. The young woman's father stepped into view. Tall, thin, and gray, he was a dentist and looked the part. Behind him, the young woman's two timid aunts emerged from the shadows.

The young woman grabbed Buck by the hand—and wouldn't let go—as she led Buck into the foyer. Speaking accented English, her father told Buck that there were no German soldiers in the house. He opened the door to the first floor, revealing his dark and empty dental office.

Buck explained the situation with the MLR. The man was appreciative, but seemed unmoved by the prospect of spending the night downrange. Where else could they go?

Someone tapped Buck's shoulder. He turned and found Janicki, Byron,

Annemarie Berghoff

and a few other members of his squad at the doorstep, having come to check on him. The father invited everyone upstairs and the others happily obliged.

The young woman held Buck back. She also spoke broken English and introduced herself as Annemarie Berghoff. Her father was Wilhelm. Buck told her his name. As she led him up the marble steps to the second floor, Annemarie exclaimed: "Buck, first American I see!"

Wilhelm Berghoff led the doughs to the second floor. But he might as well have taken them into another world. Art hung from clean, white walls. The flooring was made of polished wood. The high ceilings were patched where they had sprung leaks, but remained dry. Wilhelm offered the weary doughs a seat on plush couches. Buck and Annemarie took seats away from the other doughs.

Annemarie's aunts brought a glass pitcher out of the kitchen and served drinks.

Buck eyed the orange-colored beverage and wondered whether it was safe to drink. These were Germans, after all. Wilhelm gave a toast to the war's end and then everyone clinked glasses. Buck took a hesitant sip. The beverage had a metallic tang. He fought off the urge to cringe, but relaxed when he saw the Berghoff family drinking. He was fairly certain they wouldn't poison themselves.

A calming mood settled over the room. The doughs sunk into their comfortable seats. It was as if the war were really over. Buck shimmied closer to Annemarie as other doughs eyed her enviously.

She was absolutely glowing and kept repeating, "Buck, first American I see!" to herself. Annemarie's father and aunts conversed with Janicki. As conversation filtered around him, Byron eyed his new surroundings so intently, he looked like he was planning a heist. He was infamous among his fellow doughs for not talking for hours on end. He also had an uncanny knack for ducking out of a squad photograph whenever a camera appeared.

Annemarie's family puzzled Buck. *Why were they so happy?*

All the other Germans had seemed sullen and depressed. They lived with only sporadic power, limited water, erratic telephone service, no shops or pubs, and only food rations to fill their bellies. So why were Annemarie and her family so unperturbed?

There had to be something more at work.

In the course of their conversation, Buck learned that Annemarie worked as an assistant in her father's dental office, twice a week, between attending an abbreviated version of school. But all Annemarie wanted to talk about was the aerial bombings. For more than four years of her life, that was all she'd known.

Even though she didn't shy from the subject, the bombing campaign had obviously affected her. She told Buck about the unexploded bunker-buster bomb she'd found. She spoke of her classmate whose house was bombed. When she and her father arrived to help, they discovered the family's bodies burned and shrunken, half the size in death that they were in life.

What Annemarie neglected to mention was the time she was injured in an air raid in the city center. Before she could reach a bomb shelter, a white phosphorus target-marker landed nearby and seared her leg. Buck meant to ask about the whereabouts of Annemarie's mother. He had seen her in a photo on the way in, but erred on the side of being polite.

After about twenty minutes, Lieutenant Boom's runner knocked on the front door to order Buck and the others back across the avenue.

Annemarie darted to her bedroom and returned with a photograph. It was a portrait of her wearing a checkered red dress. She wrote her name and address on the back before handing the photo to Buck and pointing at the address: Eichendorf Street 28.

Buck was touched. She wanted him to come back. He had dated here and there in college, but none of those relationships seemed serious. This felt different. In the heightened state of wartime, his run-in with Annemarie felt like fate.

Annemarie led Buck to the door. She wouldn't release his hand until he promised he would return. It was an easy promise to make, but would be a hard one to keep.

That night from across the street, Buck gazed at the outline of Annemarie's house in the light of a half-moon. He swore he felt her eyes on him, as if she were gazing back at him from behind the darkened windows.

Beyond her house lay Cologne's inner city—the one thing that could prevent him from ever seeing her again. If the enemy were going to fight for Cologne, that's where they would make their last stand.

Tomorrow.

The next day, March 6, 1945
Cologne, Germany

In the cool light of an uneasy dawn, a Mark IV tank crossed the Hohenzollern Bridge toward the city of Cologne.

The battered structure could collapse at any moment.

Gustav leaned over the side of the tank from the radio operator's compartment and looked down with concern. Countless steel plates patched the bridge, and through the gaps between them he could see the murky rushing waters of the Rhine.

The Hohenzollern was the last bridge into Cologne still standing. The smaller Hindenburg Bridge, just downriver, had already collapsed, and this one would fall too, sooner or later. The bridge's serpentine arches and supporting spans had been weakened to the point of failure by countless bombs and shellfire. Hopefully today wasn't the day.

Gustav's company had no choice but to send their tanks across one at a time, an agonizingly slow process. Gustav gripped the hatch so tightly that his knuckles turned white. The 28-ton tank was a lot of weight.

Mercifully, the engine drowned out any anguished groans from the dying bridge.

Sitting high in his seat beside Gustav, the new driver steered carefully. Since more than half of the bridge's surface was lined by train tracks, the road across was unusually narrow. With one wrong slip of the controls they would plummet over the side.

The driver and the tank's gunner were replacements, new to the crew. Second Company had arrived the night before and Gustav had met them during the crew assignments only that morning. Now one of these strangers held his life in his hands.

From his hatch, Rolf kept a watchful eye on the new driver. He had fought in a Mark IV in Russia and wasn't thrilled to find himself in one again, especially with a crew unaccustomed to serving together.

There was one other potential for disaster. Everything beneath the tank had been rigged to blow. The brigade's pioneers—as the demolition men were known—had wired the bridge with explosive charges. If it didn't collapse of its own accord, they were going to blow it up—and there was a timeline for that.

Gustav and his fellow tankers had been ordered to travel into Cologne where they would take up positions in the inner city. Their mission: to hold off the Americans for as long as possible. Then they would escape back the way they'd come and once they were safely across, the pioneers would demolish the bridge in their wake.

As with everything in a fighting unit, the plan hinged on trust. Gustav drew assurance from the knowledge that the pioneers hailed from his own brigade. Theirs was an understanding between comrades—the pioneers would wait. This wouldn't be a one-way trip.

A pair of medieval castle turrets guarded the entrance to Cologne, standing tall against the low, gray clouds. Gustav stared with wonder as the tank passed through the gate and came down from the bridge.

It was like driving into another realm.

On Gustav's left, the city's iconic cathedral reached toward the sky, adorned with countless Gothic icicles and towering twin spires. Gustav could see how it could compel devotion. He had to tilt his head all the way back to see the top.

The cathedral's first stones had been laid in the 1200s. It had taken generations of German workers more than 630 years to finish construction and about five years for the Second World War to nearly destroy it. Mass had not been celebrated in the cathedral since a crippling RAF raid in June 1943. By the time Gustav rode into the city, a dozen high-explosive bombs had breached the cathedral's roof and raked its exterior. But it was still standing, a source of inspiration to its defenders.

The driver immediately turned right, heading toward the train station. Situated side by side, the cathedral and train station shared a plaza between them.

Gustav couldn't fathom the devastation laid out in front of him. Only the burnt ribs of the train station's arched glass ceiling remained, and the long galleria was full of rubble. All the buildings in the station's surrounding plaza were skeletons of their former selves, their bombed-out windows empty like eye sockets. The area had been ground zero for the British bombing campaign.

Two Panthers from Gustav's company that had crossed the bridge before them now idled in front of the station, waiting for the Mark IV. The decimated station would serve as the Germans' defense headquarters on this side of the Rhine. Rolf guided the Mark IV alongside the waiting Panthers. They were it. The German Army's last hope to delay the Americans' conquest of Cologne.

Three tanks.

No one else was waiting for them. No one else was coming to their aid.

Second Company's other tanks, which were in poor mechanical shape, remained back on the other side of the Rhine. Their sister companies in the Rhineland were missing or wiped out; no one knew which, because radio communication had broken down. The 9th Panzer Division had at least twenty tanks in the northern outskirts, but the Americans had them pinned against the Rhine.

Wilhelm Bartelborth

Three tanks.

In the heart of Cologne, that was it.

While they lacked adequate manpower, at least they had leadership.

Gustav's respected company commander, Second Lieutenant Wilhelm Bartelborth, sat in the turret of the neighboring Panther. Twenty-nine, with faint blond hair, blue eyes, and a cleft chin, Bartelborth—much like Gustav himself—was descended from humble stock in northern Germany. In his life before the war, Bartelborth had been a teacher.

Gustav didn't know him personally, but had heard the man was a skilled fighter.

First Lieutenant Otto Leppla, an older officer who had once commanded the brigade for several weeks, emerged from the train station's wreckage. Primarily a desk-bound commander now, he would do his fighting by map and field telephone.

Rolf and the other two commanders dismounted from their tanks to hear Leppla's briefing.

Gustav knew there would be no holding off the inevitable, the city would fall. But maybe Leppla had a plan? Maybe they could survive long enough to hear the call to retreat?

When Rolf returned, he was tight-lipped about the meeting, telling the driver only to follow Leppla, who was gesturing directions in front of the tank.

Gustav could read Rolf like a book. He could tell something was amiss. Gustav looked behind the tank and saw the Panthers turning in the opposite direction. They were headed back toward the train station—away from the enemy.

"Where are they going?" Gustav asked.

"They're staying back to defend the bridge," Rolf said. He sounded dejected.

It didn't make sense to Gustav. The Panthers should have led the way toward the enemy, not them. Especially not in an outmoded Mark IV. According to the tactical manual, during a coordinated attack, the Mark IV should defend the flank "while the Panthers quickly press on and drive a wedge into the enemy position."

At last glance, Gustav saw Bartelborth's tank heading for a tunnel that ran beneath the rail lines that joined the bridge and the train station. With orders to make his stand here, his intent was obvious.

The company commander was laying an ambush.

Leppla guided the Mark IV through Cologne's financial district, glancing both ways at intersections to get his bearings before proceeding.

Known as "Cologne's Wall Street," the once proud banks in the area were covered in soot, their tall columns pocked with white pits where they had sustained bomb damage. The morning sky streamed through roofless buildings.

Riding in his open hatch, Gustav searched for the reassurance of friendly forces.

He expected to find German soldiers buzzing behind barricades and around command posts. He expected to find antitank guns covering the enemy's avenues of approach. But the reality was shocking.

The few scattered troops that he did see peered from windows in ones and twos or stood smoking in doorways. Many were former policemen or firemen with no experience as soldiers, who had been conscripted. Of the city's Volkssturm, only about 60 out of 600 showed up to fight. And those who did were armed with outdated foreign rifles and Panzerfausts that only their officers had been trained to use.

And where were the illustrious Waffen SS?

A climatic, suicidal battle for a major German city seemed like the perfect stage for those who answered only to the Nazi Party, and who believed that death on a battlefield was a straight ticket to Valhalla, a warrior's lodge in the heavens.

Yet the SS was nowhere to be found in Cologne.

Ever since a July assassination attempt on Hitler's life by senior German Army officers, the rift between the SS and the army had deepened. Hitler himself now favored his SS units over the army and often spared the SS in desperate late war situations, leaving the army to serve as a sacrificial rear guard.

And where were the city's Nazi overseers?

Known derogatorily by many Germans as the "Golden Pheasants," they, too, were long gone. After incinerating their incriminating papers and slipping into civilian clothes, they fled in boats to the east bank of the Rhine at the first sounds of gunfire. Their gauleiter had joined them after posting a manifesto urging Cologne's citizens to resist until the bitter end.

Gustav and his fellow tankers were on their own.

The Mark IV had traversed about half a mile when artillery began falling. They had reached the Gereon quarter by then, an office district named for its patron, Saint Gereon.

Each blast tossed sharp rubble into the air. Leppla pointed frantically to a five-story building on the right where the tank should deploy, and beat a quick retreat back toward the station while holding on to his hat.

The Mark IV's walls closed in as Gustav shut his hatch cover. Across from him, the driver's instruments glowed in the dark confines. The tank had never felt so small. Rolf guided the driver as he backed the tank alongside the chosen building. Rolf had the driver edge the front of the tank to the right so the gun was aiming into a massive four-way intersection while the building still shielded their position. If the Americans came hurrying down the road in a rush to reach the train station, they would drive into their ambush.

There was nothing left to do but wait.

"How many Americans are coming?" a crewman asked Rolf.

Rolf said he did not know.

"What are our orders?" another asked.

"Fight them," Rolf said.

Gustav couldn't believe his ears. It was as if someone just wanted to be rid of them, and worse, Rolf wasn't resisting in the least.

In every burnt, honeycombed building he came across in Cologne, Rolf must have envisioned his beloved Dresden. During the firebombing campaign against his native city, fifteen square miles had been charred, which surpassed the ten square miles of Hamburg that had been incinerated in 1943.*

Between the initial British attack and follow-up raids by American bombers, it was believed that as many as 25,000 Germans had died in Dresden. The truth was horrific enough, although Goebbels broadcast an inflated death toll of 250,000.

Rolf had not received any mail from home, so he assumed the worst: his family was dead and his home was demolished. His best-case scenario at this point was a POW's future in Siberia, as Goebbels

---

* Was firebombing Dresden going a city too far? Sir Arthur Harris, commander of RAF Bomber Command, would never waver from the decision. During the German "Blitz" bombing of London and towns such as Coventry, some 40,000 Britons lost their lives, and by war's end, 55,000 airmen of Bomber Command would die combating the German world threat. The bombing of Dresden was also strategic, as Harris explained in 1977: "The bombers kept over a million fit Germans out of the German army . . . manning the anti-aircraft defenses; making the ammunition, and doing urgent repairs, especially tradesmen."

had predicted for those who failed to secure the final victory. The propaganda minister had even devised a battle cry for German soldiers in the war's last days: "Victory or Siberia!"

For men with nothing left to lose, fighting to the bitter end seemed like a good way to die.

No one came or went through the empty intersection in front of Gustav. The minutes felt like hours. Gustav couldn't tell the difference anymore. He missed his clock.

During a lull in Alsace, beside a barn he'd found an abandoned car that still had a clock in its dashboard. Gustav had never owned a wristwatch, let alone a clock, so he removed the screws and took it. He was thrilled that it still worked and kept perfect time. When a friend earned a furlough home, Gustav loaned him the clock so the man wouldn't miss his train. He never saw the clock again.

Gustav fiddled with his radio but every channel hissed with static. He checked his machine gun to ensure that the ammunition belt was secure. It would be useless against an American tank, but it made him feel better nonetheless.

So why keep fighting? There was no way to end the war, short of deposing the Nazi leadership, an impossible scenario to envision. As one soldier posited after the war, "This had been an undiscussable subject due to the Nazis among us who still had the power to terrorize us even up to the last day."

Gustav believed that what mattered now was *how* they lost.

With the Red Army preparing for its final assault just forty-five miles from Berlin, he and other soldiers clung to a forlorn, naïve hope. Maybe if they fought hard enough, the Western Allies would seek a peace treaty with terms that wouldn't destroy the German people.

If that possibility failed, all that remained was their duty.

Gustav felt a duty to his company, to his brigade, to his army, and to his people—even those who had turned against him—to help avert the slavery that Goebbels had forecasted. Casting any doubts aside, Gustav leaned into his gun sight and checked his field of fire.

. . .

That morning, about a mile away from Gustav's position, Buck's platoon of doughs took cover behind a series of empty storefronts.

A German sniper was firing at another platoon, almost rhythmically. Buck shuddered at every bullet crack. But Janicki—who was right by Buck's side—wasn't overly concerned. Based on how the sound of the shots carried, the sniper was firing from one hundred yards away and maybe farther.

Before the sniper appeared, Buck's morning had been off to a great start. As A-Company departed aboard tanks, Annemarie and her father waved at him from the sidewalk. Buck's squad chided him mercilessly, repeating Annemarie's mantra from their first meeting: "Buck, first American I see!"

A-Company had been clearing the commercial district, making steady progress toward the Gereon quarter. Then the sniper struck, sending everyone scrambling for cover.

The platoon gathered around Lieutenant Boom and his runner as they approached. Boom had a plan. Across the street, doughs were advancing toward the sniper's purported position, but they needed the platoon's help. With forty sets of ears and eyes, they could spot the sniper and steer the other doughs to his position with suppressing fire.

Boom reminded the men not to venture too far from safety. They were still new to urban warfare, and he didn't want anyone getting shot. He told Buck and two men from a sister squad, who happened to be standing next to him, to post up in the nearest building, an abandoned flower shop. He then led Janicki and the others away, dispersing them up and down the block. The hunt was on.

Only a three-foot-high ledge of wall remained beneath the shattered storefront window. It didn't offer much cover, but it would have to do. Buck and the others darted forward before sliding behind the ledge to take cover. Withered flower petals scattered across the floor.

Rising in unison, the three men peered over the last jagged fringe of glass left in the windowpane. An industrial area of small factories and overgrown greenery dominated the landscape across the street. The moment transported Buck back to his childhood. It reminded him of hunting squirrels with his brothers, when the kid with the best eyes prevailed.

Buck wanted to see the sniper before anyone else. His eyes settled on a crumbling three-story factory set back from the street. Each floor held at least a dozen dark windows.

To Buck's left, Private First Class Robert Morries was also searching as he swept his carbine from side to side. A short nineteen-year-old with deep bags under his eyes, Morries had quit elementary school after third grade to help his mother and sister run the family farm in Peach Orchard, Missouri.

"I see him," Morries whispered. From the direction of Morries's gaze, Buck deduced that the sniper had to be hiding on one of the factory's higher floors. Morries raised his carbine and aimed it at the sniper. But before he could get a shot off, the German fired first.

The bullet zipped under Morries's trigger hand, snapping through the carbine's wooden stock and entering his shoulder. The impact knocked him to the floor. Buck and the other dough hit the ground as the rifle's report echoed down the block. The other dough hollered for a medic. Buck asked Morries if he could move.

"Barely," came the reply.

Staying low, Buck and the dough pulled the wounded man behind a shelf. Morries's head came to rest on Buck's thigh. His dark eyes stared through Buck to the ceiling.

A medic arrived and went to work. Using scissors, he cut off Morries's shirt, which revealed a jagged black hole in his shoulder that was seeping blood. Buck cringed. The bullet had mushroomed as it passed through the stock.

"How bad is it?" Morries asked. The medic said it wasn't pretty, but that the wound wasn't bleeding badly either. The explanation seemed to comfort Morries.

The medic sprinkled sulfa powder and was reaching for a bandage when blood suddenly began spurting from the wound like a fountain. The bullet must have pierced an artery wall.

The medic compressed the wound to stanch the bleeding, but the bandage turned crimson in no time. As the medic reached for another bandage, Morries began coughing. "Raise him up!" the medic shouted. Buck lifted Morries, cradling him in his arms. The young man was turning pale at an alarming rate.

More blood shot into the air when the medic swapped bandages. Buck could tell that Morries was slipping away. Morries looked up at

Buck, gasped one last time, and abruptly closed his eyes. He would never return to the farm to see his mother, Cinda, or his sister, Clara May, again.

The medic tossed aside the bloody bandages and departed in disgust. Buck was horrified by Morries's lifeless face, still resting on his knee.

The other dough, Private Richard Baughn, wasted no time in seeking revenge. Buck joined him as he crept back to the ledge beneath the window. They were both eager for the same thing.

Baughn's round, ruddy face was clenched with anger. A little older than Buck at twenty-three, Baughn was a former factory worker from Oklahoma, where he had left his wife and daughter in the care of his parents.

Buck's fingers wrapped around his rifle's hand guard. He was ready.

Baughn swung his M1 above the ledge and took aim. Buck popped up beside him, once again affirming his reputation: *Shorty thinks he's invisible.* With his heart pounding and the blood thumping in his eardrums, Buck searched the empty windows for the glint of the sniper's scope. But he couldn't see any trace of the enemy.

Buck's stomach sank when he realized his error. They'd never see the sniper because he was probably set back in the shadows. But Buck and Baughn were in the light. And *he* could see them.

That instant, another crack split the air and Baughn spun to the floor. Buck dropped below the ledge and lay there, panting. Baughn rose to his hands and knees and crawled toward the back door through Morries's blood, leaving a crimson streak behind him. He dropped to the floor short of the doorway. Buck screamed for the medic, darted to Baughn's side, and rolled him over. Baughn was gurgling blood.

"Where are you hit?"

"I don't know."

Buck unclipped the man's harness and spotted a hole on the left side of Baughn's neck where the bullet had entered. On the other side, a massive lump swelled and turned black with blood.

The medic returned and cursed at the sight of another wounded man. He examined Baughn's wound, looked at Buck, and just shook his head. It was that bad. The medic shouted for a stretcher bearer.

Baughn held a hand over his eyes as they carried him away. He'd die the following day, never to return to Oklahoma to reunite with his wife, Opal, or his daughter, Carolyn.

Buck was frothing with desire to kill that cowardly sniper. This time would be different. This time, he was ready. Just when he was about to sprint back to his position, a voice floated into Buck's mind with a competing thought: *Don't.*

Buck focused on the streak of blood that pointed from Morries's corpse like an arrow to the shop's exit. The sniper hadn't fired since shooting Baughn. He was probably still waiting, zeroed-in on the storefront window that had twice brought him success.

Would there be a third target?

Buck wouldn't give him the satisfaction.

He turned on his heels to go warn Lieutenant Boom and the others—maybe they could handle the sniper together? He was done trying to win the war alone.

Buck left the flower shop a different person from the one who entered.

He wasn't "invisible" anymore.

Several hours later, sometime after noon

The four tanks moved forward like knights entering a great hall.

With three Shermans trailing, the Pershing led the way between the shattered buildings of Cologne's inner city.

A dark boulevard lay ahead, crisscrossed with sagging streetcar cables. Propaganda leaflets dropped on the city by bombers skittered across the street. The destruction was worsening by the yard.

This was a job for the entire company, not four tanks. The trouble was, the Timberwolves Division in the southern half of the city had failed to keep up, so Easy Company had to leave a tank behind at each intersection to guard their right flank.

Clarence held his eyes to his periscope as the turret traversed with a buzz. At the end of the long hall, the twin spires were gazing down at the tanks' approach.

Outside, Earley hunched low in his hatch and held the pork chop close. Every so often, he ducked down into the turret as streetcar cables grazed the top of the tank with a grating sound.

Four- and five-story buildings towered over him but now only ghosts watched from their ornate, sculpted balconies.

The Pershing passed an arrow-shaped sign nailed to a tree pointing to the bridge. Earley consulted his map and alerted the crew. One mile remained. The men remained silent, dreading the countdown. Their orders were not just to reach the bridge but to charge across it and take the other side.

It was a suicide mission. The enemy had fortified the far bank and would pick off the tanks as they lumbered across if the bridge didn't blow up beneath them. Clarence yearned for the tank to go slower. The only thing awaiting them was certain death.

With Cologne's collapse imminent, the gunfire had dropped off. The enemy had stopped darting through the streets, jockeying for firing positions. Instead, they were fleeing. They could see the handwriting on the wall. Even the American doughs had dropped behind the tanks and shied to the sides of the streets. German foot soldiers were no longer their primary concern. In these wide streets, one great fear remained: German tanks.

At one P.M., a distant explosion ripped the air, followed by the groan of crumpling steel.

When Earley saw a plume of gray smoke rising from behind the cathedral's twin spires he knew exactly what it was: the Germans had demolished the bridge.

The Pershing stopped abruptly after the explosion. Inside, Clarence flashed DeRiggi a smile. Sighs of relief and outpourings of joy could be heard throughout the tank.

Crews were also celebrating in Chuck Miller's tank and on down the line in their meager column. The race to the bridge was over. They had been spared.

Maybe they could wait here for the rest of the company to catch up? The crew listened in with hope as Earley radioed headquarters.

When word came back, it wasn't good. The bridge *had* been blown, but there was to be no letting off the gas until American units reached Germany's sacred river. They were to keep going to the Rhine.

The crew groaned and cursed. The death march was still on.

The driver fired up the Pershing. Drive sprockets turned and track links began clacking forward again. Earley reminded his men to remain alert. Any German soldiers left behind had just lost their means of escape. With their backs to the wall, they would fight for their lives.

The Pershing pulled up to a massive four-way intersection, but instead of crossing the space it held back in the shadows, plotting its next move. The road continued on to the Gereon quarter, across the way.

Clarence gazed far and wide as he scanned with his 6x zoom sight. Tall buildings on all four corners of the intersection had been smashed to pieces, as if a giant had lumbered through. With walls shorn away, he could see inside an empty office where employees once typed. Scanning to the side, he saw the wallpaper in an apartment and a staircase climbing to a missing floor.

The buildings appeared deserted. But what about the street?

A gray car lay by the roadside. Its roof had been ripped off by an earlier shell burst or bomb and the remains of a German soldier—likely the car's driver—lay nearby. He was wearing black boots, gray pants, and his body ended there. The man had been cut in half. Cars were fair game in Cologne.

Clarence had been told that anything on wheels belonged to the German military, since German civilians weren't allowed to buy gasoline given the widespread wartime shortages.

With no need to distinguish between friend and foe, the rules of engagement were simple: *Shoot anything that moves.*

Rolf was restless in the turret. He wanted to peek around the corner, but the five-story building to his right obstructed his view.

Were the Americans massing across the four-way intersection? Would they come in ones and twos or in a massive wave?

There was only one way to find out. Rolf ordered the driver to bring the tank forward just enough for him to catch a glimpse. Gustav tensed behind his gun. It sounded like a terrible idea. The driver put the tank in gear, drove forward, and idled.

Above the turret, Rolf cursed and ordered a hasty retreat. He didn't like what he saw. The tank roared back into the shadows before

Gustav could even crack his hatch cover to take a look. A chorus of voices begged to know what Rolf had seen.

Rolf told the crew: a lone American tank.

"Did they see us?"

Rolf wasn't sure.

"A Sherman?"

Rolf didn't have an answer for his men. The tank he had seen matched no known description from the American arsenal.

Clarence cursed his bad luck.

He had turned the turret far to the right when he caught a brief glimpse of a German tank pulling out on his left. He had swung the 90mm gun toward the enemy, but the turret wasn't fast enough, and the enemy tank backpedaled from his reticle.

It was a German tank. But Clarence didn't know what type.

Earley studied the area with binoculars. He had missed the enemy's appearance altogether. "You're sure?" he asked Clarence.

"Trust me," Clarence said. "He's hiding behind that building."

Earley radioed the Shermans to stay back.

Clarence set the reticle where he'd last seen the tank.

Try that again.

His index finger gently wrapped the trigger.

Shaking with terror, Gustav pressed an eye to his gun sight.

They were sitting ducks. Surely the American tank had spotted them. The enemy didn't even have to venture out into the intersection to kill them; they could just send a bazooka squad on foot.

He angled his MG 34 machine gun toward the intersection, as close to the enemy as he could get it. Across the street lay a pile of rubble and steel beams—perfect cover for a bazooka man.

His scope was narrower than the width of his thumb, and the sight was scratched. He couldn't be sure, but Gustav swore he saw rifle muzzles already poking above the rubble. He fired a panicked burst or two. Green tracers cut the air above the pile, stirring up a maelstrom of dust.

"What is it?" Rolf asked.

Gustav told him what he thought he saw.

"Then fire like you mean it!" Rolf said.

Gustav squeezed the trigger and swept the gun from side to side, sending a hail of bullets at the pile itself, hoping to shatter bricks and fling deadly splinters in the enemy's direction.

Green tracers weaved through the debris.

Clarence was miffed by what he was seeing downrange.

A hose of green German tracers were firing at an innocuous pile of rubble. Either the enemy was spooked or this was an attempt to create a distraction.

Clarence wouldn't allow himself to blink. The German tank could dart out at any moment. The rattle of the idling engine drowned out any other noise in his ears. The black sides of the zoom sight squeezed his vision.

Sweat poured down the leather side flaps of his tanker helmet and beneath his wool shirt and jacket. No one moved or whispered. The intercom twitched with static.

An armor-piercing round was locked and loaded and Clarence was ready to fire at the drop of a hat.

Farther to the east, a black Opel P4 car raced toward the massive intersection. Its wheels bounced on the rutted street and stirred a swirl of dust in its wake.

In the passenger's seat rode twenty-six-year-old Katharina Esser.

Brunette locks draped her shoulders and flat eyebrows framed meek brown eyes. She was dressed as if for a journey, wearing a short red jacket and pants tucked into boots.

The third of four sisters, "Kathi" was a nurturer. Before the evacuations cleared away most of Cologne's civilians, she had cared for her sickly father and could be found in the park with her nieces and nephews, pushing them on their scooters. Someday she hoped to be a mother herself, and had attained a degree in home economics. Until then, she worked at a small grocery store in Cologne's Old Town.

Kathi Esser

At Kathi's side, forty-year-old Michael Delling, the grocery store's owner and Kathi's boss, gripped the wheel of the speeding car.

Delling's car was an exception to the city's ban of civilian vehicles. As a grocer, his work was deemed important to the war industry, so he was permitted the use of the car, strictly for business.

But today's was no pickup or delivery run.

Rather than languish in an air-raid shelter awaiting the uncertainty of liberation by foreign troops, Delling and Kathi were making a run for the bridge.

Either they hadn't heard the noise of its collapse, or they had and still harbored hope that it might be passable—no one knows. All that is certain from eyewitness accounts was that Kathi—gripped by a sense of impending doom—had encouraged the attempt.

All three of her sisters had lost husbands to the war, most recently the youngest. Eleven days earlier, it was Kathi who discovered that her brother-in-law Friedel had fallen—even before her sister received word.

"My dear ones," Kathi wrote to her parents, who had taken refuge outside the city. "I received both of your letters and want to thank you for them. . . . But the matter I have to tell you about now will take your breath away. The letter I wrote to Friedel last Christmas was sent back to me with the remark that recipient fell for greater Germany."

Kathi lamented that it was impossible to obtain a train ticket to Dortmund, otherwise she would go to notify her sister and comfort her.

"Life only has these (sad) things to offer us nowadays," Kathi wrote in closing. "I don't believe in a good outcome anymore. I think there will be a time soon when we start to envy Friedel and all the others who already passed away."

Clarence was peering straight across the intersection when the sudden motion took him by surprise. A black blur crossed into his sight picture from the left.

"Staff car!" Earley shouted.

Sure enough, a black car with gray blotches that resembled camouflage darted into the intersection at top speed. Instinctively, Clarence's thumb shot to the machine gun trigger. He mashed the trigger and the coaxial machine gun hammered, shattering the silence that had fallen over the tank.

Fiery orange bolts zipped downrange after the car. Near misses blazed past the car and skipped from the street, stirring the dust.

Tracers chase Delling's car as it crosses the intersection.

Clarence chased the fleeting target's tail end with the reticle. Just before his bullets could catch it, the car swung a hard left turn toward the German tank.

It was getting away.

Clarence reversed the turret's motion and clamped the trigger, snapping a desperate whip of fire after the car.

The car veered out of control as his tracers cut the air.

Gustav flinched at the orange shafts of light that slanted in front of his tank.

"Get ready!" Rolf said.

Gustav gritted his teeth and gripped his machine gun. If it was the American tank, he would go down shooting.

The dark shape came from the right, pursued by the orange shafts of light. Gustav clenched the trigger, the bolt blurred, and the machine gun spat a steady stitch of green.

Green tracers interwove with orange as the car drove through the flaming crosshatch. The windscreen blew out and the rear window shattered before the car veered into the nearest curb.

Gustav released the trigger and the bolt reappeared. The heat rising from the sizzling barrel made his line of sight wavy. When the haze had cleared, Gustav gazed at the scene with disbelief.

A black car was stopped and its driver was slumped over the wheel, dead.

Gustav was outraged. *Why would anyone drive through a battle!*

Military or civilian, the person shouldn't have been there.

A door swung open from the passenger's side and a body crumpled to the street.

Gustav swore he saw a fling of curly brown hair.

A woman?

Clarence, too, saw the car's door swing open, but the rubble impeded his view. He couldn't tell if he had hit the car or if the driver had come to his senses and pulled over.

Clarence had more pressing concerns. He had seen the green

tracers. The German tank was still there, lingering somewhere just beyond his sight.

Clarence faced a life-or-death decision. With orders to keep going to the Rhine, they couldn't just wait the enemy out. But if they rolled forward, the German tank would surely get the first shot, an advantage that Clarence was reluctant to concede. He had to do something.

"Ears," Clarence said, which served as a warning to the crew that he was about to fire. He set the reticle low on the building, where he estimated the enemy tank was hiding.

With a deafening crack, Clarence blasted an armor-piercing warhead downrange. The shell left behind a smoking hole as it cut straight through the building. Bricks tumbled down from a higher floor.

"No effect," Earley reported.

DeRiggi threw another shell into the breech and Clarence fired again.

No sign of a hit this time either, just more falling bricks. The building was obviously unstable after suffering damage in air raids. Clarence looked closer. A predictable pattern was forming after each shot, of bricks plunging from the building's higher stories.

The bricks. They were falling in the direction of the enemy tank.

He could work with this.

Clarence fired a third time. "Keep 'em coming!" he urged DeRiggi.

Earley remained silent atop the turret. He could tell Clarence was up to something. But what exactly? That remained to be seen.

Smoking shell casings piled up on the turret floor as Clarence repeatedly punched holes in the same wall, each time shifting his aim to the left.

Dust billowed from the building's ground floor. Clarence fired again and again, chopping at the building's shadowy legs. A pile of bricks cascaded down the façade. The entire structure was crumbling. A four-story wall wobbled before losing its support and falling backward. With a final well-placed shot, the upper floors of the building imploded in an avalanche of bricks.

Through the swaying streetcar lines, Earley couldn't believe his eyes. Clarence had cut the building practically in half.

· · ·

Gustav braced his hands over his head as he cowered in the darkness.

The avalanche from the collapsing building had come crashing down on them and even now, after the initial wave, a trickle of bricks continued to slam the ceiling above him.

Dust streamed inside, dimming any trace of light. The men hacked and coughed.

As soon as they had their wits about them again, the crew flew into a panic. Surely the American tank was coming to finish them off. On Rolf's command, the driver backed the tank farther behind the collapsed building.

The gunner tested the turret to see if it was operational, but it made a grinding sound and wouldn't budge. In all likelihood, bricks were wedged between it and the hull.

Gustav tried to open his hatch, but the cover wouldn't budge. He grunted and pressed harder. His arms quivered from immense effort, but the hatch was weighed down by bricks. He was trapped. Again.

His breath quickened. The walls seemed to tighten. He put his shoulder against the cover and pushed with all his might. The bricks gave way and the hatch flung open. Gustav sucked in the fresh air and glanced wildly about. But since he wasn't sure where the Americans were, he quickly sank back into the tank and shut the hatch.

Rolf had emerged from the turret and was shouting to someone outside. A civilian had approached, curious about the progress of the battle. After a brief exchange, Rolf chased the man away, dropped into the turret, and closed the cover.

"The bridge is gone," Rolf said.

Gustav didn't believe it. He pressed the commander for answers. The civilian had told Rolf the news on good authority. Rolf and his crew had simply failed to hear the explosion over the engine's noise.

It took a moment for the enormity of the news sink in.

Normally quiet and obedient, Gustav felt a new sensation stirring— anger. He began trembling.

Our own guys did this! They abandoned us!

One of the crewmen proposed a new course of action. He suggested that they back the tank into a cross street and let the Americans come to them. An ambush.

"What are we supposed to do," Rolf said, "throw bricks at them?"

The gunner reminded Rolf that they could still fire forward. They could position the tank using just the tracks like a self-propelled gun, and maybe get a side shot on an American tank using the element of surprise.

Gustav couldn't believe it. They wanted to keep fighting, even if their tactic could work only once before the Americans converged on them with overwhelming forces.

A third crewman was in agreement with the suicidal plan.

By now, Gustav was fuming. He'd just shot a car and might have killed innocent people. His own people. And now his crew was petitioning to trade their lives—and his—for the chance to kill some lone American tank crew.

"This is senseless!" Gustav blurted.

A crewman snapped at Gustav, reminding him of their orders.

There was no reasoning with the others, so Gustav spoke directly to Rolf. "What do we owe them anymore?" he said. "They sent us here to die!"

Rolf remained silent. He was waffling, having already resigned himself to an honorable death in his tank.

But it didn't matter. Gustav had made his decision. The young radioman who valued duty to his family, to his comrades, and to his countrymen had forgotten someone important.

He had a duty to himself.

Rolf never issued an order to abandon the tank, but that didn't stop Gustav. He was finished being a pawn for the Third Reich. He flung open his hatch cover and made one last appeal to Rolf, his only friend left in the war.

"Come on, Rolf! Why get killed for nothing?" With that, Gustav tore off his headset and lifted himself from the tank.

Gustav bolted behind the tank to the nearest street corner but then hesitated. He was unsure which way to run or what to do next. Freedom was a fresh sensation.

Rolf stood from the turret and spotted Gustav. In one swift motion, Rolf pushed himself up and out of the turret. Then he jumped down to the engine deck and then the street. Gustav braced himself as Rolf dashed after him. He wasn't sure if his friend had come to punish him or join him.

"Let's go," Rolf said. He grabbed Gustav's arm and pulled him in a new direction. They went down a street where civilians were standing in the entrance of a building and motioning for the duo to join them.

Gustav and Rolf ran for shelter.

Behind them, the Mark IV pulled a U-turn in the rubble and plunged into a cross street without them.

The tank—and the three men who chose to remain aboard—would never be seen again.

Clarence's plan had worked like a charm—the intersection was safely behind them.

The Pershing idled about fifty yards behind the bullet-riddled car.

Clarence fixed his aim far beyond, in the direction of St. Gereon's Basilica, a Catholic church, ready for any threat that might come around the bend.

Doughs ducked around the fallen building to his left, searching in vain for a buried enemy tank beneath the rubble. Clarence felt fortunate that he had seen the German tank at all. The thought of what would have happened had they driven past it sent a shiver down his spine.

Now and then, his eyes drifted down to the wrecked car. The Opel P4 was a civilian model often used by the German Army. Bullets had studded the trunk and shattered the rear window.

Clarence was surprised. What had looked like camouflage from a distance was actually blotches of gray dust on the car's black paint.

Three medics reached the car. The driver was dead from a head-shot, but there was someone else lying alongside the passenger side. The medics set about tending the second victim. Doughs passing on the sidewalks watched the medics work by glancing over their shoulders. Clarence followed the doughs' eyes, but the car's fender obscured most of his view.

The medics rolled the victim over and Clarence swore he saw a flash of long, curly hair. But it happened so quickly, he wondered if his eyes had deceived him. He felt a pit open up in the depths of his stomach.

Did I shoot a woman?

His mind swirled with panic. Was she hurt badly? What was she doing there in the first place? Then, he remembered. This was Cologne. Only the Nazis had cars here.

To drive through a gunfight, the woman and her driver had to be running from something. Were they a pair of Golden Pheasants who had waited too long to get out? Was he a general, and she his mistress?

Clarence absolved himself of any guilt.

Whoever she was, she had to be one of the bad guys.

Behind the Pershing, Chuck Miller watched the curbside triage through his telescopic sight.

The medics had given up. It was hopeless. With grim looks on their faces, they stood and stepped away, revealing the patient they had struggled to save—a young woman curled in the fetal position.

A civilian witness would later recount having seen the young woman reaching to aid the wounded driver when she, too, was struck by bullets.

A medic took a long coat from the car. He tenderly covered her up to the shoulders before departing to aid someone else in need.

The woman's face was turned toward Chuck. Her eyes were glassy and distant. She reminded him of one of his sisters and Chuck wondered if she was already dead.

Then, she blinked.

Chuck reeled back from his telescopic sight, horrified and guilt-stricken. It felt as if she had caught him looking, watching her die.

He couldn't tell Clarence, he wouldn't, not with the darkest depths of Cologne—a place that no American crew wanted to go—still ahead.

That man at the Pershing's gun was Chuck's best hope of ever reaching home again. Chuck had seen enough of this place to know it.

In the Fortress City, anything could be lurking around the next corner.

Later that afternoon, around two P.M.
Cologne

Everything they'd fought for was finally within reach.

A pair of hesitant Shermans crept down a narrow street toward the bright light at the end.

The lead Sherman's flanks were laden with shields of logs. The commander crouched low and watchful in his turret.

Part of the cathedral and its opulent square could be seen between the buildings at the end of the block, and some of the railroad station as well. But they weren't out of the woods yet.

These last yards were treacherous.

The final push to the Rhine was a job for the Pershing, but the Super Tank had fallen behind after the firefight at the intersection. So the task fell to the Shermans of F-Company.

After F-Company seized the cathedral, the Stuarts of B-Company—now queuing in the background—would make a run for the Rhine. Together they would share the glory as the conquerors of Cologne. But first, they had to get past this street, blocked by a landslide of debris from a collapsed building.

The lead Sherman stopped beneath a street clock whose hands had frozen in the six o'clock position. The second Sherman pulled up parallel on the left. From the lead tank's turret, Second Lieutenant Karl Kellner searched for a way around the barrier.

With a receding hairline and thin glasses, the deeply religious

Karl Kellner

twenty-six-year-old looked like a prime candidate for the priesthood. In actuality, back home in Sheboygan, Wisconsin, he had worked at the Jerry Miller Food Market and had a fiancée waiting for his return.

If anyone might be worthy of reaching the cathedral first, it was Kellner. He'd already received a Silver Star for his actions in Normandy, and twice he'd been hospitalized from wounds, then earned a battlefield commission to lieutenant just two weeks prior.

But the road ahead was impassible. Kellner had no choice other than to call for a dozer tank—the triumph would have to wait.

In a nearby doorway, an army journalist by the name of Staff Sergeant Andy Rooney kept his camera close. Short in stature, with tight-set, almost pugilistic features, Rooney was poised to document the culmination of a "major news story." Rooney—destined for acclaim in the television era—wasn't your typical journalist. As a writer for *Stars and Stripes,* he had flown aboard B-17s in combat. He had also shared a tent in Normandy with the legendary reporter Ernie Pyle, and had been present for the liberation of Paris.

Behind him, other reporters were discussing the world-class hotels around the cathedral and making plans to rush the Hotel Excelsior's wine cellar, but Rooney kept ahead of the pack. Something told him that this story was far from over.

The shot came without warning from the railroad station.

A green bolt of German tank fire angled from the front left, through the ruins of a building, before it slammed obliquely into the gun shield of Kellner's Sherman, spraying shrapnel into the gunner's legs inside.

The deep, brassy clang from the strike had barely ceased resonating when a second green bolt punched the tank again, so close to the first point of impact that the holes overlapped. Kellner's Sherman ruptured from the detonating shell. Hatch covers burst open from turret to bow.

The driver of the neighboring Sherman threw his machine in reverse, but it was too late. Another green bolt followed him and clipped the front end of the tank's right track. Desperate to escape the line of fire, the second Sherman veered backward and left. When a building stood between them and their assailant, the crew came pouring out.

Thin, steamy smoke rose from Kellner's Sherman. Kellner emerged from the turret bareheaded and clutching a carbine. In the midst of his labored movement, he dropped the rifle, falling to the engine deck. His left leg had been violently amputated at the knee and the stump was smoking. The gunner exited the tank behind Kellner and nose-dived off the turret to avoid exposing himself to any more fire.

Kellner rolled back across the engine deck before stopping at the edge. With only one leg to land on, it would be a long fall. A medic, a tanker from the other crew, and Rooney darted forward—almost in unison—to lend a hand. Together, they carried Kellner to safety before resting him on a pile of rubble.

Rooney elevated Kellner's leg, which was "a blur of gore and bone," according to an onlooker. A tanker removed his shirt and tied the sleeve around Kellner's thigh in an attempt to stem the bleeding. As Rooney held him, Kellner stared back at the newsman blindly. But the tourniquet was too little, too late. Kellner died in his fellow soldier's arms.

"I had never been present before at the moment someone died," Rooney would write. "I didn't know whether to cry or throw up."

Like a survivor loitering around a car wreck, Kellner's bow gunner lingered in a daze. He had no idea how he or the gunner had survived. A reporter overheard his words: "I don't know how I got out . . . I don't know how he got out. The sons of bitches."

The U.S. Department of War would soon be wiring a telegram to Kellner's parents and his fiancée, Cecelia, to tell them that Karl had been killed in action, "somewhere in Germany."

Inside the turret, Kellner's loader lay in pieces. And his driver, Private First Class Julian Patrick, the youngest of four brothers who all fought in the war, was dead at the tank's helm, still seated beneath an open hatch. Patrick's tanker helmet had come to rest tipped back. The blood from his nose had dried, and one eye stood half-open.

The smooth rattle of a German tank approaching from the square sent Rooney and the other survivors running.

The killer was approaching.

• • •

The Panther trundled past the cathedral and stopped in the corner of the square, facing the derelict Shermans head-on.

The tank had fired from the tunnel beneath the railroad tracks before emerging from the shadows to stake its claim on the battlefield. The light revealed the tank's commander.

Bartelborth stood tall in the turret.

Without a bridge to defend, German soldiers were desperately swimming over the Rhine, using stray doors and planks as rafts to aid their crossing to friendly lines. But Bartelborth and his crew had chosen a different course.

Inside the Panther, Bartelborth never ordered his men to resist to the last bullet.

There was no need.

They had stayed to fight to the death.

The last battleground. The train station can be seen to the left of the cathedral, and beyond both landmarks lies the Rhine.

• • •

One street over and three hundred yards back, the Pershing idled on the Wall Street of Cologne.

Sculptures in the classical Greek style towered over the entrance of the Commerzbank. The train station's iconic arched roof and burnt ribs could be seen two blocks away at the end of the street.

Inside the Pershing, Clarence and the crew followed the flurry of radio transmissions. The last they'd heard, doughs had been dispatched to pursue the marauding enemy tank.

A shout from outside the Pershing rose above the engine's jangle. "Hey Bob!"

Earley rose from the hatch and saw his friend Tech Sergeant Jim Bates, clutching a small motion-picture camera.

With thick cheeks and dark hair, the twenty-eight-year-old Bates was a small, scrappy combat cameraman in the 165th Photo Signal Company. He was the type of man who would have been at home in any cigarette smoke–filled newsroom back in the States.

Bates told Earley that there was a "monster" of a tank guarding the cathedral. Earley knew that much already.

"You can see him around the corner!" Bates said.

Earley pondered the notion, then told Clarence to assume command. He was going to investigate on foot.

"What?"

Jim Bates

It was foolhardy. Clarence reminded Earley that there were no friendly troops ahead; the Pershing was the front line. But Earley couldn't be swayed. He wanted to see what they were up against with his own two eyes.

He lowered himself from the Pershing and conferred with Bates. "Jim, let's go down and see what we can see on that tank," he said. "I don't know what we're going to run into—we may never get back."

Earley and Bates crept down the block through a no-man's-land populated by propaganda posters—here, a German worker hammering with a rivet gun, and there, the lurking shadow of an Allied spy.

Bates thrived amid danger. The cameraman had jumped with the 82nd Airborne on D-Day, and in the Ardennes he put himself in the bow gunner's seat of a Stuart tank to get the best shots. He was fearless, which made his film a cut above the others'.

At the end of the street, on the left, the duo approached the German Labor Front Building, which was home to the nation's trade unions. If they went any farther, the Panther might see them. Earley and Bates ducked inside.

From the mezzanine-level windows, they saw it. Two streets over, the sandy-yellow Panther idled in the corner of the bright square. Its gun was still pointed directly at Kellner's incapacitated Sherman, an ominous warning to anyone who dared follow in Kellner's footsteps.

And there, Earley saw his opportunity.

He laid out his plan to Bates: his tank would continue up its current street, nose into the intersection, and blindside the Panther with a side shot.

"You get all ready for it," he told Bates. "When you hear me coming up underneath you, you'll know where I am."

Earley departed for his tank as Bates took the stairs higher to position himself for the best possible view of the daring attempt.

This was personal, for Bates too.

In the Ardennes, he had been riding in a Stuart when its crew spotted a German tank, sidelong to them and ready to fire. Bates bailed out with the crew moments before the German shell landed. Bates's peers weren't all as lucky as he was. Of the sixty-five army cameramen who'd reported to Europe with him, fewer than half would come home.

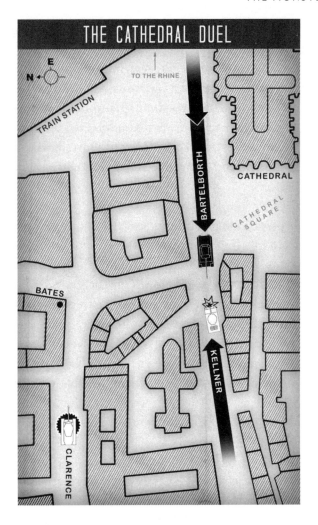

Bates steadied his camera out the window and prepared to capture the action.

The time had come to settle "a nine-month-long dispute" that had been brewing since he first witnessed the dominance of German armor at Normandy: Could an American tank finally stand on equal footing against a Panther?

The answer was long overdue.

Inside the Panther, the minutes felt like hours.

Condensation formed on the ceiling. The crew peered through their periscopes searching for the enemy as the engine's thrumming drowned out their thoughts.

Bartelborth, the former teacher, had been fighting in tanks since 1941 and had even served a stint as an instructor. Maybe it was experience. Maybe it was instinct. But a sixth sense told Bartelborth that the Americans might come at him from an unexpected direction.

Leaving his Panther's hull facing forward, Bartelborth ordered the gunner to turn the turret to the right—toward an entirely empty street.

From his third-story window, Bates saw the Panther's turret turning toward him. He hit the floor, certain the German tank commander had seen him. When the room around him failed to explode, Bates raised himself up to take a peek below. What he saw horrified him: the Panther's super-velocity gun was aimed at street level—facing the exact spot where Earley said he would pull out.

The tank had Bates trapped.

There was no walking out the front door. There was no time to warn his friend. Even if he screamed at the top of his lungs, it wouldn't do any good.

The Pershing was about to roll into an ambush.

The smooth note of the Panther's exhaust system reverberated through the empty streets.

Ready for action, Buck and the rest of his platoon followed Lieutenant Boom toward the sound. One dough clutched a bazooka; another carried shells. The tank sounded close, perhaps as close as the other side of the building to their right.

Rather than turn the corner and fight the tank face-to-face, Boom led the men inside the building. A shot from a window made more sense. Hopefully, the Panther would never see it coming.

The squad ran through the building's empty cross section before bounding up the rubble-filled stairs. At each floor they came to, a dough darted to a window to survey their surroundings. And after each floor, the report was the same: "No Panther!" They still didn't have a shot.

Lieutenant Boom led the men higher.

As he chased the pounding footsteps in front of him, Buck's mind was still back in the flower shop. By the time that A-Company had converged on the three-story factory, the German sniper had escaped— albeit without shooting anyone else. Janicki had tried to console Buck by reminding him, "It's not your fault. Your head was sticking up next to theirs."

But that wasn't the point.

Buck was angry with himself because he should have known better. He should never have gone back to that window a second time, let alone contemplated a third attempt. The lesson was as indelible as Morries's blood that remained soaked into his trousers.

If he was going to survive this war, it was time to start thinking like a veteran.

Before they knew it, Boom ran out of floors. In the ceiling above, a scuttle led to the attic. It was the highest vantage point the doughs would get. Someone would have to go up there and that someone would have to be lightweight. Everyone expectantly turned to Buck.

Buck wanted to groan. He'd never escape the role of first scout now. He had never fired a bazooka before and doubted the wisdom of firing a backblast weapon in a tightly confined space.

Boom took a knee and motioned for Buck to ascend.

"Fine," Buck said. He handed over his rifle. The Panther had whacked two American tanks and someone had to stop it, even though Buck wished it wasn't him. He stepped onto Boom's thigh as Boom grabbed the back of Buck's belt and pushed him up through the scuttle in one motion.

The bazooka had already been loaded when it was passed up to Buck. Buck armed the weapon and dropped to his belly. He shimmied forward, following the ceiling's downward slant toward the windows that overlooked the street, while sliding the bazooka alongside him.

The cacophonous noise of the Panther flooded the attic as soon as he propped open the window. From his perch, he was above the roof-tops and eye-level with the cathedral.

Buck looked down on an empty street and cursed.

They were a block too far.

A sound rose from below. It was the mechanical noise of another tank approaching from the right, where friendly forces were positioned. Its powerful engine was gunning as its tracks slapped the ground.

Buck was horrified. An American tank was moving forward toward the idling Panther. *Didn't anyone tell them?* He and the doughs hadn't killed the Panther yet. They needed more time.

Buck cringed at the noise as it came closer. It sounded like an American crew driving to their deaths.

Earley radioed instructions for the Shermans to hold back as the Pershing rolled forward.

The Pershing would handle this on its own.

The plan was simple. They would edge into the intersection and then it would be Clarence's show.

"I'll go for a hull shot," Clarence volunteered. It was the largest target, so there would be less chance of missing in the heat of battle.

"Shoot wherever you want," Earley said. "He's just sitting there like he owns the place."

Earley had cause for confidence. Even a 75 Sherman could knock out a Panther from broadside. And shooting a tank when it was blind? It almost felt unsportsmanlike.

The intersection was fast approaching.

Across the turret, DeRiggi cradled a 24-pound T33 armor-piercing shell, poised for a speedy reload.

Clarence announced to the driver that he was pre-positioning the gun. "Keep us on a line, Woody," he added.

Clarence lowered the reticle to where the enemy tank would sit and swung the 15.5-foot barrel as far right as he could without scraping the buildings. With his family's lives in his hands, he wasn't taking any chances. Even if the enemy was broadside and blind, it was still a Panther.

A bird passing overhead would have seen two armored beasts blindly searching for each other. Going up one street—a Pershing with its gun pointed to the right as it prepared to breach the corner. Around that corner—a stationary Panther with its gun targeting the intersection the Pershing was heading toward.

McVey fed the tank more gas. The Pershing quickly gained speed. Smokey held on for dear life.

Earley brought the pork chop close to his mouth.

Clarence set his eyes to the periscope for the widest possible view. *Don't miss.* It was them or his family.

When the Pershing entered the intersection, Smokey saw it first. The enemy tank was sitting in the intersection, bathed in light, and he was looking directly down its rifled barrel.

Smokey cried out in terror.

McVey panicked and stomped on the gas, which sent the Pershing lurching even farther into the intersection and harm's way.

The crew uttered a collective gasp.

Clarence's heart seized as the Panther slid into his sights. Between the rubble and the dangling streetcar lines, all he saw was the black hole of its muzzle.

Inside the Panther, Bartelborth saw the dark, blurry vehicle leap from the shadowy street. The green tank was low and sleek behind a wedge of frontal armor. It was no Sherman.

"Stop!" Bartelborth screamed to his gunner. "That's one of ours!"

Clarence had no time to aim. There was no time for the tank to stop. There was no time for anything. The reticle rested on the Panther and that would have to be good enough.

Clarence fired and the 90mm's muzzle flash illuminated the shadows.

Earley saw it all from his perch above the turret.

An orange bolt streaked like a flaming telephone pole and punched into the Panther's engine bay with a leap of sparks and a crack like lightning. Dust swirled from the rubble and behind the cloudy tentacles came flames licking from the Panther's engine.

The commander's hatch slid open, releasing a gush of smoke from inside the Panther. The German commander wiggled free from the turret. Using his tank to shield himself, he jumped to the ground on the far side. The driver rolled over his side of the hull to safety.

Inside the Pershing, Clarence couldn't even tell if he had hit the Panther. The 90mm's blast had stirred up so much dust that the Panther appeared to be just an outline, angular and threatening, with its gun still pointed at him.

"Another T33!" Clarence demanded.

DeRiggi slammed another shell into the breech as Clarence shifted his aim forward along the hull, stopping just beneath the rise of the turret. His finger squeezed the trigger. Through the dusty gloom, another burst of sparks split sidelong from the Panther as if the tank had been struck by a massive chisel.

"Hit!" Earley yelled.

The holes in the Panther's hull began glowing with light. A fire was rapidly spreading along the length of the tank—from the rear to the front.

A disoriented German crewman pushed himself up from the turret and flopped over the Panther's side. Another dove from the loader's rear hatch with his uniform ablaze—a "living torch," as he would later describe himself. They, too, scattered behind the wall of the tank.

Inside the Pershing, Clarence called for another armor-piercing shell. Was this butchery? An excessive use of force? Not when the Panther's gun was still pointed at Clarence and his crew. If a German crewman reached the trigger in his last gasp, he could still kill them all.

Clarence would not let that happen. The dust was settling and this time he took aim. Clarence lowered the reticle to the deep recess between the Panther's wheels and hull.

His finger crushed the trigger. In a blinding flash, the shell punched through the Panther's heart and straight out the other side with the sound of a metallic splice.

This time, Clarence saw it all.

A volcano of flame surged from the turret, the front hatch covers blasted open, and flames stood where men once sat. The fire soared twice the height of the tank as it roared like a blowtorch. Clarence swore he felt heat around his eyes.

All three shell holes in the Panther's flank glowed and pulsed as fire consumed the tank's interior. The gunner's optical sight flickered at Clarence like a cyclops's eye.

From above, Earley had seen enough: "Driver, reverse!"

The engine growled as the Pershing rolled backward into the shadows. The turret smelled acrid from the empty shell casings, so DeRiggi opened a hatch and tossed them out. One. Two. Three casings clanked on the street.

The Pershing stopped. The crew listened. From around the corner came popping and crackling sounds as the Panther's ammo cooked off in the heat.

Clarence sat back from the periscope, still stunned by the previous forty or fifty seconds of furious action. *Did that really happen?*

DeRiggi, Smokey, and McVey remained tightlipped out of a mix of deference and awe for Clarence's abilities. Earley sank into his seat and leaned forward to catch his breath as if he were going to vomit. No one had been more shocked at the sight of the Panther's barrel than he was.

Earley laid a hand on Clarence's shoulder.

After some time, Clarence broke the silence in the tank. "That was close," he said.

"Really close," DeRiggi agreed.

Clarence returned to his periscope and resumed scanning for threats. Earley found his footing and settled his elbows outside the turret.

Over the rooftops, the Panther's smoke rose like ash from Vesuvius.

It was about three P.M. when a figure emerged from the German Labor Front Building before making a mad dash toward the Pershing.

It was Bates. He shouted up to Earley, "I think I got it!"

"What?" Earley responded quizzically.

Despite the 90mm's shockwaves rattling his camera, Bates had filmed the duel between the two tanks. He needed just one last shot: a picture of the Pershing's crew.

"It'll take less than a minute," Bates promised.

Earley checked his surroundings. The other three Shermans had pulled up behind the Pershing. He figured it was safe enough, so he spoke into the pork chop. Hatches opened and the crew stood one by one against a backdrop of pitted columns and blown-in windows.

Pershing crew

Earley moved forward alongside the turret to make way for Clarence, who rose from the commander's hatch.

Bates began filming.

McVey looked past the camera, his eyes casting a thousand-yard stare, Smokey chomped a cigarette. Earley looked nothing short of disturbed. Bates told him to tip back his helmet, the shadows were hiding his face. DeRiggi squeezed a tight grin and Clarence cast a hesitant smile.

To Bates, this crew were the messengers. After all the Nazis did to Russia and Poland, these men carried word to Germany "that its men and cities could be dealt with in the same manner."

True to his word, Bates capped the camera's lens just shy of a minute after he started filming.

The tankers could go back to war.

The patrol of four tanks rolled bravely forward toward the remains of the Hohenzollern Bridge.

With their guns fanning half the clock face, the Pershing and the three Shermans probed for any remaining pockets of resistance.

Beneath a cold, dark afternoon sky, Earley halted the patrol by the tracks that spilled from the train station.

Inside the Pershing, the turret buzzed as Clarence searched for an enemy gun that could spoil their survival.

Nothing.

The train station was cold and cavernous. The murky Rhine streamed around the bridge's sunken arches. And the cathedral was now the headstone to a lifeless city.

Earley raised the pork chop to his lips and made the call at 3:10 P.M. His patrol had reached Germany's sacred river. "Any further and we'll be swimming."

Before he could release the Transmit button, the crew erupted in shouts of joy. Clarence and DeRiggi, McVey and Smokey, everyone whooped and hollered and looked for one another to shake hands. During his crew's celebration, Earley remained above the turret, still tangled in the emotion of their close call.

Clarence sat back in his seat with the impression of his zoom sight still encircling one eye. He lit himself a cigarette and took a long drag.

Cologne was theirs.

Later that evening

Sounds of hushed voices drifted as Gustav and Rolf sat at a table in a damaged building's cellar.

Civilians—including two older couples and two young women—conversed nearby with relief that the war would soon be over for them. Flickering candles illuminated beds and other furniture set against whitewashed walls.

The civilians had shared their bread and schnapps with the tankers to calm their nerves, but Gustav remained on edge. It was only a matter of time before the Americans searched this block.

The wait was torturous. What worried Gustav the most was the Panzer Wrap uniform that he wore beneath his camouflaged coveralls. Like many Wehrmacht tankers before him, the black uniform now made him a target and the skull collar tabs made things even worse. Would his captors confuse him with an SS man and shoot him on sight?

Gustav thought of tearing off the emblems, but stopped short of doing so. It could be worse if the Americans thought he was hiding something. He hoped his captors would know the difference between the uniforms.

Gustav remembered how his family had treated "their" POW. Due to manpower shortages in Germany while the men were away at war, every farm in Gustav's region received a POW laborer. One day, a young Russian appeared on the family's doorstep. He had a shaved head and still wore his Red Army uniform, which covered his slim frame.

Gustav worked his family's fields with the Russian during furloughs from his military training. Each night, after a long day of toil, authorities would collect the POW to take him back to his prison camp. But first, the farmer's family was to serve him supper.

The Nazis had a strict rule: POWs could not, under any circumstances, eat at the same table as the farmers "hosting" them. But Gustav's mother, Mina, wouldn't have it. The young Russian was as hard a worker as the rest of them. So, each night she prepared a side table, complete with a full set of cutlery, just in case the authorities came knocking. And each night, the young Russian dined at the same table as the family.*

Shouts from the street drew all eyes in the cellar to the wooden ceiling. One of the old men went upstairs to investigate. After a few moments, he returned with news. The Americans were approaching. Rather than endanger the civilians by their presence, Gustav and Rolf moved for the stairs to confront their fears.

"Bubi." Rolf stopped Gustav at the top of the steps and wished him luck, for whatever the future held for him.

Outside, twilight had settled across Cologne.

In the fading light, Gustav and Rolf raised their hands in a sign of surrender. Two American doughs cradled rifles across the street. As they approached their captors, Rolf spoke in English. The effect was disarming and the Americans relaxed. They searched the Germans' pockets and confiscated Gustav's compass.

---

* French POWs were the first to arrive in Gustav's area and, despite the authorities' best efforts, some befriended the farmers and would return to visit after the war. Many Russian POWs, who arrived later, lobbied the farmers to let them remain there after the war, for fear they'd be executed by the Communists when repatriated.

When Gustav heard a Sherman tank rumbling on a parallel street, he tensed up.

The doughs passed Gustav and Rolf off to an American intelligence officer who spoke German. The officer asked them how many tanks the Germans had remaining in Cologne.

"Three tanks in the center," Rolf said. That was all he knew.

At this point, there was nothing to hide. Throughout Cologne, in a seemingly endless trickle, German soldiers were emerging from hiding places waving white handkerchiefs tied to sticks. Others would wait for their captors to come to them, out of necessity.

Inside a massive bunker on the south side of the cathedral, three army cameramen and a war correspondent found the crew from the Panther that Clarence had destroyed. Bartelborth had suffered leg wounds and his gunner had received burns to his face. A third crewman lay nearby in a charred uniform. He appeared to be dying, but would ultimately pull through. The remainder of their crew was missing.

The American officer asked Gustav and Rolf for their *Wehrpässe*, or soldier's identification booklets. The officer thumbed through Gustav's before glancing up at him. "So you belong to the 'Fire Department of the West'?"

Unsure of how he should react, Gustav just smiled and nodded. At Gustav's response, the officer's demeanor flipped like a light switch. He punched Gustav in the side of the face. Gustav staggered from the blow and came back nursing his cheek. This time he remained tight-lipped.

On the officer's orders, the doughs led Gustav and Rolf to the nearby ruins of the Gereon Hotel, which was serving as a makeshift holding facility for some of the 326 Germans who would surrender to Spearhead that day. There, the men sat in a corridor, opposite a guard with a flashlight.

That night, Gustav's mind couldn't escape visions of the day. The same images replayed, over and over. A car door swinging open. A woman's hair unfurling. He still couldn't figure out what she was doing in the middle of a battle. It made no sense, but troubled him regardless.

Had he shot her? Or had the American gunner?

Perhaps he'd never know.

And perhaps that was for the best.

CHAPTER 18 **THE CONQUERORS**

That next morning, March 7, 1945
Cologne

At the crack of dawn, Clarence sneaked toward the cathedral. Having gazed at its jagged façade so often from his turret, he wanted to see what lay within.

The towering spires looked majestic in the light of a new day.

Clarence found the square in front was shadowy and empty as he approached the tall double doors. Entry was forbidden because of an informal truce. The Germans hadn't used the cathedral for observation during the battle, and there was an implicit understanding that the Americans wouldn't either in the aftermath.

Finding no one guarding the front doors, Clarence simply walked inside.

The stained glass had been removed, the pews were gone, and rubble lay where people once had prayed. But even in the cathedral's diminished state, when the sun streamed down on the altar, it was a humbling sight.

Clarence removed his cap.

There was one last item that he wanted to cross off his list.

More than five hundred steps later, he gazed over the ruined city from the northern spire. Clarence held his hat against gusts of wind and simply spoke to God, offering thanks for bringing him through his journey this far.

. . .

Word of their triumph over the Panther traveled quickly, and every newsman wanted a piece of the heroes of Cologne.

Later that morning, the war reporters located the Pershing parked in a side street near the train station plaza. The crew wasn't far from their home away from home. The weather was pleasant as the newsmen gathered around Clarence and the rest of the crew.

Army Signal Corps men wanted to record Earley for *The Army Hour*, a radio program that aired stateside. Bates took some still photos of the crew before he left for Paris to process his film of their heroic duel. But the focus of the reporters' frenzy was the man who felled the mighty Panther.

All the attention made Clarence nervous.

One journalist was writing a segment called "Killing a Monster." Everyone's questions boiled down to "How did you defeat it?"

The honest answer was Clarence didn't know. The Panther had them dead to rights, but for some reason the German gunner didn't pull the trigger. The victory was a mystery to Clarence. But how could he tell them that? "It was him or me. I just shot first," Clarence told the reporters.

In the course of the interview, someone asked the young corporal from Lehighton, "What are you looking forward to when this is over?"

Clarence and his comrades often dreamed about where life would take them after the fighting was over. Before the war, Earley had been a machinist in an aircraft factory, but now he dreamed of owning a quiet farm in Minnesota. Chuck Miller simply wanted to purchase a car. And Clarence, who had never had much growing up, dreamed simple dreams.

He harbored no illusions about the future. He told them he just wanted to get a factory job when he returned home. He hoped he might someday become a manager, so he wouldn't always be subject to someone else's orders for the rest of his life.

That answer didn't satisfy the newspapermen. When the reporters pressed him, Clarence reminisced about an even simpler pleasure. "I just want to get this thing over with," Clarence said, "so I can get back to roller-skating at Graver's."

The answer gave everyone a chuckle.

Later that morning, Clarence followed Smokey across the cathedral square. He had to hustle to keep up. The diminutive bow gunner was practically running.

Smokey and DeRiggi had caught a whiff of something loot-worthy across the square in the Dom Hotel. DeRiggi was already there, and Smokey had returned only to recruit reinforcements.

Clarence's pace slowed as they approached the Panther on their way to the hotel. Even though the fire had finally gone out that morning, the tank still looked like a glowing ember—black and charred on top and orange everywhere else. The inferno had altered the color of the paint.[*]

Smokey powered past the derelict tank without a second thought. But Clarence gave its burned-out shell a wide berth. A "coffin on wheels" in the words of Bates, it had only one man—the radio operator/gunner—dead inside. But Clarence assumed the worst. He believed the entire German crew had died in there, but wouldn't dare take a look to confirm his suspicions.

That could have been us. Clarence shivered at the thought.

The once palatial Dom Hotel was in ruins. An entryway of classical columns stood intact, but bombs had scooped out several floors and hammered the roof's Byzantine domes into new shapes.

Clarence followed Smokey down into the basement. The temperature dropped as they descended deeper, then came jubilant voices and sounds of breaking glass.

Clarence and Smokey stepped into a vast wine cellar with walls like

---

[*] Bartelborth resumed teaching after the war but never forgot the duel at the cathedral. In the 1990s he wrote to an acquaintance, "Even today it seems miraculous that I made it." He died in 1998 at age ninety-three, believing to the end that the Pershing was a German tank that had been captured by the Americans and repainted.

a castle's. Everywhere they could see was stacked with bottles of wine that stretched from floor to ceiling, and a flurry of Easy Company tankers were going rack to rack, shuttling bottles into wooden cases as fast as they could. A jingle filled the air like sleigh bells.

The biggest drinker on the crew, Smokey grinned from ear to ear. This world-renowned collection of wine and spirits was theirs for the taking. Smokey dove into the fray. They needed to grab as much as they could before officers arrived and ruined the fun.

Clarence found a wooden box and joined the free-for-all. His boots crunched broken glass and stuck to patches of a syrupy liquid as he waded through the cellar and its anterooms.

DeRiggi passed by balancing a full case of bottles. He departed, but would be back for more. Earley had agreed to open the Pershing so the men could stow their loot inside.

Clarence didn't know much about wine, so he reached for vodka and gin, which he could mix with grapefruit juice and use to make Greyhounds.

A religiously devout tanker lamented that they were stealing. But his laments didn't stop him from filling a crate of his own with bottles. Meanwhile, another man reframed the narrative in a more positive light—"We're saving this stuff from the Germans!"

Clarence sampled the merchandise, taking swig after swig.

Other tankers were ravenous for whiskey, but they found very little. After opening a bottle, a man would take a hesitant sip to test the waters and see what liquor he was getting. But more often than not, it was sweet brandy, which resulted in a bitter reaction—a spit, curse, and toss of the offending bottle. The men delighted at shattering German property and denying the spoils of war to anyone but their comrades.

When General Rose's staff arrived later that day they would find brandy running two inches deep on the floor of the ransacked wine cellar. By that point, the racks had been picked clean, except for "a couple of cases of overlooked Vermouth."

Upstairs in the hotel, Clarence opened the door to a suite and set his full case of alcohol aside. The cocktail of vodka, gin, and exhaustion had taken him by surprise. The hotel bed was strewn with bits of debris from the ceiling, so Clarence collapsed on a couch. The cathedral filled his view through a massive shattered window. It was the beacon around which the rest of the city revolved.

After more than 221 days in combat, Clarence didn't care what happened next. He would do what he was told and go where he was sent. But that didn't stop him from believing in the rumor that he—and many other men in Easy Company—had heard.

The war might end here in Cologne.

During the First World War, the Germans surrendered when the battle lines hit the fringes of their empire, before the fighting could reach the German heartland. Was it too much to hope that Europe's Second World War would end here, nearly three hundred miles from Berlin?

"The yarn was either accepted as accurate or laughed to scorn," the divisional history would record.

Clarence closed his eyes.

Only time would tell.

The sun was setting that evening as Buck emerged from a five-story-high air-raid shelter to the north of the train station. A gray BMW motorcycle, outfitted with a sidecar, roared down the street in his direction. The bike pulled to a halt in front of Buck.

Janicki sat behind the vibrating handlebars. After some mechanical tinkering, he had brought the ex–German Army bike back to life and summoned Buck from A-Company's quarters. A pair of goggles was set high on Janicki's helmet. It was time for a test ride.

"Hop in!" Janicki shouted.

Buck hedged. He was unarmed, and besides, riding in a seized vehicle was forbidden. Just the day before, the First Army had reminded the men of Spearhead that all recovered enemy vehicles were to be turned in "to the nearest Ordnance Collecting Point."

Janicki dismissed Buck's concerns. He had seen his young friend sulking, and heard him talking as if Morries's and Baughn's sacrifices were all for nothing. "Don't you want to go back to that fräulein's house?" Janicki asked.

Janicki promised it would be a quick trip. No one else would know. It would be their secret. Buck relented and prepared to hop in the side-car. Two bottles of looted wine occupied the seat. Janicki handed him both bottles. "For you and the fräulein," he said with a mischievous smile.

"Oh, jeez!" Buck settled in and held on tight.

The motorcycle's throaty putter reverberated through Cologne's hollow streets. Janicki shifted gears by hand and gave a hoot when they ramped the streetcar tracks. The few German civilians who remained stared from the sidewalks in a state of bemusement.

Janicki's tight-set eyes were wide and bright behind his goggles—the glaze was gone. A grin traced his thick jaw. Buck was amazed to finally see the real Bob Janicki.

And he knew why Janicki was suddenly so ebullient. The promotion. Word had trickled down that Janicki would become a half-track driver in two weeks. From here on out, he'd be sitting pretty. Janicki would drive the squad into battle then wait around for their return. But it was so much more than just a promotion. It was a ticket to what Janicki wanted above all else: to make it home to his wife in one piece.

Every bomb-blasted street looked exactly the same. Numerous times, Janicki pulled over and Buck hopped out to ask Germans for directions. He'd show them Annemarie's address on the back of her photo, and the civilians gave directions by hand signal. They were eager to help the Americans. It was almost as if there had never been a war at all.

A *Yank* magazine reporter labeled these citizens of Cologne the "Who? Me?" Germans.

"When you talk to them about the misery they have brought on the world and on themselves their reaction is: 'Who? Me? Oh, no! *Not me.* Those were the bad Germans, the Nazis. They are all gone. They ran away across the Rhine.'"

That generalization might have overstated the case, especially in the city of Cologne.

During the elections in 1933—before Hitler seized power—44 percent of Germans across the country voted for the Nazi Party. However, in Cologne, the vote was 33.1 percent in favor of the Nazis. About two-thirds of the city's populace voted against the regime. And that was before Cologne's citizens had weathered a brutal decade living under the shadow of the Gestapo.

The Party's secret police were still executing people in Cologne—including a fifteen-year-old local, a Russian POW, a Polish slave laborer, and seven others—up to four days before the Americans reached the city.

When Buck and Janicki finally arrived at the address on the back of the photo, Annemarie's father, Wilhelm, opened the door.

The man warmly greeted them but hovered behind the door, gauging their intent. He hadn't forgotten the young American's romantic enthusiasm for his daughter.

Buck played their only ace card in hopes of breaking the ice. He smiled and raised both bottles of wine. It helped. Wilhelm invited them in and Buck handed over the wine. Janicki winced, but it was the price of admission.

Upstairs, the family was in the middle of a party. One of Annemarie's aunts was celebrating a birthday with family and several neighbors. Annemarie was overjoyed to see Buck. She threw her arms around him and they embraced.

Wilhelm took the men's helmets, and Annemarie's aunts served them cake and beverages. For the first time in ages, Buck felt at home among friends.

At one point in the party, Annemarie fetched a candle and led Buck away for a "tour" of her father's dental office so the two of them could be alone. Janicki gave his young friend a wink as he departed. A little romance would work wonders for Buck's mood.

Annemarie proudly led Buck around the office, opening drawers and picking up dental tools. Once this had been her grandfather's barbershop, where wealthy clients would stop each morning for a shave while they smoked cigars and drank coffee enhanced with cognac.

Annemarie confided that she had once worked side by side with her mother, Anna. Buck remembered seeing her in the photo album, but not in person, and asked the indelicate question. Was Annemarie's mother still alive?

Annemarie's mood turned somber. But she resolutely told Buck what she knew.

It started with a rumor in September 1942. In those earlier days of war, all young men had to serve six months in the Reich Labor Service, constructing fortifications and tending the West Wall. And it wasn't just the men; young women were being drafted too.

Annemarie's teacher told her female students that when they reported to the Reich Labor Service, they would have to bear a child for the Führer. They wouldn't need parental permission and the Party would raise the babies for them.

Horrified at the prospect of having a child for the regime, Annemarie told her mother, and when an officer in the Reich Labor Service came to the office for dental work, Annemarie's mother asked him point-blank about the rumor. Was it true?

The Gestapo provided a definitive answer.

For simply broaching the question, they arrested Annemarie's mother, imprisoned her, and put her on trial three months later for making a "false assertion that could indeed damage the nation and the reputation of the government and the NSDAP party."

"Her statement could provoke the impression that governmental institutions would tolerate such immoral practices," prosecutors asserted.

A conviction on the charges seemed certain and the punishment would undoubtedly be a trip to a concentration camp. As Cologne's Jewish population was being deported to ghettos and extermination camps in the east, the Gestapo was sending its remaining enemies to Buchenwald and Theresienstadt at the time.*

The worst didn't happen, in this case. Annemarie's mother was spared when a judge contradicted conventional wisdom and ruled in her favor. He freed Annemarie's mother on grounds that she had

---

* The Gestapo's punishments could be unpredictably cruel. In Cologne, a middle-aged seamstress named Paula took "a few minor clothing articles, an empty suitcase, and two cans of coffee" from the rubble of her apartment complex after an air raid in 1942. When she couldn't prove that the belongings were hers, the Gestapo executed her as a "parasite of the people" in Cologne Prison, where the Third Reich murdered more than 300 people by guillotine.

merely sought an answer from a Reich Labor Service leader, without spreading the rumor publicly.

But even though she escaped the camps, irreparable damage had been done. Annemarie's mother was so traumatized by her treatment at the hands of the Gestapo that the family had no choice but to commit her to a psychiatric asylum. She hadn't come home since.

Buck comforted Annemarie when she started to cry. Now he realized why she had been so happy to see him. He and his fellow Americans had liberated her from the people who had destroyed her mother. The realization made Buck feel better about the sacrifices he'd witnessed.

Maybe they were for something after all?

The young couple rebounded quickly from the sad story of Annemarie's mother and returned to the party. They had each other now to rely on.

Someone rapped heavily on the front door, silencing the partygoers.

One of Annemarie's aunts went downstairs to investigate. She returned in a hurry. Three American MPs had arrived to search the house. Buck cursed. Under the nonfraternization policy they could bust him for "cohabitation" with a German woman. The punishment was a fine of $65, which was $5 more than his monthly salary.

But there was a way out.

Annemarie followed as her father quietly led Buck and Janicki to a fire escape at the rear of the house. It was almost dark outside. Everyone had lost track of time. Buck paused to steal one last moment with Annemarie as her father and Janicki descended the fire escape. She kissed him quickly.

"You'll come back?" she asked.

Buck knew it was unlikely that he'd see her again at this decisive juncture of the war. But he didn't want Annemarie to think he would abandon her by choice.

"I will, someday," he said.

Tears streamed down Annemarie's face, but she understood. Their time together was spent. Buck's hand slipped from hers before he climbed down the fire escape.

Back on the ground, he found Janicki and Annemarie's father searching for the motorcycle. It had disappeared from the alleyway. The MPs must have found it, triggering their search of the house.

After bidding Annemarie's father farewell, the doughs took off running, following the dark streets back toward the cathedral. Buck looked repeatedly over his shoulder.

The city was much more menacing at night than it was during the day.

"I'm sorry I fixed that motorcycle up," Janicki said at one point.

"I'm not," Buck said. "I just wish we went earlier."

The duo was halfway through an intersection when an American voice yelled, "Halt!"

Buck and Janicki froze. They had stumbled upon a checkpoint. There was probably a .30-caliber machine gun aimed at them from a corner building, with a trigger-happy GI ready to light up the intersection.

The American gave the sign of the day, then waited for the intruders to give the countersign.

"We don't know your signs!" Buck shouted. His voice was unmistakable, high and Southern. A pair of GIs approached with flashlights. They wore patches of the Timberwolves Division, green disks with the silver head of a wolf, on their sleeves. The Timberwolves had taken the southern half of the city and apparently their lines had shifted northward. Buck explained the situation and the astounded GIs gave a laugh before letting them proceed.

After five hours on foot, Buck and Janicki slipped into the air-raid shelter sometime after midnight. Safe in the warm bunker, they regaled their buddies with tales of how they had survived at least five checkpoints. The stories screeched to a stop when their squad leader barged into the room.

"Sorry, fellas," he said, "but I had to report you as 'missing.'" The report was already with the company clerk and would be in the officers' hands by morning.

Janicki nearly collapsed with anguish, and Buck knew why: his friend's promotion—the ticket home to his wife—was in jeopardy.

Heads would roll.

Several days later

Clarence moved slowly through the back streets as he made his way back to the tank. Contrary to the menacing nature of Cologne at night, the deserted streets seemed innocuous in the light of midmorning.

Whenever he wasn't on duty, Clarence went wandering through the city like a tourist.

Once, he had returned with a dagger that he found in a train-station locker. Another time, he came back with a charcoal portrait of himself under his arm. A GI artist was sketching Cologne and drew Clarence with the iconic cathedral in the background. The portrait wasn't flattering—Clarence looked forlorn in his depiction—but he bought the sketch anyway.

Where he had roamed that day has been long forgotten, but when he turned a corner near the train station, he knew immediately that he was in trouble. At this point, he had to hold his course. There was no going back.

At least five young German boys and girls—all under the age of twelve—were sitting on the staircase of a ruined building. The kids perked up at the sight of an American soldier.

A young woman watched over them from the front doorstep. Clarence didn't think she was their mother; she was too young to have that many children already. Some of the children were probably orphans.

The kids flocked to Clarence's side. He wasn't surprised by the attention—this happened everywhere a GI went in Cologne. The kids kept pace with him and tugged his sleeve, begging him for bubble gum. Clarence cringed. He wasn't supposed to talk with them. Even contact with children was forbidden under the fraternization ban, and on top of that there were the health risks.

Typhus was spreading through Cologne's lice-ridden air-raid shelters, medical clinics, and even an entire neighborhood north of the city. American troops had been warned that "all civilians are potential carriers of typhus fever and other communicable diseases."

But the kids were relentless.

Clarence stopped and searched his pockets while the kids bounced with excitement. He pitied them. They were pale from living underground, having spent more of their lives in wartime than he had. Their eyes hinted at a psychological trauma that Clarence couldn't imagine.

"The fear of airpower is so deep in them that you will see little children with their heads buried in their mothers' aprons shuddering, or peeping fearfully up at the terrible skies," wrote a reporter.

Clarence's childhood hadn't always been easy, but he'd never worried for his life.

The only things Clarence had in his pockets were cigarettes, and he couldn't share those with children. He squatted down to the kids' level and broke the bad news to them in German. "I'm sorry, guys, but I don't have any gum."

The kids' faces sank, but they weren't buying it. Certainly every American soldier carried gum. Thinking that Clarence was holding out on them, they turned on the charm even more.

Clarence directed the kids toward the young woman, asking her to explain things to them. But before he could clear up the situation, the throb of an engine drew everyone's attention. An American jeep slowly turned the corner.

Clarence cursed under his breath. The jeep pulled over and two MPs hopped out. Full of fear, the children bolted to the young woman's side.

An MP sergeant approached Clarence and opened his pad. He eyed the 3rd Armored Division patch on Clarence's sleeve, triangular with yellow, red, and blue sectors, and asked for Clarence's documents.

Clarence tried to make his case, but the MPs weren't buying his explanation. They'd caught him red-handed talking to a German mother with at least five kids tugging at his sleeves. It was an open-and-shut case. The sergeant recorded his name and serial number before announcing that Clarence was getting reported for fraternization.

Satisfied that they'd done their duty, the MPs drove away.

The kids were still watching from behind the young woman. Clarence gave them a little wave and resumed his trek. There were worse fates that could have befallen him. The fine wouldn't pinch his pocket too badly. He had been warned and he had learned his lesson. It was just embarrassing for a former candy salesman.

Next time he came back this way, he wouldn't be caught without a few packs of gum.

Soon after, stateside

The postal carrier dropped mail through the slot of a two-story home in suburban Kansas City. A slender, gray-haired woman picked it up.

Hattie Pearl Miller's quiet eyes hid behind wire-rim glasses. Raising Chuck and his six siblings had aged her far beyond her fifty-seven years, but she still wore cheerful floral dresses when she did her seamstress work from home.

Hattie Miller

A devout Methodist, Hattie prayed often. To honor her sons' sacrifices, she kept their photos above the fireplace—Chuck in his army green and his older brother, William, in the tropical uniform of the Army Air Forces.

Among the ordinary mail, one envelope in particular drew Hattie's attention. It bore the return address of her sister, Beth, who lived in Washington, D.C. Inside was a newspaper clipping from *The Washington Post* accompanied by a short, handwritten note: "Is this our Chuck?"

A quick glance at the clipping gave Hattie cause to fret. "Nazi Tanks Excel Ours, Troops Say," the headline declared above a photo of a smoldering Sherman tank. Chuck had hoped that his mother would be proud when she saw his name in the article by Ann Stringer, but instead, the story terrified her.

"Don't talk about the superiority of American tanks to men of this Third Armored unit," Stringer had written. She went on to describe the slaughter at Blatzheim, observing, "In one field alone, this company lost half its tanks."

Hattie might have cried as she read the quotes from Earley, Villa, and her son, disparaging their Sherman tanks, but she never admitted this to Chuck. She wasn't the only one dismayed by the news. Eisenhower sent an inquiry to General Rose to ask if the claims were true, and Rose had backed up his tankers. But by then, the damage was done. The story had been syndicated from coast to coast and the families of countless tankers were shocked by the headlines.

"American Tanks Not Worth Drop of Water, Crews Say."

"U.S. Tanks No Good in Battle, Say Crewmen After Losing Half of M-4 Machines."

"American Tanks No Good, Assert Troops in Reich."

But there was a curious sidebar in the clipping that Hattie held. To counter the negative fallout from Stringer's article and any public outcry, the army had rushed forth an announcement of a new American "Super Tank." It was a machine that the assistant secretary of war called "one of the strongest weapons of the war . . . the most powerful tank we have ever built."

The Pershing.

The juxtaposition was strange—a blurb hailing a new tank within a story disparaging the older models. But whatever a Pershing was, it offered a glimmer of hope for the distraught families back home.

Hattie set aside the clipping. The article had said that Chuck was in Cologne. She opened an atlas and located the city on the Rhine. Chuck was still a long way from Berlin. Hattie was no military tactician, but the map spoke volumes. There was only one direction that her son could travel—deeper into the heart of Nazi Germany.

She would pray for Chuck and the boys, and prepare herself for more news she didn't want to hear. If things were as bad as Stringer's story suggested—half the tanks lost in one field—the worst might be yet to come.

CHAPTER 19 **THE BREAKOUT**

About a week later
Fischenich, Germany, five miles south of Cologne

The scent of the Rhine was in the air. It finally felt like spring.

The men of Easy Company were lounging at their tanks in a small, grassy field fenced in by trees. It was morning, but the time of day didn't matter. While other GIs were swimming, fishing, and kayaking in the Rhine's cold waters, Easy Company was holding a riverside party. Almost everyone was drinking. Some drank from canteen cups. Some straight from the bottle. Tankers strolled past to shoot the breeze and offer their fellow crews refills.

Between halfhearted attempts at maintenance, Clarence, DeRiggi, and the crew were imbibing around the Pershing . . . all except for Earley. It was possible that he was the only sober man left in the field. There was no telling how long this party would last. Wooden crates full of alcohol—the spoils of Cologne—were lashed to their tanks' engine decks. But Earley would let his platoon enjoy the downtime while they could.

Cologne had not been the end of the road that many hoped it would be. American troops had already crossed the Rhine at Remagen, and soon it would be Spearhead's turn. "Most of the tankers and infantry-men, as much as they hated combat, would have felt left out of the party if the division was indeed pulled out of action," the 3rd Armored unit history observed. "These men had been the first team of the First Army since Normandy. They were the first through the

Westwall, the first to take and hold a German town. The 3rd had a reputation."

A tank crew from B-Company drifted through the gathering, searching for Clarence. The tank's driver, Harley Swenson, and his gunner, Phil Dest, had something to say. Back in Cologne, they had been one of the Stuart crews ordered to prepare for a mad dash to the Rhine. They were certain that if it hadn't been for Clarence, the Panther would have killed them. They assured Clarence that he had saved their lives, and for this, they were forever grateful.

Clarence was uncomfortable with the attention. He didn't feel he had truly bested the Panther as everyone thought. He had run through countless scenarios, but still couldn't figure out why the German gunner had held his fire. "I didn't save your lives," Clarence joked with the Stuart crew. "I saved my life and yours were along for the ride!"

The Stuart crew laughed as they raised their glasses in his honor, and Clarence grudgingly accepted their tribute. He wasn't about to spoil their celebration by revealing the truth about the Panther: he had just gotten lucky.

Later that morning, a jeep pulled up next to the Pershing.

"Smoyer?" the enlisted driver behind the wheel asked.

Clarence ambled forward. Captain Salisbury wanted to see him.

"Oh, shit," Clarence said. How was he going to fake sobriety in front of the captain?

Earley thrust a canteen of water into Clarence's hand and made him chug the contents.

Clarence racked his foggy mind, trying to discern why the captain had summoned him. It couldn't have anything to do with Stringer's newspaper story—he hadn't sounded off to the reporter. It had to be something else.

"Don't talk any more than you have to," Earley advised.

Clarence dropped into the jeep's passenger seat and gave a sloppy salute.

This wouldn't be pretty.

• • •

An aide ushered Clarence into Salisbury's office on the first floor of a German farmhouse.

The captain sat behind his desk, sipping a drink as he scribbled away on paperwork. He had just returned from Paris, with his curly hair neatly clipped and his uniform meticulously pressed.

Clarence saluted and remained standing uneasily. The floor felt like a boat's deck on the Rhine.

Salisbury looked up. His commanding stare fixed squarely on Clarence. "I never realized what a great gunner you were until you knocked those chimneys off," he said, referencing the firing demonstration in Stolberg. "It made me proud."

Clarence breathed a deep sigh of relief. He wasn't in trouble after all.

"Then you got that Panther in Cologne and you did the unit proud," Salisbury added. The captain informed Clarence that Lieutenant Stillman had recommended him for the Bronze Star.

Clarence was shocked and honored.

Salisbury took a written report from the desk and waved it in front of Clarence.

"And then you go and do this."

Clarence's mind raced. *What did I do?*

Salisbury read the MP's report, which detailed how he had caught Clarence fraternizing with a German woman and her kids. Clarence couldn't believe his ears. After he had led Easy Company up to the doorstep of Blatzheim and across the apocalyptic cityscape of Cologne, the captain was holding a trivial offense against him?

He tried to explain himself, but to no avail. Salisbury was unmoved by his defense.

"I can fine you," he said, "or give you KP."

The dreaded Kitchen Police.

Clarence's blood began boiling. Being assigned to the potato peelers in the rear of the formation was supposed to be a punishment. It was intended to be emasculating and degrading.

Clarence couldn't bottle it up any longer. "Sir, KP sounds like a vacation to me."

Salisbury was blindsided by Clarence's display of defiance. He reminded Clarence that they'd given his crew the best tank in the battalion. They were *lucky* to have the Pershing.

Clarence couldn't let that go. Earley, DeRiggi, Smokey, and McVey never had a chance to be candid with their captain, so he would speak for them all.

"Yeah, and because of it we're always the first over the goddamn hill," Clarence said. "Whenever we turn a corner, we don't know if it's going to be our last."

Salisbury held himself back. He couldn't afford a rift with his top gunner, not when the company was days from crossing the Rhine. And having spoken his mind, Clarence remembered his place. Salisbury was still his company commander.

"Sir," Clarence said calmly, "one of these days we're going to end up dead in a ditch."

Salisbury's stance softened. He asked if Clarence would like a transfer to another crew in the rear. After all he'd done, he deserved a breather. Salisbury was offering Clarence nothing short of survival.

"I'll stay up front with the guys," Clarence said. He would never leave his family, even if it meant saving himself. He told Salisbury that it would be nice if there were a few more Pershings, so the crews could take turns leading the way.

Salisbury agreed. The Pershing would be in demand, now more than ever. The Germans had retreated from Cologne, ceding the territory to save their forces for the next round of fighting.

"There's a big drive coming," Salisbury said, "that's all I can tell you." He crumpled the MP's report, threw it in the trash, and told Clarence to go sober up.

Clarence saluted, but didn't even attempt a turn on his heels. There was no way that he could execute it in his current state.

He had just talked himself out of a Bronze Star, but that wasn't as important as what he'd achieved. He had spoken for the crew. Even if nothing changed, the captain had heard them, loud and clear.

Clarence had made sure of that.

About a week later, March 26, 1945

A spring shower fell that morning as the armored column raced through the misty forest.

The Pershing set the pace.

It was late in the morning, approaching noon. Doughs clad in ponchos rode the Pershing and every tank behind it as Task Force X sped along a dirt road near Altenkirchen, traveling deeper into Germany. Already the column was more than fourteen miles east of the Rhine.

The bridgehead breakout was under way.

Three days earlier, Spearhead had made the leap across the Rhine and by now the First Army, the Third Army, the Ninth Army, and the British forces under Field Marshal Montgomery had all crossed the sacred river. Everyone was gunning to beat the Red Army to Hitler's doorstep.

"This was the beginning of the big push," the 3rd Armored history recorded. "There was victory in the air and it was contagious." The mood was so ebullient that a new slogan emerged: "Berlin or Bust!"

From above the Pershing's turret, Earley and DeRiggi kept a watchful eye on their surroundings. In the bow, McVey drove with his hatch open.

The men were soaking wet from riding in the rain, but had no choice about it. Frustrating columns of drizzle leaked down the tanks' periscopes, distorting any view from the interior.

The forest they were passing through was foggy and mysterious, undulating with rocky rises and deep gullies. Cold black streams gushed with snowmelt as winter thawed. Abandoned Reich Labor Service camps were deteriorating in clearings.

Some tankers wondered, why hadn't the Germans built the West Wall here? If they had, this region would have been unconquerable.

When vertical white sticks appeared by the roadside, Clarence sounded the alarm. They were approaching an intersection. The chain reaction reverberated through the column as the Pershing slowed. Clarence checked both approaches before the tank went forward. The day before they had blasted through a four-way intersection without looking before they leaped. Parked in the woods to their right, a German self-propelled gun was lurking in the shadows, its barrel wrapped in foliage.

Luckily, Earley spotted the vehicle before it was too late, and Clarence sprang into action. He swung the tank's gun around and blasted the vehicle through the flank, setting it afire.

The self-propelled gun had the sloped front of a Jagdpanther or Jagdpanzer, either of which could be lethal to a Pershing. The enemy crew may have been distracted or had already abandoned the vehicle, but that wasn't the point.

Clarence and his crew had almost fallen victim to the curse of the lead tank. "Sooner or later somebody is going to get the first shot," he told Earley, "and we're not going to be around here anymore."

Earley agreed. But what could they do? The lead tank would always be the first target.

It was a bitter pill for Clarence to swallow. *It's just a matter of time.*

By noon, the column was back to speeding.

A Sherman drove behind the Pershing, its engine deck laden with doughs. Janicki and his fire team rode with their legs dangling over the sides. In a battle zone like this, they left the half-tracks behind since tanks allowed for a quicker, more nimble egress to confront any threats.

Janicki was miserable. He and the rest of the fire team wore their poncho hoods under their helmets. Rain dripped from their brims, which made it hard to see. And it wasn't just the awful weather. The higher-ups had torn away his stripes for breaking curfew and rescinded his promotion to half-track driver. He was right back to fighting on foot. But he never blamed Buck—the motorcycle had been his idea alone.

Buck hadn't gotten in trouble at all. He was already the low man on the totem pole and couldn't be demoted any further. Instead, Lieutenant Boom awarded Buck a pass to a rest facility in Viviers, France. He was there now, enjoying three days of hot food, clean sheets, and all the motion pictures he could watch.

Janicki and the rest of the squad were envious. But everyone knew Buck deserved it. As first scout, he'd kept them safe on the road to Cologne and in the city itself. They'd rely on him again—if he could catch up to the unit after his vacation.

The road ahead curved to the right to avoid a rocky rise in the forest. Earley raised his binoculars as the Pershing made the swing.

About one hundred yards ahead, a log roadblock stretched across their path. It was a disconcerting sight in the otherwise empty woods.

Earley halted the column to assess the situation. Only three or four tanks had made the turn. The rest were still somewhere behind the bend.

Clarence took aim and set his reticle on the logs. This was doable. He could blast through them. DeRiggi just needed to replace the armor-piercing shell that was in the breech with a high-explosive round. Clarence called for a shell change.

No reply came from DeRiggi.

Clarence glanced across the turret to see what his loader was doing.

DeRiggi was standing head and shoulders above his hatch, studying the curious roadblock. So were Earley and the doughs from three or four other tanks. And all the while, the enemy was watching them.

High atop the rocky rise, eight German antiaircraft trucks were parked end to end in the misty drizzle. A gun crew stood around a Flak 38 cannon in each truck bed.

The gunners swung their cannons toward the American column below. Their round gun sights were meant for targeting an aircraft's wingspan, but these were not planes. Their 20mm explosive shells wouldn't penetrate the tanks' armor, but that wasn't their target now either.

Tank crews were visible outside their turrets and doughs were just sitting there with their legs dangling over the edge.

The cannons' rhythmic thumping split the air as the German gunners stomped their firing pedals.

Inside the Pershing, Clarence shrank in his seat as a flurry of shells shattered against the turret. Earley ducked inside and slammed the hatch just in time, but DeRiggi wasn't quick enough. The loader fell to the turret floor amid a spray of crimson, writhing and clutching his face. His blood sprayed the white interior and his screams competed with the crackle of splitting shells that streamed inside from his open hatch.

Clarence rose to help his friend, but Earley stopped him. "Stay on the gun!"

Earley unplugged his helmet from the intercom and moved to the loader's side.

. . .

Directly in the line of fire, Janicki and the doughs didn't stand a chance.

A rain of glowing red shells the size of golf balls came down on them. Explosions rippled across the tank's flank. Doughs pressed themselves flat against the engine deck, but the shrapnel found them anyway.

The sizzling steel pierced a smoking hole in De La Torre's boot and lodged in another man's hip. A direct hit landed against Janicki's left leg in a flash of sparks and a haze of blood. When Janicki looked down, his left leg was hanging by a thread below the knee.

Many men would have given up and simply lain there, waiting to die, but Janicki was a fighter. Clutching his wounded leg, he rolled away from the fire with the others, across the blistering engine deck and over the side of the tank.

It wasn't his day to die.

It was all too much for the driver of the third tank in line. Doughs were being swept from the tanks ahead of him as the fire slanted down over them.

In a panic, the driver floored the throttle and his Sherman took off like an unbridled horse as it careened through the formation.

On the engine deck, Byron Mitchell—Squad 3/2's master looter—and his fire team held on to the runaway tank for dear life. They went left around one Sherman, then right around the Pershing, before skidding off the road and slamming sidelong into a tree. Doughs went flying head over heels, except for one unfortunate man who found himself pinned between the tank and the tree by his ankle.

When the Sherman reversed, the dough dropped to the ground, his ankle crushed.

Inside the Pershing, Earley desperately wrestled with DeRiggi in a furious attempt to save his loader's life. DeRiggi was thrashing and Earley was trying to stick him with a syrette of morphine.

Shrapnel had torn a hole in the side of DeRiggi's face. Between spurts of blood, his crewmates could see his teeth. DeRiggi's screams tortured the others. Clarence's chest heaved. His friend was bleeding out, but there was no space on the loader's side for a third person, and even if there had been room for him, there was nothing he could do.

Earley had shut the loader's hatch in the turret ceiling, but the steady cadence of shell bursts against the armor sounded like someone was trying to break in using a sledgehammer. Clarence had to act. And there was only one way he knew to help.

He swung the turret toward the thumping sounds and elevated his gun. Through the streaky periscope his view rose from the roadside up the wall of rock, but stopped short of the top.

Clarence cursed. The gun couldn't elevate enough to see the enemy.

A cacophony of fast-talking voices filled his earphones. Commanders in the rear were alarmed about what was happening up front. Meanwhile, panicked commanders in the front wanted to regroup in the rear. Voices overlapped and talked past one another. No one had a shot at the enemy and men were suffering. Five tankers had head wounds and ten doughs were injured, the majority with leg wounds. They had to get the injured men to safety.

Salisbury called for a fighting retreat. The lead tanks would reverse and provide a moving wall of cover for the doughs.

Clarence alerted Earley—they had the green light to ferry DeRiggi to safety, but Earley had his hands full.

"Tank's yours," Earley shouted. "Get us out of here."

Clarence leaped to the commander's position, plugged into the intercom, and stood to see what was behind him using a periscope. The Shermans that had been following were already rolling backward, so there was space to move.

Clarence summoned a calm voice and called for a reverse. Without a rearview mirror, McVey would steer blind. Clarence told him to go steady. He would be his eyes.

Byron and four doughs hugged the dirt in a roadside ditch as the flaming golf balls cut the air and shattered trees behind them.

The runaway tank had left their fire team stranded far ahead of the column.

Everyone else had retreated. Tanks had rolled back the way they'd come, firing blindly toward the rise, and the rest of A-Company had gone with them, dragging Janicki away by his suspenders.

Now, Byron and his fire team were isolated, just the five of them. And the Germans knew it. The enemy fire came to a sizzling stop, which could only mean one thing—some of them were coming down from the rise to eliminate any resistance. The fire team was left with one sane option: surrender. But even that presented its challenges.

Byron removed his jacket and opened his sleeve to reveal a wrist full of German watches. He began loosening them one by one before sliding them up and under his shirt sleeve to hide them.

Carrier, the dough from backwoods Kentucky, somehow found humor in this predicament. With an unsettling grin on his moon-shaped face, he removed his holster. Carrier had taken the collar tab from an SS prisoner and pinned it to his holster as a war trophy.

If any SS man saw those silver runes now, the holster would be a death sentence. Carrier tucked the holster against the dough with the shattered ankle. Revolted, the wounded dough passed it back, which led Carrier to shove the holster toward another man. But it came straight back to him, like a twisted game of hot potato.

Carrier tried to tear off the collar tab, but the pin wouldn't budge. So he opened the holster and tried to bite the pin's silver stud in half with his teeth. When that failed, he buried the holster beneath the leaves and hoped for the best.

A handful of German soldiers approached cautiously from across the road while their comrades covered them from the rise. Their rifles were leveled toward the stranded Americans.

One of the doughs was waving something white—a handkerchief or T-shirt—the undisputed sign of surrender.

And then came an error of war. The American column had fallen back in the forest, but they hadn't retreated so far that they couldn't watch over the road. A machine gun barked as a burst of orange tracers zipped across the road from the left. The Germans scattered. Byron and the others dived for the ditch to take cover.

The dough leaned from the ditch and waved his flag more furiously. The gunner must have seen him because the firing ceased. Was it a rear guard of doughs or a trigger-happy tank gunner? No one remembers. Either way, it was too late. Several dead Germans lay in the road.

Even Carrier stopped grinning.

The Germans marched the prisoners to their headquarters, a farmhouse in a forest clearing.

The dough with the shattered ankle hobbled with his arms draped over his buddies' shoulders. The enemy jabbed and prodded the Americans with their rifles along the way.

The Germans were fuming. They paraded the Americans to the side of the farmhouse before throwing shovels at their feet and instructing them to dig. Their comrades had been lured to their deaths by the false promise of a white flag. Someone had to pay.

Byron and the others knew there was no need for foxholes alongside a house; the placement offered no field of fire. A stretch like this was only suited for one thing—graves.

The German soldiers eyed the doughs' progress. The holes were nearly deep and wide enough to hold bodies.

The Germans' trigger fingers were getting itchy. Gunfire was thundering from the forest and their fellow troops were walking and riding past the farmhouse in retreat. The ambush had delayed the Americans for only so long.

A throaty snarl drew everyone's attention—prisoners and guards alike. A camouflaged German tank rumbled by the farmhouse. From atop the turret, the commander eyed the shoveling prisoners and spoke into his microphone. The tank stopped abruptly.

The commander climbed down and stormed toward the Americans and their captors. Shovels froze in midair. The commander's face was tight with rage. He grabbed a fistful of the nearest German guard and pulled the man aside. It didn't take a course in German to understand his blistering screams.

"Yes, but did *they* shoot your men?"

After the commander finished lecturing his fellow soldiers, the doughs were instructed to put down their shovels. The newly humbled German guards steered the Americans into the farmhouse. Byron gave one last glance before he disappeared inside and saw the German tank commander watching the guards with folded arms, a clear look of disappointment on his face.

The German tank gave a grunt and departed. The guards vacated the house. Lift gates slammed shut and the trucks carried them away, leaving the Americans unfettered.

Soon, new vehicles could be heard, pulling up and idling outside the farmhouse. The engine rattle was familiar, but the doughs didn't dare stir from the floor.

A boot kicked the door open and a man stepped inside with a weapon in his hand and the patch of the 3rd Armored Division on his sleeve.

The doughs erupted with outpourings of relief.

They had lived to tell the tale.

CHAPTER 20 **THE AMERICAN BLITZ**

Three days later, March 29, 1945
About fifty miles farther east

The pack of Spearhead vehicles stretched along the highway for as far as the eye could see.

Tank after tank, half-track after half-track, more than 150 vehicles were all headed in the same direction, north of Marburg, Germany. "This show looked like the beginning of the last rat race in Europe," noted one GI.

Near the middle of the convoy, the Pershing's crew drove unbuttoned, with their faces buffeted by the wind. It was midmorning and they had been on the go since six A.M.

The concrete below the tanks was slick from a recent rain. Ominous storm clouds still lingered in the sky, with only meager cracks of blue sky shining through. The crew rode with their goggles lowered as the convoy roamed through broad valleys bordered by evergreen forests, past hunters' tree stands and a crumbling castle. The familiar scenery reminded some men of their hometowns back in Wisconsin and Minnesota.

McVey followed the Sherman ahead while Smokey took in the sights like a tourist. Easy Company's Task Force X had relinquished the lead position for a change and was tagging along behind Task Force Welborn, which was named for its colonel, Jack Welborn.

Atop the turret, Earley occupied one hatch. Clarence stood in the other, having convinced the replacement loader to share his perch. A white silk scarf fluttered from Clarence's neck. He had found a parachute hung up in a tree and fashioned it into a scarf, perfect for a moment like this. Standing there in a tanker's orchestra of howling motors, Clarence couldn't help but grin. He was relishing the speed of the formation, a sensation only possible when no one was shooting at him. And there was something else that sent his spirits soaring.

There was the feat that they were attempting.

Spearhead had punched more than sixty miles east of the Rhine as of that morning—well into enemy territory—before the order came to hit the brakes. Eisenhower's headquarters had its mandate to end the war by targeting "the heart of Germany." But where exactly would that be? There were two candidates: Berlin and the Ruhr Valley.

Capturing Berlin before the Russians would be a symbolic, political coup, whereas the Ruhr, known as "Germany's Detroit," would represent a strategic military victory. The Ruhr was the source of 80 percent of Germany's coal and 66 percent of its steel. If they could isolate the Ruhr from the rest of Germany, the enemy's war machine would starve.

Given its strategic importance, the choice was clear.

The higher-ups issued new orders and at first light Spearhead made a ninety-degree turn to the north to make another of its legendary mad dashes.

But this time, they wouldn't be charging into trouble alone.

As the 3rd Armored plowed north, the 2nd Armored, Hell on Wheels, would cut across Germany's northern flatlands and swing south. With luck, the army's two heavy armored divisions would link up near the German town of Paderborn to "slip a steel wall around the great industrial Ruhr," an accomplishment that would send a blunt message to Berlin: *It's over.*

There was just one hiccup: getting there.

Depending on the route, Paderborn lay more than one hundred miles away. To pull off the link-up, Spearhead would have to make one of the longest, fastest drives of the war, an American "blitz," behind enemy lines the whole time. But if it worked, it would deliver what the division called "a haymaker to the heart of Germany."

So General Rose spread Spearhead across four parallel roads and set a course for Paderborn. As his division rolled forth, Rose radioed

CLOSING THE RUHR POCKET

the task force commanders to offer a bounty: "One case of Scotch for dead or alive Guderian, Himmler, Kesselring, or Dietrich—one bottle for Hitler."

Rose issued the challenge over unsecured radio channels in hopes that the dispatch would be intercepted by the Germans and the words carried back to Berlin.

He wanted Hitler, himself, to hear the voice of Spearhead.

The gunner's seat felt stiffer by the hour. Eventually, Clarence sought comfort by sitting on the turret floor. There was nothing new to see outside anyway, just the tail ends of an endless parade of Shermans.

On the other side of the breech rode a short, dark-haired kid named Mathews, who had been brought in to replace DeRiggi. Clarence liked him already. He was quiet and capable, although he lacked DeRiggi's pluck.

"Johnny Boy" had survived, that was all the crew had heard after they laid him into a ditch where medics were caring for the wounded. Clarence hoped he'd see his loader again.

To pass the time on the way to Paderborn, Clarence reread his mail. The words bounced on the page before his eyes as the floor vibrated beneath him. One particular letter from his mother brought a smile to Clarence's face every time.

At the urging of friends and family, his parents had gone to the movies. His mother had worn her best dress and his father had ditched his laborer's jacket and boots in favor of a suit. They went to the theater specifically to see the newsreels that ran before the main feature.

And there they saw Clarence and had never been so proud.

The Bates film that showed the Pershing's duel with the Panther was everywhere. Theaters across America were showing the gritty tank battle, transporting audiences closer to the fighting than they'd ever been before. It culminated with a steady pan of the Pershing crew, which featured Clarence standing in the middle, staring impassively at the camera.

Bates would later receive the Bronze Star, in large part for his film work in Cologne. Earley would receive one too, for taking down the Panther, and so would Clarence's friend Joe Caserta, for tossing burning musette bags—lit by passing tracers—off his turret during a firefight. Clarence knew that no such award was in the cards for him, but he was okay with that.

He was simply amazed at what his parents had done in order to see him on the big screen. They'd gone to the movies for the first time in their lives.

Buck Marsh was back from his sojourn in France. He sat beside the driver in a half-track behind Easy Company, fiddling with a single-burner stove that he'd set on the floor to hard-boil some eggs.

Buck had rejoined the squad a day after the forest ambush.

Four seats that had been occupied when Buck had last seen his buddies now stood empty in the passenger compartment behind him. Janicki—his left leg destined for amputation—was on his way to England. De La Torre and two others were still in a field hospital recovering from their injuries. Meanwhile, Byron and Carrier were telling the story of a German tank commander who had spared their lives to anyone who would listen.

"We were lucky he was a good guy," said Byron, who seldom had much to say.

Buck found solace in the lone bright spot to emerge from an awful situation. At least Janicki was going home to his wife.

Scalding water leaped from the pan as the half-track swayed back and forth. Buck and the squad leader, who stood in the gun ring, lifted their legs to avoid the hot splatter, but the driver had to keep one foot on the gas.

He yowled as a splash of hot water landed on his pant leg.

"You all better like those eggs," he shouted, "I'm getting scalded up here!"

"Oh, stop," Buck said. "You're the one hitting the bumps!"

The whole squad snickered. The driver was lucky that this was the worst wound he could possibly get.

As the convoy plunged deeper into the wild that afternoon, the tension steadily mounted.

Through his periscope, Clarence kept an eye out for any and all potential threats. No one had taken a shot at Easy Company yet, which meant it was only a matter of time before someone did.

From the front of the convoy came the occasional clap of American guns and soon after, the results drifted past Clarence's sight. A vehicle burning by the side of the road. A handful of German prisoners heading in the opposite direction, searching for someone who would take their surrender. At the fearsome sight of the convoy, most German soldiers scattered from their guard posts. They were astonished to behold American armor so far from the Rhine.

The radio suddenly buzzed to life with alarm: a tank commander had spotted movement in the pine forest to the right of Easy Company.

Brake lights flashed from half-tracks as the entire convoy slowed. A company's worth of tank turrets turned in unison toward the threat.

Clarence took indiscriminate aim at the tree line, which stood a field's length from the road. Nestled deep in the shadows of the forest, dark shapes were paralleling the column.

Earley gave a range estimate as Clarence hovered his thumb over the machine-gun trigger. The reticle bobbed with the tank's motion, as if the machine itself were breathing.

The dark shapes burst forth from the trees. As they charged the convoy, they took the form of a bounding herd of deer.

Clarence lifted his thumb away from the trigger. *They're just deer!*

But other gunners didn't hesitate as the deer bounded right at them.

Tracers converged on the defenseless herd as every gunner for a mile opened fire. Deer crashed to their knees or cartwheeled across the ground. Spooked out of their senses, the herd split, with some veering toward the road, and others back to the tree line.

A few tanks in front of Clarence, Chuck Miller tracked a fleet-footed pair of deer. They were approaching the road faster than his turret could turn. After months of tasteless rations, he had venison on the brain.

Chuck moved his foot off the trigger as a half-track of doughs slid into his line of sight.

Damn!

The deer pranced between the vehicles and kept running. They were seemingly in the clear until several doughs stood in the half-track and raised their rifles to their shoulders. A quick fusillade of bullets sent both deer tumbling. Chuck gave a joyful shout.

The convoy ground to an abrupt halt. The voices of officers yelling at one another crackled over the radio. They were assessing whether an enemy force had flushed the deer from the woods.

There was still time to salvage the impromptu hunt. Chuck leaped from his seat and his baldheaded commander, Red Villa, made way for him to exit the turret. Summoning a fellow crewman's help, Chuck darted to the fallen deer. They were met by doughs with the same idea. The men struck a quick bargain.

When the convoy set in motion again, a dead deer was lashed to the Sherman's engine deck. For the first time in a long time, Easy Company would eat like kings.

As the convoy pushed farther into enemy territory, pit stops were a necessity.

When the column halted, men rushed the fields to answer the call of nature while MPs hammered signs to remind anyone who followed not to stray far—"Jerries cleared to the edge of the road."

Supply trucks raced from the rear of the formation to deposit five-gallon cans of gas alongside each vehicle.

Clarence took his place on the engine deck, lifting the forty-pound gas cans from his buddies' hands. The tanks were thirsty. The Pershing managed a half mile to the gallon while a Sherman got about a mile to the gallon, depending on the model.

Although they were gas guzzlers, the American tanks had reliability on their side. Up and down the column, few tanks, if any, fell from formation. The Pershing was too new to know its limits, but the average Sherman kept ticking for more than 2,000 miles with only minimal maintenance.

Whenever Clarence returned to the turret after a pit stop, Earley seemed to be poring over the exact same piece of mail—a "Dear John" letter that his girlfriend had sent him. But no matter how many times he read the letter, the message didn't change. She had found someone else, another man who hadn't gone away like he had. Earley was heartbroken.

Clarence would take his seat and pretend that he didn't notice. It was a conversation that he had never had and didn't know how to handle.

Clarence's sister regiment, the 33rd Armored Regiment, was positioned at the spearhead of Task Force Welborn. As one crew were stretching their legs, a jeep pulled up beside their Sherman.

Corporal John Irwin, a rookie gunner, saw an unfamiliar figure in the jeep's passenger seat.

"He had a crew cut, stiff graying hair, a serious, handsome face, and a big frame," Irwin recalled. "He looked up at us and touched a forefinger to his brow in salute and said, 'My helmet's off to you men—keep it up!'" Irwin still had no idea who the man was until his buddies razzed him for not recognizing General Rose.

Rose was beaming for a reason. His division was on the verge of driving farther in a single day than any other unit in military history.

· · ·

The lights of the column rolled headlong into the chilly darkness as night fell over the German countryside.

Chuck Miller dozed in his seat to the soft lullaby of the tank's engine. As Chuck slept, his driver followed the thin blackout taillights of the Sherman now ahead of him.

Under the cover of darkness, any trace of violence was magnified. The smell of burning wood preceded a spectacle of destruction as the convoy rolled past. "The plains and valleys were dotted with burning villages set ablaze by tank shells when foolish German soldiers offered some resistance from houses," recorded one war reporter.

In the headquarters section, a jeep's headlights swept across a German staff car sitting by the side of the road. The corpses of two enemy officers sat upright in the car's backseat. They had both been beheaded by .50-caliber bullets.

From the turret of Chuck's Sherman, Red Villa caught sight of headlights approaching from the rear. Puttering sounds emanated from the dark. The sounds and lights drew closer as three motorcycles emerged from the shadows. They kept pace with the Sherman before accelerating and pulling ahead of the tank.

As the motorcycles drove through the tank's thin headlight beam, Villa nearly leaped from the turret. The motorcycle riders wore gray rubberized trench coats and German helmets.

Villa shook Chuck awake and shouted, "Eleven o'clock!"

Chuck swung the cannon leftward but didn't see anything through his periscope, just darkness.

"Thirty-caliber," Villa said. "Fire, right where you are!"

The machine gun's bright flame blinded Chuck as he stood on the trigger. Glowing tracers zipped into the dark and momentarily illuminated a slice of the road, the tank ahead, and the German motorcyclist bringing up the rear.

Chuck had aimed too high, but it was enough to get the job done.

A shower of sparks burst at ground level as the motorcyclist spun out. He hadn't been hit, but the fire flying overhead had made him lose control of his bike. Chuck let off the trigger as the tank roared past the fallen German.

Shortly thereafter, the convoy halted and coiled for the night at 9:50 P.M., but Chuck couldn't fall back to sleep.

He wouldn't stop shaking for the next hour.

The convoy powered along a high, curvy road as the sun rose over the neighboring valley.

The Pershing rose and fell on its suspension. Rubber that had worn off the tracks and tires of the vehicles ahead littered the road before them.

Earley spoke into the pork chop as he guided Smokey, now driving in place of McVey. On the left stood a wall of rock. To the right, the road dropped off to the wide valley. It was a tight fit, offering no room for error. But Paderborn couldn't be far now.

Throughout the company, drivers' arms had cramped so badly that bow gunners had shifted to the driver's seat to make good on their training as assistant drivers. And one gunner's rear was so bruised from sitting for extended periods of time that he "took to kneeling on the floor of the turret, just to relieve the pressure."

It was a small price to pay to make history. It was official: the prior day's drive had been "the greatest one-day advance in the history of mobile warfare," according to the 3rd Armored unit history.

One task force had clocked 102 miles on the odometer, another 100, and the tanks ahead of Easy Company had logged 90. As a whole or in parts, Spearhead went farther through enemy territory than any German, Russian, or British unit, even eclipsing Patton's epic drive through France.

But this wasn't France—this was the Third Reich.

It began like any other refueling stop.

The convoy edged to the side of the road to give the fuel trucks the right of way. The tanks shut down and the crews climbed into the daylight.

Clarence paused atop the turret. The view was as good as any high-way's scenic overlook that he'd ever seen. But something wasn't right. His eyes settled on sharp lines that stood contrary to nature, on a road that crossed the valley.

Clarence rubbed his eyes and looked closer. They were vehicles and looked to be the size of tanks. The task force to the east must have bypassed them. He dropped into the turret and swung the gun to the right, setting the reticle on a target. His 6x zoom sight would give him a closer look.

They *were* tanks. It appeared that some column had begun to pull from a forest and had stopped, perhaps to consult a map. They looked like light tanks, maybe Stuarts or the division's new M24 Chaffees.

Clarence shouted to Earley.

Earley raised his binoculars but couldn't discern their identity.

"I'm pretty sure they're American," Clarence said.

Earley radioed Salisbury and reported that Clarence had eyes on tanks, possibly friendly forces.

Salisbury replied quickly. Too quickly. "There's no troops of ours down there, fire on them."

Clarence was aghast. "I can't knock out our own tanks!"

Earley was torn. Whoever the tanks were, they were in enemy territory.

"Can you see their identification panels?" he asked Clarence.

Their engine decks were bare, which didn't help his case, but Clarence didn't waver. Earley was sweating the order, so he stalled and pleaded for Salisbury to reconsider.

"Goddammit, I told you they aren't our tanks!" Salisbury said. "Fire!"

On any other day, Earley would have resisted. The stoic, homespun commander usually landed on the moral side of any argument, siding with logic over the hot tempers of the war zone.

But Earley wasn't himself that day. The crew's father figure was worn down physically and emotionally as the war and the long drive and the bad news from home were taking their toll on him. So, it wasn't really Bob Earley speaking when he gave Clarence the command: "Well, you heard him—fire."

Earley sunk into his seat. He couldn't bear to watch.

Clarence turned and looked him straight in the eye—*Are you serious?*

"Want them to put us in chains?" Earley said.

Clarence returned to his zoom sight with his jaw clenched in frustration. He worked the hand crank, inching his aim leftward. Clarence squeezed the trigger. The 90mm gun blasted the shell with an ear-piercing crack.

He counted down the time until the tracer made impact. One thousand one, one thous—

A splash of dirt burst from the road ahead of the lead tank. Clarence had missed—intentionally.

Hatch covers flung open and crewmen came pouring out. The men frantically waved colored panels toward the shooter to identify themselves.

They're Americans, all right!

The Stuart tanks or Chaffees were probably scouting ahead of the other task force.

"That would have stayed with us!" Clarence snapped at Earley.

Earley leaped to his feet and raised his binoculars. He muttered in astonishment before getting on the horn to give Salisbury the news. "Well, Captain," Earley said, "looks like they *are* our tanks."

The only response from Salisbury's end was a stunned silence.

Several hours later, the convoy descended into a world of trouble.

The column had stalled about eight miles south of Paderborn. Small-arms fire crackled and Panzerfausts thumped in the distance. SS men were firing from a ridge and Task Force Welborn was doing the brunt of the fighting.

Through his periscope, Clarence saw traces of the battle raging ahead.

Smoke was rising from behind the brown, dead woods as officers traipsed back along the convoy searching for a particular tank or person.

Clarence was thankful to be seated right where he was, nestled in the idling line of tanks. The landscape outside looked cold and foreboding. Narrow country roads wound through dull green fields and hills bristling with thin trees.

An awful truth had spread from vehicle to vehicle in the convoy by then: Paderborn wasn't just a name on the map. It was much more than just a gap in the steel wall being slipped around the Ruhr. Paderborn was the "home port" for the armored forces of the Third Reich, the "Nazi Fort Knox," as GIs would call it.

Every German tanker spent a stint in training there. The German Army's elite tank training base was located at Paderborn, as was the SS's armor school. In fact, the SS—whose spiritual headquarters lay nearby at Wewelsburg Castle—would lead the fighting to come.

To defend Paderborn, the SS had assembled SS Panzerbrigade Westfalen, a mixed battle group of troops from the SS, army, air force, and Hitler Youth. And they would pull out all the stops. Even battle-scarred instructors from both tank schools would be coming out to fight.

Spearhead had put itself deep behind enemy lines, deeper than they ever had before, and that worried Clarence. This was tank country after all.

German tank country.

That night, March 30, 1945
Seven miles south of Paderborn

Deep in the darkness of Böddeken Forest, Clarence and the crew stood horrified alongside the Pershing. Other Easy Company tankers lingered around their mounts nearby.

They couldn't look away from the terrible sight that stretched above the treetops, a little after seven P.M. Over the Paderborn countryside, the clouds were glowing red.

The bark of German tank guns knifed the woods.

Chaos was reigning just a mile to the north but there was nothing that Clarence and his crew could do. Easy Company was forbidden from going forward to help. Until the higher-ups could get a handle on the situation, no one else was to enter the maelstrom.

In its haste to reach Paderborn that night, Task Force Welborn had forged ahead, leaving Easy Company and Task Force X behind in the forest to coil for the night.

And now Clarence's crew and the others were stuck here, tugging at the reins. Task Force Welborn was in trouble, it was unmistakable.

Americans were dying out there.

A mile north

The line of flaming American tanks and half-tracks choked the country road.

German guns thundered from seemingly every direction. Vehicles ruptured. The enemy gave no sign that they were about to let up.

Task Force Welborn had driven into an ambush.

General Rose and his entourage abandoned their vehicles and leaped into a roadside ditch. Tankers and doughs crisscrossed the road seeking cover. Only a few men were able to return fire, using small arms.

There was no going forward—in front of the column, from the slope of a field, ten German tanks blasted away. There would be no retreat—behind the American column, another five German tanks shot down from a hilltop, silhouetted by the moon.

The woods were a killing zone too. The tree line blinked with small-arms fire from SS infantry stationed at both ends of the route.

With nowhere to run, all that remained for most Americans was to hide.

Rose and his entourage flattened themselves against the walls of the ditch. The general gripped a Thompson submachine gun, while the others clung to pistols and carbines.

Enemy tank shells whizzed overhead as they skipped from the road and bored into the fields.

SS Panzerbrigade Westfalen had struck the convoy with deadly efficiency. Only Colonel Welborn and some of his Shermans had escaped before the Germans cut the column by blasting vehicles at both ends, which trapped everyone else in the middle. Having seized the tactical advantage, the enemy could now afford to be methodical.

A German tanker would recall that it was "like hunting from a raised platform."

The German tanks walked their fire down the column as they pumped shells into every vehicle along the way. Another German tanker wrote that the burning vehicles flickered "like ghostly torches."

American tank crews jumped from flaming hulls. Squads of doughs tumbled from their half-tracks, screaming, burned, and bleeding. Men darted into the fields and hid from the enemy behind haystacks.

Gas tanks popped. Ammunition cooked in the flames and crackled like firecrackers. Standing tall in the gun ring of a half-track, one dough fired a .50-caliber machine gun toward the Germans in an act of futile resistance before he was silenced.

Several tankers made a run for it. Unfortunately, their escape route to the rear sent them darting toward their general. Rose climbed out of the ditch and caught the fleeing men by their arms, pushing them back toward their tanks.

The general was desperate to reverse their fortunes. This night was supposed to be the triumph of his career, the culmination of his division's record-breaking drive. Beneath his raincoat, he was wearing riding breeches and polished boots. He had abandoned the safety of commanding from the rear, opting to ride with his lead task force, and had even brought a stenographer along with him to record the moment when his division reached Paderborn.

With his crowning achievement ruined, new priorities took hold. Now he would fight just to see another day. The vehicles that Rose's entourage rode in on—three jeeps, two motorcycles, and a Greyhound armored car—were close at hand, and two of the jeeps were equipped with radios. If he could get to them, Rose could radio headquarters to call for backup.

On Rose's command, two drivers braved the enemy's fire as they maneuvered the jeeps into the ditch. It worked. Rose told his artillery colonel to bring in fire "on top of us." He then moved to the other jeep, where a soldier handed Rose the handset. On the line was his headquarters.

"Smith," Rose said, "send somebody to close up this column. We have been cut."

Enemy shells were finding targets with an alarming regularity, as if they couldn't miss. One of Rose's jeeps exploded on the road. Then, behind the column, a shell felled a tree across the road, dashing any remaining hope of retreat.

Through the light of the burning vehicles at the front of the column, Rose and his men saw a wedge of tan enemy tanks with green swaths of camouflage plowing through the field like icebergs. They were coming to finish the job.

"We're in a hell of a fix now," Rose said to a colonel at his side.

The German tankers fired flares into the air to illuminate any remaining resistance. German voices could be heard screaming commands over the hissing flames and the roar of motors. They rammed the lead American vehicles off the road and fired flares into their open compartments to destroy whatever, or whoever, was left behind inside.

Behind the column more German tanks snarled closer to Rose and his men. Some of the entourage advocated a run for the woods, but the general wanted to link up with Colonel Welborn, who had found refuge in Hamborn Castle, a ninth-century stronghold on a wooded hilltop. The castle was about two miles away from Rose's current position—a tenuous but passable trek.

Rose and his entourage ran for their vehicles. They would try for the castle.

Two colonels piled into the lead jeep, Rose leaped into a second jeep, and men ran for the Greyhound. Rose insisted that they leave the motorcycles behind because they were too noisy.

Rose's loyal driver darted to the front of the jeep and ripped off a red license plate that identified the vehicle as the general's. Engines surged and the entourage peeled to the right, dropped into the field, and raced forward alongside the burning column.

German tracers zipped through the flames and chased the getaway vehicles while American radio waves echoed with voices trying to reach Rose: "Big Six, come in Big Six!"

The next morning, around eight A.M.

Easy Company was finally unleashed to lead a rescue party. In the clear light of day, the Pershing led Task Force X from the Böddeken Forest.

As the forest opened up, Clarence pressed his eyes into his peri-scope. Gray smoke drifted over the fields like fog. He searched far and wide, hoping that there might still be time to save someone.

They were too late.

The crew remained silent as the Pershing neared the carnage.

As many as thirty-seven American vehicles lay strewn along the road like broken toys. Tanks and half-tracks, jeeps and trucks, every-thing was burned and many were still smoldering.

The destruction spread before them would soon be known as the Welborn Massacre.

Clarence was shaken. He had never seen so many American vehi-cles destroyed. And he had certainly never expected such an outcome at this stage of the war—when America was supposed to be on the verge of winning.

With his face held tight to the periscope, Clarence swept the turret from side to side, reconstructing the battle. His aim slowed across the hills. The German marauders who had laid waste to the column might still be watching.

"You seeing this?" It was the replacement loader, his voice trem-bling. "You seeing this?"

"Shut up!" Clarence snapped. "I'm looking for the gun that's pointing at us!"

Earley restored the peace. Everyone was emotional. The last thing they could afford was to turn on one another.

The Pershing pulled up to a crossroads.

Satisfied that the enemy had vacated the area, Clarence resumed scanning for survivors.

To the left, the decimated American column stretched for several hundred yards. Derelict Shermans lay frozen in confusion with their turrets pointed haphazardly in various directions.

Bullet-ridden half-tracks leaned into ditches. Torn canvas flapped from trucks. The vehicular death toll was huge. Nine Shermans. Twenty-one half-tracks. A Stuart. A pair of jeeps and trucks.

One tank had sought cover behind a barn to the right of the road, only to have been shot point-blank in the rear. The hull of a Sherman from their sister regiment, the 33rd, sat nearby. The tank was headless. Its turret had been blown off and had come to rest alongside the body.

A dead tanker lay nearby. His arms, legs, and head were all gone, and all that remained was a torso with skin that had been roasted red from the heat of his burning tank. He no longer looked like a man at all. In Clarence's eyes, he resembled a "baked ham." It was no way to die.

Clarence felt his stomach turn and had to sit back from his periscope before he lost it. After a moment, Clarence regained his composure and resumed scanning, even farther down the line.

At the lead of the ghostly column lay an abandoned Pershing, its suspension damaged by a shell strike, where the road ran uphill to Hamborn Castle. It was a rare tank to behold on any European battlefield, and to see a Pershing grounded in defeat was even more shocking.

Maybe it hadn't been fast enough to keep up with the escaping Shermans. Maybe the Germans had targeted it specifically. No one would ever know.

Clarence felt a cold, hollow pit in his stomach as he gazed upon the mangled spearhead of Task Force Welborn. A pattern was forming, at the forefront of every advance.

Two companies of doughs made a slow sweep of the fields, coming from the opposite direction.

Joined by the doughs of B-Company, Buck and the men of A-Company waded through grass littered with spent shell casings. Buck covered his mouth and nose to guard against the sickening scent of burning rubber.

Up close, the carnage was even worse. The enemy tanks had rammed aside or flattened anything on wheels in an effort to save ammunition. A German tank had bowled right over a jeep's hood. A half-track had been completely flattened from nose to tail.

Doughs from Buck's sister company, F-Company, had been riding in these vehicles. And many hadn't escaped. In the rear compartment of one half-track, several doughs were dead in their seats, still being consumed by the fire.

Small groups of men wearing olive-drab uniforms emerged from the tree line. They were tankers and doughs, many in a state of shock after hiding all night in the cold woods.

Rather than waiting for the enemy to stomp each and every trapped vehicle, most of the men of Task Force Welborn had bailed from their machines before the German shells could reach them, dramatically reducing the death toll.

Doughs discovered the motorcycles that had belonged to Rose's bodyguards, abruptly abandoned on the road. But what had become of the general?

Around the same time that morning, a reconnaissance patrol set out from Hamborn Castle in search of the answer.

Two sergeants from the 33rd Regiment's Headquarters Company broke from their comrades and traveled farther up the road than the task force had made it during the fighting. There, they came upon a jeep that had been smashed against a tree, as if a boulder had rolled down into it.

The heavy footprints of German tanks were everywhere.

The night before, Rose and his escape party were nearly in the clear. They had bypassed the burning column and returned to the road. Against all odds, they'd left the ambush behind them.

But just when they thought they were finally safe, a tank appeared on the road, headed straight for them. The colonel at the wheel of the lead jeep was relieved. The tank was broad with a long barrel and it looked American, like a Pershing under Welborn's command.

"That's one of Jack's new tanks," the colonel said to his passenger as he passed the behemoth on the left.

From the passenger's seat, another colonel looked over his shoulder and caught sight of the tank's two vertical exhaust stacks. German exhaust stacks. "Holy shit! It's a Tiger!" he shouted. "Get off the road."

The jeep jumped from the road and fled cross-country.

Rose's jeep was the next vehicle to come face-to-face with the shadowy German tank. Rose's driver also tried to veer to the left, but before he could make a clean escape, the German driver swerved the nearly 70-ton beast into the Americans' path and rammed Rose's jeep against a plum tree.

The Greyhound behind Rose's jeep darted around the collision but didn't make it much farther. It was quickly stopped by more German tanks up the road.

Rose, his driver, and an aide stepped from the disabled jeep with their hands held high. The outline of a German tank commander stood in the tank's turret clutching an MP 40 machine pistol.

The enemy commander screamed rapid-fire orders in a guttural voice. Rose spoke Yiddish, which shares similarities with German, but he couldn't decipher the words.

No versteh, Rose repeated. "No understand."

Rose's driver suggested that the German commander wanted their pistols. Rose agreed. It was a small price to pay for their lives. Rose's aide moved first. Using a thumb, he removed his shoulder holster and set it on the tank. Rose went next. He unlatched the belt from around his hips. Then he let the belt and pistol fall to his feet.

Rose brought his hands up to eye level and was raising them farther when the German's machine pistol crackled to life. A spurt of flames split the darkness. Witnesses heard the German fire three more bursts and saw the general's helmet spin through the air.

When the German commander moved to reload, Rose's driver and aide bolted into the dark.

The two sergeants from the reconnaissance patrol found their general dead in front of his jeep. He lay on his back, with fourteen bullet holes spanning from his thigh to his face.

His pistol—still in its holster—lay at his side, and his helmet, punched with bullet holes, lay nearby.

Why had the German commander killed Rose?

After the battle, the culprit—a young daredevil sergeant—revealed the answer to his fellow commanders. He said that he had almost been shot "by a very tall American," but had acted faster and fired first.

Had the darkness played tricks on his mind? Why would he imagine an act of hostility that never occurred? The truth will never be known.

During a reconnaissance mission several days after the massacre, the German daredevil would be killed in a shootout with American troops.*

One of the American sergeants removed a blanket from Rose's jeep and wrapped his body in it. He and his fellow sergeant each lifted an end, and together they half carried, half dragged the body of their fallen leader up to Hamborn Castle.

Hardened fighting men were reduced to tears when they realized what the bundle held. "He was mourned as a GI tanker mourns a dead crew-mate," the unit history would record, and for a simple reason. A signal wireman put it best: "We felt like he was one of us."

Thirteen men had died and sixteen had been wounded from Task Force Welborn during the day and night of the massacre. But it was this fourteenth body that rattled the division.

The following night

In darkness, Buck led four doughs behind a long line of American tanks parked on the high ground overlooking Paderborn.

Other doughs had pitched shelter halves for the night, but Buck wasn't taking a chance on the weather. He had his eye on a particular tank at the left end of the line, one that was wider than the others, offering more room to sleep between its tracks.

He rapped the tank's hull with the butt of his rifle to draw someone's attention. Bob Earley leaned over the side and looked down from the turret.

"Mind if we sleep here?" Buck asked.

---

* A decorated German tank commander, First Lieutenant Dieter Jähn, described the confusion the night of the massacre. From his turret, he heard vehicles approaching. A jeep emerged from the dark, followed by a massive tank. Jähn's gunner fired at the tank, but the shell bounced off. A German voice shouted from the oncoming vehicles: "You asshole!" A fellow commander by the name of Koltermann was at the wheel of the jeep, and the tank behind him was German. Jähn told his friend it was foolish to return in a captured vehicle, but Koltermann was enamored with the jeep. POWs accompanied him, including Lieutenant Colonel Sweat, Rose's operations officer. Sweat urged the German tankers to surrender, but Koltermann said it was up to the "bigger ones" in Berlin, Washington, Moscow, and London to stop the war.

Earley was fine with it. He said he'd wake them if the tank had to move unexpectedly.

Buck crawled underneath the tank and his charges followed.

The doughs following Buck were green replacements who had been sent to fill the empty seats in his half-track. They were his responsibility now.

Lieutenant Boom had promoted Buck to assistant squad leader and the sergeant had even given him a fire team of his own—the rookies—while the sergeant took the remaining veterans, including Byron and Carrier.

The men spread blankets over shelter halves before lying down side by side between the walls of wheels. The low ceiling was like camping in a cave, but the ground was warm from the machine's engine.

Hammering and wrenching noises emanated from the barns in a nearby village, where mechanics were readying the tanks for battle. A tank or two rumbled past to assume their positions in the line.

The rookies fell easily asleep, but Buck's mind was restless. At dawn they would attack the "Nazi Fort Knox," and now he'd have to fight with rookies hanging on to his belt. They were all privates and reminded Buck of himself when he first arrived in the company, which didn't inspire confidence.

There was Clyde Reed, one of thirteen brothers and sisters. He'd been a sheltered kid, and the first thing he said when he met Buck was that he "didn't want to have to kill anybody."

There was Dick Schneider, with an unusual hatred of chicken. When the kitchen truck served a hot chicken dinner as a perk on the night before battle, Dick traded his for a K-ration.

There was Stan Richards, slender and quiet, who acted like his M1 rifle wasn't actually that heavy.

And there was Luther Jones, the eldest of the bunch at thirty-one; he would summon any passerby to show off photos of his children back home in West Virginia.

These men weren't ready for the intensity of an armored clash, and Buck knew it. Lying there, he worried about the choice he would have to face at dawn. How could he keep himself safe—and his men? When the bullets started flying, whom would he choose?

• • •

Inside the Pershing above Buck, Clarence prepared to sleep. The crew would take turns performing watch duty from the loader's hatch, but it wasn't his shift yet.

Clarence removed his seatback and laid a wooden board from his seat to Earley's.

He scrunched a blanket up into a pillow, turned off the ceiling light, and lay back while he rested his feet on the gun mount.

The commander's hatch loomed over him as the tank creaked and hissed beneath him.

Word had circulated around the company that the Germans had never searched Rose's body. Apparently they didn't know they'd just killed the highest-ranking American to die by enemy fire in the European theater—and a father.

A correspondent for the *New York Sun* remembered Rose's briefing for reporters before the record-breaking drive to Paderborn:

"This thing is almost over now," one of us had said. "When it is, what are you going to do?"

"I have a son," the general had said. "He's four years old now, and I don't know him. We're going to get acquainted, and that's going to take a lot of time."

Now his son, Mike, was fatherless, and so was Spearhead.

Beyond the sorrow that was sapping the division's morale, Rose's death was proof of Clarence's worst fear: *It's just a matter of time.*

No one was untouchable.

Found often at the forefront of the action, Rose had been the exception to the rule. He was the glimmer of hope for Clarence and any man who repeatedly faced the enemy.

No matter how tight the scrapes were, if Rose always landed on his feet, so could any GI. But that belief died when they laid the general's body on the dining-room table in Hamborn Castle.

That's what leading got him.

That's what it got Paul Faircloth as he ran toward the wounded men at Mons.

Or Charlie Rose, killed at Hèdrée a week and a half after his son was born.

Or Bill Hey, who hit a mine at Grand-Sart but didn't turn back.

Or Robert Bower, the "college kid" with a chess set in his bag at Blatzheim.

Or Karl Kellner, the former grocery clerk who fell within sight of a cathedral.

Leading had gotten them all killed.

And come dawn tomorrow, Clarence would be leading again. The men had been briefed, the tanks had been fueled and racked with ammo. The Pershing would lead a task force against SS Panzerbrigade Westfalen in Spearhead's last major fight of the war, and surely the enemy would target the tank out in front of the others, the one with the biggest gun.

Trapped within the Pershing's cold steel walls, Clarence felt like it was the night before his own execution. He reflected on his twenty-one years of life and pondered the hereafter as he counted down the hours. But there was one crucial difference between Clarence and the condemned.

The army hadn't locked his cell.

The hatch was right there in the ceiling above his face. He could walk out, disappear for a day, and get to live the rest of his life. Or he could stay and let fate carry him to his ending.

There in the darkness, Clarence searched for the answer to the riddle of the American tanker:

Why would any man saddle up for this?

The next morning, April 1, 1945
Paderborn, Germany

Easy Company greeted the dawn on a rise overlooking Paderborn. The long line of tanks stretched to the east, alongside the armor of two other task forces.

Dark clouds hung low. Only thin beams of golden sun dotted the distant hills and woods.

At the far left end of the line, Clarence nervously smoked a cigarette in the Pershing's commander's position. It was around 6:15 A.M. and Earley was away at the last briefing.

Clarence's white scarf was cinched around his neck in preparation for battle. Behind the Pershing and every tank in line, doughs were gathering their packs and rifles. All motors were silent. Clarence took long drags at the cigarette. Not even the nicotine could calm his anxiety. There was no escaping the sight in front of him.

The Pershing's gun pointed the way to Paderborn.

Located two miles away, the old German town stood out like a beacon amid the surrounding darkness. Five days earlier, an RAF air raid had stomped across Paderborn's white, half-timber homes and shattered the Gothic cathedral where Charlemagne had once stood. Some areas were still smoldering.

But Clarence's concerns were far more immediate.

Easy Company was sitting in position to attack Paderborn's rail yard, on the southwest fringe of the town. Their orders were to take the rail yard and hold it until they were relieved by reinforcements. From a tactical perspective, the rail yard was a tanker's nightmare. Enemy armor could utilize its abandoned train cars for concealment and make use of its long lanes of tracks and platforms as a shooting gallery.

However, reaching the rail yard would be a battle in its own right. Easy Company would first have to cross two miles of treacherous, bomb-pocked fields that had come to resemble a moonscape thanks to the carpet bombing's spillover. And then the company would have to punch through a tidy row of houses with slate roofs that had only suffered partial ruin during the bombings.

Unlike other civilian homes that Clarence had seen, these had no bed sheets furled from the windows to signal the occupants' surrender. And that in itself was a warning sign.

By now, Clarence could sense the enemy even where he couldn't see them. SS Panzerbrigade Westfalen was out there, waiting. He could feel them. As he burned through cigarette after cigarette, Clarence couldn't shake the thought: *Why? They know it's over, why don't they just let this end?*

A rumble over Clarence's right shoulder drew his attention. Had F-Company finally come?

A gap lay between Easy Company and the next task force down the line. A number of vital troops belonging to Task Force X—including F-Company's Shermans and two companies of doughs—still hadn't reached the line of departure.

Instead of F-Company, four M36 Jackson tank destroyers appeared on a higher rise. The M36s—each armed with 90mm guns—had come to provide fire support for Easy Company's attack. The M36s' firepower would come in handy. It was all but guaranteed that Easy Company would face enemy tanks.

The Sennelager base, the "Nazi Fort Knox," lay on the other side of Paderborn, but Spearhead wouldn't go there. This time, the enemy would be coming to them. The German armor schools at the base were deploying 25 tanks, a sizeable force at a time when Germany had only around 200 tanks and armored vehicles operational in the entire Western theater.

"Mount up!"

The men of A-Company moved to their tanks.

Doughs climbed aboard for a ride to the rail yard and men on the ground passed machine guns hand over hand and tossed rifles up to the waiting arms of their buddies.

"Mind if we come aboard?"

Clarence looked and saw Buck and his four rookies waiting behind the Pershing. They assumed he was the commander.

Clarence didn't mind. He flicked away his cigarette and descended to give the doughs a hand.

"Scooch forward," Buck advised the rookies, "or you'll fry your butts." Clarence chuckled at the sight of the four rookies shimmying away from the grates over the radiator.

Earley returned from the briefing. Clarence leaned over to get a good look at his commander's pipe as he climbed aboard. It was worse than he thought. The pipe was vibrating between Earley's chattering teeth.

Clarence would spare the crew and keep this observation to himself. "Where's F-Company?" Clarence asked. Their plot on the starting line was still empty.

Earley shook his head. He said the other half of the task force was late, but the attack couldn't wait for them.

Clarence cursed. F-Company was supposed to secure Paderborn's airfield—and whatever forces were still stationed there—on the way to the rail yard. Now, Easy Company would have to drive right past them.

The battalion chaplain, a tall, fit, white-haired man wearing purple vestments over his shoulders, approached the Pershing.

"How about a blessing?" he asked.

Earley was eager to receive one. He shouted inside the turret, which drew the crew from their hatches.

The chaplain took his place in front of the tank and removed his helmet. Clarence and Earley removed their headwear as Buck and the young doughs crowded forward to hear.

"I just want you all to remember that it's Easter," the chaplain said, "the day when life conquered death."

Easter! Amid the frenzy of preparing for battle, Clarence had totally forgotten about the holiday. He bowed his head alongside his fellow soldiers. The chaplain prayed aloud as he asked God to make

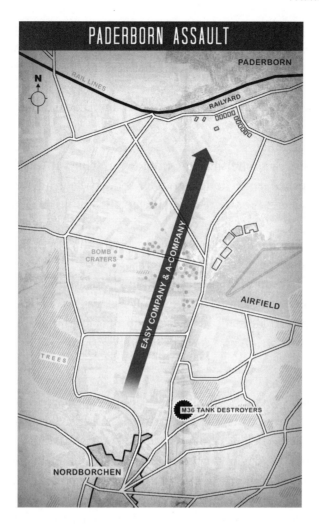

the crew his instrument to bring peace back upon his earth. When the blessing was finished, the chaplain wished the men a safe journey and moved on to the next tank.

A hush settled over the tankers and doughs.

Clarence watched men come down from their Shermans and assemble in front of their tanks, while others stood in place as the chaplain worked his way down the line. Some men took a knee while others bowed their heads as the chaplain's blessing cut through the silence.

Clarence was struck by the sight of the staggered ranks of men ascending to their Shermans, silhouetted by the sun rising from behind them.

He had always fought for his family. It had always been just the five of them—Earley, Smokey, McVey, DeRiggi, and himself—against the Germans. But on Easter 1945, Clarence saw the bigger picture for the first time.

His family was more than just the men in his own tank.

Hatch covers slammed shut up and down the line. It was time to go. Clarence turned to the doughs to offer some parting advice.

"Guys, when I fire you're going to get a hell of a scare, so just hold on tight."

Buck thanked him for the warning.

Clarence dropped inside the turret.

The field ahead of him held nothing but death, but Clarence was exactly where he wanted to be. Paul Faircloth, Bill Hey, General Rose—they had all made a choice. And that morning, Clarence had too: *We've got the biggest gun, we belong up front.*

As soon as his watch struck 6:30 A.M., Earley spoke to McVey: "Wind it up." The phrase was a holdover from the early days when a Sherman's engine needed to be hand cranked before starting.

The Pershing's engine roared to life, quickly finding its pitch among a mechanical symphony of Shermans. A devout Catholic, McVey gave no "big bullet" prayer today. The chaplain had already said it best.

From a Sherman down the line, Salisbury issued the order to attack.

A snarl of horsepower bellowed from the Pershing as it set out for the houses. The next in line, a Sherman, paused for about ten seconds before it launched forward. Ten seconds later, the next tank took off. And so on down the line.

Rather than going line abreast, the tanks cut a "left echelon" slant across the field, so each crew could guard the flanks of the tank next to them.

Perhaps the war's last great victory lay ahead of the formation. Paderborn was a lifeline for the German forces in the Ruhr. Everything—road traffic, rail traffic, communications—flowed through Paderborn to the rest of Germany. And the town could still prove to be the escape

The Pershing approaches the Cologne cathedral after its clash at the four-way intersection.

With the cathedral in sight, a second Sherman moves alongside Kellner's tank, which is obscured from this angle.

Kellner rolls from the turret after his Sherman absorbs a second hit. The urge to escape was so desperate that his gunner would dive headfirst off the turret.

The Pershing advances through "Cologne's Wall Street," bound for its duel with the Panther.

This motion picture frame captures the moment the Pershing fired at Bartelborth's Panther. The train station is visible beyond the Pershing, at the end of the street.

This sequence from the camera of Jim Bates shows Bartelborth and crewmembers emerging before the Panther erupts in flames.

Bartelborth's Panther burns in this photo taken from Bates's vantage
in the German Labor Front building.

A bulldozer clears the street that cost the lives of Karl Kellner and two of his crew. Their knocked-out Sherman can be seen on the far right.

The Hohenzollern Bridge—part roadway, part railway—having collapsed into the Rhine, as seen from the cathedral.

After reaching the Rhine, the Pershing stands guard in the plaza alongside the cathedral.

The defeated Panther, as seen from the cathedral's northern spire.

Gareth Hector's painting Spearhead depicts the conquest of Cologne, as Clarence directs Earley's attention toward the enemy-held bank of the Rhine.

American infantrymen explore bomb damage to the Cologne cathedral. The tall windows and hollow interior proved key to its survival by funneling the blasts outside.

Army cameramen brought Smokey (far left) and DeRiggi to tour the Panther the next day. Kellner's Sherman can be seen in the distance, on the far right.

Inspecting the Panther for the PR men. Left to right: Smokey, unidentified, and DeRiggi.

DeRiggi can be seen here cradling his captured German K98 rifle. In the background stands the Dom Hotel, where tankers would discover a well-stocked wine cellar.

A-Company doughs relax after securing Cologne. Lieutenant Boom is standing at the far left, and Buck is kneeling, second from the right, alongside De La Torre.

Soon after crossing the Rhine, this Spearhead crew gazes on a defeated Panzer IV G. The Sherman's hull is supplemented by an additional steel plate.

The GI artist's sketch of Clarence with the cathedral behind him.

*One of Buck's rookie replacements,
Stan Richards, stands atop Squad
3/2's half-track.*

*A Spearhead crew comes out for a breather
after silencing some resistance during the
drive to Paderborn.*

In the painting Unstoppable, *by Gareth Hector, this Spearhead M4A3E8 charges
deeper into Germany as a Tiger I smolders, knocked out by American air support.*

Easy Company commanders confer. Photographed around the time of the Paderborn assault, Earley is facing the camera and "Red" Villa stands on the far right.

An M24 Chaffee hauls a wagon of German prisoners taken by Spearhead in spring 1945.

*"Red" Villa parked his M4 at this defunct German gas station not far from
the Elbe River so Chuck Miller could take this picture.*

*Chuck cleans his tank's 76mm gun near the Elbe. The war in Europe
would end the following day.*

*McVey poses with the Pershing's .50-caliber machine gun
during some downtime in the war's waning days.*

Clarence (far left) relaxes with his fellow tankers at the war's end.

route for the Ruhr's 370,000 German troops—unless Spearhead got there first.

If the division could take Paderborn and link up with Hell on Wheels, the steel wall would be complete. They would be the victors in the "largest encirclement battle in history" and the Third Reich would be doomed to wither on the vine.

But first they needed to get to the Paderborn rail yard.

Buck held on to the turret for dear life. As a wall of small trees blurred past on his left, he noticed that the trees were already bearing blossoms in the spring weather.

On his right, tanks charged forward with their guns leveled like lances. Doughs were riding with their legs dangling over the sides. Byron, cradling his BAR in his arm, rode on the neighboring tank along with the other half of 3/2. As the tanks bobbed on the terrain, his icy eyes met Buck's.

The formation reached the soot-ringed bomb craters and sped past one shell hole after another. Buck shouted, "Hang on!" to his rookies as they were violently jostled by the tank's movement. The obstacles slowed the Pershing down, but not by much.

On the other side of Easy Company, closer to the airfield, the craters were denser. Those tanks slowed dramatically as their drivers snaked back and forth to avoid the holes.

If the war was really all but over, SS Panzerbrigade Westfalen hadn't gotten the memo.

As the tanks chugged past, enemy soldiers rose from shell holes, clutching Panzerfausts.

A faraway Sherman exploded. Its doughs were tossed into the air by the force of its rupturing fuel and ammunition.

A dough on a neighboring tank leaped to the turret and blazed away with the machine gun, seeking revenge. But his defiance was momentary. A Panzerfaust whizzed up from a shell hole and slammed the turret, blasting him to the ground with a fatal head wound.

Doughs fired back from their perches. Buck pressed himself against the turret and blasted away at the enemy. The rookies, following Buck's lead, joined in the firing.

Accuracy was impossible with tanks bouncing over the pockmarked terrain. Within a few seconds, any Germans they saw in the craters were far behind.

Another Panzerfaust struck a Sherman's left track, which caused the tank to fall out of formation with its driver dead or wounded at the controls. Stunned doughs fell off the sides and had to run from the crippled tank, which began corkscrewing haphazardly. If they didn't carefully time their scramble to safety, they would be crushed.

When Lieutenant Boom's tank bypassed a German machine-gun crew, Boom had had enough. He shouted for the commander to stop, and jumped down to earth to carry the fight to the enemy. He and his squad were last seen tossing grenades into the crater that sheltered the German gun crew.

The Pershing slowed further to prevent the formation from disintegrating. Buck rose from his crouch to take a peek at their progress. The airfield was slipping past on the right. Despite the resistance they'd faced, the formation was more than halfway there.

But they weren't in the clear yet.

Without warning, dozens of red glowing orbs sprang from the airfield and arced toward Easy Company. From positions around the hangars, a Luftwaffe flak regiment had turned its eight 20mm flak guns on them.

Across the company, doughs made themselves small. Buck and the rookies flattened themselves on the hot engine deck as the orbs descended upon them. The orbs picked up speed. At the last second they blurred over and between tanks, snapping the air.

The pulsating shells focused on a Sherman near the airfield, beating a drum rattle on its flank and blasting a dough off the back, as if the man had been flicked by a giant finger.

Another driver was so terrified by the incoming fire that he drove his Sherman into a shell crater. With a metallic crunch, doughs were flung headlong over the turret.

A radioman picked himself up and limped toward cover in a crater, but a shell felled him mere feet from safety.

The red hose of orbs swept far and wide and zoomed toward the Pershing in lazy arcs.

Buck clutched his helmet as shells landed in front of the tank, showering him with dirt. A hit smacked the Pershing's side skirt armor, tossing a wave of sparks over Buck and the rookies.

Buck crawled forward to the left side of the turret so only his legs would be exposed.

"The hell with this!" a rookie shouted. Gripping a handle on the left side of the Pershing's hull, the rookie jumped to the ground and ran alongside the tank, carrying his rifle in his other hand.

Another rookie followed his lead and dropped down from the tank as well. Yet another followed soon after. Before Buck knew it, all four rookies were running alongside the tank. He remained flat where he was, and watched with detachment.

The glowing orbs stopped hosing across the tanks.

Buck lifted his head. What had crimped the Germans' fire?

Far behind him, command had made up for F-Company's absence by dispatching an "assault section" of three Shermans armed with 105mm howitzers to storm the airfield.

Earley was silent as he rode head and shoulders above the turret. Suspiciously silent.

Clarence could only endure it for so long. "How are we looking, Bob?" he asked.

"Not good," Earley replied.

Only about six Shermans remained in formation, and there were wide gaps between them. A long trail of derelict tanks stretched in their wake. Easy Company had been whittled in half. And the fighting was just beginning.

From ahead and to the right, a green bolt rocketed into the formation at ground level. A violent strike of steel on steel sent Earley ducking for cover. Down the line, a Sherman was stopped cold in its tracks. The shot was terrifyingly precise. Shouts of alarm filled Clarence's earphones.

Easy Company continued plowing forward as more green bolts, cracking like bullwhips, zipped through the ranks and out the other side. A ricochet struck a tank and spun skyward with a wobbling noise.

Commanders reported muzzle flashes on the east side of the rail yard. Shermans fired blindly in that direction. One crew turned back after a gun stoppage. Salisbury tried to rein in his men.

Another Sherman lurched to a stop after absorbing a heavy hit. The crew rolled from their hatches before a fountain of flames leapt from the turret.

The platoon leader of the M36 tank destroyers radioed a warning: they had eyes on enemy tanks. Clarence's blood ran cold at the news. The M36 crews reported seeing a Tiger and what looked like a Panther and two self-propelled guns. The Germans were firing from the northeast, where they were hidden in the rail yard.

Earley hunted for a target with his binoculars, but was coming up empty. Clarence grew increasingly frustrated. The only thing he saw were the shadowy rail-yard buildings off to the right of the houses.

Orange tracers soared over Easy Company from behind like flaming arrows. Over Earley's right shoulder, the M36s were firing back from their rise.

The tank destroyers' gunners poured volley after volley of shells into the rail yard. From 2,600 yards away, they couldn't see the impact of their shells, but that wouldn't stop them from collectively firing seventy times.

Clarence followed the flight of the tracers as they landed in the rail yard's shadows.

With the shells pointing the way, he took aim at the gap between buildings. There was little point in firing without seeing the target. The reticle was bouncing, which made it difficult to fix his aim. Besides, these German tank commanders wouldn't be intimidated by a near miss.

They were the school's cadre of instructors, veterans who had relocated here with their wives or girlfriends and made Paderborn their home. In tanks once used for drivers' or gunners' instruction, they were now leading their students into the ultimate classroom.

Clarence's finger tightened on the trigger.

Whoever the enemy was, and wherever his shells would land, none of that mattered to him. He had a message for the Germans at the rail yard: if he was going to die here, it wouldn't be sitting on a full load of ammo.

• • •

The Pershing's 90mm belched one earsplitting roar after another. Buck gripped a ring alongside the turret and held on. The violent muzzle blasts slapped him "like a wet dishcloth," and he swore they lifted him from the engine deck.

Buck's ears rang and his lungs struggled for air. His vision wavered through watering eyes. And the worst of it was that there was no anticipating the next blast. It could come at any moment.

We're never going to make it! Buck thought to himself.

The Pershing's crew must have been thinking the same thing. The tank's engine suddenly blasted out a gust of heat as it gunned beneath Buck's feet. The forty-six-ton tank surged forward, kicking clumps of grass in its trail. The neighboring Shermans went to full throttle as well.

"Get up here!" Buck shouted to the rookies, still running beside the tank.

Setting his rifle aside, Buck leaned over, keeping one hand on the turret ring, and helped lift a rookie up and over the tank's spinning road wheels. He then grabbed a second, and a third, until just one rookie remained on the ground.

The last rookie was flying alongside the speeding tank even though he kept a grip on the handle. Each time he got his feet beneath him, he lost his footing and went back to flying with his heels kicking beneath him. With the other rookies' help, Buck managed to pull him back aboard.

Earley rose from the turret and shouted at the distracted doughs: "Prepare to dismount!"

The Pershing slowed to a stop fifty yards from the row of houses— still dangerously within a Panzerfaust's range.

Clarence saw nothing but trouble through his periscope. The enemy had dug foxholes in the front yards of the houses and there was movement at ground level. Helmeted heads rose up for a peek. In the background, German soldiers darted between houses. Clarence brought the coaxial machine gun to life with a press of the trigger. The chopping tracers sent German troops shrinking from sight.

"Tell the doughs the yards are full of them!" Clarence said.

Earley ventured outside for a quick look before returning. "Too late, they're off," he said. "Watch your fire!"

Buck and his fire team surged forward while the Pershing held back. A Sherman pulled up to the neighboring home and disgorged the other half of 3/2. The area was too risky for tanks until the doughs cleared the houses.

A German machine gun sent green snaps of fire across the yards from a house down the block to the right. Buck dropped to the lawn, where a mailbox would normally stand. Two rookies hit the dirt next to him.

The other two rookies didn't get the message and went charging headlong into the yard.

At that moment, a realization struck them. There were foxholes all around them. Foxholes full of German soldiers. The rookies just stood there with stunned expressions as bullets tore the air around them.

"Get down!" Buck shouted.

One rookie ran to the nearest foxhole. A German looked up at him with hands raised in surrender.

The rookie motioned frantically with his rifle: *Out!*

The American jumped inside as soon as the German vacated the foxhole. Facing the choice of surrender or being run over by American tanks, the enemy in the yards were compliant.

The other rookie disappeared into the nearest foxhole.

Another Sherman pulled up to the right, delivering Lieutenant Boom with his headquarters squad. Buck was relieved to see that Boom had caught up.

With three or four men, Boom charged the house where the enemy machine gun was tearing away. They kicked in the door before disappearing inside. After a few moments, the enemy machine gun went silent. When he reemerged, Boom motioned for Buck and the others to join him.

Buck shoved two of his rookies to jump-start the shell-shocked doughs. He then rousted another rookie from his foxhole with a shout.

Buck stopped in his tracks as he ran through the yard. He was one rookie short.

He located the missing rookie in a foxhole to his left. The inexperienced dough was standing face-to-face with a German Wehrmacht soldier. The two boys, about the same age, were clutching their rifles to their chests and shaking in their boots.

Buck motioned for the German's rifle, grabbed it by the muzzle, and tossed it away. Then he reached down and hauled the rookie out by the collar, leaving the German behind.

The rookie's feet were moving so slowly that Buck had to drag him forward. Buck plunged into the house, pulling the rookie inside behind him.

CHAPTER 23 **COME OUT AND FIGHT**

That same morning
Paderborn

Buck felt an immense sense of security inside the house, as if he had left the war behind him. He caught his breath while the rookie he had rescued steadied himself against the wall.

The interior was buzzing with the activity of more than a dozen doughs. Byron watched the back door with his BAR while Boom deployed lookouts.

Buck discovered a white Easter cake sitting on a table. He was amazed that no one—not even Carrier—had touched it.

The front door flew open and A-Company's commander—a be-spectacled captain named Walter Berlin—entered, followed by other doughs. Buck was glad to see Captain Berlin; the man exerted a steadying influence. Outside, doughs were coming in from the fields on foot and clearing the adjoining homes.

A worried look settled across Berlin's long face as he took a radio call. He handed the headset back to his radioman and asked, "Anyone know if our Pershing got in?"

"Yes sir, we rode in on it," Buck said.

Berlin was relieved. Two German tanks had been spotted moving amid the buildings east of them, where the M36s had been firing ear-lier. If they came any closer, the Pershing would be desperately needed.

The attack would go on.

The captain briefed Lieutenant Boom on the assault plan. Behind the house sat the railroad yards. Reconnaissance photos revealed a switch house on the grounds, which would provide observation along the length of the tracks. Boom was tasked with taking twenty men to secure the switch house. Once he did so, friendly tanks would move forward.

There was no time to waste. Buck checked his ammunition and turned to his fire team. The four rookies were standing so close to one another that they could have fit on a sofa.

Buck warned the rookies to watch their spacing when they went outside. "If there is a German machine gun and you're clustered, you're going to be their first target."

The twenty or so doughs streamed out the back door of the house. Lieutenant Boom was not among them, having stayed behind to brief the tank crews on A-Company's plan. In his place, the platoon sergeant led the men toward the switch house, about one hundred yards away.

It was strangely quiet here as the men entered the rail yard. The clash of battle sounded from behind them, where other task forces were encountering heavy resistance on the other side of the airfield. No other units had reached the city, nor would they for the next three hours.

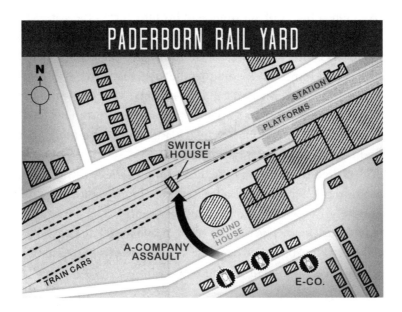

Buck and the doughs charged forward, unaware of just how alone they were.

The men darted past a roundhouse for locomotives on their right and kept going. The two-story brick switch house lay ahead.

Buck glanced backward at his rookies. They had taken his advice to the extreme, keeping a wide berth—twenty yards or more—from one another. If the gap between two doughs narrowed, each would frantically wave the other away. At any other place or time, Buck would have found humor in the spectacle.

The doughs crossed several sets of tracks and came to the rear door to the switch house. The tracks on the opposite side of the building were full of stranded train cars. Bomb craters littered the industrial landscape.

Buck and several doughs burst inside the switch house with their rifles leveled. The first floor was windowless and empty, save for a few supply barrels and a desk or two. Through the grated metal floor above they saw that the second story was empty as well. The building was clear.

"*Hilfe!*" A German voice moaned for help. "*Hilfe!*"

Outside, a dough discovered a badly wounded German soldier. He was carried inside and laid on the concrete floor. Buck cringed at the sight when a medic lifted his shirt. The man's stomach was torn open. It looked like a bullet or shrapnel had hit him across the gut.

The German begged for water with an outstretched hand. Buck uncapped his canteen, but before he could give the enemy water, the medic stopped him: "He's going to die, but the water will only kill him faster." It pained Buck to cap his canteen. Even if it wouldn't help the man, he wanted to offer the German some comfort in his final moments. The German laid his head back and started moaning again as the medic tended to him as best he could.

Buck spotted them just in time. His rookies were working their way up the staircase like moths drawn to flame. Light slanted down from wide observation windows on the second floor.

"Stop!" Buck said. The rookies froze in midstep. The key to looking outside was to stay back and peer out the windows from the shadows— something the rookies had yet to learn.

Buck held them back while three veteran doughs pounded up the metal stairs.

The windows looked eastward down the long avenues of tracks toward a Victorian-era train station with three covered outdoor platforms. From their higher perch, the veterans gazed down into open-topped train cars containing bits of iron ore and a rust-colored soil-like substance.

There was movement below.

A scope flashed in a train car about thirty yards away as a German sniper lifted his rifle to his shoulder. The men ducked just before a bullet punched through the glass, splintering the top of the window frame. The three veterans lay flat on their stomachs above, cursing after their close call. The rookies backpedaled from the steps. "That's why!" Buck admonished them.

The staccato tap of bullets drew everyone's undivided attention to the northern and eastern walls. Bullets were splattering against the outside of the switch house. Glass shattered and rained from the second-floor windows and a torrent of machine-gun fire stitched the bricks.

The Germans were mounting a full-blown counterattack.

Lieutenant Boom bolted breathlessly into the switch house. He briefed the platoon sergeant on what he'd seen outside. German soldiers were pouring from the train station and advancing toward the switch house.

The doughs had fought the Luftwaffe and the Wehrmacht that morning. But the enemy outside was a different breed of soldier, the type who would pin himself in a train car with little chance of escape. Many of the troops darting through the rail yard wore the lightning-bolt runes of the SS.

Boom gazed up through the floor. He moved toward the staircase with his eyes locked on the broad windows.

"Sniper has it zeroed," a dough warned him. But that wasn't about to stop Boom. Buck tried to block Boom's path at the base of the steps, but the lieutenant brushed past him. He was determined to take charge and hold the switch house as ordered.

Buck grabbed his sleeve. "Please don't, Lieutenant. That sniper's just waiting."

Boom shook free and turned to face Buck. "I have to see what we're up against." He flashed a nervous smile and continued up the stairs.

Buck was overcome by dread. He knew Boom. And he knew what Boom was about to attempt. A hush fell over the first floor. Everyone looked up except Buck, who couldn't bring himself to watch.

Boom raised his carbine to his shoulder as he turned the corner at the top of the stairs. The men could see the soles of his boots moving through the grates. With the body of a basketball star, he was a lanky target.

Buck flinched when the shot rang out. Boom crashed backward to the floor and his carbine and helmet rattled.

Buck glanced up in disbelief. A man ran to the top of the stairs and returned shaking his head. Lieutenant Boom was dead, shot through the throat. From there, the bullet had probably hit his spinal cord. He never stood a chance.

Buck slumped against the nearest wall, his helmet scraping brick. He buried his face in his hands, overwhelmed by a swirl of grief, fear, and anger. He had tried to stop Boom from giving the sniper the satisfaction.

Buck returned to his senses and found the rookies looking to him for guidance. He dried his eyes and wiped his nose. All of their lives were on the line now.

A cloud of red dust from shattered bricks filtered down from the second floor as bullets continued to splatter the building. Their shelter was being chewed apart.

Over the racket of gunfire, the platoon sergeant radioed Captain Berlin to inform him that Boom was dead. Buck and others turned an ear to the platoon sergeant's conversation while a few doughs kept an eye on the back door. "Sir, we can't make it back, it's too hot!" the platoon sergeant said.

From what Buck could gather, A-Company didn't have the manpower to send a relief force, and air support couldn't help them either. A flight of eight P-47s was just arriving above the clouds, but couldn't descend because of the overcast conditions.

Buck's mind cycled through their options for escape.

Where are our tanks? he thought. Then, Buck remembered. For the tanks to advance, the doughs were first to have gained observation over the tracks. And that hadn't happened.

Buck's stomach sank at the realization. The armor that had brought them in wouldn't be coming to their rescue. That simply wasn't part of the plan.

The Pershing was idling back between houses when the radio calls reached Earley's ears. The doughs in the switch house were making pleas for help to anyone listening.

They desperately needed tank support, and therein lay the problem.

The division had committed three task forces to the attack, but only Easy Company had reached Paderborn.

And how many of their tanks had made it in? No one knew for sure. Salisbury's tank had limped to the houses but was unable to continue due to mechanical problems. Lieutenant Stillman's vehicle was also out of commission. So the officers had passed command to the last platoon sergeant still standing.

Bob Earley.

Earley reached for the pork chop. He couldn't just sit there and listen to his fellow Americans in distress, regardless of what the plan had been. "We're pushing on the railroad," Earley announced over the radio. "Anyone who's left, fall in with us."

The Pershing rolled forward with Earley standing head and shoulders above his hatch.

To his right, a 76 Sherman pulled out from the houses, with Red Villa in the turret and Chuck Miller at the gun. Farther down the line a second 76 emerged. Its gunner was Clarence's friend Private John Danforth. A twenty-eight-year-old Texan built like a football player, Danforth was so broad that he had to turn to squeeze through a hatch.

Three tanks. Three crews. It was all that Easy Company could muster.

The tanks moved slowly, side by side, as they approached the switch house from behind. At the sight of American armor, the enemy's fire slackened as their foot soldiers took cover.

Each tank gunner kept an eye on a different sector. On the left flank of the formation, Clarence covered the front left. In the middle tank, Chuck Miller aimed forward. Holding down the right flank, Danforth watched the front right.

The tanks had barely edged over the first tracks when Danforth saw trouble.

"Tank!" his commander broadcast the alert over the radio. "One o'clock, behind the station."

Everyone halted. Earley swung his binoculars.

An enemy tank peeked out from behind the train station across the tracks. Only a fraction of its frontal armor was visible. Its gun, however, was pointing toward the switch house, which provided the Easy Company tanks with an opening to hopefully land the first shot.

Danforth's 76mm barked and recoiled back into the gun shield.

Sparks leapt from the German tank downrange. Danforth had delivered only a glancing blow. The enemy tank threw itself in reverse and slipped from sight.

Profanity bemoaning the missed opportunity coursed over the American airwaves, then the chatter cut out abruptly.

The enemy tank was not alone.

A second German tank rolled forward from the same position, eager to try its luck. But Chuck Miller was waiting for him. Chuck's Sherman spat a length of flame as it rocked back on its heels. The tracer shell struck the enemy tank then ricocheted skyward like a harmless flare—another strike that failed to penetrate.

The second German tank retreated without firing a shot. Where it would relocate next was anyone's guess. A German civilian would later write of having witnessed "a running conflict between firing steel giants."

Earley radioed Task Force X from the Pershing. They recorded his message at 8:51 A.M.: "At least two enemy tanks here, as usual our shots bounced off."

Clarence had seen enough. *Now we've got two pissed-off German tanks!* If they were going to fire, they needed a weapon that would kill. He swung the 90mm toward the station and set the reticle where the enemy tanks had been.

"I've got my gun on the spot," Clarence told Earley. "Tell the guys to watch the flanks."

Earley radioed directions to the others. But it was too late.

From the front right came a green lance of tracer. Danforth's tank shuddered as the clash of steel going through steel rippled the rail yard.

The sound of the punch raised the hair on the back of Clarence's neck. Was Danforth okay? His eyes drifted for a view. A slap on his right shoulder brought Clarence back to reality.

"Three o'clock!" Earley shouted. The shot had originated from the far end of the station.

Clarence swung the gun farther to the right and took aim through the covered train platforms. The German tank had already vanished from sight.

Clarence felt a shiver run down his spine. *This guy's good.*

From his perch outside, Earley counted aloud as Danforth's crew abandoned their tank. At last came the big Texan, squeezing himself free. Some of the crew limped as they fled for the switch house, but they had all made it out alive.

It was time to get back to business.

If the enemy commander was as smart as Clarence thought he was, he might regroup and attack from their flank.

"Bob, watch the right," Clarence said. "He knows this place better than us."

Earley agreed with Clarence's assessment.

Villa came over the radio, sounding shaky. *What now?*

The choice was in Earley's hands. They could fall back, but a retreat would likely embolden the enemy to swarm the switch house. Or they could stand their ground.

Earley didn't hesitate with his decision. The Pershing and Sherman edged forward past Danforth's abandoned tank, wheeled to face the train station, and stopped.

A 180-degree front line stared back at them.

Side by side, with hulls pointing forward, the tanks' guns spread apart like a wishbone.

Each could cover only about half of the battlefield, but this was better than running away.

With one tank, they could never do it.

With two, they just might be able to hold.

It was as if someone had rung a bell, announcing open season on the two remaining Easy Company tanks. A sniper's bullet clanged the hatch cover. Earley dropped inside to take shelter.

Bullets cracked and zinged against the turrets. When the machine guns joined in, a shower of sparks flew over the tanks' open hatches. German soldiers were gunning for the tanks' commanders, firing from shell holes and rising up from train cars. Machine guns blinked rapidly from the station house.

Villa ducked into his turret and slammed the cover shut.

Earley reached up quickly and gave his lid a tug. With his eyes pressed to the periscope, Clarence didn't know where to begin. Flashes were coming from every direction.

Clarence steadied the reticle on a train car. His finger hovered over the coaxial trigger as he waited for a German soldier to reappear.

Then, he remembered. He could still reach them.

His finger wrapped the main gun trigger and the 90mm spit out an armor-piercing shell. The train car shattered on impact, which sent a cloud of red minerals—and whatever remained of the enemy soldier—skyward.

The new loader, Mathews, slammed home a fresh shell. Clarence shifted his aim and another train car popped.

Each red cloud that Clarence sent billowing into the sky doubled as a smoke signal to the enemy—"Come out and fight!"

Smokey's bow gun sprang to life as it fired orange tracers that dotted boxcars and hosed shell holes. Clarence joined in with the coaxial, and now two orange hoses poured downrange. A third followed, and a fourth joined the party as Villa's tank added its firepower to the mix.

The four orange streams were beautiful as they weaved and criss-crossed one another. The noise from the multiple guns blended into one long rip that sounded like tearing fabric.

A yellow shape flying through the air seized Clarence's attention. From the front left, the blur fell directly in front of the Pershing before it burst with a blinding flash. Clarence reeled back from the periscope as shrapnel smacked against the tank's armor. He recognized that explosion all too well. It was fire from a Panzerfaust.

Clarence returned to his periscope. Outside, cinders were still raining down when another Panzerfaust approached from the same direction as the first.

The yellowish warhead soared over the distant train cars like a football until its propellant ran out and it landed with another flash. Moments later, more warheads followed, leaving thin trails of black smoke in their wakes.

Villa's tank pulled forward to escape the line of fire. Inside the turret, Chuck Miller kept his eyes peeled for enemy tanks at the station. He'd leave the Panzerfaust soldiers to Clarence.

Clarence tracked the smoke trails to the opposite side of the tracks, where the rail yard abutted a residential neighborhood. It was there that enemy soldiers were darting onto a footbridge, firing, then retreating out of the line of fire, shielded by boxcars.

Clarence raked the bridge with machine-gun fire repeatedly. But despite his efforts, the Germans refused to cede the bridge. Several daring souls dashed forward gripping a Panzerfaust. Most were felled by Clarence's fire, but a few were able to launch shots in his direction.

With every Panzerfaust that streaked toward the Pershing, Clarence grew increasingly desperate. Sooner or later, the enemy would land a direct hit.

Someone had to destroy the footbridge.

Clarence had a plan in mind, but it was risky. It required a high-explosive shell, which meant that they would have to go without an armor-piercing shell in the breech—momentarily—leaving them sidelined with German tanks in the neighborhood.

Shrapnel clattered against the Pershing's armor. From inside the tank, it sounded like a hailstorm hitting a tin roof. The Panzerfausts were landing closer and closer to their position. Clarence had to act. "HE!" Clarence called.

The loader tugged a handle and opened the breech. He removed the black-tipped shell by the rim, racked it, retrieved a silver-tipped high-explosive shell, and slid it into the breech. The seconds ticked by slowly. Finally, the breech closed with a clang. Clarence was in business.

He settled the reticle on the center of the bridge as his finger tensed against the trigger. It was just then, right as he was about to squeeze the trigger, that he saw it.

A Panzerfaust warhead was flying straight at him, in what seemed like slow motion.

Clarence gasped. All he could do was watch. At the last second, the warhead dipped. A white flash filled the entirety of Clarence's periscope as the explosion rocked the tank. The concussive force raced straight down the 90mm's barrel, causing the gun to discharge without Clarence even touching the trigger.

A flaming ball of gases escaped the breech and rose toward Earley. The commander howled in pain as the flaming ball singed the side of his face. The turret turned dark with smoke. McVey and Smokey were screaming.

Clarence bent over, heaving for breath.

"We're on fire!" Earley shouted. "Bail out!"

Clarence turned just in time to see Earley's boots abandon the turret. Sunlight poured inside when the loader threw open his hatch and climbed up and out.

The sight of a smoking American tank invigorated the enemy. Machine-gun bullets plinked a steady rhythm across the frontal armor.

Clarence scrambled back through the turret and snatched a Thompson submachine gun from its rack on his way out. Even if he had to abandon the tank, he wasn't going down without a fight.

He felt the breath of passing bullets hot on his face as he emerged from the commander's position. Clarence dropped to the engine deck, then rolled off the back of the Pershing before he fell hard to the ground between pairs of train tracks.

Earley and the loader waved Clarence toward them from a drainage ditch about twenty yards behind the tank. Bullets nipped at Clarence's heels as he ran to safety, sliding feet-first into the ditch like a baseball player going for home plate. The shallow depression was only about two feet deep. Smokey and McVey were missing.

Clarence rose to the lip of the ditch and searched for his friends.

A murderous flood of green machine-gun tracers was still splashing the Pershing. Both men were frantically crawling beneath the tank, having dropped through the escape hatch in the belly instead of going over the sides.

"Come on!" Clarence shouted, waving them toward safety.

Smokey and McVey made a run for it. As they hurtled themselves toward the ditch, tripping and tumbling to the edge, Clarence and the others pulled them inside.

Smokey lay on his back and cursed a blue streak at the sky.

Earley and the others racked rounds into their 1911 pistols while Clarence worked the action of his Thompson. They might have to shoot their way out of this tight spot. He glimpsed over the top of the ditch before a snap of German bullets sent him diving back down. Green tracers kicked up the dirt just inches above his face and tinged off the steel rail tracks like fireflies.

Earley gritted his teeth, saying nothing. Clarence's chest felt tight with dread.

The turret of Villa's tank wheeled from side to side as it fired indiscriminately out of sheer desperation. The coaxial hammered from the gun shield and the bow gun wagged and spat fire. The interior was no doubt filling with spent cartridges.

They wouldn't stand a chance alone. They couldn't defend themselves from all directions, and when the enemy advanced with Panzerfausts, the last tank would go silent.

Pinned in his shallow grave, Clarence feared that the end was near. *It's only a matter of time.* It was a mantra Clarence had recited, a recrimination of his circumstances, and now his time had come.

And the Germans realized it as well. Everything lay in plain view.

A Pershing, abandoned and smoking. A crew, pinned like rats. The enemy must have called their command center to the north and urged them to send in the big guns—to "Strike them now!"

That was the only explanation for what was to follow.

CHAPTER 24 **THE GIANT**

That same morning
Paderborn rail yard

Buck kept the rookies close by his side, deep in the shadows of the switch house.

The Germans were converging on their position.

Machine-gun bullets tapped on the walls as if they were searching for an entrance. Panzerfausts burst through bricks, sending streams of red dust filtering down. In the words of one eyewitness account, the building was being "shot to pieces."

Byron and the other doughs crowded the doorway. One at a time, each man made a mad dash outside and fired around the corner before scrambling breathlessly back to safety.

The wounded German was still pleading for assistance, but now he focused his entreaties on Danforth and his battered crew, who sat against the wall with pistols across their laps.

One of Buck's rookies wanted to make a break for it, back the way they'd come. But Buck held him from bolting.

"You'll just get cut down!" Buck said.

Out there, death was everywhere.

From the ditch, Clarence saw it too. The Germans' focus had shifted. They were crossing the tracks and leaping between shell craters, stopping only to fire their weapons as they bore down on the men in the switch house.

The enemy's plan was apparent: subdue that strong point first, and then they could silence the last functioning tank and end the valiant stand of Chuck Miller and his crew.

Clarence took aim over the top with his Thompson, ready for the first German to dash forth with a Panzerfaust. If the Germans were going to get to Chuck, they'd have to get past him first. As he surveyed his field of fire, Clarence's eye settled on the Pershing.

Wait a second.

The tank was still idling in place, with its gun aimed leftward. The smoke had stopped rising, providing him with a clear view of the damage.

My God.

Clarence saw cause for hope.

The Panzerfaust hadn't hit the Pershing's barrel as he'd thought, only the muzzle brake at the tip. The jet of flaming plasma had bored a hole in the casting large enough for daylight to stream through, but that looked to be the extent of the damage.

Clarence drew the crew's attention over the clash of battle— "I think that gun can fire!"

Everyone crept to the lip to take a look. It was hard to tell from this distance.

Earley squinted at the tank. It was risky. If the gun barrel was fractured, a shell could detonate prematurely or get stuck, which would send the blast right back into the turret.

Clarence's eyes darted from Villa's tank to the doughs darting and firing from the switch house. They couldn't hold the Germans off for much longer. Time was running out.

"The tube looks okay," Clarence said.

"That's a heck of a gamble," Earley said. If they were wrong, the mistake could wipe out the entire crew. "Are you certain?"

All eyes turned to Clarence. "No," he said. "But we have to try something."

Smokey and McVey had been there at Mons, and so had Earley, with another crew. The words coming out of Clarence's mouth sounded a lot like those of someone they had once known.

Paul Faircloth.

"Let's go, then," Earley said.

He vaulted from the ditch and led the way as Clarence and the others followed in a mad dash to the Pershing.

Countless German troops swung their rifles and machine guns at the sprinting American crew from across the rail yard.

Earley climbed aboard and crouched behind the turret, making way for the turret crew. He urged them to hurry.

Bullets snapped overhead and dinged against the Pershing as Clarence and the loader clambered atop the turret and dropped inside. Earley followed them and deadened the noise of gunfire as he slammed the hatch cover shut.

Beneath the Pershing, McVey wormed his way to the escape hatch and pulled himself up and into the tank, but Smokey was lagging behind and struggling to catch his breath.

McVey patched into the intercom. He was eager to escape the relentless fire.

"Put us up there with Red," Earley ordered.

The Pershing rolled toward the lone fighting Sherman as McVey fed the engine some gas. No one had noticed Smokey's empty seat.

Unable to pull himself inside, the bow gunner was being dragged forward on his back as he gripped the escape hatch with all his might beneath the moving tank.

"Stop, goddammit!" Smokey screamed into the hull.

McVey heard him and looked over and realized that Smokey was missing.

The tank screeched to a halt, allowing Smokey to pull himself inside. Once he was safely on board, a tempest of curse words flooded the intercom.

Earley asked what had happened. Clarence fought not to snicker as Smokey explained.

Earley radioed Villa. His voice was all business. "We're back," he said. "They got us down, but not out."

Villa sounded relieved as he welcomed the crew's return.

Soon after the Pershing had started rolling again, Clarence asked Earley to stop. He had spotted a machine-gun nest blinking near the station, one of the same guns that had targeted them during their dash to the tank.

At Earley's command, the Pershing ground to a stop about thirty yards behind Villa's Sherman and slightly to its left.

Clarence called for a high-explosive shell.

The loader threw a fresh shell in, and the breech snapped shut. Clarence's finger hesitated against the trigger. Firing was a heck of a gamble. If the barrel was fractured, they wouldn't survive to figure out they'd been wrong.

Earley opened his hatch to spot with his binoculars for Clarence.

It was then that he heard it. The unmistakable sounds of metal squeaking on metal, and steel tracks slapping the ground. The raspy snarl of an engine accelerating. Earley glanced over his right shoulder. The noise was originating from about fifty yards *behind* them.

Something was traveling coming down a corridor between the rail-yard buildings, which amplified the sound and funneled it in their direction.

"TANK!"

Clarence heard the call and felt Earley's heavy grip on his right shoulder, the signal to turn the turret. "Five o'clock," Earley said.

Clarence couldn't believe his ears. *Five o'clock?* Someone was practically behind them.

Clarence turned the turret so hard to the right that he nearly broke the pistol grip and the turret whined in recognition of the order.

"What is it?" Clarence asked.

Earley replied with the word that every American tanker dreaded: "Panther."

All of a sudden, Clarence felt cold.

Earley's muttering certainly didn't help. "Faster, faster, faster." Earley held on above the rotating turret, powerless to do anything but watch.

The brownish-green Panther cut through the shadows as it approached the roundhouse. It was so close there was no need for binoculars.

Whoever the enemy commander was, he was a professional. Not only had he managed to outflank them, he had come stalking with his

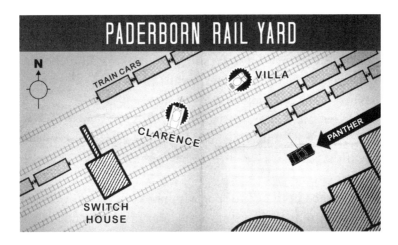

gun pre-positioned. The Panther's turret was already turned ninety degrees to the right, in position to fire a quick broadside.

From Earley's vantage point, something didn't add up. The Pershing was the closer target, but the Panther's gun was pointing elsewhere. Earley traced the trajectory of the enemy's aim to the rear of Villa's tank.

The German had likely received a radio call that the Pershing was abandoned, its crew seeking refuge in a ditch. And the Sherman was ripe for the picking.

But that was ten minutes ago.

Now, the Pershing had risen from the dead. And the Panther had taken notice.

Inside the enemy tank, the crew was likely urging their gunner to shift his aim to the Pershing, the tank with a gun turning toward them. Sure enough, the Panther's gun began swinging left while the Pershing's gun swung right, both guns turning toward each other like gates closing. Someone wasn't going to drive away from this.

Inside the turret, Clarence held his eyes to the periscope. He watched the train station with its platforms and tracks blur past before he remembered: they had the wrong shell loaded.

A high-explosive shell was locked in the breech. It was the right firepower to take out a machine-gun nest. But it wouldn't dent a Panther.

Gotta clear the gun! Clarence thought in a panic. "Ready an AP!" he yelled to his loader.

The youngster heaved a black-tipped T33 shell from the ready rack, anticipating a shell change.

"Not yet," Clarence said. "On my call."

A shell change would take time, and Clarence didn't have a second to spare. He'd have to do it differently from how any instructor would ever dream of teaching in gunnery school.

Above the turret, Earley kept silent. He could sense that Clarence must have had a plan. If he didn't, they were all already dead.

Clarence reached with his left hand and gripped the wheel that controlled the gun's elevation as he waited for his first glimpse of the Panther.

The brownish-green tank appeared on the right side of Clarence's sight.

Clarence spun the elevation handwheel counterclockwise, using every ounce of muscle.

Outside the tank, the 90mm gun dipped—taking aim toward the ground—and the turret kept turning until it reached the Panther.

The 90mm roared.

The HE shell slammed the ground in front of the Panther, kicking a gray cloud of cinders and dust in the enemy tank's face. The Panther momentarily disappeared behind the cloud.

Inside the turret, Clarence righted the pistol grip—he'd turned the turret far enough.

"Now!" he shouted.

The loader slammed the AP shell into the open breech. With spins of the elevation wheel, Clarence returned the 90mm to its level position. He set his eyes to the periscope.

The huge, angular shape of the Panther reappeared as the cloud of dust settled down. Its gun was still turning, its black muzzle hole searching for him.

Clarence's finger crushed the trigger.

The 90mm spoke with an earsplitting crack. A blinding flash illuminated both tanks.

The 24-pound shell went spinning through the air at 2,774 feet per second and covered the distance in a blink.

A screech of sparks blasted from the Panther's slanted front armor as the shell bored through more than five and a half inches of steel and kept going into the tank's guts.

"Hit!" Earley shouted with elation. The loader locked another shell in the breech.

Clarence's finger hovered over the trigger in a rare moment of indecision.

Wait.

As the dust around the enemy tank settled further, he saw figures—the Panther's crew. They were leaping from the turret and the driver was opening his hatch.

There was a gaping black hole in the Panther's armor between where the driver and radio operator had once sat, but no fire ensued.

The driver flopped over the side of the tank and fled to the rear.

Clarence tracked his retreat through the periscope sight. Instincts took over. An enemy soldier was downrange, a man who, mere moments before, had tried to kill Clarence and his crew.

The driver disappeared behind his tank, then reappeared again to the left of it, mindlessly following the road back the way he'd come.

He may have been injured or in shock, because he staggered and dropped in the road. Clarence fixed his eye to the 6x zoom sight and set the reticle on the man.

At that exact moment, the German turned and stared back at the Pershing.

The zoom sight brought his face close, as if Clarence were standing a few feet away from him. The driver was young, with brown hair. His eyes welled up with despair as he realized his mistake.

Clarence balanced the power of life and death in his index finger. With a few pounds of pressure, his coaxial could wipe one more enemy soldier from the earth.

Those were his orders, after all. This was his duty too.

But Clarence hedged.

Fighting to the end. Killing to the end. That's what *they* did. The Germans he'd been fighting all these months.

And he wasn't about to become someone like them.

Clarence nudged the pistol grip to the left. The 90mm slid off the man and stopped, its muzzle brake bobbing like a nod.

It was a signal. The Panther was out of the war and that was enough for Clarence.

The German driver's eyes changed. He stood up and ran away in disbelief.

The effect of the Pershing's shot reverberated across the rail yard. The Germans could see their incapacitated Panther sitting there frozen in defeat, with its hatches pried open. And they could hear the rattle of two American tanks that had taken everything thrown at them and still refused to go away.

The enemy stopped advancing and their fire tapered off. There was nothing left to win here.

As if pulled by a marionette's strings, the German forces retreated back across the tracks and into the residential neighborhood on the other side.

The Pershing's engine shuddered to a stop after it returned to the switch house, parking about thirty yards in front of the abandoned Panther. Villa's tank pulled up beside the Pershing before its engine also shut down. Both American tanks were speckled silver by bullets or shrapnel.

The sounds of gunfire had shifted deeper into Paderborn.

A chain of exhausted A-Company doughs slogged from the switch house without looking back. Relief had finally come. F-Company's Shermans had secured the rail yard with two companies of doughs, claiming ninety-three prisoners in the process, before continuing their sweep into town.

"It was disgusting to watch how the Third Reich died," wrote a German sergeant. "None of its leaders came to the foxholes to defend it to the last man as they had promised. They all abandoned their posts and fled, afraid of being held responsible, or cowardly died by suicide."

Clarence came down from the turret and joined his crew as they examined the hole in the muzzle brake. Another inch to the side and the Panzerfaust warhead would have landed in the barrel itself. His gamble to fire the gun had paid off, but it was riskier than even he had imagined.

Still shaken by the ordeal, Earley puffed away at his pipe. He had never seen anything like Clarence's first shot, a deliberate miss. Later on, he wouldn't hesitate to tell him so.

If Clarence had called for a shell change as soon as he realized that the wrong ammunition was loaded—as gunners were trained to do—he would have condemned himself, and his entire crew, to death.

But luckily, Clarence had never been formally trained as a gunner.

Red Villa's crew gathered around the Pershing and its tankers. Chuck Miller approached Clarence with a wry smile. "I hear you missed with your first shot," Chuck said.

"Yeah, but not the second!" Clarence said.

Chuck laughed and hugged his friend tightly.

Danforth bypassed the congregation altogether. Hobbling on an injured leg, he beat a path straight for his derelict Sherman, the third tank that he had lost in the war and one of more than six hundred Shermans that Spearhead would write off as scrap—the most of any U.S. division.

The broad Texan squeezed inside the turret and reemerged moments later with a bottle in his hand. Danforth found Clarence in the scrum of tankers and presented him with a bottle of champagne.

Clarence was surprised by the gesture. The champagne was from the Dom Hotel.

"My last one," Danforth said. "I was saving it for something special." He thanked Clarence for saving his life. "That Panther wasn't coming to take prisoners," he said.

Clarence's quick thinking had given Danforth a new lease on life, but neither man could know how short that tenure would last. In two days, Danforth would be promoted and given command of his own tank and three days after that, his Sherman would drive in front of a German tank while crossing a small village.

He was killed at age twenty-eight. Danforth's fourth tank would be his last.

Buck lingered in the switch house long after everyone else had departed.

Lieutenant Boom's eyes were closed, but Buck took a knee alongside his body and spoke to him as if he were still alive. Buck told Boom that everyone had made it, and thanked him for keeping them safe.

Boom would be buried in the Netherlands American Cemetery, near the grave of General Rose, and his name would appear in his hometown paper one last time, but not in the sports highlights column where it usually appeared.

This time, the elements that appeared in print were his name, a photo, and a caption: "Makes Sacrifice."

Having returned to A-Company's headquarters—the home with the untouched Easter cake—Buck settled his eyes on a curious sight down the block to the east. A knocked-out German tank blocked the road, as if frozen in motion.

Byron lingered nearby, looking bored, so Buck gave him a shout. The duo went to investigate with the rookies tagging along.

Buck looked up in awe from alongside the enemy behemoth.

It was a Tiger I, Germany's most legendary tank of the war, a monstrous machine that looked as if it had been chiseled from a block of stone. Its interlacing wheels were wrapped in tracks that stood chest-

Tiger I

high on Buck. Byron circled the Tiger as the rookies climbed aboard. The tank was camouflaged with foliage and, curiously, its barrel had been hewn down to less than half its original length.

Buck assumed that the Pershing had destroyed the beast. Later accounts would attribute its destruction to airpower, although no aircraft had attacked that morning. The tank's shattered barrel hinted at a possible explanation. The German crew may have suffered a mechanical failure and disabled their own tank with explosives as they abandoned the vehicle.

A commotion to the left of the Tiger drew Buck's attention. An Easy Company tank crew was pushing and prodding a German tank crew against the brick wall of a building. They were searching for one man in particular.

A rough American tanker from the Deep South, like Buck, singled out the German tank commander and threw him down to the ground. He then began kicking him over and over again. The German's crew watched, powerless to intervene.

Buck cursed. Hadn't there been enough violence already? He told the rookies that they might want to look away.

Buck and Byron moved in behind the angry American crew. Buck expected to find SS runes on the German's collar, but saw only silver Panzer skulls. The man was a Wehrmacht tanker, probably the commander of the Tiger.

The rest of the American tank crew encouraged the abuse. Buck shot Byron a look that asked: *Is it worth interceding?* Byron shrugged in response.

Maybe the tankers had lost a buddy that morning?

Doughs and tankers, everyone had bled taking the rail yard. A-Company had suffered seventeen casualties, and Easy Company fifteen, not to mention their five tanks destroyed and others disabled. For the next two years, Shermans would lie rusting in the fields of Paderborn.

The irate tanker drew his 1911 pistol. Even his own crew gave him space when he pointed it at the German. The tanker turned red as the pistol shook in his hand.

"You don't need to do this," Buck said aloud. Even the tanker's own crew agreed with Buck. From his knees, the German commander removed his peaked cap and pleaded for mercy.

Byron saw something and began shaking his head—No, no, no. He couldn't take his pale blue eyes off the German commander's face. It was a face that was burned into his memory. He'd recognize it anywhere.

The rough tanker shucked a round into the pistol, but before he could make a move, Byron thrust himself between the gunman and his target. It was an audacious move. There was no telling what this enraged man was capable of. Byron took a closer look at the German before turning to face the incensed American.

"Don't shoot him," Byron pleaded.

"What the hell, boy?" said the tanker. "Are you a Kraut lover?"

"This fellow saved my life," Byron said, "and if you'll get that damn gun out of my face, I'll tell you about it."

The tanker uttered a harrumph of disbelief, but lowered his pistol all the same. Buck felt a wave of relief wash over him.

Byron explained how he and some other doughs had been captured and forced to dig their own graves when a German tank commander—this same man—had driven past, seen what was happening, and prevented their execution.

Buck was floored by his friend's revelation. Nevertheless, he stepped to Byron's side with palms raised. "He's telling the truth." Buck said he had heard the same story from several others in their squad.

The American tanker's eyes shot back and forth between Buck and Byron. "Are you sure this is the same Kraut?" he asked.

Byron was certain and turned the question back on the tanker. How could he forget the man who saved his life?

The tanker almost spat as he holstered his pistol. "Get him out of my sight before I change my mind."

Byron pulled the German commander toward his fellow prisoners. The American tank crew moved on, their anger having subsided. Buck and Byron lingered with the prisoners until someone came along to claim them.

The German commander laid a hand on Byron's shoulder. "Thank you," he said in English.

Byron gave the man a nod.

As Buck and the doughs returned to headquarters, Byron was as white as a sheet and couldn't go any farther. He sat on the curb, his lip quivering. Byron buried his face in his hands as all the emotions that he'd bottled up came flooding out.

Buck gave his friend some space.[*]

As Buck and the squad readied for the next round, Panzerfausts could be heard bursting in Paderborn. The enemy was waging a delaying action so the remnants of SS Panzer Brigade Westfalen could escape eastward. But the worst was over.

The rail yard was theirs. So was the airfield. And it was only a matter of time until Paderborn would be theirs as well. The division was so certain of its conquest that it had dispatched a task force west to Lippstadt, where history was unfolding.

A radio call would soon go out: "Spearhead to Powerhouse," and at 3:45 P.M., the tankers of Spearhead would clasp hands with the tankers of Hell on Wheels to complete the steel wall around the Ruhr.

The prize? More than 325,000 German troops—including twenty-six generals and one admiral, all trapped inside the "Ruhr Pocket." It would be a greater blow to the enemy than the losses of Stalingrad or Africa.

In America, word would break on April 9 that the army had decided to rename the Ruhr Pocket; it would be henceforth known as the "Rose Pocket," in honor of General Rose.

And from Paderborn, Spearhead would steamroll eastward, where they would come face-to-face with the crimes of the Nazi regime. At the foot of the Harz Mountains, two task forces would liberate the Dora-Nordhausen concentration camp, releasing slave laborers from across Europe, including Jewish prisoners transferred from

---

[*] Author's note: We searched for the German commander's identity with help from a colonel in the present-day German tank forces, but due to spotty late-war records, all we discovered was that a staff sergeant "Oberfeldwebel Böving" commanded the Tiger knocked out at the rail yard. Was he the one? We may never know. To hear Buck tell this story of mercy in his own words, take a look at my video interview with him on my website.

Auschwitz, while Clarence's task force rammed down the walls at the nearby copper mines of Sangerhausen, liberating five hundred British and Russian POWs.

As for Berlin, the men of Spearhead would never lay eyes on the enemy capital. General Omar Bradley estimated that the battle for Berlin could cost 100,000 American casualties—"a pretty stiff price for a prestige objective"—and Eisenhower concurred. The brass would stop Spearhead at the Elbe River, sixty-six miles from Berlin, leaving Hitler to the Russians.

But all of that was to come.

Buck went from Clyde to Dick to Stan to Luther, checking their ammo levels and finding them disturbingly low. Shaking his head in bewilderment, he harangued them: were you expecting the Germans to share?

If his old classmates had voted again that day, Buck would no longer be elected the boy with the best personality.

He'd become something better.

The Panther attracted Clarence like a magnet. He approached the German war machine slowly. Its armor was pitted from earlier scuffles and weld lines ran like scars up the seams.

Clarence felt the jagged shell hole. His shot had gouged right through the Panther's breastplate, revealing a thick, dark core, like a vein of coal.

Clarence climbed aboard. The layer of *Zimmerit* felt gritty beneath his boots, as if the tank were made of concrete instead of steel. The driver's hatch was open. He looked behind the tank in the direction its driver had fled. But the street was empty.

Above the hull, where the radioman/bow gunner would sit, Clarence took a knee. He had seen all but one member of the Panther's crew come pouring out in the aftermath of his hit. He had to know.

He lifted the hatch cover.

Below, a young German tanker sat dead in his seat. He was fair-haired, with light eyes that remained open as if he were only dreaming and would wake up soon.

Clarence didn't cringe at the sight of the man he'd killed. He didn't lose his stomach. He didn't even look away. He just wished he could speak with his fallen foe. He'd ask him one simple question: *Why?*

Why fight to the last hour, to the last breath, to try to kill him and his friends? The war was lost. *Why didn't you just let this end?*

The enemy's mind-set was one he'd never understand. There was no sense in trying.

Clarence focused on the black holster at the man's side. He reached inside and drew the German's pistol. It was a Walther P-38, stamped with Nazi proof marks and all. Clarence wiped the pistol on his coveralls and stuffed it inside his tanker jacket.

It was his by right, he had fought for it.

He was once a loader, but not anymore.

He was a tank gunner now.

Clarence shut the hatch.

Nine months later, Christmas Eve 1945
Mourmelon-le-Grand Airfield, France

The party in the base canteen was in full swing. Gustav carried plates of piping-hot doughnuts as he moved between tables full of festive American soldiers.

Tall black letters were stitched to the back of his green American training uniform: "PW," an abbreviation for "prisoner of war." The canteen resembled a beer hall, with a high wooden roof. Garlands draped the walls. Hundreds of conversations buzzed above the music from a military band, which played holiday tunes from the stage. Snow flurries streaked the darkness outside the windows.

Once home to P-47 squadrons, Mourmelon-le-Grand was now a transition camp for American soldiers leaving Europe or beginning their tours with the occupation forces.

Dinner had ended and it was time for dessert. Gustav cheerfully delivered the doughnuts—plain, with a dusting of powdered sugar— to a table of GIs. The Americans were appreciative. Other German POWs poured coffee from stainless pitchers and the smell flooded the room.

Gustav's specialty on the kitchen crew was making doughnuts, an assignment that he treasured. He was paid 80 cents a day for his work and the job came with an undeniable perk—he could eat as many doughnuts as he wanted.

He wasn't the least bit homesick. He had sent his family a postcard through the Red Cross, so that they knew he was alive and well. He had survived the *Endkampf,* and that was all that mattered. The resistance in those first five months of 1945 had cost Germany more than 1 million fighting men—25 percent of those who died during the entire war—not to mention the 3 million troops marched into Russian captivity. Of those unfortunates, 1 million would never return.

When he was first captured, Gustav didn't think he'd survive a week.

From Cologne, he and Rolf were transported by train across Belgium. They rode huddled against the cold in an open-top train car with about fifty other POWs. If a prisoner dared entertain thoughts of jumping with a glimpse over the side of the car, an American guard would fire warning shots from a machine gun over everyone's heads.

Halfway across Belgium, the train stopped and the POWs were served soup without bowls or utensils. Gustav and the others used their caps as bowls, but the soup quickly soaked through the fabric.

News of the train carrying German POWs spread through villages along the route.

From their position in the middle of the car, Gustav and Rolf saw Belgian civilians waiting on an approaching overpass with bricks in their hands. *This can't be good,* Gustav had thought. He didn't fully grasp the peril he was in until the bricks came raining down upon them from above. Gustav and Rolf covered their heads. Due to the train's momentum, the bricks missed Gustav's car and landed in the car behind them, killing several POWs.

The assault was repeated at the next overpass. And the one after that.

The Germans were separated upon their arrival at the camp. SS men went one way, Wehrmacht soldiers another. Ranks were further separated and Rolf bid Gustav goodbye with a nod. Gustav hadn't seen his friend since.

The Americans were unprepared for the vast numbers of prisoners they'd taken. As a result, the POWs' rations were meager. They were typically allotted a single loaf of bread, per day, split between ten men. POWs became sickly from malnourishment, often to the point of death.

Sympathy was in short supply. To their American overseers at the time, the Germans were not fellow soldiers or human beings—they were war criminals. After the war ended, Gustav discovered an explanation for the hostility. He and other POWs were herded into the camp theater and shown a film reel taken inside a newly liberated concentration camp.

Since 1933, the Nazis had told Gustav and other Germans that concentration camps were prisons for society's degenerates. But the film showed a different reality, one far worse than anything that Gustav could have imagined. It was sickening and Gustav buried his face in his hands. While he was fighting on the front lines, the Nazis were committing genocide.

Gustav eventually found sympathy where he least expected it.

Due to his small stature—deemed unsuitable for breaking rocks to build roads—Gustav was assigned to the kitchen crew, where he struck up a friendship with an African American GI while he cleared the men's trays after meals. Gustav was puzzled that white and black Americans sat separately. His new friend explained segregation this way: "You are Prisoner number 1, and we are Prisoner number 2!"

When Gustav cleared the black GIs' trays, he found something curious—morsels of food untouched in the corners. A smear of peanut butter. A slice of fruit. Some crackers. Gustav devoured the leftovers when his guards weren't looking. The black GI flashed Gustav a wink and other black soldiers gave him a nod. The leftovers were no accident.

Their generosity would pull him through.

That was nine months ago. Now, the party was swinging. As Gustav collected empty plates to refill them with doughnuts, he noticed his guard going from prisoner to prisoner.

Was something wrong?

At each POW, the guard whispered a message and the POW abandoned whatever he was doing to head back to the concession counter.

The guard approached Gustav and told him that he could visit the chow line. Gustav didn't understand.

"Everyone gets the same tonight," the guard said—commander's orders.

Gustav swore he was dreaming.

The bounty in the chow line was plentiful. As Gustav moved from station to station, the cooks—his fellow POWs—filled his tray high with turkey and all the trimmings.

At the end of the line, he faced a choice: Bottled beer? Or a can of cola?

Other POWs had taken seats at the end of a table of GIs, but Gustav hesitated. *Is this permitted?* he asked himself.

The GIs didn't seem to mind. Neither did the guards, who had turned their attention to the band. So, Gustav took a seat and experienced his first bite of turkey. It was toasty, meaty, and marvelous. The bland rations of the last few months made it taste even better.

Gustav had chosen the cola. He had never experienced a canned beverage before. As he carefully popped the lid, the cola hissed. Gustav took a sip and nearly coughed from the carbonation.

It was the single best sip he'd ever taken.

A hush fell over the canteen as the American bandleader drew everyone's attention with a tap on the microphone. GIs lowered their coffee cups and POWs' forks hovered over their suppers.

The bandleader asked the audience to sing along to the next song with them. The song was "Silent Night," an Austrian Christmas song composed in the early 1800s.

The bandleader translated the title, so the Germans would understand him—"Stille Nacht."

Gustav was surprised. The Americans wanted them to sing too?

The music began filtering through the canteen.

At first, only American voices carried the tune.

Silent night. Holy night.

Gustav looked to the POWs at his sides. A few joined the Americans in singing.

All is calm—Alles schläft.
All is bright—einsam wacht.

With each verse, more German voices joined the chorus and the two languages blended throughout the cavernous room.

Gustav found his voice and sang along.

Heav'nly hosts sing Alleluia—Tönt es laut von fern und nah.
Christ the Savior is born!—Christ, der Retter ist da!
Christ the Savior is born—Christ, der Retter ist da.

As the song continued, Gustav's eyes moistened with tears. He dabbed at them, but tears kept slipping despite his efforts.

The sound of everyone singing together told him it was true.

The war was really over.

Two months later, February 1946

Gustav walked the empty road as the sun set at his back.

The last miles were the longest. And the hardest.

A ceaseless cold wind swept across the flats of northern Germany. The weather typically blew from the north, as if the turbulent sea lay just beyond the horizon.

Gustav carried his belongings in a small sack over one shoulder. His boyhood home sat in the middle of the British zone of occupation, so it was their troops who had delivered him to the nearest city and set him free.

Gustav paced with his head hung low as he walked the remaining fifteen miles home. After the time he'd spent as a prisoner, freedom felt unnatural to him. It was overwhelming and uncomfortable, like an itch he couldn't quite scratch.

He had stayed at Mourmelon-le-Grand as a volunteer, working up to the day the camp closed. He had even inquired about emigrating to

America. At one time there had been a program that allowed POWs to seek asylum there, but it ended quickly after too many Germans applied.

Life was just simpler as a POW. He knew how the day would begin, how it would end, and where his next meal would come from.

Gustav was apprehensive about coming home. There were too many questions. What would tomorrow hold? How could he just resume his life as if nothing had happened?

Part of him wished he could keep walking forever.

The Schaefer family was finishing their work in the fields for the day when they saw Gustav coming.

They dropped their tools and ran toward him. Gustav's father bounded among them. By some miracle, the Russians had released him from captivity, due to his age.

Gustav's face lit up as he embraced his family—it'd been two years since they'd been together. Since last he'd seen him, Gustav's brother had grown taller than Gustav. His grandmother and grandfather wept as they held him. Gustav's mother pulled him by the arm toward the ranch. She declared that they would celebrate that night with a ham, schnapps, and bread with slabs of butter.

As his mother entered the house, she flipped a switch. The sight was wondrous.

Lightbulbs illuminated the entire room.

Gustav marveled at the spectacle of his boyhood home cast in brightness. That summer his family had invested their meager savings and had a power line attached to the house.

Gustav couldn't stop smiling as he examined the new lightbulbs up close.

The darkness of the war felt far behind him.

CHAPTER 26 **THE LAST BATTLE**

Thirty-seven years later, winter 1983
Fort Myers, Florida

Clarence pedaled his three-wheel cruiser bike in an easy rhythm on a path across the dunes. Tropical bushes slipped past on both sides as the dunes rolled down to the white sand of Fort Myers beach.

Clarence was sixty, balding, and tan from head to toe. He had embraced the Florida lifestyle, wearing just the essentials—shorts, boat shoes, and sizeable sunglasses.

Amid this paradise of blue skies and towering clouds, Clarence had found peace.

His wife, Melba, rode a matching bike at his side.

Just a few weeks after Clarence returned from the war, he bumped into Melba—the young admirer who had sent him the homemade fudge when he was in combat—at his local skating rink. She was eighteen and petite with cherubic cheeks and gentle eyes. She often wore a bow in her curly brown hair. They were married within a year and had lived a wonderful life ever since.

Clarence and Melba

When Clarence retired as supervisor of an industrial cement plant earlier that year, the couple had become snowbirds. They now split their time between a mobile home in Florida and another in Pennsylvania, where their two daughters resided.

And they roller-skated. They brought their skates along in the trunk of their green Rambler station wagon whenever they made a road trip. They belonged to a skate club in Pennsylvania and would travel with other couples to "Old Timers' Nights" at rinks that still played live organ music. Melba could skate backward, but Clarence struggled with his coordination. The only way he could pull off what seemed to come so naturally for her was when Melba steadied him by the hands.

Clarence held on and didn't look back.

In these, his golden years, the war seemed far behind him.

Twelve years later, November 1996

Clarence emerged from his trailer in Palmerton, Pennsylvania, on a cool fall morning. The Forrest Inn trailer park was neat and tidy, tucked beneath a canopy of trees.

Clarence walked toward a bank of mailboxes at the park's entrance. Every day for the past week, he'd checked the mail obsessively, hoping it would come.

Today was the day. It had finally arrived. The package was just the size of a book, but even holding it made him nervous.

Melba was out running errands, so the trailer was quiet. Clarence unwrapped the package revealing a VHS cassette entitled *Scenes of War*. For fifty-one years, he had waited to see the contents of this tape. By the time Clarence had returned from Europe, Jim Bates's film of the fighting in Cologne had disappeared from theaters and was nowhere to be found.

Until now.

A war buddy had sent a letter alerting Clarence to the tape's whereabouts. Apparently, Bates had held on to a personal copy of the film and had recently donated it to his local library in Colorado Springs,

Colorado, and the library had produced a documentary using the footage. Clarence wasted no time in ordering a copy.

But now, with the tape in his hands, Clarence was having doubts.

Is this a bad idea?

For fifty-one years, he had waged an epic battle of will. If a war movie played on TV, he'd skip over the channel. When fireworks popped off on the Fourth of July, he'd shut the windows. No 3rd Armored Division license-plate holder would be found on a car of his, so no one would ask questions or figure out the truth: the wounds were still there.

Clarence could still blink and see Paul Faircloth lying upside down on the bank as blood gushed from the stump of his leg. Even all these years later, he imagined the torso of the tanker at the Welborn Massacre, roasted like a "baked ham" on the table at holidays. And he saw the events at Blatzheim, where an entire crew had to work together to remove a dead buddy from their tank after the concussion force of a shell's impact had shattered his bones—turning a man to Jell-O— with just his skin holding him together.

Despite his misgivings, Clarence inserted the VHS tape into the player.

It's just nostalgia, he told himself. *It's harmless.*

After all, his parents had seen this film back then. So how bad could it be?

Clarence pressed Play. Bates's black-and-white film flickered as the documentary began.

Clarence watched a dough advancing through the streets of Cologne, firing a machine gun from the hip. A narrator gave a play-by-play in a pitchy voice while an orchestral soundtrack stoked the tension.

The cathedral's spires loomed large.

The footage showed the Pershing idling, stalking someone or something.

Clarence watched eagerly. It was like opening a time capsule.

A massive four-way intersection appeared on-screen. Clarence recognized this place. The Gereon neighborhood was on the other side, where the German tank had taken cover behind a building. Bates steadied his camera on the spot where the enemy tank had been, hoping to catch another glimpse. Instead, he filmed something totally unexpected, a dramatic event that took Clarence by surprise once again, all these years later.

A black Opel P4 car suddenly raced into the intersection from the left, driving wildly.

Clarence edged forward in his seat—he remembered this.

Machine-gun tracers chased the car. Misses skipped from the street like stones off the water. Puffs of dust—the sign of hits—leapt from the car itself.

The film flickered. . . .

The fighting had ended on-screen and the setting had changed. Bates was tagging along as the doughs secured the opposite side of the intersection. He turned his camera on the bullet-ridden car that had come to rest against the curb. A trio of American medics had already found one victim—a man who lay dead behind the wheel, killed by a headshot. His identity had become known in the intervening years.

He was no Nazi general fleeing justice, as Clarence had thought at the time. The driver was Michael Delling, the owner of a grocery store. He was just a civilian trying to escape the carnage that surrounded him.

Clarence stared at the screen, dumbstruck by what he was seeing.

The film flickered. . . .

On the passenger's side, the medics tended to the second victim. The young woman lay on her back against the curb. Her eyes were closed and she was barely breathing.

Clarence watched in horror. Back then, he had only seen the flash of her long, curly hair and had wondered if his eyes were playing tricks on him. Now there was no doubt.

A medic gnawed on his pipe as he opened the woman's jacket, revealing a lightly colored sweater with embroidered flowers. The medic checked beneath the sweater for entry or exit wounds before rolling the woman onto her side with the assistance of his fellow medics. When he lifted her sweater, he discovered her pale skin was streaked with blood.

Clarence had never seen any of this back then. He had been too busy maintaining a lookout for enemy tanks. He had not seen the look of defeat on the medic's face after he bandaged the woman's wounds.

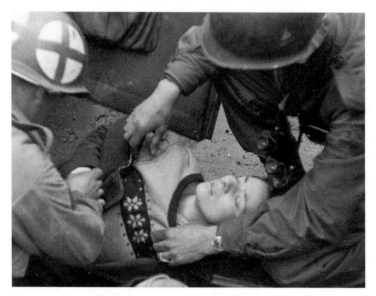

American medics tend to Kathi Esser

He had not noticed the man checking for a pulse before tenderly lowering her hand. The car had shielded Clarence from the heartbreaking details, but it hadn't impeded Jim Bates from keeping his camera rolling so people on the home front could see the tragic face of war.

The film flickered. . . .

Two of the medics moved to rejoin the doughs, while a third remained with the wounded woman. The remaining medic retrieved a briefcase from the car before placing it under the woman's head to serve as a makeshift pillow. Next he found a jacket to drape over her like a blanket. Curled in the fetal position, the woman gazed into Bates's lens with glassy eyes.

She was dying and there was nothing anyone could do for her. But as the documentary revealed, that didn't stop the medic from trying to make her last moments a little less painful.

Inside the briefcase resting under her head were her letters, photos, and a degree in home economics. She was no Golden Pheasant or general's mistress. She was an innocent young woman, a grocery clerk named Kathi Esser who would die soon after Bates lowered his camera.

Clarence lurched forward and turned off the TV.

He stared at the black screen in disbelief, his chest heaving as the thought took hold: *Did I kill her?*

A decade later

Clarence had never imagined that in his eighties he would fear the dark. Nighttime had never frightened him as a child, but now he lay awake at Melba's side, afraid to close his eyes.

A full night's sleep was now an exception to the rule, ever since he had first laid eyes on the Bates documentary. In the few hours he did get, Clarence often dreamed that he was wandering around Cologne on foot, trying to get to safety. But every sound or shadow that he chased led him back to the black car, where he found Kathi dying on the curb all over again. Every time he came across her body in his dreams, he would bolt wide-awake, soaked in sweat.

It was unlike any traumatic memory of the war that he'd experienced. This wasn't some dusty, lingering memory from 1945. This guilt was fresh, born the moment that her face appeared on his television screen.

And the torment wasn't restricted to the dark of night. It often spilled into daylight. On any given day, Clarence would sit on his couch, listless from lack of sleep. His hands trembled. He was irritable, disheartened, and depressed.

And he suffered in silence. Melba was by his side, typically curled around a pillow, but the spark had vanished from her eyes. She was in the grip of Alzheimer's. Sometimes she recognized Clarence's face. His voice still had a calming effect when she became agitated. But after sixty-one years of marriage, she had forgotten his name.

Clarence was faltering and he knew it. He had promised Melba he would never place her in a nursing home, but her care consumed what little energy he had. It was only a matter of time before his fatigue led to sickness and sickness claimed him too. If he was going to be there to care for Melba until the end, Clarence knew he had to fix himself, somehow.

The past could destroy the present—he had seen it happen before.

When Captain Salisbury, Clarence's company commander, had returned home from the war, he finished his degree at Yale, attended Columbia Law School, and went on to become a lawyer at a prestigious New York firm.

In late November 1950, he spent the weekend at his parents' mansion on Long Island. He played tennis on Saturday and dined with his mother and his father, a general retired from the National Guard, on Sunday.

The following morning when his father opened the garage, he was floored by a rush of exhaust fumes. A car had been running all night long in the garage. Inside was his son, Mason.

Clarence's commanding officer had committed suicide at thirty years old. No one had seen it coming. When the press came calling, General Salisbury hinted at the contents of a note that Mason had left behind. As one reporter wrote, "General Salisbury said that since the war his son had been increasingly depressed over the battlefield loss of friends."

After surviving more close calls with German shells than he could count, Captain Salisbury had been stalked and cut down by the unseen killer: the mental toll of war.

About five years later

Clarence paced through the sterile hallways of the VA hospital in Wilkes-Barre, Pennsylvania. He'd been here so many times by now that he knew the corridors by heart.

Prior to this, a VA psychiatrist had diagnosed his symptoms and told him the name of the demons that kept him up at night: "PTSD." Post-traumatic stress disorder. His psychiatrist had prescribed him an antianxiety pill and another for depression, which would help him sleep. The medications masked his pain, but no dosage could erase his guilt. So his psychiatrist urged Clarence to try another approach to treat his problems.

As Clarence neared the conference room's open door, upbeat conversation poured forth from within. A group therapy session was about to begin. A collection of strangers—mostly Vietnam War veterans and some of the new generation who had fought in Iraq or Afghanistan—were gathered inside.

Clarence slowed his step and paused outside the door. He had forced himself to come this far, but now he was wavering. The men in there were all younger than he was. Why would they want to hear about the problems of an old man? Especially when the wounds of their wars were still so raw.

It was embarrassing for him. He was a World War II veteran—he wasn't supposed to have PTSD. His peers had all sorted out their problems six decades ago. And they'd done it without needing to sit in a circle with strangers.

If that's what they did, then that's what he would do.

Before he could second-guess his decision, Clarence resumed walking, straight past the open door.

With a notepad in hand, Clarence scoured Bates's film for clues.

He had acquired the original uncut footage from the National Archives and now watched it over and over again, searching for an explanation as to what really happened that day so long ago.

Maybe it wasn't his fault? Maybe someone else had shot Kathi and her driver?

The film showed several doughs carrying the same type of machine gun as his. Clarence tracked their movements from frame to frame, pausing to take notes.

What about Smokey? Smokey, in his role as bow gunner, had been aiming down the same field of fire. And so were three more Sherman tanks behind them.

Clarence played the film in slow motion, tracking the tracers' trajectory to discern the truth: Did the bullets that killed Kathi really come from his gun? But his hunt for answers was inconclusive. No matter how many times Clarence watched the film, it showed only the same frustrating narrow slice of the battlefield.

If only he could talk to someone who had been there. But Bates, Smokey, Earley, and the rest of the crew had all died of old age by then.

Chuck Miller was still alive, but he had been parked behind the Pershing and hadn't seen the car dart into the intersection and come under fire.

Then, out of the blue, an idea struck Clarence. An epiphany. There *was* someone else, another man with his finger on the trigger that day.

The German.

Clarence had seen the enemy's hose of green tracers, although Bates's film had failed to capture it. But by the time the Pershing drove past the collapsed building, the enemy tank had slipped away. Clarence had always assumed that someone else had finished the job that he'd started and bagged the enemy tank around the next bend. But what if he was wrong?

What if the German from that tank *had* survived?

What if he was still alive?

More than a year later, March 21, 2013

On a cold winter afternoon Clarence stood in front of the Cologne Cathedral once again.

A biting wind rustled through the vast square. If the clouds overhead had suddenly burst with flurries, he wouldn't have been surprised. Clarence flipped up the collar of his gray U.S. Army running jacket. A combination of nervousness and cold kept him fidgeting. He had fought here at this time of year, long ago, but had forgotten how frigid Cologne could be.

With his back turned to the cathedral, Clarence studied the people who crisscrossed the square. Cologne on a Thursday was far less deserted than the setting in his nightmares.

The square was full of activity. Businessmen wearing long coats strode past on their way to the train station. Nuns filtered through the cathedral's double doors. Tourists snapped photos of the spires.*

---

* Clarence allowed this author to accompany him, to record the dialogue and events as they played out. In the city's modern glass architecture, Clarence, always the gunner, saw targets everywhere—"It would have been nice to shoot at that!" A glass building shaped like an Easter egg? "We could have done a lot of damage there!"

Clarence was looking for a fellow World War II veteran, but not just any veteran. A German veteran.

With the help of a Cologne journalist, Clarence had found him: the last living German tanker of the three crews who had fought for the inner city. And the German had agreed to meet Clarence, today, here.

But where was he? Their agreed-upon meeting time had come and gone twenty minutes ago.

Had his German counterpart had second thoughts? Was *he* crazy for ever thinking it could work? Clarence was eighty-nine. Senior citizens just didn't attempt things like this.

He had left Melba in their daughter Cindy's care and traveled four thousand miles to a foreign city just to talk to someone about something that had happened sixty-eight years ago. And to top it off, that "someone" happened to be the man who had been trying to kill him.

"Hey, Clarence!" A high-pitched Southern voice called his name.

Buck Marsh approached Clarence from a side of the square, where he had been helping to keep an eye out for the German veteran.

Buck, now eighty-nine as well, had recently retired from his construction company and still looked the part of a CEO—he was balding, with small glasses, and wore a sweater vest beneath his jacket. He and Clarence had reunited and become close friends in 2006, after Buck had hosted Clarence as the guest of honor at an A-Company reunion in Harrisburg, Pennsylvania.

Buck sidled up to Clarence. "Any sign of our guy?" he asked.

"Afraid not," Clarence said.

A third American veteran approached Clarence from the other direction. Now eighty-eight, Chuck Miller moved with a cane but hadn't lost his telltale squint and wry grin.

Chuck's hair was thick and white now. He wore a yellow Spearhead ball cap littered with pins in the style of many veterans. But Chuck wasn't just any veteran.

He was "Major Miller" now.

Back when the Cold War was heating up, Chuck had reenlisted in the reserves and gone on to command a tank battalion. He always credited Clarence as the greatest tank gunner he'd ever known. When Andy Rooney's book *My War* mistakenly credited a bazooka man with destroying the Panther in Cologne, Chuck was the first to write and correct him.

Chuck took his place with the others. "Well, any luck?"

Clarence shook his head in defeat. "What if he walked right past us?" he said.

Buck and Chuck reassured Clarence that there was no way that could have happened, not with the three of them maintaining a lookout. Cologne was a busy city, they said. The German was probably stuck somewhere in traffic.

The three men stood in silence, rubbing their hands together against the cold.

Buck chuckled when a schoolteacher herded a group of children past the veterans.

"Well," Buck said, "at least there are no kids running around who look like Clarence."

"Yeah, they're all too small," Chuck added. "Look for a bigger one."

Clarence cracked a rare smile.

He hoped that he hadn't dragged his friends all this way for nothing.

When Clarence had asked Buck and Chuck if they would accompany him to Cologne, their enthusiasm took him by surprise—*When do we leave?*

In their minds, Clarence had kept them safe through some of the worst battles of the war and this was their chance to repay him. Besides, from what they could tell, this was a journey that their friend needed to make.

After coming home from the war, Buck and Chuck had done one thing that Clarence had not. They had faced their trauma.

While attending Auburn University, Buck spent afternoons on the sun porch discussing the war with a fraternity brother, the budding author Eugene Sledge, who had fought as a Marine in the Pacific.

As soon as Chuck returned, he bought himself a present—a new Studebaker—then set out on a road trip with his brother, who was also a veteran. On those desert highways on the way to California, Chuck told his brother all about the horrors he'd seen.

Talking. That's what had healed them—and that's what they hoped might help Clarence now. And Clarence was thankful for their encouragement. Frankly, he was amazed that his friends had dropped everything to join him on this long shot of a journey.

Buck had a wife, Wanda, and a beautiful lake house in Auburn, Alabama, where he fed the ducks each morning and spent days volunteering at his church, mowing the lawn during summertime. And when Chuck wasn't helping run his legion post and serving as treasurer of the local cemetery, he and his wife, Winona, were adoring grandparents to nine grandkids back in Versailles, Missouri.

Yet both men had come so far and showed no signs of quitting now.

So Clarence would wait in the cold, windy square as long as it took. This was his last chance at healing, even if the reality might be difficult to accept: only his enemy could save him now.

The three veterans were no longer alone.

"I see him," Chuck said.

"That's gotta be him," Buck concurred.

Clarence followed their eyes to the city side of the square. There, a diminutive older gentleman stood with his arms tucked timidly behind his back.

Gustav Schaefer looked as lost as they did.

Now eighty-six, Gustav wore his black winter jacket open at the collar, his shirt and tie peeking out. His white hair was neatly combed. Gustav glanced from side to side, hoping he hadn't missed the Americans. His glasses' dark transition lenses hid worried eyes.

His son, Uwe, had driven him and they had hit heavy traffic during the four-hour drive, which made matters even worse. After all, he was here to meet the American who had brought a building down upon his tank. And even though his former enemy had seemed friendly in his letter, he also mentioned bringing two comrades along with him.

What will they be like? he wondered. *And what have they come all this way to talk about?*

"That's him, all right." Clarence moved toward the German veteran. After all the thought that went into getting here, he was now operating on instinct.

Buck and Chuck held back. Their role was complete—this was Clarence's show now.

Gustav saw the American approaching from the cathedral side of the square and moved hesitantly in his direction.

The American was intimidating, a far taller man than Gustav had expected.

Clarence moved faster with each step he took toward Gustav, like a train picking up speed. He felt a knot forming in his throat and feared he wouldn't be able to speak. Still many feet apart, a nervous grin spread across his face and he reached out an open hand to his enemy.

A smile appeared on Gustav's face as he extended his hand to meet Clarence's.

The towering American and the diminutive German shook hands and kept shaking while extending greetings to each other. Although one spoke German and the other English, they understood each other perfectly—Clarence remembered enough German from his boyhood and Gustav had picked up some English during his POW days.

Clarence leaned close to Gustav's ear with something to say. "The war is over and we can be friends now."

Gustav nodded, visibly relieved. *"Ja, ja, gute,"* he replied.

Gustav had been thinking the exact same thing.

In a nearby hotel bar, Clarence and Gustav sat side by side, sipping beers as they talked. For the next two nights, Gustav and his son would stay at the same hotel as the Americans.

Buck and Chuck hovered nearby as Clarence asked Gustav—through an interpreter they'd hired—about his life after the war.

Gustav said that he had been so accustomed to sleeping on wooden planks covered with straw in the POW camp that he slept on the floor alongside his bed for the first week after he came home.

With his family's farm in good hands, Gustav found work of his choosing and spent his life operating bulldozers and, later, Caterpillars, converting marshland into farmland.

And these days? Gustav said he resided on a small ranch within sight of his boyhood home. Since his wife, Helga, had died in 2006, he passed his time with a new hobby: Google Earth. Seated at his computer, Gustav spent most days exploring the world using the satellite imagery program to travel without leaving the comforts of home.

He had already looked up Clarence's house and had questions about the things he saw. What kind of car did Clarence park outside? How was his home decorated inside?

Clarence chuckled at the line of questioning.

As the men became more comfortable, they discovered a shared sense of humor.

"Did you have a bathroom in your tank?" Clarence asked Gustav. "Because they forgot to put one in mine."

"Yes, we did," Gustav said, "in the empty shells!"

"We had a chargrill in the Pershing," Clarence said. "And a refrigerator."

Gustav nodded, playing along. "We also had a refrigerator," he said, "but only in wintertime!"

Buck and Chuck roared with laughter from the sidelines.

Several beers later, after Buck and Chuck had departed, Clarence and Gustav's conversation took a somber turn.

Clarence revealed that his nightmares of Cologne still woke him in the night. "I can see her in my dreams," he said. "The woman from the car."

Gustav knew exactly whom Clarence meant. A decade earlier, he had stumbled across the same film as Clarence, while watching a documentary about the battle on television.[*]

Gustav admitted that he, too, had lingering nightmares, but his played out differently. In his dreams, he was trapped inside his tank and all he could see outside was the shattered car and Kathi Esser lying wounded on the sidewalk.

Clarence leaned close and spoke in a hushed tone. "Did you ever tell anyone about what happened?"

---

[*] Author's note: I'm still astounded by the powerful film that accompanies this story. There's Bates's wartime footage of Clarence fighting in Cologne—including his duel with the Panther—as well as film of Clarence's reunion with Gustav, and more. I've posted all of this for you to view on my website, AdamMakos.com.

A deep frown settled across Gustav's face. "Who would have understood?" he asked.

Clarence knew the feeling all too well.

With little to do but to wait for their friend, Buck and Chuck ventured from the hotel on a side mission of their own.

Both men wore their collars raised against the cold as they stepped out of a cab onto Eichendorf Street in a stately neighborhood of northern Cologne. Buck led the way toward a house on the corner while Chuck—who had come along simply out of curiosity—followed.

"Maybe she'll be sitting on the front porch, waiting for you?" Chuck joked—"Without any teeth."

Buck chuckled at the thought.

The duo stopped across from the cream-colored stone house numbered 28. Even after all these years it still had the same impressive carved window flourishes.

In Buck's hands was the sepia-tone photograph given to him by Annemarie Berghoff. The address she had written on the reverse side had guided him back.

Buck had always wished he'd handled things differently.

After losing Lieutenant Boom at Paderborn, Buck made no attempt to return to Cologne, as he assured Annemarie he would. He was just twenty-one then, and wanted to go home.

Only in his old age did the thought occur to him: how many times had she run to the door when someone came knocking, thinking he was back, only to be disappointed? He wished he'd at least written to inform her of his change in plans.

And now he found himself wondering, with a hint of guilt: *Did she have a good life?*

Buck had asked his wife, Wanda, if he could investigate what became of Annemarie while he was in Cologne, and Wanda was understanding, up to a point: "I hope she's fat."

Sounds of hammering and buzz saws emanated from the house's open side door. Contractors were hard at work inside, dividing the grand single-family home into separate apartments.

It was now or never.

Buck waded inside while Chuck lingered at the doorway.

No stranger to a construction site, Buck located the building engineer on a familiar stone staircase. The engineer spoke English, but because of confidentiality laws he couldn't reveal the name of the home's owner.

Buck was crestfallen, but he understood the rationale. He gave the engineer his business card and the name of his hotel, just in case the engineer encountered the owner.

Deflated, Buck stepped outside and into the cold. He had waited too long.

Bundled in winter attire, Clarence and Gustav shared the city side-walk the next morning as if they were simply two old buddies headed to the bus stop.

Clarence wore a yellow Spearhead ball cap, while Gustav wore a black beret. Their noses were red from the cold, but their spirits were high with the zest of a fresh start.

The boulevard to their right was thin with traffic. The workday had just begun and most Cologners were already at their desks. Citizens shuffled past the veterans sporadically, wearing long jackets and knit caps. Exhaust puffed from Mercedes taxis idling at the stoplights.

Buck and Chuck had stayed behind at the hotel so Clarence and Gustav could complete their journey alone, just the two of them. It was time to confront the past.

Gustav gauged their position by the buildings across the street as he and Clarence worked their way toward a familiar massive intersection that was awash with light.

Gustav's transition lenses had turned dark again. His face was tight with concentration. It had been sixty-eight years since he had last been in this neighborhood—could he even find the street again?

After a short search, his face lit up with recognition. This was it.

Gustav stopped and directed Clarence's attention across the boule-vard. On the other side stood a corner building with a pub at ground level. It was bordered by a quiet cross street lined with apartments.

Gustav explained that this was where his tank crew had retreated after spotting the Pershing, before Clarence demolished the building and the bricks came tumbling down.

But the building he had destroyed years earlier had been rebuilt and Clarence marveled at its new height. The building was tall again. It was as if nothing had ever happened.

Revisiting the memories sent a shiver running down Gustav's spine. "Back then I wasn't as afraid as I should have been," he said. "But in discussing it now, I am afraid for my eighteen-year-old self!"

Gustav revealed that during postwar reunions of his brigade, other soldiers often chided him for abandoning the tank and running away. "You should have just cleared the bricks," they had said, to which Gustav replied: "Yeah, we should have gotten out of the tank and asked the Americans to stop shooting at us while we fixed our gun!"

Clarence smiled a guilty grin—"Sorry about that."

"No, I'm glad you shot the building on us," Gustav said. "If I had stayed in that tank, I would have died in it."

Farther along the sidewalk, the men stopped short of the massive intersection. Small cars bustled around a median bristling with frozen trees. Warm light shone down on the square from the surrounding office buildings.

A somber mood settled over the two tankers.

This was where their lives collided all those years ago.

In front of Clarence, a bicycle was locked to the lamppost where the bullet-ridden black car had come to a screeching halt. He looked down at the sidewalk.

"This is where I see her in my dreams," he said softly.

Gustav frowned and nodded. His lenses hid his eyes, but the emotion was there, internalized in his stoic, Germanic manner.

Clarence gazed across the intersection. A line of cars sat parked where his Pershing had once idled.

Everything was much closer than he remembered.

Back on that fateful day, the boulevard had been emptier too.

Standing there, seeing the reality of the scene, Clarence dispelled any doubt about what had happened when the car darted into his field of fire.

The boulevard was a shooting gallery. It would have been impossible for him to miss. His worst nightmare was a reality, but at least he finally knew the truth. Clarence turned to Gustav. With his lip quivering, he admitted that everything had happened so fast, he didn't have time to study his target. He thought the car belonged to the German military—so he shot it.

What Gustav said in reply stunned Clarence. "Well, that's why I shot it too."

"You shot it too?" Clarence said, his voice shaking with disbelief.

"Oh, yes," Gustav said. "The car came to a stop right in front of me."

Gustav explained that he thought the car was the American tank coming for them, so he squeezed the trigger and didn't let go until it was too late.

Clarence looked at where Gustav's tank had been, then to where his had been. It was unmistakable. Their respective lines of fire converged on this very spot. His eyes teared at the revelation: *We both did it.*

Something was bothering Gustav, something he hadn't said. He couldn't hold back any longer. Gustav said that it was irresponsible of Delling to have been on the road in the first place. He and Kathi should have sheltered in a basement instead of driving into a battle—if they had just waited two more hours, none of this would have happened.

Clarence nodded. Gustav had a point.

"It's war," Gustav said, shaking his head. "It's in the nature of it. It can't be undone."

It's in the nature of it. The words gave Clarence pause. During the course of sixteen years of guilt and self-loathing, he had never considered that he might have been a victim of that day as well.

None of them should have been in that intersection.

Clarence should have been home in Lehighton on roller skates at Graver's skating rink. Gustav should have been watching the trains on the Hamburg-Bremen line. And Kathi should have been playing with a niece or nephew in a park, not driving through a raging battle.

Clarence felt a weight lift as this realization set in.

It's in the nature of it.

It wasn't their fault, or hers.

It was war.

The wrought-iron fence swung open with a groan. Clarence and Gustav stepped inside the grotto of St. Gereon's Basilica, the ancient church about two hundred yards from where they had once fought.

The shady grotto was enclosed by evergreens and walls crawling with vines. It was cold here, colder than the neighboring streets. And it was eerily quiet.

Gustav wore his black beret snugged tightly and Clarence kept his coat zipped high. Each carried a pair of yellow roses, brought along for a special purpose. Clarence's connections in the city had assured him: this was the place.

The men followed a path of stepping-stones through a sea of leafy shrubs. Gustav's lenses had become clear in the dim light, revealing eyes that were serious with remorse.

Stone crosses rose up out of the undergrowth around the men.

The grotto was a small cemetery.

Clarence and Gustav stopped at a particular stone cross and read the inscription:

MICHAEL JOHANNES DELLING

1905–1945

Clarence looked on with regret. Forty. Delling was only forty when he died behind the wheel that day—still a young man, in Clarence's eyes.

Gustav laid a rose at Delling's grave and Clarence did the same.

From there they moved across the cemetery to a knee-high wooden cross that held an iron crucifix.

A plaque on the cross read: THE UNKNOWN DEAD.

Clarence's and Gustav's heads sunk lower. This was where Kathi's story had come to an end.

After the battle, her body had been separated from her briefcase for reasons yet unknown. Without identification papers on her, she was buried in this shared grave.

A small pail for flowers sat in front of the cross. Empty.

Clarence shook his head. It was painful enough to accept how Kathi's life had ended, but this made it even worse, seeing her forgotten, as if she had never lived.

Gustav leaned forward and placed his rose in the pail before stepping back to make way for Clarence. Bent at the waist, Clarence leaned forward with his rose clenched in a shaking hand. He became unsteady and was on the verge of losing his balance. Before he could fall, Gustav grabbed him by the arm. Steadied by his former enemy, Clarence placed his rose in the pail and righted himself.

Clarence and Gustav stood side by side without speaking. Wind stirred the trees and the vines and the yellow roses. Where he was and what he was doing still seemed surreal to Clarence.

An innocent woman—once a stranger, now someone somehow familiar to him—lay buried at his feet and his former enemy stood beside him.

Nowhere else in Cologne was the tragic truth more plainly on display. *War touches everyone.*

Clarence shut the gate behind them after he and Gustav emerged from the grotto. But he wasn't finished here. He lingered outside the grotto, gazing into the dim environs as his fingers gripped the fence. Even if she lay in a nameless grave, he knew she was there.

In silence, Clarence made a vow to Kathi Esser.

He would never forget her.

As Gustav watched an unmoving Clarence fixate on the wooden cross, he became worried. Gustav urged the interpreter to check on his friend.

"You okay, Clarence?" the interpreter asked.

Clarence released his grip from the fence and stepped away.

He shrugged and nodded. "I'm okay now."

Clarence and Gustav removed their hats when they entered the narthex of St. Gereon's Basilica. Faded medieval frescos lined the dark antechambers, but the dome overhead was full of light.

The men approached a row of candles still burning from the morning Mass. Clarence and Gustav dropped coins into the poor box before lighting a pair of votive candles. Each man added his own candle to the row of flickering flames.

In stillness they paid their respects, silent words the world would never hear.

Clarence's German journalist friend had arranged for an unexpected meeting after Clarence and Gustav left the basilica.

A slender young man wearing a long winter coat was waiting for them. He was a history professor at the University of Cologne who had slipped out between classes to meet the veterans who had fought so many years earlier in the city he called home. His name was Marc Hieronimus. He was thirty-nine, with glasses and a closely cropped beard, but more important, he was Kathi Esser's grand-nephew.

Clarence froze.

This man was Kathi's family, after all. Gustav hovered behind in Clarence's shadow, leaving his larger friend to sort out the situation.

Marc defused any tension with a smile as he greeted the men in English. Clarence grinned and Gustav emerged from hiding.

Marc wasn't here to judge them. Instead, he had come to offer his help. Would they like a tour of his aunt Kathi's life? He would be their guide.

The silver van rumbled across countless streetcar tracks as the driver wound through Cologne.

Marc narrated from the passenger's seat while Clarence and Gustav sat behind him, listening with boyish awe as the sights passed outside their windows.

Kathi's home, a row house made of red brick.

Her park, where the entrance to an air-raid shelter still stood.

The street that she had bicycled down each day to go to Delling's grocery store.

After a morning spent in somberness, Clarence and Gustav were back to smiling again. Marc's tour was uplifting, a fond remembrance of the life that Kathi had lived.

At the tour's conclusion, the van pulled over near a gate in the city's Roman wall.

Marc spun around in his seat. Before returning to the university, he wanted to extend an invitation to Clarence and Gustav: "Next time you come to Cologne, let's have dinner together?"

And it wouldn't just be dinner with him. His invitation was for dinner with Kathi's family—as friends.

The gesture wasn't lost on Clarence. Marc was offering them forgiveness.

Clarence couldn't stop smiling.

It was a good thing that Buck had stayed behind that morning. A call from the front desk summoned him from his hotel room. He had a visitor.

Buck discovered a lady waiting in the lobby to meet him.

She wore a long black jacket, neatly accented by a tan scarf. Her shoulder-length blond hair framed a face with an unforgettable beauty that stirred Buck's memory.

She looked like Annemarie.

But how could that be? She wasn't even half the age she should be.

The lady introduced herself as the owner of the home that Buck had visited—the engineer had passed Buck's business card along to her. Her name was Marion Pütz. She was Annemarie's daughter.

Buck took Marion's hand and held it. He couldn't get over her likeness—"You look just like your mother!"

Marion said that meeting Buck was special for her. Her mother had passed away a decade before and this was a chance to remember her by learning a bit more about the life she had lived.

The pair settled into seats on the side of the lobby.

Buck told Marion how he had met Annemarie and the story of their brief friendship. He expressed his lament that he had forgotten her so quickly after the war, but Marion urged Buck not to feel any guilt.

"You were there at the right time for her," Marion said. "When things were difficult, you gave her hope."

Buck leaned forward to ask the question that had been burning inside him ever since he came to Cologne: "Did she have a good life?"

Marion said that her mother had studied dental medicine and continued working in her father's practice. She became one of the first women in Cologne to get a driver's license and one of the first to buy a car—a Volkswagen Beetle.

Annemarie went on to marry a wealthy factory owner, she gave birth to Marion, and although her marriage didn't endure, she lived a happy life, splitting her time between Germany and a house on a Swiss lake that she loved to cruise in her motorboat.

Buck was pleased to hear all this—and thankful.

Marion gripped Buck's hand as she stood to leave. "I want to thank you for making my mother happy," she said.

Buck choked up at the sentiment. "Well, she made me happy too."

The next morning

While Gustav's son retrieved his car, the veterans approached the Cologne Cathedral. They had become a team in their short time together. A reunion of enemies had become a gathering of friends, and none of them wanted the visit to end.

But Gustav's son had work the following day. And the Americans had families waiting at home. There was just one thing left to do.

The veterans stopped in the cathedral square and posed for photos together, passing their digital cameras back and forth.

Buck hopped into a photo with Gustav and joked about their matching heights.

Chuck took a turn alongside Gustav. Seeing Clarence aiming his camera and hearing him shout—"Say cheese!"—Chuck knew that the journey had been worth it. His friend was going to be all right.

Ultimately, Clarence and Gustav wound up smiling for the camera with their arms intertwined right in front of the cathedral. Cameras beeped and flashed. Buck, Chuck, and even their interpreter kept snapping pictures.

Then, Clarence did something unexpected. He reached down and hugged Gustav. He held the hug for the cameras and refused to let go. Gustav returned the hug with equal enthusiasm.

Passing teenagers might have laughed at the two old men—the towering American and the diminutive German—chuckling as they embraced in the bustling city square. But a passing group of teenagers would never have known just who these men were.

The veterans found Gustav's son waiting with the idling car at the hotel. He was ready to drive his father home.

Clarence knew what this meant. This would likely be the last time he would ever see Gustav.

The little German veteran had confided that his health was poorer than he let anyone, including his family, know. But even so, he hoped to stay in touch with Clarence for as long as he possibly could.

They parted ways that morning with an understanding. Whatever guilt remained from the war—they would share it. Whatever nightmares surfaced—they would face them together.

Before Gustav stepped into the car, he gave the interpreter one last message for Clarence.

What he said made Clarence dab his eyes.

"Tell Clarence, in the next life, we will be comrades."

As America's largest fighting force in Europe during the Cold War, the **Spearhead Division** went on to hold the line against the Soviet Union, ready for the tank-on-tank clash that never came.

The division's next battlefield would instead be in the desert. Summoned from Germany, the 3rd Armored Division spearheaded the ground assault during the Persian Gulf War, waging the first major tank engagement since World War II. After battering the Iraqi Republican Guard, Spearhead helped bring the war to a cease-fire—in one hundred hours.

And that would be its final battle.

The Cold War had ended. Terrorism was the new threat to freedom. So the mighty armor division was retired and its units spread piecemeal among the U.S. Army. Now Spearhead remains a slumbering giant, at rest until the day when machines will again fight machines.

In September 2017, the WWII veterans of the 3rd Armored Association held their last reunion in Philadelphia. Just three tankers were able to attend. Two were Easy Company men: **Clarence Smoyer** and **Joe Caserta.**

. . .

Clarence's crew died long before they could gather again. At reunions, Clarence learned how their lives played out.

Homer "Smokey" Davis became an electrician and lived out his years in the woods of rural Kentucky.

William "Woody" McVey worked in an automotive repair shop near Detroit, where his skills were put to use test-driving cars.

John "Johnny Boy" DeRiggi's facial wounds healed during a year spent in army hospitals—from Greenland to Valley Forge—and he later became a steelworker in Levittown, Pennsylvania.

Bob Earley attained the farm of his dreams in Fountain, Minnesota, trading his perch in a tank turret for a seat on a tractor. He married, raised sons, and was known for riding his motorcycle cross-country to attend reunions.

Clarence never saw Earley after they'd parted in Germany, but was at peace with how they sealed their friendship—with a long handshake and thankfulness that they'd made it through together. Earley died in 1979. After staring down the barrel of the Panther in Cologne, every additional day of life was a gift, and Bob Earley spent his well.

Seeking information about **Paul Faircloth,** Clarence called countless numbers in the Florida phone book before finding Paul's nephew.

The nephew informed Clarence that it would be difficult to visit Paul's grave because he was buried far away, at Épinal American Cemetery in France.

Determined to see his friend remembered on his native soil, Clarence donated money in Paul's name toward the construction of the 3rd Armored Division Memorial that now stands in a park at Fort Knox, watched over by a silent Sherman tank.

According to **Chuck Miller**, his trip to Cologne with Clarence was "the thrill of a lifetime."

Chuck died the following year. In his funeral procession, his grandson's motorcycle club escorted the hearse, filling the air with thunderous noise, reminiscent of an armored column on the move. Everyone who knew him said the same thing: Chuck would have approved.

· · ·

Frank "Cajun Boy" Audifred married the company sweetheart, his girlfriend, Lil, a month after returning from the war. Despite being nearly deaf in both ears from that day at Blatzheim, Audifred spent a career as a machinist with Standard Oil of Louisiana.

Now ninety-six, his body is still shedding German shrapnel. When dental hygienists find slivers of steel in his mouth during routine checkups, Audifred just chuckles.

In 1955, **Buck Marsh** and **Bob Janicki** attended their first division reunion together in St. Louis. Buck discovered that his battlefield mentor hadn't lost a step, despite wearing a false leg. Using his disability compensation, Janicki had opened a motorcycle dealership in Freeport, Illinois, a business that would later expand to three stores, allowing him to purchase—and fly—his own private plane.

In the 1960s, Buck found **Byron Mitchell** living in Atlanta and phoned him. Never one for words, Byron's report was brief: "I'm driving a concrete truck and I really like it."

These days, Buck serves as the honorary sergeant major of his former unit, the army's **36th Infantry Regiment,** and he makes appearances at schools to teach children about World War II.

Without exception, some youngster will always ask: "How many Germans did you kill?"

Amused by the naïveté of youth, Buck gives the same answer every time: "I wish the number was zero."

On the other side of the Atlantic, **Gustav Schaefer** attended reunions of **Panzer Brigade 106** for decades, hoping to see **Rolf Millitzer.**

The gatherings were small enough to fit in any restaurant's back room—the brigade had been all but wiped out—yet Rolf never walked through the door.

After his POW sentence, Rolf was likely repatriated to his home in the Soviet-controlled zone of East Germany, and there he vanished behind the Iron Curtain.

. . .

It didn't take until "the next life" for Clarence and Gustav's friendship to take root.

The duo became pen pals, exchanging letters and Christmas cards. Clarence gave Gustav a gift: a small, die-cast Panther tank.

They even Skyped on their computers. With an interpreter joining in, the veterans would talk face-to-face, despite being thousands of miles apart. In the background behind Gustav was a clock with a pendulum, a bookshelf filled with atlases, and the little model of a Panther tank.

After hanging on four years longer than even he had thought possible, Gustav succumbed in April 2017 to cancer. At his funeral were flowers from family and friends, and one ribboned bouquet bearing these words:

I WILL NEVER FORGET YOU!
YOUR BROTHER IN ARMS,
CLARENCE

When he stood at the grotto of St. Gereon's Basilica, Clarence had vowed that he would never forget **Kathi Esser**. Every year since his visit, yellow roses are placed on the unmarked grave where her body remains.

On March 6, they will appear once again.

After he met Gustav, Clarence's nightmares disappeared. Painful memories from the war remain—and always will—but he can live with them.

It took some time for him to revisit the VA hospital, but he did.

Clarence approached the conference room's open door. Familiar upbeat voices poured forth—another group therapy session was about to commence.

This time around, a different Clarence Smoyer paced those sterile hallways.

A survivor.

He had faced his PTSD and emerged victorious. Talking about it, with someone who listened and understood, had saved him.

And maybe that's what those younger veterans needed to hear. Maybe he could encourage them to keep talking—or maybe he could be that someone who would listen?

When Clarence reached the open doorway, he didn't slow his step or pause beyond sight. There was no turning back from what he'd come to do.

Someone has to help those guys.

Clarence stepped inside.

ACKNOWLEDGMENTS

I'd like to extend my deep thanks to the following people for their help with *Spearhead:*

To the World War II veterans at the heart of this story—Clarence Smoyer, Buck Marsh, Gustav Schaefer, Chuck Miller, and Frank Audifred— you relived the most difficult years of your lives so that we might discover the human cost of war. Thank you for entrusting me with your stories.

To the armor and infantry veterans whose technical advice and supplemental interviews brought poignancy and depth to this book: Joe Caserta, Harry Chipp, Bill Gast, John Irwin, Robert Kauffmann, Marvin Mischnick, Ray Stewart, George Smilanich, Walter Stitt, Harley Swenson, Les Underwood, and to German tank commander Dieter Jähn, who taught us about the hopes and fears of men on the other side. You're each worthy of a book of your own.

To the Cologne journalist Hermann Rheindorf, it was your research that first identified Kathi Esser and brought Gustav, as well as Kathi's family, into Clarence's life. You are the unparalleled documentarian of your great city—Cologne.

To Clarence's daughter, Cindy Buervenich, you watched over your mother, Melba, so your father could travel overseas to meet Gustav. This book was born of that trip—thanks to your support.

To Frank Audifred's daughter, Sherry Herringshaw, you unearthed priceless wartime letters and relayed our countless questions so that we might discover an amazing Cajun—your dad.

To Kathi Esser's grandnephew, historian Marc Hieronimus, you stepped away from your classroom to give Clarence and Gustav an unforgettable day and the greatest gift: the chance to heal.

To Marion Pütz, who opened the doors to her family's history to us—you're everything that one would expect from the daughter of Annemarie Berghoff.

To our "man on the ground" in Cologne, Dierk Lürbke, whose study of the cathedral tank duel is so forensic that even Clarence learned a thing or two. Thanks for always being on call to lend a helping hand.

To the family and friends of our "cast of characters," your memories, documents, and myriad contributions enriched these pages: Glenn Ahner, John DeRiggi, Craig Earley, John R. Faircloth, Patricia Fischer, Bernard Makos, Wanda Marsh, Jim Miller, Dr.-Ing Günter Prediger, Deborah Rose, Charles Rose, John Rose, Luke Salisbury, Charles Stillman, Deborah Stillman, Carol Westberg, Helene Winskowski.

To my dedicated agent, David Vigliano, who deftly guided *Spearhead* into the hands of Ballantine Books, and to my former editor, Ryan Doherty, who gave life to this book. To my current editor and literary mentor, Tracy Devine, whose impeccable sense of "story" polished the manuscript to its final form. To the president and publisher of Random House, Gina Centrello, and the publishing team at Ballantine Bantam Dell: Kara Welsh, Kim Hovey, Susan Corcoran, Greg Kubie, Quinne Rogers, Lexi Batsides, Evan Camfield, Simon Sullivan, David Stevenson, and everyone on the sales and marketing team, thank you all for bringing *Spearhead* to the world.

To our guides to Paderborn, who took me and my research team "back to the battle": Dr. Friedrich Hohmann, the region's grandfather-historian, and Colonel Wolfgang Mann, a tank commander of the modern-day German Bundeswehr. To our escorts in the Ardennes, the incomparable expert Reg Jans, and to Bob Konigs, who welcomed us to his Guesthouse BoTemps.

To our armor advisers: Bill Boller, the armor guru and trustee of the Collings Foundation, who could be found crawling over a World War II tank with a measuring tape in hand to answer our toughest of questions. Rob Collings, CEO of the Collings Foundation, who made his stable of tanks available to us and lent his historical input for this, our third book in a row. To Kevin Wheatcroft, the world's preeminent expert on German armor and the owner of the Wheatcroft Collection, a jaw-dropping tank collection in England, thanks for ensuring our accurate portrayal of the machines of the other side. And ultimately to "The Chieftain," Nicholas Moran, who gave the manuscript its final check ride, summoning his encyclopedic knowledge of all things armor and bringing to bear his real-world experience as a tank platoon leader in Iraq.

To the historians who made the Spearhead Division come alive for us: Vic Damon and Dan Fong, who run the 3rd Armored Division History Foundation at 3ad.com; Jan Ploeg, who remembers the doughs at 36air-ad.com; A-Company historian Dan Langhans; and Steven Ossad and Don Marsh, authors of *Major General Maurice Rose: World War II's Greatest Forgotten Commander General*.

To the dedicated authors, experts, and researchers who provided vital data, photos, and artwork for this book: Kevin Bailey, Justin Batt, David Boyd, Rita Cann, Lamont Ebbert, Tim Frank, Daniel Glauber, Timm Haasler, David Harper, Gareth Hector, Nick Hopkins, Craig Mackey, Douglas McCabe, Jeannette McDonald, Russ Morgan, Darren Neely, Jaclyn Ostrowski, Debra Richardson, Gordon Ripkey, Matt Scales, Susan Strange, Bill Thomas, Bill Warnock, and Steven Zaloga; and to Nicolas Trudgian, whose primer on wartime train travel turned me into a rail fan for life.

To Thomas Flannery Jr., the veteran development editor who coached my writing from the first chapter to the last. Your eye for sharpening and polishing made this a better book.

To the early readers who lent a discerning eye to this manuscript: Matt Carlini, Joel Eng, Jaime Hanna, Lauren Heller, Matt Hoover, Tricia Hoover, Joe Gohrs, and Rachelle Mandik.

To my "early-warning system," my sister, Erica Makos, and mother, Karen Makos, who read every first draft—your feedback helped steer this book. To my grandparents, Francis and Jeanne Panfili, for your encouragement, to my youngest sister, Elizabeth Makos, for the entertainment; to my sister-in-law Agata Makos, whose delicious meals kept us going; and to my dear friends Helga Stigler and Georgea Hudner, who cheer me on from afar.

To my friend Pete Semanoff, who first discovered Clarence while interviewing veterans for his Eagle Scout project. You introduced me to his story and urged me to talk with him while we were in college, and after college, and even when we spoke in the desert of Iraq. Finally I met Clarence and came to know why he's your hero. This book is the result of your tireless efforts.

To our German researcher and comrade, Franz Englram. After interpreting for Clarence and Gustav in Cologne, you became one of our team, interviewing Gustav for us and poring through countless foreign documents to research his unit. During the war, your great-uncle, Gerard, died on the Eastern Front at age nineteen. By the sensitive way you treated the veterans of *Spearhead,* you honored his memory.

To my dad, Robert Makos, who "spearheaded" our interviews and countless cold calls for this book, your lifetime of experience in the psychology field made you more than a great researcher—you were irreplaceable.

To my brother, Bryan Makos, this book's research director and co-creator, you led us to Cologne three times, and to the Black Forest and back. Your task was lofty: to conduct history-gathering across two continents, five countries, and both sides of the Second World War. Clarence and Gustav, theirs is a one-in-a-million story. But your talent made this a one-in-a-million book.

Lastly, thanks to you, the reader, for riding along with us through the pages of *Spearhead.* I hope this story will remain with you long after you close this book. If you enjoyed your experience, please leave a review online, or tell others of these heroes that you've come to know. Nothing is more powerful than your endorsement.

If you're hungry to learn more, I'll be leading a tour of the European battlefields from this story and invite you to join me. You'll find details of the itinerary, along with plenty of bonus content—including the wartime footage of Clarence's tank duel and film of his emotional reunion with Gustav—on my website: AdamMakos.com.

On behalf of Clarence, Buck, and the last living heroes of *Spearhead,* I pass the torch to you, dear reader. The legacy of great men and women lies in your hands.

This book is the product of a treasure trove of historical sources. We unearthed a paper trail of after action reports, wartime interviews, original orders, radio logs, morning reports, vintage newspapers, unit histories, and more, from archives such as:

Bundesarchiv-Militararchiv Freiburg, Germany
National Archives and Records Administration at St. Louis, Missouri,
    and College Park, Maryland
National Archives (UK)
U.S. Army Heritage and Education Center, Carlisle, Pennsylvania
Dwight D. Eisenhower Presidential Library, Abilene, Kansas.
The 3rd Armored Division Association Archives at the University of
    Illinois
Maneuver Center of Excellence Museum Division, Fort Benning, Georgia.

But what was our greatest source of all? The veterans. Clarence. Buck. Gustav. Chuck. Audifred. Caserta. Each was alive during the composition of this book and shared his memories in the best detail that he could remember.

We interviewed them anywhere and everywhere: Gustav on the street in Cologne. Chuck in a frigid field at Blatzheim. Buck visited us in Colorado and we visited him in Alabama. I interviewed Joe Caserta at his kitchen table in New Jersey and my team traveled to Louisiana to work with Frank Audifred.

We dropped by Allentown, Pennsylvania, so many times to inter-view Clarence that we came to know the staff of the Holiday Inn by name. We talked with him by phone, too, almost weekly for five years. And when the manuscript was finished, Clarence, Buck, and our other core characters read this book cover to cover before giving their stamp of approval.

If I cited every fact from the stories that Clarence and his fellow veterans told us, our notes section would be longer than the book it-self. So, for any facts not directly cited, you'll know where they came from: the men themselves.

But not every historical nugget was recited verbally. The veterans supplied us with written material. There were oral histories, like the one Clarence did in 1985—now thirty-three years ago. There was war-time correspondence—Audifred's family saved every letter that he sent home. And some supplied accounts penned by their own hands, such as Buck Marsh's brilliant 200-page memoir, *Reflections of a World War II Infantryman*.

Armed with these desk-swallowing mounds of history, we married records, memories, writings, and information gleaned from the sources to follow to reconstruct this story as accurately as possible.

Gustav's interviews were translated from German into English, and I took the liberty of converting German military ranks into their American equivalents and metric measurement into imperial stan-dards for the American editions.

But everything else is as we found it.

Introduction

xii   **"workhorse unit"**: Frank Woolner, *Spearhead in the West: The 3rd Armored Division in WWII* (Frankfurt, Germany: Kunst and Wervedruck, 1945; reprinted Nashville: Battery Press, 1980), 10.

xii   **"most aggressive"**: Philip DeRiggi, "My Brother John S. DeRiggi," 3rd AD Soldiers' Memoirs, 3ad.com/history/wwll/memoirs.pages/deriggi.htm (accessed September 2, 2017).

xiii   **Patton's tankers adopted his "flair"**: Omar Bradley, *A Soldier's Story* (New York: Modern Library, 1999), 226.

xiii   **were known for their "breeziness"**: Ibid.

xiii   **"with a serious and grim intensity"**: Ibid.

1. The Gentle Giant

3   **beyond sight, was Mons:** E-Company, 32nd Armored Regiment, Morning Report, September 3, 1944, National Archives and Records Administration (henceforth NARA).

4   **were behind enemy lines:** Ibid.

4   **390 tanks:** Steven Zaloga, *Panzer IV vs. Sherman: France 1944* (New York: Osprey, 2015), 43.

5   **breakout across northern France:** Frank Woolner, *Spearhead in the West: The 3rd Armored Division in WWII* (Frankfurt, Germany: Kunst and Wervedruck, 1945; reprinted Nashville: Battery Press, 1980), 5.

5   **earning its nom de guerre:** Harold Denny, "U.S. Tank Division Honored as Heroic," *New York Times,* August 25, 1944.

5   **German Fifteenth and Seventeenth Armies:** Lt. Fred Hadsel and T/3 William Henderson, *Battle of Mons, 1–4 September, 1944,* 2nd Information and Historical Service, VII Corps, Breinig, Germany, February 16, 1945, NARA.

5 **107 miles in two days:** E-Company, 32nd Armored Regiment, Morning Report, September 3, 1944, NARA.

6 **new replacement:** E-Company, 32nd Armored Regiment, Morning Report, August 25, 1944, NARA.

7 **30,000 enemy troops:** Woolner, *Spearhead in the West*, 86.

7 **18,000 defensive fortifications:** David Crossland, "World War II Bunkers Turn into Wildlife Haven," Spiegel Online, spiegel.de/international/germany/from-wehrmacht-to-wildcats-world-war-ii-bunkers-turn-into-wildlife-haven-a-507880.html (accessed August 1, 2017).

7 **Around two A.M.:** Lt. Fred Hadsel and T/3 William Henderson, *Battle of Mons, 1–4 September, 1944*, interview with Maj. W. K. Bailey, CCR 3rd Armored Division, Breinig, Germany, February 15, 1945, NARA.

8 **A WWII tanker's helmet:** James Brown and Michael Green, *M4 Sherman at War* (St. Paul: Zenith, 2007), 60–61.

9 **Everyone else could only listen:** Ibid., 61.

10 **"the Pride of the Wehrmacht":** Frank Woolner, "Texas Tanker," *Yank* 1, no. 16 (November 12, 1944).

10 **Not a single shot:** Nicholas Moran, "US Army Anti-Armor Firing Tests of 1944," The Chieftain's Hatch, worldoftanks.com/en/news/chieftain/chieftains-hatch-us-guns-vs-german-armour-part-1 (accessed June 10, 2017).

12 **11-foot, 8-inch:** Michael Green, *Images of War: Axis Tanks of the Second World War* (South Yorkshire, England: Pen & Sword Military, 2017), 61.

12 **the Mark IV:** Zaloga, *Panzer IV vs. Sherman*, 4–5, 8, 20.

2. Baptism

14 **Thirty-three tons of tank:** Steven Zaloga, *Panzer IV vs. Sherman: France 1944* (New York: Osprey, 2015), 17.

14 **about 20 miles per hour:** "Sherman I & IC (Typical for II) Outline," War Office Records 194/132, March 14, 1945, National Archives (UK).

14 **9-cylinder radial engine:** Zaloga, *Panzer IV vs. Sherman*, 17.

15 **directed a Panther tank:** Frank Woolner, *Spearhead in the West: The 3rd Armored Division in WWII* (Frankfurt, Germany: Kunst and Wervedruck, 1945; reprinted Nashville: Battery Press, 1980), 88.

16 **perfectly blue sky:** Georges Licope, *La bataille dite de Mons, des 2, 3 et 4 septembre 1944* (Mons, Belgium: Musée de Guerre à Mons, 1973), 44–47.

17 **"delicious traffic jam":** Don Marsh and Steven Ossad, *Major General Maurice Rose: World War II's Greatest Forgotten Commander* (Lanham, MD: Taylor Trade, 2006), 227.

18 **sent out to fight:** Woolner, *Spearhead in the West*, 86.

23 **"you just want to slaughter us":** Ibid., 209.

23 **"As though drawn to the city":** Ibid., 87.

23 **come in to finish:** Ibid., 86.

23 **three generals:** Marsh and Ossad, *Maurice Rose*, 230.

23 **lowly sailor who had hitchhiked:** Lt. Fred Hadsel and T/3 William Henderson, *Battle of Mons, 1–4 September, 1944*, interviews with Maj. Jame Byron (S-3),

Maj. Thomas Curlee (Assistant S-3), Capt. Charles Echerd (S-2), Capt. Robert Russell, 36th Armored Infantry Regiment, CCR 3rd Armored Division, Breinig, Germany, February 15, 1945, NARA.

23 **"so swift a destruction":** Woolner, *Spearhead in the West,* 86.

23 **body lay at the medics' feet:** Paul Faircloth Individual Deceased Personnel File, Office of Human Resources Command, US Army, Fort Knox, KY.

24 **more men killed in action:** "Army Battle Casualties and Nonbattle Deaths: Final Report, 7 December 1941–31 December 1946," Statistical and Accounting Branch, Office of the Adjutant General, Washington, DC, June 1, 1953.

24 **lose the most American tanks:** Steven Zaloga, *Armored Thunderbolt* (Mechanicsburg, PA: Stackpole, 2008), 342–43.

3. "Bubi"

27 **strength of forty-seven vehicles:** Timm Haasler, *Hold the Westwall: The History of Panzer Brigade 105* (Mechanicsburg, PA: Stackpole, 2008), 29.

29 **two-ton slab:** Measurement and calculation by Bill Boller, president of the Military Vehicle Technology Foundation, founded by Jacques Littlefield.

29 **Equivalent to 5.7 inches thick:** Steven Zaloga, *Panther vs. Sherman: Battle of the Bulge 1944* (New York: Osprey, 2008), 21.

29 **3.5-inch front plate:** Ibid.

29 **3.149 inches thick:** Ibid.

4. The Fields

31 **losing twenty-one tanks:** Friedrich Bruns, *Panzerbrigade 106 Feldherrnhalle* (Celle, Germany: Eigenverlag, 1988), 159.

32 **more than 6,000 Panthers built:** Bob Carruthers, *The Panther V in Combat: Guderian's Problem Child* (Barnsley, England: Pen & Sword, 2013), 26.

32 **eclipsed by the 49,234 Shermans:** Zaloga, *Armored Thunderbolt,* 332.

32 **Panther came with worrisome defects:** Steven Zaloga, *Armored Thunderbolt* (Mechanicsburg, PA: Stackpole, 2008), 177–78; Michael Green and Gladys Green, *Panther: Germany's Quest for Combat Dominance* (New York: Osprey, 2012), 38, 209.

32 **operate without these necessities:** Bruns, *Panzerbrigade 106 Feldherrnhalle,* 56.

33 **32 percent fewer tanks:** Christer Bergstrom, *The Ardennes, 1944–1945: Hitler's Winter Offensive* (Havertown, PA: Casemate, 2014), 431.

33 **50th Fighter Group:** "Headquarters IX Tactical Air Command: Operation Summary #93 for Period 1100–1600 Hours," September 9, 1944, Air Force Historical Research Agency, Maxwell AFB, Alabama.

33 **Seven hundred horsepower:** Steven Zaloga, *Panther vs. Sherman: Battle of the Bulge 1944* (New York: Osprey, 2008), 11.

34 **the Panther was deemed faster:** Green and Green, *Panther,* 239.

34 **At 18 miles per hour:** Ibid.

36 **Hitler Youth had been mandatory:** United States Holocaust Memorial Museum,

"Indoctrinating Youth," Holocaust Encyclopedia, ushmm.org/wlc/en/article .php?ModuleId=10007820 (accessed August 3, 2017).

37 **column of the 34th Tank Battalion:** Vic Hillery and Emerson Hurley, *Paths of Armor: The Fifth Armored Division in World War II* (Nashville: Battery Press, 1986), 111.

37 **17-foot-long gun:** Zaloga, *Panther vs. Sherman*, 11.

37 **turret crept agonizingly slowly:** Ibid., 28.

37 **"super velocity":** Don Marsh and Steven Ossad, *Major General Maurice Rose: World War II's Greatest Forgotten Commander* (Lanham, MD: Taylor Trade, 2006), 382.

37 **within a twelve-inch circle:** Green and Green, *Panther*, 59.

38 **their turrets turned:** Hillery and Hurley, *Paths of Armor*, 110–11.

38 **sixteen-pound warhead:** Zaloga, *Panther vs. Sherman*, 28.

38 **Amazingly, of the two Shermans:** C-Company, 34th Tank Battalion, Morning Report, September 9, 1944, NARA; "Combat History 47th. Armd. F.A. Bn., 5th Armd. Div., August 6, 1944–April 26, 1945," 5ad.org/units/47AFA.html (accessed June 15, 2016).

39 **burning at 5,000 degrees:** Gordon Rottman, *World War II Infantry Fire Support Tactics* (New York: Osprey, 2016).

39 **some sort of armored vehicle:** Hillery and Hurley, *Paths of Armor*, 111.

39 **American M7:** "Combat History 47th Armd. F.A. Bn., 5th Armd. Div., August 6, 1944–April 26, 1945," 5ad.org/units/47AFA.html (accessed June 15, 2016).

40 **would execute 10,000:** Antony Beevor, *Ardennes 1944: Hitler's Last Gamble* (New York: Viking, 2015), 44.

5. The Foray

44 **vulnerable flank and rear:** Nicholas Moran, "US Army Anti-Armor Firing Tests of 1944," The Chieftain's Hatch, worldoftanks.com/en/news/chieftain/chieftains -hatch-us-guns-vs-german-armour-part-1/ (accessed June 10, 2017).

44 **On the Eastern Front:** Ray Merriam, ed., *World War 2 in Review: German Fighting Vehicles No. 3* (Hoosick Falls, NY: Merriam Press, 2017), 25.

44 **Seaforth Highlanders:** Christopher Miskimon, "Repurposing German Vehicles by Allied Troops," Warfare History Network, warfarehistorynetwork.com/ daily/wwii/repurposing-german-vehicles-by-allied-troops/ (accessed August 7, 2017).

44 **British Coldstream Guards:** Ibid.

46 **reported seeing the shells:** "Frank Bäke," WWII Forums, ww2f.com/threads/ franz-b%C3%A4ke.21649/page-2 (accessed June 13, 2016).

47 **without aerial reconnaissance:** Friedrich Bruns, *Panzerbrigade 106 Feldherrnhalle* (Celle, Germany: Eigenverlag, 1988), 49.

48 **roll into Luxembourg:** Vic Hillery and Emerson Hurley, *Paths of Armor: The Fifth Armored Division in World War II* (Nashville: Battery Press, 1986), 111.

48 **first boots on German soil:** Charles MacDonald, *The Siegfried Line Campaign* (Washington, DC: US Army Center of Military History, 1990), 3.

48 Belgian coast to Switzerland: Ibid.

48 "at the heart of Germany": Ibid.

6. Beyond the Wall

49 **a storm was boiling over:** Weather description is based on period photos and B-Company, 32nd Armored Regiment, Morning Report, September 15, 1944, NARA.

49 **punch through the West Wall:** Associated Press, "Third Armored Units Break Siegfried Line," *Tucson Daily Citizen*, October 4, 1944.

49 **capture a German town:** Haynes Dugan et al., *Third Armored Division: Spearhead in the West*, 2nd. ed. (Paducah, KY: Turner, 2001), 207.

50 **missing five tanks:** E-Company, 32nd Armored Regiment, Morning Report, September 15, 1944, NARA.

50 **"next to impossible":** Lt. Fred Hadsel, *Battle of Mons, 1–4 September, 1944: Summary Statement*, 2nd Information and Historical Service, VII Corps, Breinig, Germany, February 16, 1945, NARA.

51 **penetrating an extra inch:** Steven Zaloga, *Armored Thunderbolt* (Mechanicsburg, PA: Stackpole, 2008), 116.

51 **received maybe five 76s:** Ibid., 340.

51 **The British had up-gunned:** Ibid., 180.

52 **"12 man bunker crew filed out":** Frank Woolner, *Spearhead in the West: The 3rd Armored Division in WWII* (Frankfurt, Germany: Kunst and Wervedruck, 1945; reprinted Nashville: Battery Press, 1980), 211.

52 **"You will not stop the Americans":** Nigel Cawthorne, *Reaping the Whirlwind: The German and Japanese Experience of World War II* (Cincinnati: David & Charles, 2007), 75.

54 **German 12th Infantry Division:** Steven Zaloga, *Siegfried Line 1944–45: Battles on the German Frontier* (New York: Osprey, 2007), 17.

54 **"Honey I don't see where candle":** Frank Audifred, letter to Lillian Zeringue, December 4, 1944.

55 **"to race amok":** Woolner, *Spearhead in the West*, 10.

55 **barely 1 of 4 tanks:** Ibid., 98.

55 **"Tanks were tied together":** Thomas Henry, "Masters of Slash and Surprise; 3rd Armored Division," *Saturday Evening Post*, October 19, 1946.

55 **nearly 6,000 trucks:** David Zabecki, ed., *World War II in Europe: An Encyclopedia* (New York: Routledge, 1999), 1254.

55 **"Red Ball Express":** Antony Beevor, *Ardennes 1944: Hitler's Last Gamble* (New York: Viking, 2015), 16.

55 **from Normandy:** Woolner, *Spearhead in the West*, 98.

55 **He'd attended college for a year:** "Highpockets'" 1940 Draft Registration Card and 1942 Enlistment Record, NARA.

56 **The shells were coming from:** Woolner, *Spearhead in the West*, 101.

7. Respite

58 **"sticky ribbons of mud"**: Frank Woolner, *Spearhead in the West: The 3rd Armored Division in WWII* (Frankfurt, Germany: Kunst and Wervedruck, 1945; reprinted Nashville: Battery Press, 1980), 103.

59 **"astonished and dismayed"**: Ibid.

59 **considered the images objectionable**: Derek Zumbro, *Battle for the Ruhr: The German Army's Final Defeat in the West* (Lawrence, KS: University Press of Kansas, 2006), 388.

61 **attending Yale in 1942**: "Obituary Record of Graduates of the Undergraduate Schools Deceased During the Year 1950–1951," *Bulletin of Yale University* 48, no. 1 (January 1, 1952).

62 **he had served as secretary**: "U.S. Army 1944 Firing Test No. 2," Wargaming, wargaming.info/1998/us-army-1944-firing-test-no2 (accessed June 15, 2017).

62 **"chubby with braided pigtails"**: Ed Hoy, *From KP to Combat, Recollections of a WWII Topkick*, unpublished memoir.

62 **Easy Company remained billeted**: E-Company, 32nd Armored Regiment, Morning Report, December 1944, NARA.

63 **the port of Antwerp had been opened**: Wilson Heefner, *Dogface Soldier: The Life of General Lucian K. Truscott, Jr.* (Columbia, MO: University of Missouri Press, 2010), 330.

63 **seek cover during an air raid**: Woolner, *Spearhead in the West*, 103.

65 **"quiet paradise for weary troops"**: Antony Beevor, *Ardennes 1944: Hitler's Last Gamble* (New York: Viking, 2015), 105.

65 **"vague, general zones of contact"**: Woolner, *Spearhead in the West*, 108–9.

65 **"it's just like a movie"**: Jim Cullen, interviewed by Charles Corbin, video interview, 1995, vimeo.com/channels/ww2vets/4692409 (accessed August 17, 2017).

66 **a three-to-one edge in infantry**: Peter Schrijvers, *The Unknown Dead: Civilians in the Battle of the Bulge* (Lexington, KY: University Press of Kentucky, 2005), xiv.

66 **broadcasts of bells ringing**: Beevor, *Ardennes 1944*, 120, 138.

66 **To slow the onslaught**: Ibid., 127, 164.

66 **four inches for buoyancy**: Steven Zaloga, *Armored Thunderbolt* (Mechanicsburg, PA: Stackpole, 2008), 222–24.

66 **relief force of 60,000 men**: Beevor, *Ardennes 1944*, 366.

67 **"If one of your men"**: Dick Goodie, "The Battle of the Bulge Remembered: View from My Snowfields," Battle of the Bulge Memories, battleofthebulgememories.be/stories26/32-battle-of-the-bulge-us-army/832-the-battle-of-the-bulge-remembered.html (accessed August 18, 2017).

67 **Easy Company fell in line**: E-Company, 32nd Armored Regiment, Morning Report, December 20, 1944, NARA.

67 **"destination unknown"**: Ibid.

8. The Fourth Tank

68 **"Russian High" of frigid winds**: Danny Parker, *Battle of the Bulge: Hitler's Ardennes Offensive, 1944–1945* (Cambridge, MA: Da Capo Press, 2004), 216.

69 **largest battle ever fought:** "Battle of the Bulge Facts," Historynet, historynet .com/battle-of-the-bulge (accessed August 28, 2017).

69 **"for a second time":** Frederick Karl, *Python Tales: World War II Memories of a Young Soldier* (Self-published, printed by CreateSpace, 2014), 111.

69 **"It was a good try":** Frank Woolner, *Spearhead in the West: The 3rd Armored Division in WWII* (Frankfurt, Germany: Kunst and Wervedruck, 1945; reprinted Nashville: Battery Press, 1980), 108–9.

69 **86-mile journey:** E-Company, 32nd Armored Regiment, Morning Reports, December 20–24, 1944, NARA.

69 **Germans' ultimate objective:** Peter Schrijvers, *The Unknown Dead: Civilians in the Battle of the Bulge* (Lexington, KY: University Press of Kentucky, 2005), xiii.

70 **When the Germans delivered:** Ibid.

71 **for ten days:** Woolner, *Spearhead in the West*, 53.

72 **70 percent of the time:** Steven Zaloga, *Armored Thunderbolt* (Mechanicsburg, PA: Stackpole, 2008), 231.

73 **to the next crossroads:** 2nd Battalion, 32nd Armored Regiment, After Action Report, December 1944, NARA.

73 **2nd Panzer Division had come up:** Schrijvers, *The Unknown Dead*, 247.

73 **"Impress on every individual":** Don Marsh and Steven Ossad, *Major General Maurice Rose: World War II's Greatest Forgotten Commander* (Lanham, MD: Taylor Trade, 2006), 269.

74 **the Panther's frontal armor:** Steven Zaloga, *Panther vs. Sherman: Battle of the Bulge 1944* (New York: Osprey, 2008), 24–25.

9. Hope

77 **temperature hovered around zero:** Antony Beevor, *Ardennes 1944: Hitler's Last Gamble* (New York: Viking, 2015), 259.

78 **"I have had two tanks":** Don Marsh and Steven Ossad, *Major General Maurice Rose: World War II's Greatest Forgotten Commander* (Lanham, MD: Taylor Trade, 2006), 381.

78 **"We will pray for you":** Peter Schrijvers, *The Unknown Dead: Civilians in the Battle of the Bulge* (Lexington, KY: University Press of Kentucky, 2005), 247.

80 **avoid the Shermans on the N4:** The 32nd Armored Regiment's Journal & Log claims that the unit spent the night of December 23–24 on a gridline that passed through Hèdrée, but the veterans say otherwise; Frank Audifred remembers the unit first returned to the village durring daylight on December 24, where he resumed his pursuit of the enemy tank but discovered it had slipped away.

80 **They were a blocking unit:** Schrijvers, *The Unknown Dead*, 247.

80 **Chuck fell into his seat:** In high school, Lt. Charlie Rose's youngest brother, John, related how teachers would tell him stories about Charlie. Chuck Miller stayed in touch with the Rose family and told them that no Christmas Eve had passed since that he didn't think of Charlie.

81 **assigned a tank of his own:** E-Company, 32nd Armored Regiment, Morning Report, November 27, 1944, NARA.

81 **"And God Was There"**: "Hey Memorial Rite Conducted," *Asbury Park* (NJ) *Evening Press*, March 15, 1945.

81 **"He's a nice fellow honey"**: Frank Audifred, letter to Lillian Zeringue, December 8, 1944.

83 **full circle in fifteen seconds**: Steven Zaloga, *Panther vs. Sherman: Battle of the Bulge 1944* (New York: Osprey, 2008), 28.

83 **60-ton behemoth**: James Brown and Michael Green, *Tiger Tanks at War* (Minneapolis: Zenith Press, 2008), 19.

85 **Sun glinted from the snow**: Marsh and Ossad, *Maurice Rose*, 278.

85 **six miles north of Marche**: E-Company, 32nd Armored Regiment, Morning Report, December 26, 1944, NARA; 2nd Battalion, 32nd Armored Regiment, After Action Report, December 1944, NARA.

85 **worked bare-chested**: Schrijvers, *The Unknown Dead*, 248.

86 **"Shades of Valley Forge"**: Frank Woolner, *Spearhead in the West: The 3rd Armored Division in WWII* (Frankfurt, Germany: Kunst and Wervedruck, 1945; reprinted Nashville: Battery Press, 1980), 114.

86 **windows on First Street**: Lamont Ebbert and Gordon Ripkey, telephone interview by Peter Semanoff, April 2017.

87 **Nearly 400 B-24s**: Eric Hammel, *Air War Europa: America's Air War Against Germany in Europe and North Africa* (Pacifica, CA: Pacifica Press, 1994), 427.

87 **Royal Air Force planes**: "Bomber Command Campaign Diary: December 1944," National Archives, webarchive.nationalarchives.gov.uk/20070706054631/http://www.raf.mod.uk/bombercommand/dec44.html (accessed April 15, 2017).

87 **"Over our head, floods"**: Nigel Cawthorne, *Reaping the Whirlwind: The German and Japanese Experience of World War II* (Cincinnati: David & Charles, 2007), 91–92.

87 **overhead for thirty minutes**: Donald Edwards, *A Private's Diary* (Self-published, 1994), 264.

10. Something Bigger

88 **around eight thirty A.M.**: G-3 Periodic Report No. 195, 3rd Armored Division, January 7, 1945, NARA.

88 **A blue sky beckoned**: E-Company, 32nd Armored Regiment, Morning Report, January 9, 1945, NARA.

88 **battled thirty-six miles**: E-Company, 32nd Armored Regiment, Morning Reports, January 2–9, 1945, NARA.

88 **"Enough dirt on us"**: Frank Audifred, letter to Lillian Zeringue, January 24, 1945.

88 **stopped within three miles**: Steven Smith, *2nd Armored Division "Hell on Wheels"* (Surrey, England: Ian Allan, 2003), 54.

88 **Marche was safe**: Peter Schrijvers, *The Unknown Dead: Civilians in the Battle of the Bulge* (Lexington, KY: University Press of Kentucky, 2005), 324–25, 351.

89 **the Germans reached the Meuse**: Smith, *2nd Armored Division*, 54.

89 **"The town is in ruins"**: Antony Beevor, *Ardennes 1944: Hitler's Last Gamble* (New York: Viking, 2015), 358.

89 Easy Company had lost two tanks: E-Company, 32nd Armored Regiment, Morning Report, January 6, 1945, NARA; Frank Audifred, interviewed by Robert Makos, April 2016.

90 blind the gunner: Steven Zaloga, *Armored Thunderbolt* (Mechanicsburg, PA: Stackpole, 2008), 116.

91 entered production in early 1942: Steven Zaloga, *Panzer IV vs. Sherman: France 1944* (New York: Osprey, 2015), 16.

91 more than 17,000: Zaloga, *Armored Thunderbolt*, 346.

91 "great satisfaction": Zaloga, *Panzer IV vs. Sherman*, 16.

91 designed for everything in 1941: Zaloga, *Armored Thunderbolt*, 33.

91 built only twenty tanks: Thomas Anderson, Michael Green, and Frank Schulz, *German Tanks of World War II in Color* (Osceola, WI: MBI Publishing 291), 7.

92 it was redrawing the map: Don Marsh and Steven Ossad, *Major General Maurice Rose: World War II's Greatest Forgotten Commander* (Lanham, MD: Taylor Trade, 2006), 279; Theodore Draper, *The 84th Infantry Division in the Battle of the Ardennes* (Historical Section, 84th Infantry Division, 1945), 25.

93 It was 10:13 A.M.: 2nd Battalion, 32nd Armored Regiment, Journal & Log, January 7, 1945, NARA.

93 remnants of two Wehrmacht regiments: 2nd Battalion, 32nd Armored Regiment, After Action Report, January 1945, NARA.

93 "on foot, on bicycles, on horses": Schrijvers, *The Unknown Dead*, 357.

93 "It was only the realization": Beevor, *Ardennes 1944*, 366.

94 sometimes killed the bow gunner: Aaron Elson, *Tanks for the Memories* (Hackensack, NJ: Chi Chi Press, 2001), 77.

96 Chuck fell almost nine feet: Zaloga, *Panzer IV vs. Sherman*, 17.

96 one-in-three chance: Zaloga, *Armored Thunderbolt*, 329.

97 Only at 5:07 P.M.: 2nd Battalion, 32nd Armored Regiment, Journal & Log, January 7, 1945, NARA.

97 "It's miserable darling": Frank Audifred, letter to Lillian Zeringue, January 14, 1945.

98 one of nineteen replacements: Malcolm Marsh Jr., *Reflections of a World War II Infantryman* (Self-published, 2001), 57.

99 captured thirty-seven enemy prisoners: 2nd Battalion, 32nd Armored Regiment, After Action Report, January 1945, NARA.

99 implore for shelter: Schrijvers, *The Unknown Dead*, 357.

99 check their trousers: Beevor, *Ardennes 1944*, 176.

101 "loses his honor": Ibid., 343.

101 "If there is any suspicion": Ibid., 345.

102 "Our men haven't eaten": Schrijvers, *The Unknown Dead*, 219.

11. America's Tiger

103 their first morning back: E-Company, 32nd Armored Regiment, Morning Report, February 9, 1945, NARA.

103 lost more tanks than it destroyed: Haynes Dugan et. al., *Third Armored Division: Spearhead in the West*, 2nd. ed. (Paducah, KY: Turner, 2001), 66.

103 **had to borrow 350 Shermans:** Antony Beevor, *Ardennes 1944: Hitler's Last Gamble* (New York: Viking, 2015), 218.

104 **In a letter to Eisenhower:** Don Marsh and Steven Ossad, *Major General Maurice Rose: World War II's Greatest Forgotten Commander* (Lanham, MD: Taylor Trade, 2006), 378–79.

104 **"We're just out-tanked":** Ernest Leiser, "Shells Bounce Off Tigers, Veteran U.S. Tankmen Say," *Stars and Stripes,* February 23, 1945.

105 **"We have been lied to":** Beevor, *Ardennes 1944,* 27.

105 **"A lot of guys are getting":** Frank Audifred, letter to Lillian Zeringue, February 16, 1945.

106 **good day for shooting:** E-Company, 32nd Armored Regiment, Morning Report, February 23, 1945, NARA.

106 **"All you hear is":** Frank Audifred, letter to Lillian Zeringue, February 23, 1945.

106 **front lines were eight miles away:** "February 20, 1945, HQ Twelfth Army Group situation map," Army Group, 12th Engineer Section, and 1st Headquarters United States Army, loc.gov/item/2004631880 (accessed April 23, 2015).

107 **Homemade armor:** Steven Zaloga, *Armored Thunderbolt* (Mechanicsburg, PA: Stackpole, 2008), 283–85.

107 **A staff sergeant's rank:** E-Company, 32nd Armored Regiment, Morning Report, February 8, 1945, NARA.

107 **"America's answer to the Tiger":** "Chasing the Tiger," *Newsweek,* March 19, 1945; "New U.S. Super Tank Bears Name of Gen. Pershing," *Daily Press* (Newport News, VA), March 8, 1945.

107 **Half of the inventory:** Richard Hunnicutt, *Pershing: A History of the Medium Tank T20 Series* (Brattleboro, VT: Echo Point Books & Media, 2015), 13.

107 **advanced tank technology:** Wes Gallagher, "Gen. Pershing Tank Was Capable of Dealing with German Armor," *Harrisburg* (PA) *Telegraph,* May 16, 1945; Steven Zaloga, *Panther vs. Sherman: Battle of the Bulge 1944* (New York: Osprey, 2008), 11, 19; Hunnicutt, *Pershing,* 201; Steven Zaloga, *T-34–85 vs. M26 Pershing: Korea 1950* (New York: Osprey, 2010), 18.

109 **the most potent weapon:** "The Heavy Tank T26E3 Training Film F.B.-191," U.S. Army Signal Corps 1945, youtube.com/watch?v=XWF83bNq_LQ&t=101s (accessed August 31, 2017).

109 **southwest British seacoast:** Frank Woolner, *Spearhead in the West: The 3rd Armored Division in WWII* (Frankfurt, Germany: Kunst and Wervedruck, 1945; reprinted Nashville: Battery Press, 1980), 56.

110 **age of seventeen:** Marsh and Ossad, *Maurice Rose,* 231.

110 **climbed the ranks:** Woolner, *Spearhead in the West,* 3.

110 **commanded tank units:** Ibid., 3.

110 **"greatest tank force in the world":** Ibid.

110 **"He goes himself":** Marsh and Ossad, *Maurice Rose,* 231.

110 **assigned half of the tanks:** Hunnicutt, *Pershing,* 13.

111 **3-foot-long armor-piercing shell:** *Armor-Piercing Ammunition for Gun, 90mm, M3* (Washington, DC: Office of the Chief of Ordnance, 1945), 12.

111 **15.5-foot barrel:** *90-mm Gun M3 Mounted in Combat Vehicles* (Washington, DC: War Department, 1944), 6.

111 **football-shaped muzzle brake:** Hunnicutt, *Pershing,* 117.

112 "I'll try for the near one": Michael Green and Gladys Green, *Panther: Germany's Quest for Combat Dominance* (New York: Osprey, 2012), 180.

114 "There is no question": Marsh and Ossad, *Maurice Rose*, 378–79.

12. Two Miles

115 Rain spiraled from the tanks' barrels: E-Company, 32nd Armored Regiment, Morning Report, February 28, 1945, NARA; B-Company, 32nd Armored Regiment, Morning Report, February 28, 1945, NARA.

115 coordinated drive of the First Army: Steven Zaloga, *Remagen 1945: Endgame Against the Third Reich* (New York: Osprey, 2006), 12.

115 thanks to the Timberwolves: 2nd Battalion, 32nd Armored Regiment, After Action Report, February 1945, NARA.

115 fortified since the prior fall: Zaloga, *Remagen 1945*, 21.

116 "each with its main streets barricaded": Frank Woolner, *Spearhead in the West: The 3rd Armored Division in WWII* (Frankfurt, Germany: Kunst and Wervedruck, 1945; reprinted Nashville: Battery Press, 1980), 122.

116 Three M5 Stuart light tanks: Lt. Fred Hadsel and T/3 William Henderson, *The Roer to the Rhine, 26 February to 6 March, 1945*, interview with Lt. Col. C. L. Miller (CO), Maj. R. S. Lawry (XO), 2nd Battalion, 32nd Armored Regiment, 3rd Armored Division, Cologne, Germany, March 13, 1945, NARA.

117 buried Bill in his uniform: William Hey Individual Deceased Personnel File, Office of Human Resources Command, US Army, Fort Knox, KY.

117 "obsolete in every respect": Isaac White, *United States vs. German Equipment* (Bennington, VT: Merriam Press, 2005), 5.

117 far cry from the engineering marvel: Robert Cameron, *Mobility, Shock, and Firepower: The Emergence of the U.S. Army's Armor Branch, 1917–1945* (Washington, DC: US Army Center of Military History, 2008), 464.

118 "forgot" his objective: Hadsel and Henderson, interview with Miller and Lawry.

118 wounded men rolled over the sides: B-Company, 32nd Armored Regiment, Morning Report, February 28, 1945, NARA.

120 another shot came from the front: Hadsel and Henderson, interview with Miller and Lawry.

120 firing their tank-killer gun: HQ, 1st Battalion, 36th Armored Infantry Regiment, Unit Report No. 110, February 25–28, 1945, NARA.

120 gun with an 88mm mouth: *Technical Manual E9–369A: German 88-mm Antiaircraft Gun Material* (Washington, DC: War Department, 1943), 87; Phil Zimmer, "WWII Weapons: The German 88mm Gun," Warfare History Network, warfarehistorynetwork.com/daily/wwii/wwii-weapons-the-german-88mm-gun/ (accessed August 14, 2017).

120 fire from at least six guns: 2nd Battalion, 32nd Armored Regiment, After Action Report, February 1945, NARA.

121 held around eighty shells: James Brown and Michael Green, *M4 Sherman at War* (St. Paul: Zenith, 2007), 92–93.

121 "Once you get hit": Aaron Elson, *Tanks for the Memories* (Hackensack, NJ: Chi Chi Press, 2001), 95.

121 **One crew reported a jammed cannon:** Hadsel and Henderson, interview with Miller and Lawry.

123 **region had been a flak belt:** HQ, 1st Battalion, 36th Armored Infantry Regiment, Unit Report No. 110, February 25–28, 1945, NARA; Friedrich Koechling, "Defensive Combat of the LXXXI. Armeekorps During the Period from 25 January 1945 to 13 April 1945," US Army Foreign Military Studies, B-576, April 10, 1947.

124 **transferred over from B-Company:** B-Company, 32nd Armored Regiment, Morning Report, December 31, 1944, NARA; E-Company, 32nd Armored Regiment, Morning Report, January 29, 1945, NARA.

124 **Tall, with blue eyes, brown hair:** Robert L. Bower, 1940 Draft Registration Card, NARA.

127 **Sherman's reputation as a tinderbox:** Frederick Karl, *Python Tales: World War II Memories of a Young Soldier* (Self-published, printed by CreateSpace, 2014), 68; Blaine Taylor, "M4 Sherman: 'Blunder' or 'Wonder' Weapon?" Warfare History Network, warfarehistorynetwork.com/daily/wwii/m4-sherman-blunder-or-wonder-weapon/ (accessed August 16, 2017).

127 **The Sherman owed its fire-prone:** Steven Zaloga, *Armored Thunderbolt* (Mechanicsburg, PA: Stackpole, 2008), 117–18.

128 **to his wife, Darlene:** "World War II Casualties: Sgt. Raymond W. Juilfs," Jones County Iowa Military, iowajones.org/military/WWII_Casualties_Juilfs_Raymond .htm (accessed September 1, 2017).

129 **skull crushed beyond recognition:** Robert Bower Individual Deceased Personnel File, Office of Human Resources Command, US Army, Fort Knox, KY.

130 **"Johnny, boy, if I get hold":** Philip DeRiggi, "My Brother John S. DeRiggi," 3rd AD Soldiers' Memoirs, 3ad.com/history/wwll/memoirs.pages/deriggi.htm (accessed September 2, 2017).

130 **an American helmet rolled:** Malcolm Marsh Jr., *Reflections of a World War II Infantryman* (Self-published, 2001), 75.

132 **"all-consuming noise":** Ibid., 76.

132 **the gun pits held abandoned 88s:** HQ, 1st Battalion, 36th Armored Infantry Regiment, Unit Report No. 110, February 25–28, 1945, NARA; 2nd Battalion, 32nd Armored Regiment, After Action Report, February 1945, NARA.

133 **A-Company claimed 173 prisoners:** 2nd Battalion, 32nd Armored Regiment, After Action Report, February 1945, NARA.

133 **"unconditional defense":** Koechling, "Defensive Combat of the LXXXI. Armeekorps During the Period from 25 January 1945 to 13 April 1945," 24.

133 **sights of the battle's aftermath:** Lt. Fred Hadsel and T/3 William Henderson, *The Roer to the Rhine, 26 February to 6 March, 1945: Part III Notes on the Operation, 25 February—28 February 1945*, interview with Lt. Col. John Boles (XO), Task Force X, 3rd Armored Division, Königswinter, Germany, March 28, 1945, NARA; E-Company, 32nd Armored Regiment, Morning Reports, February 27–March 11, 1945, NARA; B-Company, 32nd Armored Regiment, Morning Report, February 28, 1945, NARA; 2nd Battalion, 32nd Armored Regiment, Journal & Log, "Annex B: Losses in Action," NARA.

134 **Chuck would be sent to Stolberg:** Oda "Chuck" Miller, *Life & Death on a Tank Crew,* unpublished memoir, 1997, Army Heritage Center Foundation Collection.

135 **"Super Tank":** "New U.S. Super Tank Bears Name of Gen. Pershing," *Daily Press* (Newport News, VA), 2.

135 **five letters of consolation:** Raymond Juilfs Individual Deceased Personnel File, Office of Human Resources Command, US Army, Fort Knox, KY; Robert Bower Individual Deceased Personnel File, Office of Human Resources Command, US Army, Fort Knox, KY; "Branning A Samuel," 3rd Armored Division Memorial Group, 36air-ad.com/names/serial/34982223 (accessed September 6, 2017); "8 Give Lives in War, 18 Wounded in Action," *St. Louis Post-Dispatch*, March 23, 1945; Fred A. Lee, 1943 Enlistment Record, NARA.

13. Hunting

137 **winter was refusing:** E-Company, 32nd Armored Regiment, Morning Report, March 3, 1945, NARA.

137 **clearing the woods toward Oberaussem:** 2nd Battalion, 32nd Armored Regiment, After Action Report, March 1945, NARA.

138 **"An American soldier surveyed":** Frank Woolner, "Drive on the Rhine," The Writings of Frank Woolner, 3ad.com/history/wwll/woolner.pages/drive.on.rhine .htm (accessed September 8, 2017).

139 **Boom had played basketball:** "Officer Awarded Silver Star Posthumously," *San Bernardino County Sun*, October 14, 1945.

14. The Fire Department of the West

143 **parallel to the Odenwald Mountains:** George Bradshaw, *Bradshaw's Illustrated Hand-book for Belgium and the Rhine; and Portions of Rhenish Germany, Including Elsass and Lothringen (Alsace and Lorraine), with a Ten Days' Tour in Holland* (London: W. J. Adams & Sons, 1896), 149.

144 **After the Germans seized the territory:** Steven Zaloga, *Operation Nordwind 1945: Hitler's Last Offensive in the West* (New York: Osprey, 2010), 13.

144 **The Panther, ever mechanically sensitive:** Steven Zaloga, *Panther vs. Sherman: Battle of the Bulge 1944* (New York: Osprey, 2008), 29; Michael Green and Gladys Green, *Panther: Germany's Quest for Combat Dominance* (New York: Osprey, 2012), 248.

144 **5,000 Allied fighter-bombers:** Derek Zumbro, *Battle for the Ruhr: The German Army's Final Defeat in the West* (Lawrence, KS: University Press of Kansas, 2006), 85.

145 **The Wehrmacht was preparing the city:** Karel Margry, "The Battle for Cologne," *After the Battle* 104 (1999).

148 **the old baroque buildings:** Paul Eisenberg, ed., *Fodor's Europe* (New York: Random House, 2004), 380.

149 **Wehrmacht tankers claimed the emblem:** Chris McNab, ed., *Hitler's Elite: The SS, 1939–45* (New York: Osprey, 2013), 80–81.

149 **Goebbels claimed the Americans:** Antony Beevor, *Ardennes 1944: Hitler's Last Gamble* (New York: Viking, 2015), 33, 99; Nigel Cawthorne, *Reaping the Whirl-*

wind: The German and Japanese Experience of World War II (Cincinnati: David & Charles, 2007), 141.

149 **"the mood there is shit":** Beevor, *Ardennes 1944,* 40–41.

150 **"Prolongers of the War":** Ibid.

151 **"Subversion of the War Effort":** "Law on Treacherous Attacks Against State and Party, and for the Protection of Party Uniforms," *Reichsgesetzblatt* 1 (December 20, 1934): 1269.

151 **Section 5 reads:** "Subversion of the War Effort," *Reichsgesetzblatt* 1 (August 17, 1938): 1455.

152 **"If our enemies think":** This joke made such an impression on Gustav that he remembered it, word for word, seventy years later.

153 **seven hundred years of German history:** Jackson Spielvogel, *Western Civilization: A Brief History,* vol. 1 (Boston: Wadsworth, 2005), 204.

153 **nearly 800 British bombers:** *Encyclopaedia Britannica Online,* "Bombing of Dresden," britannica.com/event/bombing-of-Dresden (accessed September 15, 2017).

153 **the horrors of Dresden:** Victor Gregg, "Dresden Bombing 70 Years On: A Survivor Recalls the Horror He Witnessed in the German City," *Independent,* independent.co.uk/news/world/world-history/dresden-bombing-70-years-on-a-survivor-recalls-the-horror-he-witnessed-in-the-german-city-10042770.html (accessed September 15, 2017).

153 **Eisenhower had 73 divisions:** Zumbro, *Battle for the Ruhr,* 85.

15. Going First

155 **Ominous clouds were forming:** E-Company, 32nd Armored Regiment, Morning Report, March 7, 1945, NARA.

155 **A parallel task force:** Frank Woolner, *Spearhead in the West: The 3rd Armored Division in WWII* (Frankfurt, Germany: Kunst and Wervedruck, 1945; reprinted Nashville: Battery Press, 1980), 127.

156 **Lieutenant Bill Stillman:** Bill Stamm, letter to John Huffman, March 12, 1945.

157 **still smoking from an RAF raid:** Karel Margry, "The Battle for Cologne," *After the Battle* 104 (1999).

157 **cathedral's twin spires stared back:** Ann Stringer, "Deserted Avenues Echo U.S. Advances in Cologne," *The Times* (Shreveport, LA), March 6, 1945.

157 **"An old Cavalryman":** "Traded Saddle for a 'Sherman,'" *Oriole News* (32nd Armored Regiment), July 18, 1945.

159 **A seat of Nazi power:** Dr. Horst Matzerath, *Cologne During National Socialism: A Short Guide Through the EL-DE House* (Cologne: Hermann-Josef Emons Verlag, 2011), 104; Richard Weikart, *Hitler's Ethic: The Nazi Pursuit of Evolutionary Progress* (New York: Palgrave Macmillan, 2009), 105.

159 **Panzerfaust's warhead worked:** Isaac White, *United States vs. German Equipment* (Bennington, VT: Merriam Press, 2005), 70.

161 **march into Cologne had been delayed:** 2nd Battalion, 32nd Armored Regiment, After Action Report, March 1945, NARA.

161 **linchpin of Operation Lumberjack:** Steven Zaloga, *Remagen 1945: Endgame Against the Third Reich* (New York: Osprey, 2006), 12.

162 the time of the *Endkampf*: Steven Zaloga, *Downfall 1945: The Fall of Hitler's Third Reich* (New York: Osprey, 2016), 89.

162 "unrelenting defense of Cologne": Dr. Martin Rüther, *Cologne During National Socialism: A Short Guide Through the EL-DE House*, 247.

162 gotten drunk and fell off a horse: Bill Stillman, letter to John Huffman, March 10, 1945.

163 23-pound shell: *Technical Manual 9–735: Pershing Heavy Tank T26E3* (Washington, DC: War Department, 1945), 452.

163 platoon of its tanks peeled off: 2nd Battalion, 32nd Armored Regiment, After Action Report, March 1945, NARA.

163 RAF had bombed the city: Karel Margry, "The Battle for Cologne," *After the Battle* 104 (1999).

164 "Rubble and broken glass crunched": Woolner, *Spearhead in the West*, 128.

164 biggest house-to-house battle: Ibid., 127.

165 The enemy was near: Friedrich Koechling, "Defensive Combat of the LXXXI. Armeekorps During the Period from 25 January 1945 to 13 April 1945," US Army Foreign Military Studies, B-576, April 10, 1947; Charles MacDonald, *Victory in Europe, 1945: The Last Offensive of World War II* (Mineola, NY: Dover Publications, 2007), 190.

167 "Closets are crammed with Nazi leaflets": Howard Katzander, "Allies Govern Germany," *Yank* 3, no. 44 (April 20, 1945).

167 knocked "mouse holes" in the walls: Sidney Olson, "Underground Cologne," *Life,* March 19, 1945.

169 To prop up its ranks: 415th Infantry Regiment, 104th Infantry Division, Intelligence Report, March 3, 1945, NARA.

170 Buck searched the food bin: Buck had originally believed this story to be set a few days earlier at the Erft Canal, but after our visit to Cologne and upon further reflection, he identified the setting as Cologne itself, during the first day of fighting.

170 Spearhead had ticketed 1,027 prisoners: Lt. Fred Hadsel, *The Roer to the Rhine, 26 February to 6 March, 1945: Enemy Order of Battle,* interview with M/Sgt. Angelo Cali (G-2), OB Team, 3rd Armored Division, Cologne, Germany, March 13, 1945, NARA.

170 "No [German] unit above company": Ibid.

170 "YOU ARE ENTERING COLOGNE": Ann Stringer, "Deserted Avenues Echo U.S. Advances in Cologne," *The Times* (Shreveport, LA), March 6, 1945.

171 been going since four A.M.: HQ, 1st Battalion, 36th Armored Infantry Regiment, Unit Report No. 114, March 4–7, 1945, NARA.

171 he was busted to private: E-Company, 32nd Armored Regiment, Morning Report, August 8, 1944, NARA.

171 back to being a commander: E-Company, 32nd Armored Regiment, Morning Report, March 12, 1945, NARA.

172 dubbed the "Rhine Maidens": "The Press: The Rhine Maidens," *Newsweek,* March 19, 1945.

172 scrolling, creative monikers: Woolner, *Spearhead in the West*, 66, 76, 88.

172 The men explained: Ann Stringer, "U.S. Tanks No Good in Battle, Say Crewmen After Losing Half of M-4 Machines," *Salt Lake Telegram*, March 7, 1945.

173 **killed in his jeep:** "People: William John Stringer," The Baron, thebaron.info/
people/memorial-book/william-john-stringer (accessed August 25, 2017).

173 **admonishment only spurred her:** "The Press: The Rhine Maidens," *Newsweek*,
March 19, 1945.

173 **Of the twelve Shermans:** 2nd Battalion, 32nd Armored Regiment, Tank Status
Report, March 5, 1945, NARA.

173 **three years of war without modifications:** Steven Zaloga, *Panzer IV vs. Sherman:
France 1944* (New York: Osprey, 2015), 16.

176 **They lived with only sporadic power:** Margry, "The Battle for Cologne."

176 **more than four years of her life:** A. C. Grayling, *Among The Dead Cities: The
History and Moral Legacy of the WWII Bombing* (New York: Walker, 2006),
283.

16. Victory or Siberia

178 **28-ton tank:** Steven Zaloga, *Panzer IV vs. Sherman: France 1944* (New York:
Osprey, 2015), 13.

179 **against the low, gray clouds:** E-Company, 32nd Armored Regiment, Morning
Report, March 7, 1945, NARA.

179 **630 years to finish construction:** "Cologne Cathedral," UNESCO, whc.unesco
.org/en/list/292 (accessed September 26, 2017).

179 **a dozen high-explosive bombs:** Karel Margry, "The Battle for Cologne," *After
the Battle* 104 (1999).

180 **at least twenty tanks:** Friedrich Koechling, "Defensive Combat of the LXXXI.
Armeekorps During the Period from 25 January 1945 to 13 April 1945," US
Army Foreign Military Studies, B-576, April 10, 1947.

180 **Second Lieutenant Wilhelm Bartelborth:** *March 1945—Duel at the Cathedral*,
produced by Hermann Rheindorf, Kölnprogramm, 2015, DVD.

181 **First Lieutenant Otto Leppla:** Friedrich Bruns, *Panzerbrigade 106 Feldherrnhalle*
(Celle, Germany: Eigenverlag, 1988), 36.

181 **"while the Panthers quickly press on":** Michael Green and Gladys Green, *Panther: Germany's Quest for Combat Dominance* (New York: Osprey, 2012), 150.

181 **"Cologne's Wall Street":** Louis Lochner, "Hitler Commits Germany to Suicide,
Says Lochner," *Lansing* (MI) *State Journal*, March 8, 1945.

182 **Many were former policemen or firemen:** Charles MacDonald, *Victory in Europe, 1945: The Last Offensive of World War II* (Mineola, NY: Dover Publications, 2007), 190.

182 **Of the city's Volkstrum:** Lt. Fred Hadsel and T/3 William Henderson, *The Roer
to the Rhine, 26 February to 6 March, 1945: "Volksturn in Cologne" to Enemy
Order of Battle*, March 8, 1945, NARA; Koechling, "Defensive Combat," 66.

182 **SS was nowhere to be found:** "March 6, 1945, HQ Twelfth Army Group Situation Map," Army Group, 12th Engineer Section, and 1st Headquarters United
States Army, loc.gov/item/2004631894/ (accessed September 26, 2017).

182 **Hitler himself now favored his SS:** Antony Beevor, *Ardennes 1944: Hitler's Last
Gamble* (New York: Viking, 2015), 26, 88.

182 the "Golden Pheasants": Derek Zumbro, *Battle for the Ruhr: The German Army's Final Defeat in the West* (Lawrence, KS: University Press of Kansas, 2006), 26.

182 incinerating their incriminating papers: Margry, "The Battle for Cologne"; "Fighting Fronts," *Newsweek*, March 19, 1945.

183 his native city, fifteen square miles: Alan Taylor, "World War II: The Fall of Nazi Germany," *The Atlantic*, October 9, 2011, theatlantic.com/photo/2011/10/world -war-ii-the-fall-of-nazi-germany/100166/ (accessed September 26, 2017); Robert Philpot, "The Carpet-Bombing of Hamburg Killed 40,000 People. It Also Did Good," *The Spectator*, May 9, 2015, spectator.co.uk/2015/05/the-carpet -bombing-of-hamburg-killed-40000-people-it-also-did-good/ (accessed September 26, 2017).

183 Was firebombing Dresden going city: Ian Carter, "RAF Bomber Command During the Second World War," Imperial War Museums, iwm.org.uk/history/raf -bomber-command-during-the-second-world-war (accessed August 25, 2017); Suzannah Hills, " 'I Would Have Destroyed Dresden Again': Bomber Harris Was Unrepentant over German City Raids 30 Years After the End of World War Two," DailyMail, dailymail.co.uk/news/article-2276944/I-destroyed-Dresden -Bomber-Harris-unrepentant-German-city-raids-30-years-end-World-War-Two .html (accessed August 25, 2017).

183 inflated death toll of 250,000: Ian Kershaw, *The End: The Defiance and Destruction of Hitler's Germany, 1944–1945* (New York: Penguin Books, 2011), 239.

184 "Victory or Siberia!": Beevor, *Ardennes 1944*, 99.

184 "This had been an undiscussable subject": Nigel Cawthorne, *Reaping the Whirlwind: The German and Japanese Experience of World War II* (Cincinnati: David & Charles, 2007), 122.

184 forty-five miles from Berlin: United States Holocaust Memorial Museum, "The Soviet Union and the Eastern Front," Holocaust Encyclopedia, ushmm.org/wlc/ en/article.php?ModuleId=10005507 (accessed September 26, 2017).

186 Morries had quit elementary school: Robert Morries, Report of Physical Examination and Induction, US Army, August 13, 1943, NARA.

187 see his mother, Cinda: Ibid.

187 Baughn was a former factory worker: Richard Baughn, 1944 Enlistment Record, NARA.

188 reunite with his wife, Opal: Richard Baughn, Report of Death, Adjutant General's Office, War Department, Washington, DC, March 30, 1945, NARA. In A-Company, a man's date of death was often reported days after the actual event because the company clerk and first sergeant were back with the support units and it was sometimes difficult to find a break in the fighting to notify them.

188 With three Shermans trailing: This description is based on the actual event captured on film by the cameramen of the 165th Signal Photo Company, US Army, during the Battle of Cologne, March 6, 1945, acquired from the collection of NARA.

188 to guard their right flank: 2nd Battalion, 32nd Armored Regiment, Journal & Log, March 6, 1945, NARA.

189 At one P.M., a distant explosion: Bruns, *Panzerbrigade 106 Feldherrnhalle*, 596.

192 a black Opel P4 car: Rainer Rudolph, "Katharina starb an St. Gereon," *Kölner Stadt Anzeiger* (Cologne, Germany), July 30, 2007.

192 twenty-six-year-old Katharina Esser: Marc Hieronimus, grand-nephew of Katharina Esser, interviewed by Adam Makos, March 2013.

192 The third of four sisters: Helene Winskowski, niece of Katharina Esser, interviewed by Bryan Makos, Franz Englram translator, August 2014.

193 had encouraged the attempt: Rudolph, "Katharina starb an St. Gereon."

193 All three of her sisters: Helene Winskowski, niece of Katharina Esser, interviewed by Bryan Makos, Franz Englram translator, August, 2014.

193 "My dear ones": Katharina Esser, letter to Karl and Gertrud Esser, February 23, 1945.

199 often used by the German Army: Jean-Denis Lepage, *German Military Vehicles of World War II* (Jefferson, NC: 2007), 53; Reinhold Busch, ed., *Survivors of Stalingrad: Eyewitness Accounts from the Sixth Army, 1942–43* (London: Frontline Books, 2014), 4.

200 A civilian witness would later recount: Frieda Taisakowski, "Statement Under Oath," Cologne, Germany, January 16, 1946.

17. The Monster

201 A pair of hesitant Shermans crept: This description is based on the actual event captured on film by the cameramen of the 165th Signal Photo Company, US Army, during the Battle of Cologne, March 6, 1945, acquired from the collection of NARA.

201 After F-Company seized the cathedral: Clifford Miller, letter to Clarence Smoyer, June 21, 2001.

201 The lead Sherman stopped beneath: This description is based on the actual event captured on film by the cameramen of the 165th Signal Photo Company, US Army, during the Battle of Cologne, March 6, 1945, acquired from the collection of NARA.

201 deeply religious twenty-six-year-old: "Lt. Karl E. Kellner Reported Killed in Action on March 6," *Sheboygan* (WI) *Press,* April 6, 1945.

202 a battlefield commission: Clifford Miller, letter to Clarence Smoyer, June 21, 2001.

202 call for a dozer tank: 2nd Battalion, 32nd Armored Regiment, Journal & Log, March 6, 1945, NARA.

202 "major news story": Timothy Gay, *Assignment to Hell: The War Against Nazi Germany with Correspondents Walter Cronkite, Andy Rooney, A. J. Liebling, Homer Bigart, and Hal Boyle* (New York: NAL Caliber, 2012), xiv.

202 wasn't your typical journalist: Andy Rooney, *My War* (New York: PublicAffairs, 2002), 126, 186, 212.

202 rush the Hotel Excelsior's wine cellar: Ibid., 249.

202 slammed obliquely into the gun shield: Dierk Lürbke, "Skirmish Panther vs. Sherman," Tank Duel at the Cathedral, anicursor.com/colpicwar2.html (accessed September 15, 2017).

202 **clipped the front end:** Hans Krupp report, *Kölner Stadtanzeiger,* November 4, 1980. Republished in: Hermann Rheindorf, ed., *1945 Kriegsende in Köln: Die komplette Fotoedition von Hermann Rheindorf* (Rheinbach, Germany: Regionalia Verlag GmbH, 2014), 199.

203 **Rooney darted forward:** Rooney, *My War,* 251.

203 **"a blur of gore and bone":** Al Newman, "Al Newman in Cologne: Madness, Death, Poison," *Newsweek,* March 19, 1945.

203 **"I had never been present":** Rooney, *My War,* 250.

203 **"I don't know how I got":** Mike Levin, Overseas News Agency, March 7, 1945.

203 **"somewhere in Germany":** "Lt. Karl E. Kellner Reported Killed in Action on March 6," *Sheboygan* (WI) *Press,* April 6, 1945.

203 **Julian Patrick, was dead:** "Patrick H Julian," 3rd Armored Division Memorial Group, 36air-ad.com/names/serial/15056008 (accessed September 15, 2017); "WWII: The Face of War," Getty Images, gettyimages.com/detail/news-photo/view-of-dead-american-soldier-julian-patrick-from-kentucky-news-photo/5049 6163#view-of-dead-american-soldier-julian-patrick-from-kentucky-us-3rd -picture-id50496163 (accessed September 15, 2017); Lürbke, "Skirmish Panther vs. Sherman." Also giving his life in that tank was twenty-two-year-old T/5 Grade Curtis Speer of Fort Worth, Texas.

204 **tank had fired from the tunnel:** Lürbke, "Skirmish Panther vs. Sherman"; Wilhelm Bartelborth, letter to Dr. Siegfried Grasmann, published in Rheindorf, *1945 Kriegsende in Köln,* 160–61, 171, 175, 210; *March 1945—Duel at the Cathedral,* produced by Hermann Rheindorf, Kölnprogramm, 2015, DVD.

204 **Bartelborth never ordered his men:** Wilhelm Bartelborth, letter to Dr. Siegfried Grasmann, published in Rheindorf, *1945 Kriegsende in Köln,* 160–61, 171, 175, 210; *March 1945—Duel at the Cathedral.*

206 **"Jim, let's go down and see":** *Scenes of War: Combat Photographer Jim Bates,* produced by Steve Antonuccio, Jim Bates, Ree Mobley, and Dave Richkert, Pikes Peak Library District, 1994, vimeo.com/122653345 (accessed January 19, 2017).

206 **populated by propaganda posters:** This description is based on the actual event captured on film by the cameramen of the 165th Signal Photo Company, US Army, during the Battle of Cologne, March 6, 1945, acquired from the collection of NARA.

206 **"You get all ready for it":** *Scenes of War.*

206 **Bates bailed out with the crew:** James Bates, *A Photographer at War: First Day of Closing the Bulge,* unpublished memoir, 2.

206 **Of the sixty-five army cameramen:** *Scenes of War.*

207 **"a nine-month-long dispute":** Bates, *A Photographer at War,* 4.

207 **the minutes felt like hours:** Wilhelm Bartelborth, letter to Dr. Siegfried Grasmann, published in Rheindorf, *1945 Kriegsende in Köln,* 160–61, 171, 175, 210; *March 1945—Duel at the Cathedral.*

208 **Bates saw the Panther's turret turning:** *Scenes of War.*

210 **knock out a Panther from broadside:** "US Army 1944 Firing Test No. 2," Wargaming, wargaming.info/1998/us-army-1944-firing-test-no2 (accessed June 15, 2017).

210 **24-pound T33:** *Armor-Piercing Ammunition for Gun, 90mm, M3* (Washington, DC: Office of the Chief of Ordnance, 1945), 8.

210 **15.5-foot barrel:** *90-mm Gun M3 Mounted in Combat Vehicles* (Washington, DC: War Department, 1944), 6.

211 **dangling streetcar lines:** This description is based on the actual event captured on film by Jim Bates and the cameramen of the 165th Signal Photo Company, US Army, during the Battle of Cologne, March 6, 1945, acquired from the collection of NARA.

211 **Bartelborth saw the dark, blurry vehicle:** Wilhelm Bartelborth, letter to Dr. Siegfried Grasmann, published in Rheindorf, *1945 Kriegsende in Köln*, 160–61, 171, 175, 210; *March 1945—Duel at the Cathedral.*

211 **"Stop!" Bartelborth screamed:** Hans Krupp report, *Kölner Stadtanzeiger,* November 4, 1980. Republished in Rheindorf, *1945 Kriegsende in Köln,* 199.

212 **a "living torch":** Ibid.

214 **McVey looked past the camera:** This description is based on the actual event captured on film by Jim Bates, US Army, during the Battle of Cologne, March 6, 1945, acquired from the collection of NARA.

214 **"that its men and cities could":** Bates, *A Photographer at War,* 5.

215 **made the call at 3:10 P.M.:** 2nd Battalion, 32nd Armored Regiment, Journal & Log, March 6, 1945, NARA.

217 **found the crew from the Panther:** Mike Levin, Overseas News Agency, March 7, 1945; Karel Margry, "The Battle for Cologne," *After the Battle* (104): 1999; Hans Krupp report, *Kölner Stadtanzeiger,* November 4, 1980. Republished in Rheindorf, *1945 Kriegsende in Köln,* 199.

217 **some of the 326 Germans:** Lt. Fred Hadsel, *The Roer to the Rhine, 26 February to 6 March, 1945: Enemy Order of Battle,* interview with M/Sgt. Angelo Cali (G-2), OB Team, 3rd Armored Division, Cologne, Germany, March 13, 1945, NARA.

18. The Conquerors

219 **record Earley for *The Army Hour*:** Bill Stillman, letter to John Huffman, March 10, 1945.

219 **he left for Paris to process:** Jim Bates, letter to Clarence Smoyer, October 21, 1996.

219 **segment called "Killing a Monster":** Al Newman, "Al Newman in Cologne: Madness, Death, Poison," *Newsweek,* March 19, 1945.

219 **Earley had been a machinist:** Robert Earley, 1942 Enlistment Record, NARA.

220 **Bartelborth resumed teaching:** Wilhelm Bartelborth, letter to Dr. Siegfried Grasmann, published in Hermann Rheindorf, ed., *1945 Kriegsende in Köln: Die komplette Fotoedition von Hermann Rheindorf* (Rheinbach, Germany: Regionalia Verlag GmbH, 2014), 160–61, 171, 175, 210; *March 1945—Duel at the Cathedral,* produced by Hermann Rheindorf, Kölnprogramm, 2015, DVD.

220 **"coffin on wheels":** James Bates, *A Photographer at War: The Battle of Cologne (Second Day),* unpublished memoir, 5.

221 **"a couple of cases":** Don Marsh and Steven Ossad, *Major General Maurice Rose: World War II's Greatest Forgotten Commander* (Lanham, MD: Taylor Trade, 2006), 292–93.

222 **"The yarn was either accepted":** Frank Woolner, *Spearhead in the West: The 3rd*

Armored Division in WWII (Frankfurt, Germany: Kunst and Wervedruck, 1945; reprinted Nashville: Battery Press, 1980), 130.

222 **"nearest Ordnance Collecting Point":** Lt. Colonel W. G. Barnwell, "Memo to All Units Combat Command A," 3rd Armored Division, Cologne, Germany, March 6, 1945, NARA.

223 **"When you talk to them":** Howard Katzander, "Allies Govern Germany," *Yank* 3, no. 44, April 20, 1945.

223 **During the elections in 1933:** Dr. Werner Jung, *Cologne During National Socialism: A Short Guide Through the EL-DE House* (Cologne: Hermann-Josef Emons Verlag, 2011), 87.

224 **still executing people in Cologne:** Carsten Dams and Michael Stolle, *The Gestapo: Power and Terror in the Third Reich* (Oxford, England: Oxford University Press, 2014), 34; Jung, *Cologne During National Socialism,* 40.

224 **her grandfather's barbershop:** Marion Pütz, daughter of Annemarie Berghoff, interviewed by Adam Makos, Franz Englram translator, Germany, March 2013 and August 2014.

225 **a rumor in September 1942:** Anna Berghoff trial documents, "Sondergericht 1S Js 42/43: Anklageschrift," Cologne, Germany, April 13, 1943; Anna Berghoff trial documents, "Sondergericht 1S Ms 13/43: Sitzungsbericht zu 39–266/43," Cologne, Germany, December 2, 1943.

225 **"false assertion that could":** Ibid.

225 **"Her statement could provoke":** Ibid.

225 **Cologne's Jewish population:** Dr. Karola Fings, *Cologne During National Socialism: A Short Guide Through the EL-DE House* (Cologne: Hermann-Josef Emons Verlag, 2011), 193–95, 246.

225 **The Gestapo's punishments:** Eric Johnson, "German Women and Nazi Justice: Their Role in the Process from Denunciation to Death," *Historical Social Research* 20, no. 1 (1995); Karel Margry, "The Battle for Cologne," *After the Battle* 104 (1999).

225 **He freed Annemarie's mother:** Anna Berghoff trial documents, "Sondergericht 1S Js 42/43: Anklageschrift," Cologne, Germany, April 13, 1943; Anna Berghoff trial documents, "Sondergericht 1S Ms 13/43: Sitzungsbericht zu 39–266/43," Cologne, Germany, December 2, 1943.

226 **The punishment was a fine:** Joseph Balkoski, *The Last Roll Call: The 29th Infantry Division Victorious, 1945* (Mechanicsburg, PA: Stackpole, 2015), 19.

228 **The portrait wasn't flattering:** The description of the artist's rendition of Clarence is based on observation of the drawing, which was completed in March 1945 in Cologne, Germany. Gifted to the author by Clarence, it resides as a treasured item in the author's collection.

228 **Typhus was spreading:** Katzander, "Allies Govern Germany."

228 **"all civilians are potential carriers":** Lt. Colonel W. G. Barnwell, "Memo to All Units Combat Command A," 3rd Armored Division, Cologne, Germany, March 7, 1945, NARA.

229 **"The fear of airpower":** Sidney Olson, "Underground Cologne," *Life,* March 19, 1945.

230 **gray-haired woman picked it up:** Jim Miller, son of Chuck Miller, interviewed by Robert Makos, October, 2017.

230 **"Nazi Tanks Excel Ours, Troops Say":** Ann Stringer, "Nazi Tanks Excel Ours, Troops Say," *Washington Post*, March 8, 1945.

230 **Rose had backed up his tankers:** Marsh and Ossad, *Maurice Rose, 378*.

231 **"American Tanks Not Worth Drop":** Ann Stringer, "American Tanks Not Worth Drop of Water, Crews Say," *The Pittsburgh Press,* March 7, 1945.

231 **"U.S. Tanks No Good in Battle":** Ann Stringer, "U.S. Tanks No Good in Battle, Say Crewmen After Losing Half of M-4 Machines," *Salt Lake Telegram,* March 7, 1945.

231 **"American Tanks No Good":** Ann Stringer, "American Tanks No Good, Assert Troops in Reich," *San Bernardino Daily Sun*, March 8, 1945.

231 **"one of the strongest weapons":** Stringer, "Nazi Tanks Excel Ours, Troops Say."

231 **Hattie set aside the clipping:** The clipping of Ann Stringer's article remained a priceless relic in the Miller family from that day forth.

19. The Breakout

232 **other GIs were swimming:** Frank Woolner, *Spearhead in the West: The 3rd Armored Division in WWII* (Frankfurt, Germany: Kunst and Wervedruck, 1945; reprinted Nashville: Battery Press, 1980), 131.

232 **"Most of the tankers and infantrymen":** Ibid., 130.

235 **A spring shower fell:** E-Company, 32nd Armored Regiment, Morning Report, March 31, 1945, NARA.

236 **a dirt road near Altenkirchen:** 2nd Battalion, 32nd Armored Regiment, After Action Report, March 1945, NARA.

236 **"This was the beginning":** Woolner, *Spearhead in the West*, 131.

236 **would have been unconquerable:** Ibid., 137.

237 **By noon, the column:** 2nd Battalion, 32nd Armored Regiment, Journal & Log, March 26, 1945, NARA.

238 **DeRiggi was standing:** Another account wrongly places DeRiggi outside the tank looking for a sniper when he was hit, whereas Clarence's memory of events is supported by after action records that report five tankers being wounded by an ambush of 20mm guns without mention of enemy snipers.

238 **Flak 38 cannon in each truck bed:** 2nd Battalion, 32nd Armored Regiment, After Action Report, March 1945, NARA.

238 **loader fell to the turret floor:** E-Company, 32nd Armored Regiment, Morning Report, March 28, 1945, NARA.

239 **Clutching his wounded leg:** A-Company, 36th Armored Infantry Regiment, Morning Reports, March 27–29, 1945, NARA.

240 **Shrapnel had torn a hole:** Philip DeRiggi, "My Brother John S. DeRiggi," 3rd AD Soldiers' Memoirs, 3ad.com/history/wwll/memoirs.pages/deriggi.htm (accessed September 2, 2017).

240 **Five tankers had head wounds:** E-Company, 32nd Armored Regiment, Morning Report, March 28, 1945, NARA.

240 **ten doughs were injured:** A-Company, 36th Armored Infantry Regiment, Morning Reports, March 27–29, 1945, NARA.

20. The American Blitz

244 **north of Marburg, Germany:** 2nd Battalion, 32nd Armored Regiment, After Action Report, March 1945, NARA.

244 **"This show looked like":** Frank Woolner, *Spearhead in the West: The 3rd Armored Division in WWII* (Frankfurt, Germany: Kunst and Wervedruck, 1945; reprinted Nashville: Battery Press, 1980), 138.

244 **slick from a recent rain:** E-Company, 32nd Armored Regiment, Morning Report, April 1, 1945, NARA.

244 **familiar scenery reminded some men:** John Thompson, "Tribune Man's Eyewitness Story of Armored Force's Dash in Reich," *Chicago Daily Tribune,* March 31, 1945.

244 **relinquished the lead position:** 2nd Battalion, 32nd Armored Regiment, After Action Report, March 1945, NARA.

245 **targeting "the heart of Germany":** Don Marsh and Steven Ossad, *Major General Maurice Rose: World War II's Greatest Forgotten Commander* (Lanham, MD: Taylor Trade, 2006), 303.

245 **80 percent of Germany's coal:** Rick Atkinson, *The Guns at Last Light: The War in Western Europe, 1944–1945* (New York: Henry Holt, 2013), 223.

245 **Spearhead made a ninety-degree turn:** Thomas Henry, "Masters of Slash and Surprise; 3rd Armored Division," *Saturday Evening Post,* October 19, 1946.

245 **2nd Armored, Hell on Wheels:** Donald Houston, *Hell on Wheels: The 2nd Armored Division* (Novato, CA: Presidio, 1977), 403.

245 **"slip a steel wall around":** Woolner, *Spearhead in the West,* 142.

245 **one hundred miles away:** Ibid., 244.

245 **"haymaker to the heart of Germany":** Ibid., 131.

245 **across four parallel roads:** Ibid., 244.

246 **"One case of Scotch for dead":** John Thompson, "Tribune Man's Eyewitness Story of Armored Force's Dash in Reich," *Chicago Daily Tribune,* March 31, 1945.

246 **"Johnny Boy" had survived:** Philip DeRiggi, "My Brother John S. DeRiggi," 3rd AD Soldiers' Memoirs, 3ad.com/history/wwll/memoirs.pages/deriggi.htm (accessed September 2, 2017).

247 **later receive the Bronze Star:** James Bates, *A Photographer at War: Award of the Bronze Star Medal to Tec 4 James L. Bates,* unpublished memoir.

247 **Earley would receive one too:** 2nd Battalion, 32nd Armored Regiment, Journal & Log, "Annex B: Awards," NARA.

248 **A vehicle burning:** Ken Zumwalt, *The Stars and Stripes: World War II and the Early Years* (Austin: Eakin Press, 1989), 42.

250 **"Jerries cleared to the edge":** Marsh and Ossad, *Maurice Rose,* 321.

250 **The Pershing managed a half mile:** Richard Hunnicutt, *Pershing: A History of the Medium Tank T20 Series* (Brattleboro, VT: Echo Point Books & Media, 2015), 217.

250 **Sherman got about a mile:** "Sherman I & IC (Typical for II) Outline," War Office Records 194/132, March 14, 1945, National Archives (UK); Steven Zaloga, *Panther vs. Sherman: Battle of the Bulge 1944* (New York: Osprey, 2008), 19.

250 **for more than 2,000 miles:** Michael Haskew, *M4 Sherman Tanks: The Illustrated History of America's Most Iconic Fighting Vehicles* (Minneapolis: Voyageur Press, 2016), 66.

250 **"He had a crew cut":** John Irwin, *Another River, Another Town: A Teenage Tank Gunner Comes of Age in Combat—1945* (New York: Random House, 2002), 45.

250 **His division was on the verge:** Woolner, *Spearhead in the West,* 142.

251 **"The plains and valleys":** John Thompson, "Tribune Man's Eyewitness Story of Armored Force's Dash in Reich," *Chicago Daily Tribune,* March 31, 1945.

251 **They had both been beheaded:** Ibid.

252 **convoy halted and coiled:** 2nd Battalion, 32nd Armored Regiment, Journal & Log, March 29, 1945, NARA.

252 **"took to kneeling":** Irwin, *Another River,* 41.

252 **"the greatest one-day advance":** Woolner, *Spearhead in the West,* 142.

252 **clocked 102 miles:** Marsh and Ossad, *Maurice Rose,* 2.

252 **another 100:** Thompson, "Tribune Man's Eyewitness Story of Armored Force's Dash in Reich."

252 **tanks ahead of Easy Company:** 2nd Battalion, 32nd Armored Regiment, After Action Report, March 1945, NARA.

252 **Spearhead went farther through:** Thompson, "Tribune Man's Eyewitness Story of Armored Force's Dash in Reich."

253 **the division's new M24 Chaffees:** Lt. Fred Hadsel and T/3 William Henderson, *The Roer to the Rhine, 26 February to 6 March, 1945: 83rd Recon Battalion,* interview with Capt. Joe Robertson (S-2), Lt. Russel Bonaguidi (S-3), 2nd Lt. Stephen Nicholosen Jr. (Public Relations Officer), Worringen, Germany, March 15, 1945, NARA.

254 **about eight miles south of Paderborn:** 2nd Battalion, 32nd Armored Regiment, After Action Report, March 1945, NARA.

254 **SS men were firing:** Ibid.

255 **Paderborn was the "home port":** Kurt Kramer, 3./schwere Panzer-Abteilung 507, recollections, published in Helmut Schneider, ed., *The Combat History of Schwere Panzer Abteilung 507* (Winnipeg: J. J. Fedorowicz, 2003), 134.

255 **Every German tanker spent:** In August 1944, Gustav Schaefer trained at Paderborn for two weeks, learning the particulars of the Panther.

255 **assembled SS Panzerbrigade Westfalen:** Derek Zumbro, *Battle for the Ruhr: The German Army's Final Defeat in the West* (Lawrence, KS: University Press of Kansas, 2006), 225–26.

21. The Fatherless

256 **in the darkness of Böddeken Forest:** 2nd Battalion, 32nd Armored Regiment, After Action Report, March 1945, NARA.

256 **forbidden from going forward to help:** 2nd Battalion, 32nd Armored Regiment, Journal & Log, March 31, 1945, NARA.

256 **in the forest to coil:** 2nd Battalion, 32nd Armored Regiment, After Action Report, March 1945, NARA.

257 **ten German tanks blasted away:** Wolf Koltermann, Commander 3./schwere Panzer-Abteilung 507, recollections, published in Helmut Schneider, ed., *The Combat History of Schwere Panzer Abteilung 507* (Winnipeg: J. J. Fedorowicz, 2003), 128–31.

257 **small-arms fire from SS infantry:** Don Marsh and Steven Ossad, *Major General Maurice Rose: World War II's Greatest Forgotten Commander* (Lanham, MD: Taylor Trade, 2006), 24.

257 **The general gripped a Thompson:** Ibid., 25.

257 **some of his Shermans had escaped:** Lt. Fred Hadsel, *Remagen Bridgehead to Mulde River, 25 March—25 April 1945: Task Force Welborn, Combat Command "B,"* interview with Col. John Welborn, CO, 33rd Armored Regiment, 3rd Armored Division, Sondershausen, Germany, May 1, 1945, NARA.

257 **afford to be methodical:** Ibid.

258 **"like hunting from a raised platform":** Kurt Kramer, 3./schwere Panzer-Abteilung 507, recollections, published in Schneider, *The Combat History of Schwere Panzer Abteilung 507*, 133.

258 **walked their fire down the column:** Koltermann, Commander 3./schwere Panzer-Abteilung 507, recollections, published in Schneider, *The Combat History of Schwere Panzer Abteilung 507*, 130.

258 **"like ghostly torches":** Fritz Schreiber, 3./schwere Panzer-Abteilung 507, recollections, published in Schneider, *The Combat History of Schwere Panzer Abteilung 507*, 133.

258 **one dough fired a .50-caliber:** Francis Grow and Alfred Summers, *A History of the 143rd Armored Signal Company, 1941–1945*, 3rd Armored Division, Summer 1945, University of Illinois Collection, 98.

258 **desperate to reverse their fortunes:** Marsh and Ossad, *Maurice Rose*, 8.

258 **"on top of us":** Ibid., 34.

258 **"Smith," Rose said:** Ibid., 33.

259 **One of Rose's jeeps exploded:** Ibid., 35.

259 **a shell felled a tree:** Lt. Fred Hadsel, *Remagen Bridgehead to Mulde River, 25 March—25 April 1945: Task Force Welborn, Combat Command "B,"* interview with Capt. J. Fred Gehman (S-3), 1st Battalion, 33rd Armored Regiment, 3rd Armored Division, Bad Frankenhausen, Germany, April 30, 1945, NARA.

259 **a wedge of tan enemy tanks:** Ibid..

259 **"We're in a hell of a fix":** Marsh and Ossad, *Maurice Rose*, 35.

259 **German voices could be heard:** Hadsel, interview with Gehman.

259 **found refuge in Hamborn Castle:** Hadsel, interview with Welborn.

259 **Rose and his entourage ran:** Marsh and Ossad, *Maurice Rose*, 36.

259 **"Big Six, come in Big Six!":** Ibid., 32.

259 **around eight A.M.:** 2nd Battalion, 32nd Armored Regiment, Journal & Log, March 31, 1945, NARA.

259 **Easy Company was finally unleashed:** Ibid.

260 **As many as thirty-seven:** 391st Armored Field Artillery Battalion, After Action Report, March 1945, NARA.

260 **Bullet-ridden half-tracks:** 33rd Armored Regiment, After Action Report, March 1945, NARA.

260 **Nine Shermans. Twenty-one half-tracks:** 391st Armored Field Artillery Battalion, After Action Report, March 1945, NARA.

260 **A Stuart:** 33rd Armored Regiment, After Action Report, March 1945, NARA.

260 **A pair of jeeps and trucks:** 391st Armored Field Artillery Battalion, After Action Report, March 1945, NARA.

260 **shot point-blank in the rear:** Kramer, 3./schwere Panzer-Abteilung 507, recollections, published in Schneider, *The Combat History of Schwere Panzer Abteilung 507*, 133.

261 **"baked ham":** The analogy of "a baked ham" was used by Clarence Smoyer to describe the dead tanker he witnessed.

261 **lay an abandoned Pershing:** Col. Frederick Brown, April 1, 1945 Sworn Affidavit, War Crimes, Judge Advocate General's Office, War Department, Washington, DC, NARA. This tank was likely repaired quickly and returned to action, as it was never registered as being knocked out on the logs that tracked each of the first twenty Pershings in the theater.

261 **Two companies of doughs:** Lt. Fred Hadsel, *Remagen Bridgehead to Mulde River, 25 March—25 April 1945: Task Force X, Combat Command "A,"* interview with Maj. Ben Rushing (S-2), Task Force X, 3rd Armored Division, Müchen, Germany, May 4, 1945, NARA; 2nd Battalion, 32nd Armored Regiment, Journal & Log, March 31, 1945, NARA.

261 **The enemy tanks had rammed aside:** Koltermann, Commander 3./schwere Panzer-Abteilung 507, recollections, published in Schneider, *The Combat History of Schwere Panzer Abteilung 507*, 131.

261 **bowled right over a jeep's hood:** Walter May, 36th Armored Infantry Regiment, recollections, published in Haynes Dugan et al., *Third Armored Division: Spearhead in the West*, 2nd. ed. (Paducah, KY: Turner, 2001), 93.

261 **rear compartment of one half-track:** Ibid.

262 **Two sergeants from the 33rd Regiment's:** Marsh and Ossad, *Maurice Rose*, 321.

262 **"That's one of Jack's new tanks":** Ralph Greene, "The Triumph and Tragedy of Major General Maurice Rose," *Armor*, March–April 1991.

262 **"Holy shit! It's a Tiger!":** Ibid.

263 **"No versteh,"** Rose repeated: Ibid.

263 **Rose's driver suggested:** Marsh and Ossad, *Maurice Rose*, 333.

263 **Witnesses heard the German fire:** Ibid., 341, 343.

263 **fourteen bullet holes:** Ibid., 343.

264 **German daredevil would be killed:** For more than seventy years, the German tank commanders involved in the Welborn Massacre kept confidential the identity of their comrade who killed General Rose. To get to the bottom of this mystery, the author and his staff traveled to Germany, where the culprit's identity was revealed to us, under the expectation that this book would reveal the man's motive, but not his name. The author shall respect those wishes.

264 **wrapped his body in it:** Greene, "The Triumph and Tragedy."

264 **"He was mourned as a GI":** Frank Woolner, *Spearhead in the West: The 3rd Armored Division in WWII* (Frankfurt, Germany: Kunst and Wervedruck, 1945; reprinted Nashville: Battery Press, 1980), 3.

264 **"We felt like he was one":** Robert Riensche, 143rd Armored Signal Corps, recol-

lections, in *Rolling Thunder—The True Story of the 3rd Armored Division,* produced by A & E Entertainment, 2002, DVD.

264 **Thirteen men had died:** F-Company, 36th Armored Infantry Regiment, Morning Reports, April 2–9, 1945, NARA; F-Company, 33rd Armored Regiment, Morning Report, April 4, 1945, NARA; I-Company, 33rd Armored Regiment, Morning Reports, April 1–10, 1945, NARA.

266 **"This thing is almost over now":** W. C. Heinz, *When We Were One: Stories of World War II* (Cambridge, MA: Da Capo Press, 2002), 154–55.

22. Family

268 **Dark clouds hung low:** "OPFLASH NO. 1-Y46: 386th Fighter Squadron, 365th Fighter Group," April 1, 1945, Air Force Historical Research Agency, Maxwell AFB, Alabama.

268 **Five days earlier, an RAF:** Derek Zumbro, *Battle for the Ruhr: The German Army's Final Defeat in the West* (Lawrence, KS: University Press of Kansas, 2006), 208, 214.

269 **A gap lay between Easy Company:** 2nd Battalion, 32nd Armored Regiment, After Action Report, April 1945, NARA.

269 **Instead of F-Company, four M36:** 703rd Tank Destroyer Battalion, After Action Report, April 1945, NARA; 703rd Tank Destroyer Battalion, "Tank Destroyer M36," October 27, 1944, NARA.

269 **were deploying 25 tanks:** Wolfgang Schneider, *Tigers in Combat II* (Mechanicsburg, PA: Stackpole, 2005), 339.

269 **had only around 200 tanks:** Steven Zaloga, *Downfall 1945: The Fall of Hitler's Third Reich* (New York: Osprey, 2016), 22, 39.

270 **The men of A-Company moved:** "E Company Hits Paderborn," *Oriole News* (32nd Armored Regiment), July 18, 1945.

270 **Their plot on the starting line:** Lt. Fred Hadsel, *Remagen Bridgehead to Mulde River 25 March—25 April 1945: Task Force X, Combat Command "A,"* interview with Maj. Ben Rushing (S-2), Task Force X, 3rd Armored Division, Mücheln, Germany, May 4, 1945, NARA.

272 **his watch struck 6:30 A.M.:** 2nd Battalion, 32nd Armored Regiment, After Action Report, April 1945, NARA.

272 **Paderborn was a lifeline:** Frank Woolner, *Spearhead in the West: The 3rd Armored Division in WWII* (Frankfurt, Germany: Kunst and Wervedruck, 1945; reprinted Nashville: Battery Press, 1980), 246; Steven Zaloga, *Remagen 1945: Endgame Against the Third Reich* (New York: Osprey, 2006), 84–85; John Thompson, "Tribune Writer Tells of Fight for Paderborn," *Chicago Tribune,* April 1, 1945.

273 **"largest encirclement battle in history":** Don Marsh and Steven Ossad, *Major General Maurice Rose: World War II's Greatest Forgotten Commander* (Lanham, MD: Taylor Trade, 2006), 5.

273 **clutching Panzerfausts:** "E Company Hits Paderborn," *Oriole News* (32nd Armored Regiment), July 18, 1945.

273 **with a fatal head wound:** Wilborn Bellflower, of Squad 2/2, was the brave machine gunner killed by the first Panzerfaust, whereas the third Panzerfaust claimed his squadmate, Ted Bird. Malcolm Marsh Jr., *Reflections of a World War II Infantryman* (Self-published, 2001), 98.

274 **began corkscrewing haphazardly:** Ibid.

274 **dozens of red glowing orbs:** Zumbro, *Battle for the Ruhr,* 225–26, 237; Woolner, *Spearhead in the West,* 145.

274 **blasting a dough off the back:** The dough killed by the direct hit was Walter Franklin, of Texas, from the 3rd Platoon machine-gun squad. Marsh, *Reflections,* 99; "Walter Franklin," 3rd Armored Division Memorial Group, 36air-ad.com/names/serial/14008296 (accessed September 25, 2017).

274 **felled him mere feet from safety:** The radioman, Paul "Packy" Rowley of the 2nd Platoon, would later die of his wounds. According to Buck Marsh, "Packy was an older fellow, having been a boxer and tavern owner in Johnstown, New York." Marsh, *Reflections,* 99.

276 **turned back after a gun stoppage:** "E Company Hits Paderborn," *Oriole News* (32nd Armored Regiment), July 18, 1945.

276 **Another Sherman lurched to a stop:** 2nd Battalion, 32nd Armored Regiment, After Action Report, April 1945, NARA.

276 **tank destroyers radioed a warning:** Ibid.; 703rd Tank Destroyer Battalion, After Action Report, April 1945, NARA.

276 **collectively firing seventy times:** 703rd Tank Destroyer Battalion, After Action Report, April 1945, NARA.

276 **school's cadre of instructors:** Wilhelm Tieke, *SS Panzer Brigade "Westfalen"* (Winnipeg: J. J. Fedorowicz, 2003), 13.

277 **"like a wet dishcloth":** Marsh, *Reflections,* 100.

277 **dug foxholes in the front yards:** Zumbro, *Battle for the Ruhr,* 173.

23. Come Out and Fight

280 **clearing the adjoining homes:** Lt. Fred Hadsel, *Remagen Bridgehead to Mulde River, 25 March—25 April 1945: Task Force X, Combat Command "A,"* interview with Maj. Ben Rushing (S-2), Task Force X, 3rd Armored Division, Mücheln, Germany, May 4, 1945, NARA; 2nd Battalion, 32nd Armored Regiment, After Action Report, April 1945, NARA.

281 **It was strangely quiet:** "E Company Hits Paderborn," *Oriole News* (32nd Armored Regiment), July 18, 1945.

281 **No other units had reached:** Lt. Fred Hadsel, *Remagen Bridgehead to Mulde River, 25 March—25 April 1945: Task Force Welborn, Combat Command "B,"* interview with Capt. J. Fred Gehman (S-3), 1st Battalion, 33rd Armored Regiment, 3rd Armored Division, Bad Frankenhausen, Germany, April 30, 1945, NARA; Lt. Fred Hadsel, *Remagen Bridgehead to Mulde River, 25 March—25 April 1945: Task Force Lovelady, Combat Command "B,"* Interview with W.O. A. J. Palfey, Communications Officer, 2nd Battalion, 33rd Armored Regiment, 3rd Armored Division, Tilleda, Germany, April 27, 1945, NARA.

283 wore the lightning bolt runes: 2nd Battalion, 32nd Armored Regiment, After Action Report, April 1945, NARA.

284 A flight of eight P-47s: "OPSUM 297 for the Period from 1100–1600 Hours, Part III: IX TAC," April 1, 1945, Air Force Historical Research Agency, Maxwell AFB, Alabama.

285 division had committed three task forces: Hadsel, interview with Gehman; Hadsel, interview with Palfey.

286 delivered only a glancing blow: "E Company Hits Paderborn."

286 "a running conflict between firing": Derek Zumbro, *Battle for the Ruhr: The German Army's Final Defeat in the West* (Lawrence, KS: University Press of Kansas, 2006), 237–38.

286 "At least two enemy tanks here": 2nd Battalion, 32nd Armored Regiment, Journal & Log, April 1, 1945, NARA.

288 With two, they just might: "E Company Hits Paderborn."

291 command center to the north: Wilhelm Tieke, *SS Panzer Brigade "Westfalen"* (Winnipeg: J. J. Fedorowicz, 2003), 31.

24. The Giant

292 building was being "shot to pieces": "E Company Hits Paderborn," *Oriole News* (32nd Armored Regiment), July 18, 1945.

295 Someone was practically behind them: Ibid.

297 2,774 feet per second: *Armor-Piercing Ammunition for Gun, 90mm, M3* (Washington, DC: Office of the Chief of Ordnance, 1945), 6–8.

299 Villa's tank pulled up: "E Company Hits Paderborn."

299 Relief had finally come: 2nd Battalion, 32nd Armored Regiment, After Action Report, April 1945, NARA.

299 "It was disgusting to watch how": Nigel Cawthorne, *Reaping the Whirlwind: The German and Japanese Experience of World War II* (Cincinnati: David & Charles, 2007), 123.

300 Killed at age twenty-eight: E-Company, 32nd Armored Regiment, Morning Report, April 8, 1945, NARA.

301 "Makes Sacrifice": "Lt. William Boom Killed as Yanks Fight in Germany," *San Bernardino County Sun*, April 24, 1945.

302 The tank was camouflaged with foliage: Malcolm Marsh Jr., *Reflections of a World War II Infantryman* (Self-published, 2001), 103.

302 no aircraft had attacked that morning: "Air Summary of Operations: Ninth Air Force," April 1, 1945, Air Force Historical Research Agency, Maxwell AFB, Alabama; "OPSUM 297 for the Period from Sunrise to 1100 Hours, Part II: IX TAC," April 1, 1945, Air Force Historical Research Agency, Maxwell AFB, Alabama; "OPSUM 297 for the Period from 1100–1600 Hours, Part III: IX TAC," April 1, 1945, Air Force Historical Research Agency, Maxwell AFB, Alabama; "OPSUM 297 for the Period from 1600 Hours to Sunset, Part IV: IX TAC," April 1, 1945, Air Force Historical Research Agency, Maxwell AFB, Alabama.

302 **A-Company had suffered 17:** A-Company, 36th Armored Infantry Regiment, Morning Reports, April 3–7, 1945, NARA.

302 **Easy Company 15:** Sgt. Sherman Albert, Tec 5 Nestor Flores Jr., Pvt. George Shafer, and PFC Henry Kulik gave their lives that day. E-Company, 32nd Armored Regiment, Morning Reports, April 3–5, 1945, NARA.

302 **Shermans would lie rusting:** Dieter Jähn, tank commander, Panzer-Abteilung 507, interviewed by Bryan Makos, Franz Englram translator, Germany, August 2014.

304 **"Oberfeldwebel Böving":** Wolfgang Schneider, *Tigers in Combat I* (Mechanicsburg, PA: Stackpole, 2004), 48.

304 **enemy was waging a delaying action:** Steven Zaloga, *Remagen 1945: Endgame Against the Third Reich* (New York: Osprey, 2006), 84–85.

304 **"Spearhead to Powerhouse":** Lt. Fred Hadsel, *Remagen Bridgehead to Mulde River, 25 March–25 April 1945,* interview with Capt. F. F. Flegal (S-3 Air), 1st Battalion, 32nd Armored Regiment, 3rd Armored Division, Bernstedt, Germany, May 3, 1945, NARA; Frank Woolner, *Spearhead in the West: The 3rd Armored Division in WWII* (Frankfurt, Germany: Kunst and Wervedruck, 1945; reprinted Nashville: Battery Press, 1980), 145.

304 **More than 325,000 German troops:** Derek Zumbro, *Battle for the Ruhr: The German Army's Final Defeat in the West* (Lawrence, KS: University Press of Kansas, 2006), 260.

304 **word would break on April 9:** James Long, "Last Railway Outlet Cut by Allied Armies," *Denton* (TX) *Record-Chronicle,* April 9, 1945; Woolner, *Spearhead in the West,* 145.

304 **liberate the Dora-Nordhausen:** 33rd Armored Regiment, After Action Report, April 1945, NARA.

304 **including Jewish prisoners:** Monique Laney, *German Rocketeers in the Heart of Dixie: Making Sense of the Nazi Past During the Civil Rights Era* (New Haven: Yale University Press, 2015), 148.

305 **nearby copper mines of Sangerhausen:** 2nd Battalion, 32nd Armored Regiment, Journal & Log, April 13, 1945, NARA.

305 **"a pretty stiff price":** Steven Zaloga, *Downfall 1945: The Fall of Hitler's Third Reich* (New York: Osprey, 2016), 34.

25. Getting Home

307 **Once home to P-47 squadrons:** Ian Gardner, *No Victory in Valhalla: The Untold Story of Third Battalion, 506 Parachute Infantry Regiment from Bastogne to Berchtesgaden* (New York: Osprey, 2014), 35.

308 **more than 1 million fighting men:** Steven Zaloga, *Downfall 1945: The Fall of Hitler's Third Reich* (New York: Osprey, 2016), 89.

308 **1 million would never return:** Erich Maschke, *Zur Geschichte der deutschen Kriegsgefangenen des Zweiten Weltkrieges* (Bielefeld, Germany: E. und W. Gieseking, 1967), 207, 224.

309 **prisons for society's degenerates:** Nikolaus Wachsmann, *KL: A History of the Nazi Concentration Camps* (New York: Farrar, Straus and Giroux, 2015), 73.

26. The Last Battle

313 **shorts, boat shoes, and sizeable sunglasses:** Author's description is based on a photograph supplied by Clarence that shows him and Melba on a bike ride during their first season in Florida.

319 **finished his degree at Yale:** "Obituary Record of Graduates of the Undergraduate Schools Deceased During the Year 1950–1951," *Bulletin of Yale University* 48, no. 1 (January 1, 1952); "Mason Salisbury's Services Are Held," *Scarsdale* (NY) *Inquirer,* December 1, 1950.

319 **"General Salisbury said that since":** "Mason Salisbury's Services Are Held."

335 **Annemarie went on to marry:** Marion Pütz, daughter of Annemarie Berghoff, interviewed by Adam Makos, Franz Englram translator, Germany, March 2013 and August 2014.

Afterword

338 **William "Woody" McVey worked:** "William D. (Dud) McVey," *Jackson* (MI) *Citizen Patriot,* January 18, 1985.

338 **facial wounds healed during a year:** Philip DeRiggi, "My Brother John S. DeRiggi," 3rd AD Soldiers' Memoirs, 3ad.com/history/wwll/memoirs.pages /deriggi.htm (accessed September 2, 2017).

338 **Bob Earley attained the farm:** "Robert M. Earley," *Chatfield* (MN) *News,* October 18, 1979.

PHOTO CREDITS

View through the periscope: Photograph by Jim Bates, courtesy of Special
  Collections, Pikes Peak Library District, 161–8919
Audifred and his M4A1: Frank Audifred
Spearhead crews in the Ardennes: National Archives
Clarence and McVey with shell: Clarence Smoyer
M4 in Baneux: National Archives via Darren Neely
Sherman and vanquished Panther: National Archives via Steven Zaloga
Troops on the turret: Clarence Smoyer
Pershing with muzzle brake: Clarence Smoyer
Salisbury inspects the barrel of an M4: Chuck Miller
Caserta and *Everlasting:* Chuck Miller
Pershing and Sherman: Clarence Smoyer
Eleanor and crew: Chuck Miller
Foster and Sherman: Clarence Smoyer
Abandoned Sherman: National Archives
Easy Eight: National Archives via Darren Neely
Pershing idles by underpass: National Archives
Pershing and white flag: National Archives
Spearhead dough in Cologne: National Archives
Kathi Esser and her nephew: The Esser Family
Kathi Esser and her sisters: The Esser Family
Medics tend to Kathi: National Archives

Second Insert

Pershing approaches Cologne cathedral: Photograph by Jim Bates, courtesy
  of Special Collections, Pikes Peak Library District, 161–3326
A second Sherman approaches cathedral: National Archives
Sherman absorbs a hit: National Archives
Pershing advances through Cologne: National Archives
Pershing fires at Panther: National Archives
Bartelborth and crew flee Panther (three photos): National Archives
Burning Panther: National Archives via Darren Neely
Bulldozer clears the street: U.S. Army photo by William B. Allen, courtesy of
  Dave Allen and Darren Neely
Hohenzollern Bridge: U.S. Army photo by William B. Allen, courtesy of
  Dave Allen and Darren Neely
Pershing stands guard: National Archives via Darren Neely
Gareth Hector's *Spearhead:* Courtesy of ValorStudios.com
Panther as seen from cathedral spire: U.S. Army photo by William B. Allen,
  courtesy of Dave Allen and Darren Neely
Infantrymen explore bomb damage: National Archives
Touring the defeated Panther: Photograph by Jim Bates, courtesy of Special
  Collections, Pikes Peak Library District, 161–3307
Inspecting the Panther: Photograph by Jim Bates, courtesy of Special
  Collections, Pikes Peak Library District, 161–3314

Cradling the K98 in front of the cathedral: Photograph by Jim Bates, courtesy of Special Collections, Pikes Peak Library District, 161–3328.

A-Company doughs relax after securing Cologne: Buck Marsh

Sherman passes a defeated Panzer: Steven Zaloga

Sketch of Clarence: Clarence Smoyer

Stan Richards stands atop half-track: Buck Marsh

Spearhead crew comes up for a breather: National Archives via Darren Neely

Gareth Hector's *Unstoppable:* Courtesy of ValorStudios.com

Easy Company commanders confer: Chuck Miller

Hauling a wagon of German prisoners: Clarence Smoyer

M4 at gas station: Chuck Miller

Cleaning the 76mm gun: Chuck Miller

McVey on the Pershing: Craig Earley

Clarence and his fellow tankers: Clarence Smoyer

INDEX

1st Infantry Division ("Big Red One"), 23

2nd Armored ("Hell on Wheels"), 104, 110, 245

2nd Company, Panzer Brigade 106 (Germany), 27, 29, 144, 179, 180

2nd Panzer Division, 73, 80, 83, 85, 88

3rd Armored Division (Spearhead Division), 4, 24, 33, 49, 103, 110, 134, 157, 170, 232–33, 243, 245, 252, 337

9th Panzer Division, 165

20th Panzer Grenadiers, 93

34th Tank Battalion, 37

36th Infantry Regiment, 339

48th Panzer Grenadiers, 93

50th Fighter Group, 33

82nd Airborne Division, 24, 206

84th Infantry Division ("Railsplitters"), 69, 78

88mm guns (German), 120, 145, 155

101st Airborne, 24, 69

104th Infantry Division ("Timberwolves"), 63, 115, 188

363rd Volksgrenadier Division, 165, 169

A-Company, 36th Armored Infantry Regiment, 89, 119, 122, 132, 133, 137, 209, 241, 270, 280, 281, 284, 299, 301, 322

African American GIs, 55, 309

Alaniz, Frank, 167, *167*, 168

"American Blitz" to Paderborn, 245–55, *246*

Antwerp (Belgium), 63, 69

Ardennes Forest (Belgium), 65–66, 68–87

The Army Hour (radio program), 219

Audifred, Frank ("Cajun Boy"), 74–76, 88, 97, 123–25, *124*, 128–29, 134, 339

B-24 bombing of Western Germany, 87

B-Company, 32nd Armored Regiment, 119, 161, 201, 233, 261

BAR (Browning Automatic Rifle), 160

Bartelborth, Wilhelm, 180–81, *180*, 204, 208, 211, 217, 220*n*

Bastogne (Belgium), 69, 70*n*, 88

Bates, Jim, 205–7, *205*, 208, 213, 214, 247, 314–18, 320, 326*n*

Battle of the Bulge (Ardennes Forest, Belgium), 65–66, 68–87, *71*

Baughn, Richard, 187–88

Berghoff, Annemarie, 175–77, *175*, 224–27, 327, 334–35

Berghoff, Wilhelm, 175, 224

Berlin (Germany), 245, 305

Berlin, Walter, 280, 284

Blatzheim (Germany) assault, 116–36, 172, 230, 315

"Blitz" bombing of London, 183*n*

Böddeken Forest (Germany), 256

Boom, William, 122, 132, 139–41, *139*, 158, 160, 174, 185, 188, 208–9, 237, 265, 274, 278, 280–81, 283–84, 300–301, 327

Böving (staff sergeant), 304*n*

Bower, Robert, 124–25, 128–29, 134, 267

Bradley, Omar, xii–xiii, 110, 305

Browning Automatic Rifle (BAR), 160

Burton, Z. T., *167*

C-Company, 36th Armored Infantry Regiment, 119, 161

Carrier, Bill, 167, *167*, 241–42, 247, 280

Caserta, Joe, 128, 134, 247, 337

"Cathedral Duel" (Cologne), 207–13, *207*

Cologne (Germany), 110–11, 116, 155–231
    cathedral, 157, *157*, 179, 201, *204*, 218, 222, 228, 320, 335
    Cathedral Duel, 207–13, *207*
    Dom Hotel, 220–22, 300
    Hindenburg Bridge, 178
    history of, 161

Hohenzollern Bridge, 178, 214
    later meeting between Gustav and Clarence, 324–26

Concentration camps, 304–5, 309

"Cuckoo" (captured Panther tank), 44

Danforth, John, 78, 108, 285–87, 292, 300

Davis, Homer ("Smokey"), 81–82, *81*, 86, 88, 112, 114, 156, 211, 213, 214, 215, 220–21, 235, 244, 252, 272, 288, 290–91, 293–94, 320, 338

De La Torre, Jose, 167–68, *167*, 239, 247

Delling, Michael, 193–95, *194*, 316, 320, 329, 330–32, 334

DeRiggi, John ("Johnny Boy"), 130–31, *130*, 163, 189, 195, 210, 212–13, 215, 220, 221, 232, 236–40, 246, 272, 338

"Deserter" (captured Panther tank), 44

Dest, Phil, 233

Doan, Leander (colonel), 157, 170

Dom Hotel (Cologne), 220–22, 300

Donovan (sergeant), 63, 93–94

Dora-Nordhausen concentration camp, 304

Dresden (Germany), 153, 183, 183*n*

"duck bills," 66

"Eagle" (Sherman tank), 51

"Eagle 7" (Pershing tank), 108, *108*

Earley, Bob, 49–50, *50*, 53, 54, 58, 59, 61, 62, 65, 67, 73–76, 82–84, 108, 111–14, 115–16, 119–21, 130–31, 155–56, 163, 166, 173, 188–89, 195, 205–6, 211–14, 219, 232, 235–40, 244,

247, 248, 250, 252–54, 260, 264–66, 270, 272, 275–76, 278, 285–88, 290, 293–98, 320, 338

Easy Company, 32nd Armored Regiment, 49–52, 54, 58, 61, 67, 69, 73–74, 77–78, 85, 88–89, 97, 115–17, 120, 123–24, 135, 155, 161, 165–66, 170, 188, 232, 244, 256, 259, 269–72, 274–76, 285, 288, 302

Eighth Air Force, 87

Eisenhower, Dwight, 48, 78, 104*n*, 110, 230, 305

"Eleanor" (Sherman tank), 78, 80, 89, 90, 93–96, 117, 125–26

Endkampf, 162, 308

Endsieg, 150

Esser, Katharina, 192–94, *193,* 199–200, 316–18, *317,* 320, 326, 329–34, 340

"Everlasting" (Sherman tank), 116–17, 125–127

F-Company, 116, 124, 158, 201, 260, 261, 270

Fahrni (corporal), 91, 93, 96, 117, 126

Faircloth, Paul, 5–6, *6,* 8–10, 12–16, 19–21, 23–24, 49, 70, 109, 266, 294, 314, 338

First Army, U.S., 66, 107, 115, 232, 236

Flak 41 guns (German), 123

Foster, Hubert, 121

fraternization, 59, 63, 226, 228, 229

G-Company, 32nd Armored Regiment, 58

German Army
Panther strategy, 96
POWs, 216, 216*n*
rift with SS, 182

German POWs, 308

German tanks. *See* Mark IV tanks; Panther tanks; Tiger I

Gestapo, punishment by, 225, 225*n*

Goebbels, Joseph, 149, 183–84

"Golden Pheasants," 182

Golzheim (Germany), 115–16

Grand-Sart assault, 89, 92–102, *92,* 117

gyrostabilizer, 92

Hamburg (Germany), 183

Harris, Sir Arthur, 183*n*

Hèdrée (Belgium), 70, 73

Hey, Bill, 80–81, *80,* 89, 93, 94–95, 97, 117, 266

Hieronimus, Marc, 333–34

"High Pockets" (lieutenant), 56–57

Hindenburg Bridge (Cologne), 178

Hohenzollern Bridge (Cologne), 178, 214

Irwin, John, 250

Jagdpanzer IV, 27, 144, 237

Jähn, Dieter, 264*n*

Janicki, Bob, 98–100, *98,* 123, 133, 141–42, 158, 166, 168–69, 175–76, 185, 209, 222–27, 237, 239, 241, 247–48, 339

Jones, Luther, 265

Juilfs, Raymond ("Juke"), 125–28, *126*

Kellner, Karl, 201–3, *202*, 267
Koltermann (tank commander), 264*n*
Kriegslok locomotive, 143–48
Kübelwagens, 83

L-4 spotter plane ("the
    Grasshopper"), 40
La Roche (Belgium), 69, 88
Leppla, Otto, 181, 182
Logan, Slim, *167*
Luxembourg City, 48

M3 smoke mortar launcher, 121–22
M4A1 Sherman tanks. *See* Sherman
    tanks
M5 Stuart light tanks. *See* Stuart
    light tanks
M7 artillery vehicle (the "Priest"),
    39–40
M8 Greyhound, 19–20
M36 Jackson tank destroyers, 269,
    276, 280
Marche (Belgium), 69, 70, 77, 85, 88
Mark IV tanks ("Panzer IV"), 12,
    83, 91, 144, 178, 180–83
Marsh, Malcolm ("Buck"), 98–102,
    122–23, 132–33, 137–42, 151,
    158, 160, 166, 168–70, 173–77,
    185–88, 208–10, 222–27, 237,
    247, 248, 264, 270, 272, 273–75,
    277–79, 281–86, 292, 300–305,
    322–28, 334, 339
  photos, *98, 167, 342*
McVey, William ("Woody"), 90, *90*,
    112, 114, 118, 131, 211, 213–15,
    235, 236, 240, 244, 252, 272,
    290–91, 293–94, 338
Merl, battle, 25-48
Meuse River, 69, 70, 88, 89*n*
MG 34 Panzerlauf machine gun
    (German), 36–37, 191

Miller, Chuck, 78–81, 90–91,
    94–96, 97, 117, 118, 125, 127,
    128, 134, 162, 164, 165, 172,
    189, 200, 219, 230–31, 248, 251,
    252, 285–86, 289, 300, 321,
    322–28, 338
  photos, *79, 342*
Miller, Hattie Pearl, 230–31, *230*
Miller, Wanda, 324
Millitzer, Rolf, 29–30, 32–41, 148,
    153–54, 179–81, 183, 190–92,
    195, 197–99, 215, 217, 308, 339
Mitchell, Byron, 160, 175–76,
    239–43, 247–48, 265, 280, 292,
    301–4, 339
Mons (Belgium), 3–5, 7, 14–24, 50,
    293
Montgomery (Field Marshall), 236
Morries, Robert, 186–87

Ninth Army, U.S., 107, 236
Nonfraternization policy, 59, 63,
    226, 228–29
Normandy landing, 48

Oberaussem (Germany), 137–42
Opel Blitz trucks, 83
Operation Lumberjack, 161

P-47s (Thunderbolts), 33–34
Paderborn (Germany), 245, 268
Paderhorn assault, 269–306, *271,
    281, 296*
Panther tanks
  about, 10, *27*, 29, 144*n*, 305
  claimed by American crews, 44,
    103
  in Cologne, 180–81, 204–13, 217,
    219, 220, 233, 247, 323, 326,
    326*n*

diagram, *27*
in Merl, 32-48
in Paderborn, 295–300, 305
vulnerabilities, 32, 74
Zimmerit, 32, 35, 305
Panzer IV tanks ("Mark IV"), 12, *12*
Panzer Brigade 106 ("Fire
    Department of the West"), 27,
    144, 339
Panzer Wrap uniform, 149, 215
Panzerbrigade Westfalen, 255, 258,
    269, 273, 304
Panzerfaust (antitank weapon), 159,
    164, 165, 273–74, 289–92,
    304
Patrick, Julian, 203
Pershing tanks
    90mm gun, 109, 131, 135, 277,
        286, 288, 290, 297–99
    about, 107–08, 118, 129, 133,
        135–36, 155, 231
    in Cologne, 188, 199
    crew, *214*
    gas mileage, 250
    in Paderborn, 277, 280, 285, 286,
        288, 293–99
    photo, *108*
    Ruhr encirclement, 250, 252, 261,
        277
    at Welborn Massacre, 261
Pfieffer, Resi, 63–64, *64,* 66, 67, 103,
    104–06
Post-traumatic stress disorder
    (PTSD), 319–20, 340–41
POWs (German), 308
Pütz, Marion, 334–35

"Red Ball Express" (supply
    convoy), 55
Reed, Clyde, 265
"Remagen Breakout," pushing east
    after Cologne, 236–55

Richard, Stan, 265
Rooney, Andy, 202–3, 322
Rose, Charles Crane, 79
Rose, Charlie, 72–73, *72,* 74, 79, 80,
    85, 86, 266
Rose, Maurice (Major General),
    73, 104*n,* 110–12, *110,* 114,
    230, 245–46, 250, 256–59,
    262–63, 266, 301, 304
"Rose Pocket," 304
Ruhr Pocket, 304

Salisbury, Mason, 61–62, *61,* 63, 74,
    75, 77, 80, 91, 107, 121, 124,
    135–36, 156, 233–35, 240, 253,
    254, 319
Sangerhausen (Germany), 305
Scenes of War (Bates's movie),
    314–18, 320, 326*n*
Schaefer, Gustav
    in Cologne, 178–99
    death, 340
    in Heidelberg, 148–55
    Kriegslok train incident, 143–48
    Paderborn rail yard, 281–304
    personal details, 25, 27–28, 31, 36,
        47, 152–53
    photos, *25, 342–43*
    postwar return to home, 311–12
    as POW, 306–11
    as radio operator in Luxembourg,
        25–48
    reunion with Smoyer, 324–36, 340
    visit to cemetery plots of Delling
        and Esser, 331–33
Schneider, Dick, 265
Schoener, Fred, *167*
Second Company, Panzer Brigade
    106 (Germany), 27, 29, 33, 144,
    179–80
Segregation, among U.S. troops, 309
Semanoff, Pete, xi

Sennelager base ("Nazi Fort Knox"),
    269
Seventh Army, U.S., 107
Sherman tanks
    about, 6, 14, 29, 66, 91, 91*n*, 121
    battles, 37, 38*n*
    description of inside of, 4
    diagram, 5
    "duck bills," 66
    gas mileage, 250
    gun gyrostabilizer, 92
    M3 smoke mortar launcher,
        121–22
    new Sherman known as "76,"
        50–51, *51*
    in Paderborn, 296
    reputation as tinderbox, 127, 127*n*
    reliability, 250
Siegfried Line (West Wall), 7, 48,
    49–50, 54, 62, 225, 236
Sledge, Eugene, 323
Smoyer, Clarence
    Battle of the Bulge, 68–87, *71*
    Blatzheim assault, 116–36
    Bronze Star, 234–235
    at cathedral in Cologne, 218, 228
    cemetery visit for Delling and
        Esser, 331–33
    chocolate, 70–71
    Cologne, 155–231
    death of Kathi Esser, 192–94, *193*,
        199–200, 316–18, *317*, 320, 326,
        328–32, 333–34, 340
    early life, 10–11
    encounter with German farmer,
        50–53
    fraternization with children in
        Cologne, 228–29
    friendship with Paul Faircloth,
        15–16, 23–24, 109
    and Resi Pfieffer, 63–64, *64*, 66,
        67, 103, 104–6

Grand-Sart assault, 92–102, *92*
marriage, 313
meeting with Salisbury, 233–35
at Mons, 3–10, *8*, 16–24, *17*
to Paderborn, 245–55, *246*
Paderborn rail yard, 281–304, *281*,
    296
Paderhorn assault, 269–306, *271*
personal details, xii, 3, 55, 70,
    84–85, 86, 184, 219–20, 247,
    313–20
personality, 3, 11
photos, *4, 342–43*
physical description, 3
post-traumatic stress disorder
    (PTSD), 319–20, 340–41
postwar return to U.S., 313
pushing east in Germany after
    Cologne ("Remagen
    Breakout"), 236–55
retirement, 314
return to Germany, 321–31, 321*n*
reunion with Schaefer, 324–36
at Stolberg, 54–67, 103–14
viewing Bates's wartime film,
    314–18, 320
at Welborn Massacre, 260–61
Smoyer, Melba, 70, 313, *313*, 318
Spearhead Division (3rd Armored),
    4–5, 24, 33, 110, 170, 236,
    244–45, 252, 266, 300, 304–5,
    337
Squad 3/2, 166–68, *167*, 278
SS Panzerbrigade Westfalen, 255,
    257, 269, 272, 304
St. Vith (Belgium), 69, 88
Stillman, Bill, 156, 234
Stolberg (Germany), 54–67,
    103–14
Stringer, Ann, 172–73, *172*,
    230–31
Stringer, William, 173, 230

Stuart (M5) light tanks, 116, 117, 118

Subversion of the War Effort law (1938), 151, 151n

Sweat, Wesley (lieutenant colonel), 264n

Swenson, Harley, 233

T26E3 Pershing tanks. *See* Pershing tanks

tank-on-tank engagement, 71, 91, 91n

tanker's helmet, 8, 8n

Task Force Welborn, 244, 254, 256, 262, 264

Task Force Welborn ambush, 257–67, 257

Task Force X, 115, 155, 161, 236, 244, 256, 259, 269, 285

Third Army, U.S., 107, 236

Thompson submachine gun, 290–91

Tiger I (German tank), 83, 262, 301–2, 301

Truffin (tank commander), 134

typhus, 228

über lang (extra-long) gun, 37, 37n

U.S. tanks. *See* Pershing tanks; Sherman tanks; Stuart light tanks

venereal disease, 62, 62n

Villa, Sylvester ("Red"), 171, 171, 248, 251, 285, 288–89, 291, 294, 300

Volkssturm militia, 145, 169, 182

Walther P-38 pistol (German), 306

Wehner, Werner, 41, 43–47

Wehrpässe, 217

Welborn, Jack, 244, 257, 259

Welborn Massacre, 257–67, 257

West Wall (Siegfried Line), 7, 48, 49, 50, 54, 62, 225, 236

White, Peter, 126

white phosphorus, 131–32, 135

Whitehead, Melba (later Melba Smoyer), 70, 313, 313, 318

Zimmerit, 32, 305

ABOUT THE AUTHOR

Hailed as "a masterful storyteller" by the Associated Press, ADAM MAKOS is the author of the *Sunday Times* bestseller *A Higher Call* and the critically acclaimed *Devotion*. Inspired by his grandfathers' service, Adam chronicles the stories of American veterans in his trademark fusion of intense human drama and fast-paced military action, securing his place "in the top ranks of military writers," according to the *Los Angeles Times*. In the course of his research, Adam has flown a World War II bomber, accompanied a Special Forces raid in Iraq, and journeyed into North Korea in search of an MIA American airman.

adammakos.com
Instagram: @AdamMakos
Find Adam Makos on Facebook